U.S.S. MIDWAY
CVA-41

B
H.
P,
U
to
i:

YANKEES IN PARADISE

BOOKS BY BRADFORD SMITH

Biography   BRADFORD OF PLYMOUTH
                     CAPTAIN JOHN SMITH

Social History   YANKEES IN PARADISE
                     A DANGEROUS FREEDOM
                     AMERICANS FROM JAPAN

Novels   THE ARMS ARE FAIR
                     AMERICAN QUEST
                     THIS SOLID FLESH
                     TO THE MOUNTAIN

For young readers WILLIAM BRADFORD—PILGRIM BOY
                     DAN WEBSTER—UNION BOY
                     STEPHEN DECATUR—GALLANT BOY
                     ROGERS' RANGERS AND THE FRENCH
                       AND INDIAN WAR
                     WITH SWORD AND PEN

Editor   THE STORY OF JESUS
                     A HANDBOOK OF ENGLISH AND
                       AMERICAN LITERATURE

YANKEES *in* PARADISE

THE NEW ENGLAND IMPACT ON HAWAII

by Bradford Smith

J. B. LIPPINCOTT COMPANY

PHILADELPHIA   NEW YORK

CONTENTS

1	LANDFALL	9
2	KINDRED IN CHRIST	20
3	THE ISLES SHALL WAIT FOR HIS LAW	34
4	A FAIR HAVEN	47
5	PRODIGAL SONS	66
6	PLURAL MARRIAGE AND SINGULAR PEOPLE	83
7	THE BELOVED COMMUNITY	94
8	REBELLION	108
9	THE KING IS DEAD	120
10	ENTER SAILORS, DEMANDING WOMEN	130
11	GOD SEND US A SPEEDY DELIVERY	141
12	THE CONSUL'S COW	153
13	THE FIRST DECADE	163
14	THE PRINCESS MISBEHAVES	177
15	PARADISE INDEED	190
16	A YEAR OF THE RIGHT HAND OF THE MOST HIGH	202
17	UNDER FIRE	213
18	THE CHIEFS' CHILDREN'S SCHOOL	224
19	ERUPTION	232
20	DAMN THE MISSIONARIES!	243
21	WITH BENEFIT OF CLERGY	255
22	THE POWER BEHIND THE THRONE	267
23	THE GREAT MAHELE	281
24	MULTIPLYING LIKE THE JEWS IN EGYPT	291
25	PHYSICIAN, HEAL THYSELF	298
26	SISTERS, COUSINS, AUNTS	310
27	DID THEY DO GOOD—OR WELL?	323
APPENDICES		335
	SOME IMPORTANT HAWAIIANS (1820–1854)	337
	MEMBERS OF THE SANDWICH ISLANDS MISSION	339
	SOURCES	347
	SELECT BIBLIOGRAPHY	348
	NOTES	358
INDEX		369

YANKEES IN PARADISE

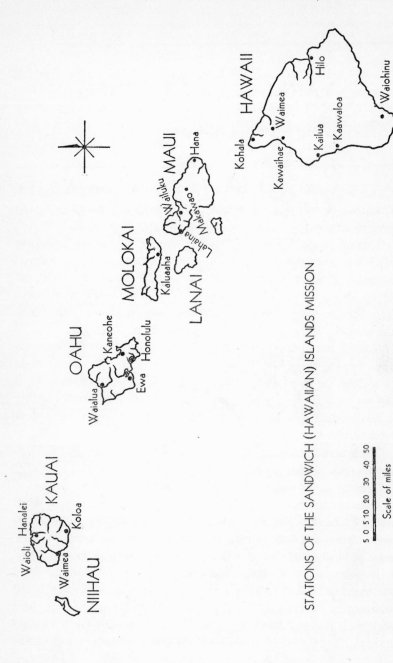

STATIONS OF THE SANDWICH (HAWAIIAN) ISLANDS MISSION

5 0 5 10 20 30 40 50

Scale of miles

CHAPTER 1

LANDFALL

A BRIGHT ROUND MOON SHONE DOWN UPON THE LITTLE BRIG *Thaddeus*. A soft tropical breeze pressed against square-rigged sails glowing like summer clouds in the moonlight.

Thomas Hopu, his body pressed to the rigging, stared across the black water to the west. His broad nostrils inflated, sensing a softness in the air. It was one o'clock in the morning of March 30, 1820, but he could not sleep. He had been a dozen years away from home, from Hawaii. He had been 159 days at sea on this voyage from Boston around Cape Horn. Now he ached for the sight of home.

Shading his dark eyes with a brown hand, he stared westward beyond the white sails and the black waters. At first he thought it might be a cloud the moonlight picked out. He blinked and looked again. It did not move or change its shape. Detached both from earth and sky, it floated with a majesty of its own—the snow-decked summit of lofty Mauna Kea.

Thomas slid down the rigging and ran swiftly on bare feet to Samuel Ruggles' six-foot-square stateroom.

"Come—come and see Hawaii," he said.

Obedient to the ecstasy in Thomas' voice, Sam Ruggles climbed out of his bunk hoping that he would not waken Nancy. He threw on some clothes and followed Thomas on deck. Sighting along Thomas' arm, he finally made out the shape of the mountain sixty miles away.

By morning the *Thaddeus* was coasting along the northeast tip of the island of Hawaii, so close that the passengers could see the rugged shoreline of the Hamakua coast, where waterfalls plunged over sheer rock walls into the ocean far below. Beyond the cliffs the land tilted upward, showing bright green fields. Beyond them came a belt of for-

9

est, and beyond that the bare mountains, Mauna Kea and Mauna Loa, crowned with snow.

Twenty-three land-hungry passengers leaned on the rail. Their five months' voyage was over. But what lay ahead of them?

For the four Hawaiians a welcome after long absence seemed assured. But would Hawaii welcome the two ministers Bingham and Thurston? The physician, Dr. Holman? The assistant missionaries Loomis, Ruggles and Whitney? Would they welcome the wives of all these men, or farmer Daniel Chamberlain with his wife and five young ones?

When Lucy Thurston, a few days before, had asked Captain Blanchard whether he thought their lives might be taken by the natives, he had answered: "Aside from intoxication which sometimes leads them on to make bold assaults, I think not—in any other way than by the use of poisons."

With this cheering reassurance in mind, Lucy Thurston—like most of the company still in her twenties—looked across the strip of water to the place which she expected to make her home for life, whether that life be long or short. She could see the little thatch houses, looking more like haystacks than habitations. Here and there a column of smoke rose into the bright, cloud-studded sky. Someone brought out a telescope, and with its help men and women could be picked out— "immortal beings purchased with redeeming blood."

The question uppermost in every mind was whether these particular immortal beings would allow this little handful of young men and women from New England to teach, preach and heal.

"Your views are not to be limited to a low, narrow scale," the American Board of Commissioners for Foreign Missions had admonished them. "You are to open your hearts wide and set your marks high. You are to aim at nothing short of covering these islands with fruitful fields, and pleasant dwellings and schools and churches, and of raising up the whole people to an elevated state of Christian civilization . . . to turn them from barbarous courses and habits . . . and to inculcate the duties of justice, moderation, forbearance, truth and universal kindness."

It was a large order, yet they had undertaken it in the conviction that they were in God's care and that if they could once get established ashore, they would be able to win this people to the Christian faith.

It was well known to them, however, that the religion of Hawaii not only countenanced but required the sacrificial murder of innocent people. The victim was hunted down in the night, strangled in his own house before he knew what was afoot, then sacrificed upon a bloody altar where hundreds had already met the same fate. So even if they were welcomed ashore, who would know whether the welcome was merely a prelude to such a sacrifice?

They knew, too, along with the rest of the Christian world, that when Captain James Cook, the English explorer, had discovered the islands in 1778 he had been regarded as a god—anointed in the temple with chewed coconut and given pork and *awa* to eat and drink after they had been chewed and spit out by reverential attendants. He and his men had been lavishly supplied with gifts of all kinds. In return, despite Cook's attempt to prevent it, his men had brought venereal disease to the women who had given themselves in the easygoing island fashion.

When Cook returned eight months later he made the mistake of overstaying his welcome. A quarrel developed, in the course of which a chief grabbed him. Cook struggled to free himself, and as he was about to fall a groan escaped him.

"He groans—he is not a god," cried the chief, and killed him.

Cook's body was carried to a temple where the flesh was removed from the bones. Some of his bones were later given back to the English squadron when peace was restored. One account says that his heart was placed in a tree, where it was found and eaten by a man who supposed it was an animal's heart, a hidden tidbit.

These things were in the minds of the young men and women who lined the rail, watching the beautiful, dramatic countryside slip past as the ship approached the northern tip of the island. Yet despite the danger they longed to be ashore. The soft tropic air, the hot sun and the innocent cotton clouds, the sight of green fields and solid mountains after the months at sea were all reassuring. Where nature smiled so beneficently, it was hard to think that man could be vile.

At four in the afternoon they turned southward, passing the island of Maui on their right. Captain Blanchard sent a boat ashore to learn the state of affairs. Thomas Hopu, eager to touch his native earth again, jumped aboard, along with John Honolii. (They had left the islands as sailors on Yankee ships several years before.) Watching them head for shore was the most distinguished of the four Hawaiians, George Kaumualii, son of the king of Kauai Island. George, now twenty-two, had been away from home since the age of six, having been sent to America to be educated. The mission group had pinned their hopes on George until the word had gone around during the voyage that he was in reality but the illegitimate son of the king and had been sent abroad to keep him from falling a victim to the malice and jealousy of Kauai's queen.

With Thomas Hopu and John Honolii went a group of sailors dressed in their shiny black tarpaulin hats, blue bell-bottomed trousers, and black kerchiefs knotted around the neck above red-checked shirts. With them also went one of the ship's mates, James Hunnewell, a young Bostonian who during 1817 and 1818 had spent ten months as a merchant in Honolulu. Then he had made the long voyage home, married, and within a few months set out for Hawaii again leaving his Susan behind him. Now he was hoping to make his fortune in the sandalwood trade.

Watching him disappear towards shore, the mission group must have felt some concern for his welfare. For on the long voyage he had proven himself a good friend, always cheerful, attentive, and a regular worshiper at divine service. A voyage of five months provides an infallible test of character, and James Hunnewell had stood the test—better indeed than one of the mission couples.

Spending much of their time in a small cabin (fifteen by twenty) which served as sleeping quarters for captain, officers and two mission couples, and as dining and sitting room for the whole group, passengers and officers had come to know each other very well. Together they had passed through a storm so violent that it had ripped up their sails and forced them to ride under bare poles. They had suffered from seasickness and cold. They had seen the table swept clean of food and dishes and found themselves sprawled in the midst of the mess on the floor. They had made the perilous passage around the Horn, and coming at last into clement weather again, they had made their landfall after wondering many times whether they would ever live to see it.

Yet their eighteen-thousand-mile voyage was not half so remarkable as the one the Hawaiians themselves had made some fourteen hundred years before. Greatest sea adventurers of all times, the Polynesians—coming in the remote past from southeastern Asia into the western islands of Indonesia—had sailed across the vast Pacific in outrigger canoes, settling upon islands all the way from New Zealand and Easter Island (off the coast of Chile) northward to Hawaii. This was a thousand years before Europeans dared to cross the comparatively small Atlantic.

After several centuries of isolation, another wave of Polynesians swept into the islands, bringing with them a higher culture than that of the original settlers. The voyages ceased, and another long period of isolation began. The newcomers had brought new customs, artifacts, religious practices, and because their culture was more developed they soon came to dominate the firstcomers. They became the *alii* or chiefs, and the *kahuna* or experts in healing, priestcraft, and other forms of learning. As the chiefs and kahuna class gained in power, the plain people became increasingly subject to them until their produce or animals might be seized whenever a chief wanted them and even their lives were not safe. Until Kamehameha * the First brought the islands (except Kauai) under one rule in 1795, they had been divided into petty kingdoms constantly changing their boundaries in the course of the wars fought by their rulers.

Every aspect of Hawaiian life—wars, crafts, relations between the sexes, household management—was subject to a tabu system administered by the priests. The system was built upon the idea that two world forces were in conflict—a sacred male principle and a common, corrupt female principle. It was forbidden (tabu or *kapu*) to men either to defile that which was sacred or to be defiled by that which was corrupt. The tabu system was therefore the keystone of the culture and the priests as its administrators had a tight hold upon the people.

Life for a Hawaiian was hedged about with tabu. He could not

---

* Hawaiian names being what they are, a list of some important Hawaiians has been placed on page 337.

eat with his wife, or even under the same roof with her. He could not stand in the presence of a chief, and even to touch his clothing by accident brought death. He must have separate houses for eating, sleeping, domestic work, household idols. During periods of strict tabu the priests enforced absolute silence. No dog must bark, no fire must be lighted, no canoe could be launched. The muzzles of the dogs were tied and chickens placed under calabashes, because everyone knew that whoever broke the tabu might have his eyes scooped out and his limbs broken before he was put to death.

Women, who were associated with the earthy and impure principle, were even more restricted than men. Many of Hawaii's choicest foods they could not eat—pork, bananas, coconuts, some kinds of fish. But perhaps this was more than compensated for by the fact that the men had to do the cooking! They also had to do the fighting, fishing, canoe- and house-building, farming, implement-making and the featherwork for which Hawaii is famous. It was the woman's job to make the plaited mats used on the floors, to make kapa from the bark of the paper mulberry for the little clothing that was worn, and to care for the children. Infanticide, however, was common. Mothers who did not want to be bothered with children buried them alive. Over twenty ways of disposing of a young or unborn baby were to become known to the mission.

Most sacred, and therefore most tabu, was the king. A man could be killed for letting his shadow fall on the king's house or for failing to prostrate himself before anything of the king's which might be carried along the road. Horrible as it sounds, the tabu system did, however, provide a principle around which the culture could organize. It regulated fishing and agriculture, fostered arts and crafts, even took the curse from taxes by giving them the sanctity of a ceremonial investment, since taxes paid to the sacred king gave a guarantee of protection against the forces of evil. The taxes, moreover, were paid at the Makahiki, a five-months' festival during which everyone took a long holiday from all but the most necessary tasks, enjoying a great variety of games and sports.

These ranged all the way from surfboarding and canoe racing to games designed to bring about sexual pairing outside the marital bond. Even in this sport, there was one rule for the common people,

another for the chiefs. The commoners played *ume,* gathering around
a big fire where a man holding a long wand trimmed with bird feathers chanted a suggestive song. When he touched a man and a woman
with the wand, they went off together into the dark. Jealousy on the
part of husband or wife was tabu. The chiefs played *kilu,* which had
the same end in view but required at least a minimum of exertion
on the part of the player, who had to throw a coconut shell at a post.
If he hit it, he could kiss the woman of his choice. Ten good throws,
and he won her fullest favors.

Other games were more strenuous. The Hawaiian form of boxing
often ended in real maiming, with a broken arm, an eye gouged out
or teeth broken. Sometimes the loser lost not only the game but his
life. There was coasting on oiled runners down a course paved with
stone, sliding down grassy slopes on ti leaves, races, sham battles,
guessing games, and a form of bowling with cylindrical stones. Children had kites, stilts, tops, skipping ropes, swings, toy canoes, jack-
stones, cat's cradles.

Though the Hawaiians had always known how to play and enjoy
life, they were also skilled craftsmen and even engineers. Lacking
metals and clay, they were still in the stone age when Cook first
visited them. Though they never developed metal crafts or pottery of
their own, working with nothing better than stone and shell tools
they made fine canoes. Their wickerwork, plaited mats, wooden calabashes and kapa beaten from bark into a kind of cloth and decorated
with colored patterns were the result of patient, painstaking work
with primitive tools. Their staple food, poi, could be produced only
by skilled water engineering to flood the banked fields in which the
taro grew. They knew how to bring in water without washing the
good earth away, they used weeds for mulch and hau branches to
turn sour soil sweet, and they understood the value of leaving fields
fallow. Their medical kahuna (expert or specialist) knew three hundred plants and their effects on the human body, understood the
therapeutic effect of heat and massage, had developed a system of
diagnosis and performed autopsies. Their arts included an extensive
mythology which was handed down by word of mouth since they had
no writing. Preserved in lengthy chants, this lore was held in the
minds of men who developed an almost unbelievable power to re-

member what they heard. Best known of all the Hawaiian arts, of course, was the hula. Far from being a mere hip-wiggling, the hula was "a religious service in which poetry, music, pantomime and the dance lent themselves, under the forms of dramatic art, to the refreshment of men's minds."

The Hawaii from which the hopeful young missionaries of New England now awaited the first word was therefore neither the paradise some would like to imagine it nor the race of ignorant savages the missionaries pictured.

Yet these "untutored heathen," these "degraded Islanders" were also "immortal beings purchased with redeeming blood." The mission group tried to remember that as they waited for James Hunnewell, Thomas Hopu and John Honolii to bring them the first word from shore.

*   *   *

The ship's boat was gone for three hours while the little group on board the *Thaddeus* waited anxiously. Did the delay mean good news or bad?

At last the boat came bouncing towards them through the choppy waters. Quickly James Hunnewell heaved himself up over the vessel's side and as the group gathered closely around him gave out the whole amazing story in a few short breaths:

"Kamehameha is dead—his son Liholiho is king. The kapus are abolished—the images are burned, the temples destroyed. There has been war. Now there is peace."

Just before reaching shore, Hunnewell and his party had met ten or a dozen fishermen in their canoes. After learning this astounding news Hunnewell had not waited to go ashore but had hurried back to the brig. He was followed not long after by canoes bearing both men and women eager to see the *haoles* (whites) and bringing heaped-up gifts of fruit.

Lucy Thurston looked out of a cabin window. In a moment a canoeful of chattering men and women, nearly naked, paddled to the ship's side. Someone handed Lucy a banana and she handed out a biscuit.

"Wahine maikai," they shouted. "Good girl."

Delighted that she understood the first Hawaiian words ever spoken to her in the islands, she passed out more biscuits and called "Wahine" (girl or woman), the only bit of repartee, apparently, that she could command on such short notice. Despite the naked torsos of the women and the brief loincloths of the men, Lucy was more impressed with the simple friendliness of the people than with their "barbarism."

The next day, March thirty-first, Samuel Ruggles went ashore with John Honolii and Thomas Hopu. They visited Kalanimoku, the prime minister, who confirmed the good news that the tabus were ended. And they returned with a gift of fish, coconuts and bananas from some of King Kamehameha's numerous widows. Then on the following day—a Saturday and April Fool's Day—Hopu went ashore to invite some of the chiefs aboard. By this time the *Thaddeus* had coasted a short distance down the western side of the island and had anchored in Kawaihae Bay. Hopu hinted that the chiefs, male and female, should wear clothes.

They came willingly—Kalanimoku, two of his wives, two of Kamehameha's widows, and a crowd of attendants. Both the men and women chiefs were huge, weighing anywhere from 250 to 400 pounds. Kalanimoku was the least Polynesian-looking of all. His prominent nose was not flat and broad, but had a pinched look. His eyes were narrow rather than round, and he wore long sideburns. He was a strange-looking man, but clearly one who expected to be obeyed. He turned up in a handsome outfit—white dimity roundabout over a black silk vest, yellow nankeen pants, white cotton hose, and shoes. (Not many Hawaiians had shoes.) Hopu introduced him first to the gentlemen. He shook hands with each and then turned to the ladies. Very few haole women had ever visited Hawaii before, yet Kalanimoku seemed to know what was expected of him. He bowed, then stepped forward and offered his hand to each one as he was introduced. *"Aloha,"* he said, with that warm, lingering accent on the full round *o*. Then he caught sight of the Chamberlain children, whose ages ranged from babyhood to thirteen. They interested him more than the women.

Now the lady visitors came forward. They wore dresses of sorts (one was of black velvet) but over them the native *pa'u*—bark cloth three or four yards long wrapped around the middle several times and tucked in at the waist. One of the old queens, taking a fancy to Lucia Holman, settled her in her huge lap and felt her all over. "Eat and grow big," she advised. Then she asked Lucia to let her hair down and show her how to roll it up on combs. Once the greetings were over, the women looked about for a place to lie down. Their weight made standing or sitting uncomfortable, and with a crowd of people to fetch for them, shoo away flies, feed and massage them, they never needed to exert themselves.

One queen stretched out full length on a bench, the other on the deck. Shown into the cabin, one of the visitors pulled off her dress and, naked to the waist, disposed her huge bulk in the favorite reclining position—hand supporting head, floor supporting elbow.

Kalanimoku accepted an invitation to dine with the mission family at the long table, but the women of the party waited until the others rose. Then they had their own food brought in, raw fish and poi, which they ate with their fingers. When they departed at sunset in their double canoe, Bingham and Thurston, mounting to the maintop, sang in close harmony the mission's favorite hymn, "Head of the Church Triumphant."

The next day was Sunday—Easter Sunday, though the mission journals nowhere mention this. Hiram Bingham, the thin-faced, purposeful-looking young man from Bennington, Vermont, preached on the text: "The isles shall wait for His law." Kalanimoku came aboard again with his company and was present at the service on deck. He also slept, but whether he did both things simultaneously, thus becoming the first Hawaiian to adopt an old Christian custom, the record does not say.

So far, the mission had succeeded beyond its farthest hopes. It had found the strong old king departed, the idolatry overthrown which it had expected to contend against, the islands providentially without a religion. Surely, they felt, this was the hand of God, preparing the way for them. Here, at the end of their long journey, the prophecy was fulfilled: "The isles shall wait for His law."

True, they had still to meet the young king and gain his permission to settle in his territory. But had it not been a providence that they had found the prime minister, Kalanimoku, so quickly, and that he seemed so well disposed towards them? Next to the king, he appeared to be the most important person in the islands. (The mission had still to learn about dowager queen Kaahumanu.) Age and experience gave him to some extent a power even greater than the king's. And here he was, dozing on the deck of the *Thaddeus* more like a snoozing roustabout than a man whose word was law. Best of all, he had agreed to sail down to Kailua on the *Thaddeus,* there to introduce the mission to the king himself. Yet not even to meet a king would the missionaries sail on Sunday, not even to put an end to the long, long voyage or to gratify their longing for the feel of firm land beneath their feet.

CHAPTER 2

KINDRED IN CHRIST

BUT HOW HAD THIS LITTLE HANDFUL OF NEW ENGLAND-
ers chosen, out of all the heathen world, these few small islands so
lost in the vast Pacific that the western world had not even been
aware of them until near the end of the eighteenth century?

With Cook when he discovered the islands was a corporal of
marines named John Ledyard. An American and a native of Connecticut, Ledyard quickly saw the importance of the islands in building up a trans-Pacific fur trade. Though the British relieved him of
his notes, he wrote a book which he published (1783) on his return
to America, advocating such a trade. Until 1789, however, most of
the ships calling at Hawaii were British. But in that year Captain
Robert Gray, two years out of Boston in the *Columbia,* stopped in
the islands on his way to China from the northwest coast with a load
of furs. Returning home by way of the Cape of Good Hope, he was
the first of many American traders to circle the earth. When he
reached Boston on the ninth of August, 1790, the man who followed
him down the gangplank was a Hawaiian who had joined the crew
when the ship was at the islands. Dressed in a feather cloak of brilliant scarlet and gold and with an equally handsome feather helmet
shaped like that of an ancient Greek warrior, he marched up Beacon
Hill to call upon Governor John Hancock.

Within two years the fur trade route from Boston by the Horn to
the northwest coast and Canton was well established. Ships left Boston loaded with goods to exchange for hides in Spanish America.
They sailed along the northwest coast trading with the Indians for
furs. They stopped in Hawaii for fresh food to ward off the scurvy
that was always threatening the crews of these long voyages, and also

to enjoy the favors of Hawaiian maidens who cheerfully gave themselves for a mirror or a bit of metal or cloth, or sometimes just for fun. Then they went on to China where furs could be converted into teas and silks for European and American markets.

After 1810 there was an additional reason for visiting Hawaii. Although sandalwood had been discovered there as early as 1790, the first shipment to China had been considered inferior and had failed to bring the fancy price this product usually commanded in the China market. For twenty years the Hawaiian forests went unravished. But then in 1811 three Yankee skippers, Nathan and Jonathan Winship and William Heath Davis, carried sandalwood to China and brought back a handsome payment to King Kamehameha. From then on sandalwood—burned for its fragrance upon the altars of China—was second on the list of things most wanted by Yankee sailors, the first of course being women.

The king promptly slapped a tabu upon the item so as to enjoy the profit himself. Yankee traders brought him everything they could think of to exchange for it. Many of these trade goods—silks and yard goods, blankets and clothing—lay moldering in royal storehouses until they had to be thrown away. Yet the smart old king did manage to acquire a fleet of six ships and a great pile of Spanish dollars.

Unfortunately for the future history of the islands, the traders also brought hard liquor and tobacco. Chiefs learned the western art of drinking to stupefaction, while the whole population, including even little children, took to smoking pipes, "drinking" the smoke until they sometimes fell down in a dead faint.

While Hawaiians were thus learning the inestimable benefits of western civilization at home, a few of them were drinking at the fountainhead. It was one of these, Opukahaia (Obookiah as he was popularly known), who brought the Hawaiian mission into being.

When Opukahaia was a lad of twelve, both his parents were hacked to pieces in the course of a war between chiefs on the island of Hawaii. Taken prisoner, Opukahaia ultimately found his way to his uncle, a priest. In 1809, now seventeen, he persuaded his uncle to let him sail to America on Captain Caleb Brintnal's ship along with Thomas Hopu, who also wanted to see the white man's world.

Opukahaia and Thomas landed at New York and soon made their way to New England, where they were both taken into homes in New Haven. One day students found Opukahaia weeping on the steps of Yale College because he was ignorant and uneducated. They volunteered to teach him. A new home was found for him with the remarkable president of the college, Timothy Dwight, and under his guidance, Opukahaia soon became a believing Christian.*

"Hawaii gods!" he said. "They wood, burn. Me go home, put 'em in fire, burn 'em up. They no see, no hear, no anything. We make them."

Meanwhile the idea had been growing that New England had a duty to convert the heathen as well as to trade with them. Religious conviction, of course, was nothing new to New England. Two hundred years before, the men and women we call Pilgrims had made a voyage more hazardous though far shorter than that to Hawaii, to settle their God-guided community in the American wilderness. Others of many persuasions had followed, but always the church had been central to the community. And always the church, while remaining separate from the state, had stressed the covenant between the state and its citizens as having a moral basis similar to that of the church and its members.

New England Puritanism had many phases, but by 1800 it had survived the inroads of deism and had entered a new phase of revivalism which recalled the Great Awakening of the early eighteenth century. Reversing the usual flow, these revivals began on the frontier and swept backward into New England.

The last decade of the eighteenth century had also seen the founding of missionary societies in several eastern states and the establishing of Williams, Bowdoin, Union and Middlebury colleges which were destined to send their young men on missions to the uttermost parts of the earth.

It was at one of the revivalist "outpourings of the spirit" in the town of Torringford, Connecticut, that a boy of fifteen named Samuel J. Mills began to wonder whether God's mercy included him. After

---

* *A Narrative of Five Youth from the Sandwich Islands* (1816) asserts that Opukahaia lived in President Dwight's home. Rufus Anderson, in *The Hawaiian Islands: Their Progress and Condition under Missionary Labors* (1864) says that Edwin W. Dwight was the one who converted him.

a period of doubt and distress, he experienced a religious conversion, prepared himself for college, and in 1806 entered Williams, already determined to devote his life to carrying the message of Christ to the heathen.

On a hot summer afternoon in 1806 Mills and four other pious young Williams men went to a grove where they had been in the habit of meeting for prayer. A thunderstorm made up and they had to scurry for protection to a near-by haystack. Here they discussed their plan of foreign missions. The Haystack Monument marks the spot where they met and where the American foreign missionary movement is regarded as having been born.

Two years later Mills, James Richards and a few others formed a secret society known as The Brethren, its members pledged to go on a mission to the heathen. In 1810 Mills went to Andover Seminary where Richards had already gone. With them went the constitution and records of The Brethren. At Andover they met other like-minded students with whom they organized the Society of Inquiry on the Subject of Missions. As yet there was no foreign missionary society in the United States which could send them abroad. So after seeking the advice of their professors, they asked the General Association of Massachusetts (the Congregational body) whether they might expect support from an American society or would have to go to Europe (presumably to England, where some of them later did go) to find support for the work to which they had dedicated their lives. The association promptly agreed to set up an American Board of Commissioners for Foreign Missions (A.B.C.F.M.). In 1812 it sent out its first missionaries, bound for Ceylon and India. Three years later James Richards followed to Ceylon. In the same year his younger brother William, who was to play a leading part in Hawaii, entered Williams.

After Andover, Samuel Mills had gone on to Yale to do graduate work and to gain other converts. There he met Opukahaia, and immediately the idea of a Sandwich (Hawaiian) Islands mission sprang into his mind. Mills himself thought of going with Opukahaia, but then he got involved in the well-intentioned scheme of colonizing freed slaves in Africa. As a result of his visit to Africa the first colony—precursor of the independent nation of Liberia—was established. But on the way back from Africa in 1818 he died and was buried at sea.

Projector also of the American Bible Society, Mills brought the whole foreign mission movement to life. The time was no doubt ripe for his dream, but the vision and the drive were his. Meanwhile, in 1816, when the American Board decided to open a school for such resident converts as Opukahaia, the people of Cornwall, Connecticut, offered an academy building and other property. The board bought a rooming house, a house for the principal, and eighty-five acres for a training farm. In 1817 the school opened with twelve students—five of whom were Hawaiian—and Edwin Dwight as their teacher.

Among the first students, in addition to Opukahaia, was Thomas Hopu, now back from adventurous years at sea during which he had fallen overboard near the Cape of Good Hope and shipped on several privateering expeditions during the War of 1812. Shipwrecked in the West Indies, he had saved the crew by getting a boat free from the wreck and rigging it with the captain's shirt. He had been captured by the British. At last he had returned destitute to New Haven in 1815 in search of his old friend. Learning that Opukahaia was at Goshen, he walked up there to find him. He found something else too—the faith to which Opukahaia had been converted.

"I hate my sins," said the converted Thomas. "I hate my heart, it is so bad. I want my poor countrymen to know about Christ." These were no idle words. Thomas walked sixty miles to find another Hawaiian, John Honolii, in order to convert him. And John also entered the Cornwall school.

Other Hawaiians who had found their way to New England with returning whalers or trading vessels were recruited. Among these was William Kanui, who had reached Boston with his brother about 1809. They had both gone to privateering, but when the brother died, William quit the sea and went to New Haven where he learned barbering. Discovered by Yale students, he was sent up to Cornwall.

Most interesting of all the group was Prince George Kaumualii who had been brought to Boston at the age of six. His father had given the ship's captain goods enough to pay for young George's care and education. But the goods were squandered and George, eventually left to take care of himself, also took to the sea where he was wounded during the fight between the *Enterprise* and the *Boxer* and then went to the Mediterranean with Decatur.

At the plain, barnlike school in Cornwall these young men were taught spelling, reading and writing, grammar, arithmetic, geography "and other branches." Prayers began and ended each day, and there was frequent reading of the scriptures as well as singing of psalms and hymns.

"I think it will be our own faults if we don't get religion," George dryly remarked to a friend, "for we have had enough said to us."

George never did get it, though Opukahaia, eloquent and well read, tried hard to convert him. Yet it was George, the scapegrace, who lived, while Opukahaia died of typhus on February 17, 1818, "a heavenly smile on his countenance and glory in his soul," as his tombstone says, thus putting an end to the hope that he would return to Hawaii to convert his people.

But then his death proved as great a stimulus as his life. Throughout New England the story of Opukahaia had flown. Books were written about him. Many had seen him as he traveled up and down, talking in churches about the unregenerate state of his people and raising funds for the Cornwall school. The growing Sunday School movement found in him a story and an inspiration just suited to its needs.

Even before Opukahaia's death, Sam Ruggles had been inspired to offer himself to the board, urging them to let him know immediately whether, with his small Latin (through Vergil) and less Greek (New Testament just begun) they would accept him. "I am destitute of anything that I can call mine," he confessed to them, and then told how he had been orphaned as a small child and brought up by friends. The board found a use for him at the Cornwall school. The Hawaiians seem to have taken to him. His big eyes, made quizzical by high arching brows, still show—in Samuel F. B. Morse's portrait of him—the look he must have given to the tales of human sacrifice and heathen rites Opukahaia and Thomas Hopu regaled him with.

It was Opukahaia's story that made Hiram Bingham offer himself too. Bingham, one of twelve children, had grown up on a farm outside of Bennington, Vermont, on the spot where Bennington College now stands. Until he was twenty-one he had farmed his father's land and learned like any young New England farmer to turn his hand to anything that needed mending or making. In the winter seasons he sometimes taught school. Although his father was deacon of the church (Congregational, of course), he was apparently unable to send his son to college. But at last, at the age when most men are launched on their careers, Hiram made his way up to Middlebury, graduating in 1816 at the age of twenty-six. By this time he felt that he wanted to be a minister. Hearing about Opukahaia, he went to Cornwall to see for himself and immediately felt the call to carry Christ to Hawaii. Turning down the offer of a teaching post at Goshen, he entered Andover Theological Seminary, center of enthusiasm for foreign missions. As his three years at Andover came to an end he visited Cornwall again, just in time to see Thomas examined in theology and Prince George in navigation. George was asked to calculate an eclipse that would occur in Kauai, his home island, in September, 1820—with the very good prospect that he would get there in time to see it. In July of 1819 Bingham formally offered himself to the board.

Hiram was now a rather handsome young man with a longish face, high forehead, and a long straight line from high cheekbones to firm chin. Intelligence, self-confidence, determination, and perhaps even a consciousness of his power to charm people and have his own way showed in his bright eyes, the slight forward thrust of the head.* Some of his Bennington neighbors thought him conceited.

Prompted by high praise from Hiram's Andover professors, the board quickly accepted him, ordering him to be ready to leave for Hawaii within a few months. This left Hiram with a problem even greater than being accepted by the board. He had to find a girl who would accept him as a husband.

So Hiram, who did all things with energy, now began the hunt for a wife. Possibly his drive scared the first prospect, for it appears that a Sarah S.—— to whom he offered his hand backed away, discouraged also by parents who could not bear the thought of having her

---

* Fortunately four of the couples—Bingham, Holman, Ruggles and Whitney —had their portraits done on the eve of departure by Samuel F. B. Morse, better known for his invention of the telegraph.

go so far. The time came for Hiram's ordination and still he had no wife, nor any prospect of one. This was serious, since the board opposed sending anyone out without a helpmate.

On September 28 Hiram was at Goshen, Connecticut, where he and Asa Thurston, the only ministers of the group, were to be ordained. Among the many interested spectators was Sybil Moseley, a young New Englander who had been teaching out in Canandaigua, New York, "in the far west." Hiram quickly swept her off her feet with his habitual fire and fervor.

"He has secured my tenderest love," she wrote. The handsome face, the deep sense of inner purpose and conviction which he not only felt but could convey with power to those about him—these had done their work. On October 11 they were married at Hartford—exactly two weeks after their first meeting.

In appearance Sybil was no match for Hiram. Her nose was too long, and it turned up at the end. Where his eyes looked wide upon the world, hers squinted as if in withdrawal or timidity. Yet everyone who ever met her spoke of her with warm affection.

A few days before the wedding she wrote to Hiram's parents (her own had died while she was still in her teens) to say how sorry she was that they could not come to the wedding. "That I might once receive the benediction of his revered parents, the embrace of his affectionate sisters, with the welcome of his brothers would be a circumstance the remembrance of which would be sweetly cherished when oceans would roll between and the confused jargon of savage tongues would fall upon my ears," she wrote. "May God of His infinite mercy grant that at the glorious day we *do* meet and hail each other in kindness and Christian love."

On the day the *Thaddeus* set sail, Sybil sent eight hundred dollars—her whole fortune—to the board, giving it for the support of missions. They were dollars she might well have used later on. But dedication to a cause was no halfway matter with Sybil Bingham.

Asa Thurston had also been looking around for a wife before his ordination. The students at Andover willingly came to his aid and one, William Goodell, offered to find out whether his cousin Lucy Goodale would consider matrimony.

She gave her permission for a visit to her home in Marlboro, Mas-

sachusetts. On September 23, robust, broad-shouldered Asa arrived
at the fine old country home at sunset and was introduced by William
Goodell to Lucy, her father, two brothers and their wives, and cousin
William's father. After supper there was talk, singing and evening
worship. Then one by one the family dispersed, leaving Lucy and Asa
at last to get acquainted. They separated at midnight "as interested
friends." The next forenoon they had made up their minds and pledged
themselves to each other "as close companions in the race of life." The
race, judging from the courtship, would be run at a swift pace.

Now Asa had to go off to his ordination on September 28. By publishing the banns on the next three Sundays, they could manage to be
married on October twelfth. And so they were.

Meanwhile Lucy, supported by brothers to pay bills and carry
parcels, went in to Boston to get outfitted. Back home in Marlboro
she had a table spread the whole length of one of the low-ceiled front
rooms, and with three friends began cutting garments by the dozen.
More helpers came in to sew, and Lucy's outfit was ready when Asa
came back to make her his wife.

A native of near-by Fitchburg, Asa had gone to Yale before entering theological school. Born in 1787, he was a full eight years
older than his bright-eyed, vivacious and intelligent wife. Asa himself, though only five feet six or eight, was sturdy and muscular, the
best athlete in his time at Yale. His broad face with its powerful self-
confident eyes, wide nostrils and ruddy good health would have suggested robust sexual power more than spiritual strength if Asa Thurston had not been a missionary. As events were to prove, he was the
most dedicated missionary of them all.

Though the Thurstons were the last to marry, there had been a
flurry of weddings during the month before the party was to sail.
Only the Chamberlains were settled in domesticity before the call
came. Older than the rest of the group, Daniel Chamberlain and his
wife, Jerusha, were in their middle thirties. Their five children, three
sons and two daughters, would of course go with them. Respected as
a successful farmer and a captain in the War of 1812, Daniel gave up
his settled way of life at Brookfield, Massachusetts, in order to reclaim the supposedly indolent Hawaiians from their idleness and
show them how to farm. A difficult assignment—though Daniel's

stiffly held head, with its firm look of command overlying features that seem about to break into a smile suggest that he, if anyone, would be capable of it.

On the twenty-second of September Sam Ruggles of the quizzical eyebrows married Nancy Wells at her home, East Windsor, Connecticut. Four years older than her husband, Nancy was pretty in a prim sort of way, her big eyes and oval face and hair curling at both temples somehow failing to overcome a tightness about the small, sweet mouth. Perhaps it was only that she had practiced single blessedness to the age of twenty-nine.

Lucia Ruggles, Sam's sister, was a handsome girl too. She and Thomas Holman had been born within a few weeks of each other at Brookfield, Connecticut. Thomas had gone away to study medicine at the Cherry Valley Medical School in central New York. Apparently he had not forgotten Lucia. When the board, reading testimonials which called him a "discreet, solid and pious young man," decided to make him the mission's doctor, he asked Lucia to marry him, which she promptly did on September twenty-sixth.

They made a handsome couple. Lucia's head, classic in features except for the dramatically heavy eyebrows, rested upon an unusually long but graceful neck. She wore her hair in a more stylish fashion than the other women permitted themselves, the part carelessly off center, the hair behind the top of her head raised up on combs in a sort of arching crown. She looked passionate, imperious, and perhaps a little spoiled. The young doctor was a match for her, with his high forehead, curling hair, and matinee-idol charm—firm chin with a slight cleft, brooding eyes, eloquent eyebrows and petulant shadow under the mouth.

Elisha Loomis and Maria Sartwell were next, on September twenty-seventh. "By a remarkable providence," as he says, he met in Utica a young lady who had long been feeling the call to mission work. He inquired about her, received flattering accounts of her character, and after spending several days in her company was satisfied that she would do. "Everything appears to be agreeable with both parties," he wrote to the board. And he promised to set out for Boston as soon as he could make her Mrs. Loomis. Youngest of all the group, Elisha had not yet turned twenty—a point his wife had reached three years ahead of him. He was to be the mission printer.

Samuel Whitney, born in Branford, Connecticut, to parents "in reduced circumstances," had been apprenticed to a shoemaker at fourteen. At eighteen he got religion, made a public profession, and then began to feel that he wished to devote himself to the missionary cause. In time he got to Yale, where the Education Society supported him for a year.

"Whitney is a young man of medium capacity," Professor Chauncey Goodrich advised the board, "patient, persevering, neither very slow nor very rapid in acquisition . . . judicious, humble and devoted to the service of Christ. His elocution is not very good, his taste is not refined, there is nothing striking in his manner of presenting a subject. He would be respectable but not distinguished . . . better as an instructor than as a preacher."

Modestly agreeing with this estimate, Whitney told the board: "I cannot feel myself qualified to be a principal in any missionary station. To engage as an assistant and instructor is my object.

"I think I am more inclined to bodily than mental exertion," he confessed. The board put him down as "mechanic and schoolmaster."

On September fourth, having heard that the board had accepted him, he wrote back to inquire whether he should take a wife.

"Though I have made no engagements," he told them with Yankee caution, "I have one in view whose piety and other missionary qualifications have been highly recommended." And would the board kindly let him know by Wednesday or Thursday next?

On October fourth, Sam Whitney, long-faced and solemn and still looking rather boyish despite his twenty-six years, stood up with pretty, round-faced Mercy Partridge in her home town of Pittsfield, Massachusetts, and took her to his wife.

With perhaps one exception, every one of these marriages was based on a deep sense of Christian discipleship. Their very haste was proof of the faith and missionary zeal of the partners. As soon as they married, the young couples began to move towards Boston. Not one of them came from Boston itself. Rather, they came from the little inland villages of New England where there was less sophistication and perhaps more piety.

By Friday, October the fifteenth they had all reached Boston—the two missionaries Bingham and Thurston, the five assistants, the wives, the five Chamberlain children, the three Hawaiian members and Prince George. In Park Street Church they drew up their covenant and articles of faith in the Congregational way as the Pilgrims had done, freely binding themselves "to walk together in a church state, in the faith and order of the Gospel."

That evening Asa Thurston opened with prayer, Hiram Bingham preached to them, and the instructions of the board were read. On Saturday the farewell service was held in a crowded church. This time Thurston preached while Thomas Hopu spoke extempore, first in English, then in Hawaiian for the benefit of five Hawaiian youths who had recently come to New England to be educated.

A week went by before the *Thaddeus* was finally ready to sail. Then, on Saturday the twenty-third, the little group assembled with their friends and families on Boston's Long Wharf for a parting all expected to be forever. Prayers were said, hymns sung. Bingham, Thurston and a friend sang in close harmony, "When shall we all meet again?" It melted nearly everyone to tears—tears that in that tearful era flowed generously from men and women alike—while the twenty-three passengers stepped down into a smart-looking fourteen-oared barge kindly provided by the skipper of the naval ship *Independence*. A patch of dirty harbor water appeared between the barge and the wharf. Hands were raised, both to wave and to hold handkerchiefs to red eyes. The space widened, the waving died down, then rose again in fitful surges as if to hold back the ebbing of tide and time and lifelong bonds of friendship and love.

The mission women were hoisted aboard the little *Thaddeus* in a chair, while the men climbed a rope ladder. The brig—eighty-five feet long, 240 tons burden—dropped down to the lower harbor and the next day put out to sea.

Within a few hours everyone except the Hawaiians was sick. The tiny cabins, piled high with baggage and supplies, offered little or nothing in the way of comfort. By the third day, however, the whole mission family managed to crawl up on deck. Here, too, the space was crowded with hogsheads, tubs, cables, a dog, cats, hens, ducks, pigs. At mealtime a pot full of soup was placed on deck. Around it the passengers squatted like children, and so they ate for several days until a proper table was finally arranged. Then the meals included coffee and hash for breakfast; meat, peas and potatoes for dinner; tea, crackers and cheese for supper.

At last the sickness wore off, returning only with storms. The landsmen grew used to the creaking of the booms, the flapping of sails against masts and rigging, the endless roll and dip of the vessel. They came to know the hoarse howl of a high wind in the rigging, the shouts of the officers, the chanting of the seamen, the rhythmic clang of the ship's bell.

And they began to know each other. Everyone had praise for Sybil Bingham. "She excels in everything that is good," Maria Loomis confided to her diary. "We have felt peculiarly united ever since we first saw each other." Daniel Chamberlain thought her "peculiarly calculated for a missionary's wife."

Hiram Bingham felt himself warmly drawn toward Sam Ruggles and his prim and pretty Nancy. Forceful and self-assured, Hiram had already begun to assume leadership even though Thurston was two years older.

As for the Chamberlain children, they had got their sea legs while the rest were still losing their dinners. Dexter and Nathan soon knew the names of all the hundreds of ropes, stays and tackle, climbing into the rigging like old hands. Young Daniel sang to the admiration of all while even little Nancy quickly learned to stand like a sailor when the ship rocked. Tutors were assigned to the three boys and to Mary. A voyage was no excuse for a New England youngster to skip school.

Life began to fall into a routine. There were classes in Hawaiian, Bible reading, daily devotions. But there were also the special events, such as sighting land after three months in the open sea, or the time several of the brethren went over the side to swim and just escaped a voracious shark. Or the time Brother Whitney offered to help paint the ship and was spilled backwards into the water when a rope broke. Someone had the presence of mind to throw him a bench until the ship could be brought round, and that bench became a permanent item in the Whitney household. When Mercy rushed to the rail in a frenzy of fear, Sam calmly raised his hat to her to show that all was well.

Two things troubled the brothers. Prince George was absenting himself from worship. Even at Cornwall he had shown little interest in religion, though sharp enough in his studies. Now, with the arguments of some deists among the ship's crew to support him, he was growing downright recalcitrant. What would happen if he openly opposed the mission when it reached Hawaii?

Even more distressing was the fact that Lucia Holman was turning out to be a self-willed, self-pampering young woman. During the voyage she made up her mind that she was not cut out for a missionary and openly said so. She also helped herself to delicacies which she claimed were her private property but which the brothers claimed came under mission control. Worst of all, her husband backed her up.

Finally, on March twenty-third, in by-laws drawn up for the mission community it was clearly specified that all property was to be held in common whether received from the Christian public or through individual barter or earning. The leaders wanted this clearly understood before they reached Hawaii, where this and all their other principles would be put to a hard test. It was impossible for them to know that a Russian commander who had visited the islands the year before was now writing in the account of his world tour:

"Were it possible to introduce the Christian faith and the art of writing among the Sandwich Islanders, they would in one century reach a state of civilization unparalleled in history. But it is not easy to introduce an outside religion to a free and strong race!"

CHAPTER 3

THE ISLES SHALL WAIT FOR HIS LAW
1820

AS THE *Thaddeus* COASTED DOWN THE WESTERN SIDE OF
Hawaii, the hump of the crater Hualalai rose more than eight thousand feet off her port bow. Halfway to Kailua a broad stream of lava
left a desolate track all the way to the ocean. It was to strike the
missionaries that the land was very much like the people—fresh, ver-
dant, sunny and cheerful in one aspect, dark, dangerous and deso-
lated in another. Their aim was to push back the darkness forever.
They had as yet no sounding of its depths.

Aboard the *Thaddeus,* now, was a crowd of chiefs and their servants, all of them happy to sail on such a proper ship. To men who
made the fifty-mile trips between islands in outrigger canoes, even
the little *Thaddeus* was luxurious. The chiefs had their mats spread
on deck where they lounged, ate and slept in a clutter of calabashes
full of their favorite foods—poi, fish, pig. At such close quarters,
Yankees and islanders began to get used to one another's ways,
though Lucy Thurston felt "a climax of queer sensations" when
crossing the deck in the evening between two rows of men dressed
in nothing but the narrow *malo* about their waists.

Queen Kalakua, who had been eyeing the dresses of the ladies,
now brought out a web of white cambric, indicating that she wanted
a dress made which she could wear ashore at Kailua, the king's residence. The mission ladies would do no sewing on Sunday, but early
Monday morning Kalakua arranged all seven of them about her on
mats. Lucia Holman and her sister-in-law, Nancy Ruggles, did the
cutting and presumably the measuring of their hefty client. The
others sewed. Then, with Yankee abhorrence of idle hands, they
brought out a pile of calico scraps and showed the queen's attendants

how to make patchwork quilts. Apparently it was a pastime that appealed, for Hawaiian women became expert quiltmakers, inventing very charming designs and patterns of their own.

While Kalakua was getting clothed, Prime Minister Kalanimoku—sometimes called "The Iron Cable of Hawaii" or sometimes just Billy Pitt—was learning to read. His teacher was young Daniel Chamberlain, who sat in his lap with open spelling book, teaching him his letters. When Billy Pitt grew tired of learning, Dan stood in the midst of the queens and chiefesses and taught them as a class, making them repeat the letters of the alphabet after him. They seemed to find it a delightful game. "And a little child shall lead them." On every hand the Scriptures were being fulfilled.

On Tuesday morning, April fourth, the brig anchored before Kailua after a voyage of 163 days from Boston. Queen Kalakua could hardly wait to go ashore in her new gown, which, as fashion decreed, came down to the tops of her shoes. Only she had no shoes. The ladies had made up for this by giving her a lace cap decorated with a wreath of roses and a lace half-neckerchief which surrounded her sturdy pillar of a neck, but gave up the attempt to cover her wide bosom. When she went ashore the waiting crowd sent up a shout of admiration and approval.

Everyone in Kailua knew about the passengers on the *Thaddeus*—about the Yankee teachers, the Hawaiian boys returning after years of exile, but mostly about the women. They were disappointed when only Thomas Hopu, Bingham, Thurston and Captain Blanchard came ashore, for they had wanted to see the women and children.

Yet their broad Polynesian faces were warm with smiles as the foreigners stepped up the lava-strewn beach. Hiram Bingham, his bright eyes taking in everything around him, noted that their noses were wide but not flat, their lips relaxed and life-loving, their foreheads high and retreating. Men and women alike were naked to the waist, their skin tattooed with animals. The women had their hair cut short, whitened and stiffened with lime above the forehead. The men shaved their heads or cut their hair to look like a helmet, the crest stained with lime. The friendly smiles disclosed wide gaps where front teeth had been knocked out in a ritual of sorrow for a departed king or chieftain. Hiram Bingham tried to ignore the nakedness, to take it for granted as the Hawaiians did themselves. Though prejudice told him it was shocking, common sense insisted that it suited the climate well and—as many a foreigner was to observe—that brown bodies scarcely seemed nude anyhow.

Pushing through the crowd, the party made their way into the little village of thatched houses. Kailua had a forbidding, desolate look which the grinning faces and warm greetings could not hide. Though the Hawaiians loved it for the broad calm ocean with its excellent fishing and fine rollers for surfing and bathing, there was little else to recommend it. Lava rock and cinders lay all about, leaving only the tiniest patches where gardens could flourish. Fresh water was miles away.

Prompted by Prime Minister Kalanimoku, the visitors marched off to call on Kuakini, governor of the island. Although Brothers Thurston and Bingham had got used to the idea that Hawaiian chiefs were generously built, they were not prepared for Kuakini—or Adams as he had been dubbed at the time when John Adams was President of the United States. For Kuakini was immense. Between four and five hundred pounds, he was as shrewd as he was tremendous. Men crouched and crawled in his presence, and the poor horse he rode sagged and nearly broke beneath him. Weight had not made him torpid. He had a keen thirst for knowledge and had already learned some English, in which he greeted Bingham and Thurston.

Next they went to call on a personality who at this point was even more interesting to them than Kuakini. This was John Young, an Englishman who had lived in Hawaii for thirty years. He had been left behind by his ship and, after wandering from place to place, was given land by Kamehameha. Young helped the king in his wars, became a trusted chief, and was given the king's niece in marriage. Striking in appearance, he looked rather frightening with his piercing eyes set in deep, dark sockets, a bird's beak of a nose, and skin furrowed and darkened by wind and sun.

Despite his forbidding looks, Young eagerly welcomed these blood brothers from the other side of the world. Though Hawaiianized and with a swarm of hapahaole * children around him, he longed for the

---

* Hapa—half; haole—foreigner, white. Haole and hapahaole are convenient and familiar words in the island vocabulary.

sound of his own language and for news of the western world. Probably he went along to the next stop, which was at the house of the king.

Crawling in through the narrow, three-foot-high doorway, Hiram Bingham could hardly see the man to whom he was presented in the windowless room. Gradually, however, he was able to make him out as he lay on his mat—a young, amiable-looking fellow with curly hair, low, bulging brows, the full Hawaiian lips and nostrils, dark skin, squinting eyes and a generally humorous look. Around him lay his five wives, all naked to the waist, all enjoying one of their frequent meals. Of the queens, Kamamalu, his half-sister, was the most beautiful. She had a rousingly generous figure and a pretty face, her large eyes accented by wide, smooth arching eyebrows, her lips full-bowed, her chin childishly round, her nostrils having a sensual fullness that must have made Hiram Bingham feel vaguely ill at ease.

A swarm of servants cared for every possible need of the royal household—separating the meat with hands which they then licked and wiped off on their legs, waving flies away with long feathered brushes, or holding out the calabash, decorated with the teeth of his ancestors, in which the king's spittle was saved. When the king drank, everyone squatted. When he had finished eating, an ever-watchful servant brought him a calabash of water for his hands, with leaves to dry them on.

While the wives moved to one corner for a game of cards, Bingham and Thurston, through Thomas, made the king a gift of a spyglass and told him why they had come.

"We have nothing to do with the political concern of these islands," they told him, though in years to come their sincerity on this point was to be questioned. Then they explained that they had come to do him and his people good.

"Let them stay," said the king's favorite, Kamamalu.

"Then I can have but one wife," said the king, "and you would have to go."

Hurt, Kamamalu got up to leave, but the king said he was fooling and ordered her to stay.

Bingham and Thurston got no promise from the king that day, so on the next they came again. This time they presented him with "the elegant Bible furnished by the American Bible Society." The king appeared grateful, but was still unwilling to say whether the group could settle in his islands. His advisers—chiefs and foreigners—were in disagreement, and the outcome was by no means certain. But Bingham did learn that rumors had begun to circulate that Great Britain, regarded by the Hawaiian court as the fatherly protector of the islands, would be displeased if American missionaries were allowed to take up residence. Hiram, always eloquent when aroused, did his best to settle these fears. Then he invited the king to dine aboard the *Thaddeus* the next day.

So on Thursday, the sixth of April, Liholiho, his wives and a troop of attendants paddled out to the *Thaddeus* over the sparkling blue water in a flotilla of canoes. The king and his ladies rode on the raised platform of a double canoe rowed by twenty men, the tall *kahilis*—ornate feather fly brushes—waving over them. This time the king was dressed in what Bingham called the princely style of the islands—breechcloth of tapa, a chain of gold on his neck, a scarf of green silk knotted over his right shoulder, and a wreath of yellow feathers on his head. The chiefs, both men and women, always had garlands of feathers or flowers and leaves about them, the Americans noted. It was graceful, it was attractive—yet from the mission point of view it was also vain.

Though it was perhaps the first time the king had ever seen foreign women, Hiram noted that he behaved with much decorum. He sat down at the head of the table and appeared to enjoy the dishes put before him. He was such an easygoing, amiable-looking fellow that Hiram could see no reason why he should not grant what they wished.

After prayers dinner was served, and after dinner the king asked for some music. The bass viol was brought out, that chosen instrument of the New England churches, and Prince George himself played it. Hiram and Asa, both fine singers, joined their voices in close harmony as they sang several hymns and psalms. The group sang in chorus too, much to the delight of the young king and all his suite. Then with words of thanks and aloha they dropped down into their canoes and swept across the shining water again.

The next day some of the ladies went ashore. Not all of them, but enough to stir up the whole of Kailua. Crowds pressed about the boat as they stepped out in their long dresses, their bonnets with deep visors. As they started down the cindery path to the king's house, men ran ahead of them in order to peer up under the bonnets and get a look at their faces. "Aloha," they said. And then, "Their necks are long—they look well." It has usually been explained that the Hawaiians nicknamed the mission women "Longnecks" because of their bonnets. But bonnets do not make long necks, and the Hawaiians were both accurate and humorous in the nicknames they gave foreigners. A glance at the portraits shows that Sybil Bingham, Nancy Ruggles and Lucia Holman all had long, slender necks.

The hubbub died down as they approached the king's house where ten or fifteen soldiers were on guard. Although it was between ten and eleven o'clock in the morning, the king as well as his attendants were sound asleep on their mats. But they soon roused, and the king asked whether the mission couples would stay to dinner. He seemed pleased when they accepted and ordered wine to be served them immediately.

Soon the five queens appeared, some in calico, some in elegant silk gowns with silk stockings and men's shoes—all with the delicately wrought coronets of yellow feathers. They were delighted to see their American counterparts again. Servants were sent scurrying. They returned with a scarlet tray cloth which they spread upon a large, round mahogany table. Then a trayful of china cups and saucers was brought in, along with a big bowl full of tea which had been boiled with sugar cane. One of the queens ladled this out into the cups which, with silver tablespoons, were then handed round. Then came sea biscuit and poi, and after that wine again.

While dinner was preparing, the missionaries walked out to have a look at the country. Men, women, children, dogs and pigs came pouring out of every house they passed, until they had the whole village following after them, and trying to get close enough to see around the visored bonnets. Naked, noisy, uninhibited and happy, the crowd trailed along as the foreigners walked on to look at the ruined temple near by. Lucia Holman, though exasperated by the peering, pushing crowd, was impressed by the vast ruin. There was stone enough there, she thought, to build a city. Holding tight to her handsome husband, she looked at the ugly wooden gods and shivered at the thought that but a few months ago anyone who had stepped, even accidentally, into these premises would have been put to death.

Walking back, the group looked more closely at the huts along the road, wondering how human beings could exist in them and noting that dogs, pigs and chickens shared the cramped quarters with the rest of the family. They were to learn that some families lacked even these frail, dark and verminous houses, living instead in caves or cracks in the lava.

When they returned to the king's house about one o'clock, dinner was ready. Elegant, wrought Chinese gilt chairs had been arranged around the table for the foreigners, but the king and his queens preferred the floor. With its layers of pebbles, grass, coarse and then fine mats up to twenty thicknesses, it was as comfortable as a bed. While the king ate his favorite dishes—fish and poi, baked dog, breadfruit and sweet potatoes, those at the table were offered roast pig, fowls, vegetables, and then wine again. It was a good meal, but meticulous Lucia Holman thought that it was like going home when she reached the brig.

On the next day, the eighth, the two leaders again pressed the king for his decision since Captain Blanchard was getting impatient to put his passengers ashore and get on with his voyage. Specifically, they asked permission to settle at Kailua and at Honolulu on the island of Oahu. It was not wise, they explained, for all of them to settle in a place so unproductive as Kailua. If only some of them could settle on fertile land, they could raise enough food for all, and be no burden to the king or his people. The king, however, wanted them all settled at Kailua where he could keep an eye on them. He offered them a large house, thirty by ninety feet, with no partitions.

When Sunday had passed in prayers and petitions, all the brethren went ashore in a body on Monday the tenth, visiting John Young, Prime Minister Kalanimoku and Naihe, another powerful and apparently friendly chief. But in the midst of their negotiations a great shouting and shuffling of bare feet arose in the village. Attendants rushed out to join the melee. It was only two youths getting ready to hula, but the whole village was bent upon seeing them. The talks had to be broken off. Against their will, the Americans followed their hosts to an open space where about two thousand people had collected. Half a dozen men sat in the midst of them beating on gourds and singing a tuneless chant. In front of them the dancers, with wreaths on their heads and wrists, gaiters thickly set with dog's teeth on their legs and fold after fold of tapa wound around their waists, moved their bodies in a smooth, sinuous and skillful undulation which the missionaries thought disgusting. Worst of all, it was a "time-killing" activity. Here, at the very moment when they were trying to bring the message of salvation to the land, the people were dancing their way to perdition.

Perhaps it was John Young who told them frankly what was working against them. Among the king's companions was a Frenchman named Jean Rives, a shady character who served as the king's bootblack, cook and bottle companion, who cherished his malign influence over the king, which depended upon the encouragement he gave to the king's carousing, and who naturally enough looked upon the missionaries as a dangerous threat. Rives was smart enough to see that if the missionaries were allowed to land, his days were numbered. So behind the scenes he was using all his influence against them. They would seize control of the country, he told the king, persuading Liholiho that the reason Bingham wanted to take part of the mission group to Honolulu was in order to put the island of Oahu under his own power. He also told the king that the true religion would have to come from France.

The arguments Rives put forward were supported by the notions the Hawaiians had acquired for themselves. Long accustomed to priests to whom murder of innocent victims was an item of faith, the plain people feared that the missionaries would bring a similarly heartless regime back again. When Bingham closed his eyes to pray, they fled in a panic, thinking that he was about to pray them to death. Hawaiian kahunas had actually possessed this power. So great was the belief of the people in the priestly power that they literally lay down and died when convinced that they were being prayed against.

Beneath all their petty objections many Hawaiians seem to have known instinctively that opening the door to these well-meaning, powerful men would mean the end of life as they liked to live it. Having just overthrown their tabus, they were enjoying a release and freedom that promised well. They were happy; they needed nothing. Why submit to a new god, new priests, new ways?

But in the end John Young persuaded the king to let the mission remain. Recalling Vancouver's failure to send the English preachers he had promised, Young said: "These men worship the same God and teach the same religion. Let them stay."

The next day the king—supported by the approval of the powerful dowager queen—gave his permission, but with conditions. The doctor and one of the two preachers must remain with him at Kailua. The others could go to Honolulu where he would have quarters built for them. But they were to send for no reinforcements, and permission to stay was limited to one year.

Now the group had to settle the question: Would the Binghams or the Thurstons stay at Kailua? Neither wanted to do so, partly from a dislike of the dismal, lava-strewn location and partly because of the uneasiness towards the Holmans which had developed during the voyage. So a vote was taken and Asa Thurston lost. Thomas Hopu and William Kanui, taken into the king's service, were also to stay and help the Americans.

Tuesday, April twelfth, was "a busy, trying, joyful and important day," according to the mission journal. From the *Thaddeus,* anchored a mile offshore, boats plied busily back and forth, carrying trunks, boxes and supplies for a full year, since no one knew when a ship might come this way again. Losing no time at their work, the missionaries gave the king a book with which to begin his studies. He worked at it with as much diligence as he could muster.

After tea, at nine o'clock in the evening, the Holmans, Thurstons and the two Hawaiians sundered themselves, in Lucy Thurston's phrase, "from close family ties, from the dear old brig, and from civilization." Ashore, they were led to a thatched hut with one room, about twenty rods from the beach. This was to be their home. Its floor was the usual grass covered with mats, its windows two open holes. Piled here and there all over the room were the trunks and barrels and boxes from the ship. Lucy, the methodical Yankee housekeeper, saw that everything would have to be moved out for a thorough house cleaning before they could settle themselves properly. So for the first night they merely moved enough boxes and trunks to make platforms for their mattresses. They listened to a reading from the Bible, sang a hymn, knelt in prayer, and then lay down.

But not to sleep. Though they were guarded outside by a detachment of soldiers, the enemy had already stolen in. The hut was alive with fleas who made the night sleepless.

In the morning, while the two Hawaiians went calling on the chiefs dressed in broadcloth suits, ruffled shirts and heavy watch chains, the preacher and the doctor, urged on by Lucy, went to work in their shirts with sleeves rolled up. They threw out all the old grass and mats, vigorously swept down the thatch from ridge to floor, and spread new grass and mats. Thurston, who loved exercise, seemed to enjoy it. This scouring of the old was a vigorous symbol of what the mission intended toward every department of Hawaiian life, and to a Yankee who firmly believed cleanliness to be next to godliness, this was as good a place as any to start. Dr. Holman, smaller and fastidious, approved the end but was not so happy over the means.

The *Thaddeus* had been too small to carry any furniture. When Queen Kamamalu saw Lucia trying to spread a bed on top of chests and boxes and learned from Hopu what was needed, she went off and came back triumphantly leading a contingent of servants who bore on their backs two large, elegant, high-post mahogany bedsteads with cane bottoms. The grateful women had the beds placed in opposite corners of the room and hung curtains all around them. By placing the beds a few feet from one wall and then running another curtain from wall to bed, they created little dressing rooms safe from prying eyes. A large chest in the middle of the room did for a table until, on the fourth day, the king sent a handsome round mahogany table which served the Thurston household for fifty years. Boxes and buckets were used as chairs until, a few weeks later, two friendly whaling captains called and gave not only chairs but badly needed crockery.

For three days the king's steward kept three pewter platters full of fish, taro and sweet potatoes for them. Meanwhile a craze of reading had swept the royal household. Three or four times a day the queens swarmed into the house with their crowd of attendants, demanding to be listened to while they read. Since the king had decreed that royalty and the chiefs must learn before the common people could be taught, the house outside was surrounded with people who could at least hear, though they could not see, the *palapala* (reading). Soon they trotted about repeating what they had heard. Everywhere the new-comers went they heard "ABC."

The effort soon grew too much for the king, but he insisted that his little seven-year-old brother and heir to the throne, Kauikeaouli, should keep at it. And he ordered two of his favorites, Kahuhu and Ii, the lighter of his pipe, to take to their books. "Teach these," he told Thurston; "it will be the same as teaching me. Through them I shall find out what learning is." Several months later, returning from a trip, he was so delighted with the progress they had made that he seized Asa's hand in both of his own and kissed it.

Running a Yankee household in the Pacific paradise was still full of difficulties. The cookstove had to be set up in the front yard, where swarms of curious people came to see the women at work. Fresh water had to be carried from two to five miles in gourds, and when Lucy let some of the Hawaiians wash her delicate tropical fab-rics, they came back full of holes. As for personal bathing, for which the mission ladies also required fresh water, the Hawaiians could never understand why Americans should not do as they did—take off their clothes and step into the ocean in front of their door. The no-tion that nudity was nasty simply did not exist in the Hawaiian mind.

When the king moved into a new set of houses, he gave his old one to the Thurstons and Holmans. Though still a grass shack, in con-trast to the first hut, it was a palace with two front doors—one only two and a half, the other little more than three feet high. There was no way to lock it up, so someone had to stay home to guard the pos-sessions. This became a serious matter when the Holmans, after three months at Kailua and without permission from the brethren, sailed off to the island of Maui in search of a pleasanter place to live. Lucia Holman had been at Kailua only three days when she confessed to Lucy that she "would never be willing to exercise that degree of self-denial which was called for by a situation among this people." Pam-pered by an adoring husband, irritated by the lack of privacy, the lack of water, the vexation of trying to direct Hawaiian servants, and the "heathenish" taste of the food they generously provided, she found her only solution in flight. With the king's permission she and her husband went to Lahaina on Maui where they moved in with a Mr. Butler and his hapahaole family until a house could be readied for them.

That left Lucy Thurston, when her husband was away, to face the crowds of the curious alone. She was teaching the young prince, Kauikeaouli, one day when a half-drunk priest of the old religion wandered into the house. With motions whose suggestiveness Lucy recognized easily enough, he pulled off his breechcloth and stood naked before her. The prince and his retainers, still awed by the recent life-and-death power of the priesthood, scurried out of the house. The priest advanced; Lucy moved back. In this manner they circled the room again and again. Reaching the big bed, the priest threw himself onto it, rolling voluptuously from side to side. Then he started chasing Lucy again. She ran out one front door, but having no refuge to go to, ran in at the other. In and out they went until she decided to make her stand in the courtyard. Trapped at last in a corner, she grabbed a stick and brought it down with all her force on the man's arm. When he drew back, she started running. She ran through the watching crowd, not one of whom had dared lift a finger, and on towards the palace a quarter of a mile distant where she knew her husband would be. On the way she met Asa, who had been summoned by Thomas Hopu. Trembling, Lucy held to his strong arm.

They had hardly reached home when the house was filled with the chiefs and queens, the latter rubbing noses with Lucy and telling her, "Very great is our love to you." In the midst of all this the priest had the truculence to return. Immediately the people prostrated themselves. But Asa, after ordering him to leave and failing to get an immediate response, grimly threw him off the premises.

The priest's visit to Lucy brought to the fore one of the many cultural differences which made it hard for Hawaiians and Yankees to understand each other. To the Hawaiians sex was fun. Like eating and sleeping, it was one of the natural pleasures and, like them, to be as naturally enjoyed. It was the obvious way of expressing love and affection. Exchanging wives was a common act of friendship, while brothers often had their wives in common. To refuse an invitation to sexual intercourse was, to the Hawaiian, unnatural, ill-mannered and mean.

When the first ships had sailed in from the west, fathers had offered their daughters, husbands their wives and brothers their sisters
to the visitors. To do less would have been downright unfriendly. The
eagerness with which the girls had been welcomed made it clear to
the Hawaiians that they had done the right thing.

But here were men who never thought to offer their women in
friendliness, who resented any advances and who taught that the
whole thing was tabu—as tabu as eating bananas had once been to
women. It was all very puzzling. What kind of men were these?

CHAPTER 4

A FAIR HAVEN
1820

EARLY ON THE MORNING OF APRIL FOURTEENTH THE *Thaddeus,* passing the islands of Lanai and Molokai, brought the diminished mission group within sight of the island of Oahu. The young wives who had been depressed by the lava and cinders of Kailua felt their spirits revive at the sight of this lovely island. A living green swept all the way up to the sharp peaks of the mountain range running through its center. Remnants of old volcanic action, the slopes dropped steeply to the narrow valleys below, their fluted sides looking as if giant canoes had been upended, bottoms out, against sheer cliffs.

As the *Thaddeus* coasted towards Honolulu—Hawaiian for Fair Haven—its Yankee passengers noted the clustered huts of thatch here and there along the shore, the coconut groves with the lazy, inviting tilt of long, slender trunks, the deep gashes where narrow valleys ran between sudden crags. Rich velvet greens, mottled to blue by cloud shadow and the shadows the crowded hills threw upon each other; blue ocean running from a hue almost black in the depths to a delicate turquoise inshore; and always the scud of cottony clouds over the mountains—this was the real Hawaii.

Ahead of them rose Diamond Hill, an extinct crater at the water's edge which marked the approach to Honolulu. The *Thaddeus,* stopping short of the narrow gap in the coral reef which made Honolulu so safe a harbor, put down a boat. Captain Blanchard, Hiram Bingham and a few other members of the mission landed near the fort. Begun by a party of Russians in 1816, it was completed by the Hawaiians after Kamehameha had ordered the Russians to leave. Accustomed to building great stone platforms for their temples, the

47

Hawaiians had only needed foreign advice on how to use stone for defense. The fort was about three hundred feet square, its walls of adobe and coral twelve feet high and twenty feet thick at the base.

The party headed for the most prominent landmark of the town itself—the stuccoed and whitewashed house of the Spaniard Don Francisco de Paula Marin. A resident of the islands for more than twenty years (no one knew exactly when or whence he had come), Marin had introduced most of the fruits and vegetables of the western world. In his beautifully tended gardens he raised lemons, oranges and pineapples as well as all the familiar vegetables. He made cigars from his own tobacco, butter from his own herd, wine from his own grapes. He salted beef for ships, worked as a mason or ship's carpenter, and lived in his neatly enclosed buildings with his second Hawaiian wife (whom he beat occasionally) and a swarm of hapa-haole children, some of whom were by now grown up. He had served Kamehameha I as physician. He had been present when the old king had died and the people, throwing off all restraint, had indulged in a general sexual orgy. This and other items of interest he had noted from day to day in his journal, as well as the growth of his possessions which had by now made him at forty-five a wealthy man. Needless to say, his wealth combined with his frugality had made him about as unpopular as he was useful.

He was also the official interpreter for the government, which was why Bingham now made his way towards the wall of coral and mud which enclosed Marin's buildings and from which flocks of beautiful doves rose in graceful circles. Marin received the Americans kindly and told them that Boki, governor of Oahu, had gone to another part of the island. As soon as he heard what the missionaries proposed, he sent two Hawaiians off on horseback after Boki.

Bingham then presented a note from Captain Nathan Winship of Boston. Winship, who owned a thatched house in Honolulu, asked Marin to unlock it for his countrymen, who were to use it until they had something better.

The delegation next called at the fort and then walked about the village among the hundreds of dilapidated-looking thatch huts, each of which had its patch of tobacco, melons, sweet potatoes and sugar cane. Inside the dark and verminous hut a whole family lived together in one room, sleeping naked on one mat and under one covering of tapa, sometimes with pet pigs and dogs mingled in amongst them. So great was the affection for these members of the household that a woman would often suckle a favorite puppy even though she might neglect her own infant. Sometimes she carried it in a sling of tapa, letting it nurse as she walked the street. Most of these dogs were short legged and small, with sharp noses, black mangy coats and long bodies and ears.

The party, followed and preceded by a pack of friendly, chattering Hawaiians, climbed up Punchbowl, the extinct crater just behind the town. Here they had a magnificent view of the central spine of mountains, the treeless plain leading out to Waikiki and Diamond Hill (not for many years to be known as Diamond Head), the fish ponds and the pools for salt-making along the shore, the harbor with the *Thaddeus* riding outside, and a valley full of wet fields where taro was growing, as Bingham noted, "with its large green leaves beautifully embossed on the silvery water, in which it flourishes."

Until Governor Boki returned, the mission did not feel at liberty to move on shore. It was the sixteenth before Boki appeared, and then he was too drunk to do any business. But when he came aboard the next day he was mild and courteous enough, though showing no great enthusiasm for having the mission take up residence. A handsome young man, with charcoal-black eyebrows accenting eyes that had depths of sadness in them, his round face and heavy, bow-shaped lips suggested a sensual, haughty, quick-tempered person—as in fact he turned out to be.

Boki permitted the brig to enter the harbor, which it did on April eighteenth, anchoring close to shore. When the ladies went to see the Winship house, and two others near by which had also been offered by Captains Lewis and Navarro, they were followed as usual by crowds who laughed and shouted, *"Aioeoe*—Longnecks." The next day they moved in—the seven Chamberlains to Winship's house, the Bingham, Ruggles and Loomis couples to Lewis's two hundred yards away, and the Whitneys to Navarro's between the other two.

With their goods piled helter-skelter, they were delighted to accept an invitation to supper that evening from Captain Pigot of New York. That night they got what sleep they could. They were only a hundred and fifty yards from the fort where once every hour a watchman struck a bell and gave a loud shout to indicate that all was well. The next morning they put up their cookstove, that symbol of western civilization, in one of the yards. Though they surrounded it with a fence of slender poles, a hundred Hawaiians at a time gathered to peer through the gaps at the strange white women who labored over the hot stove clothed from neck to ankles in superfluous, constrictive coverings.

They had very little in the way of furniture to trouble them, however, and hardly a chair amongst them. The crockery when they opened the box turned out to have been reduced to rubble. The women had a six months' wash to do, with no fresh water near by. Yet Maria Loomis could write, "Our trials are nothing to what we expected."

On the twenty-third of April they celebrated their first Sunday ashore with a meeting for worship at which Hiram Bingham preached from the text, "For behold I bring you good tidings of great joy." Assembling with the crowd of curious Hawaiians were some of the hundred to two hundred haoles—traders, sailors who had jumped ship, or escaped convicts from Australia who lived near by, some of whom had not been to church in twenty years. The sound of the familiar old hymns moved one long-time resident, Oliver Holmes, to tears. Prince George delighted the congregation with his singing and sawing on the bass viol.

A week later he departed tearfully from the brothers in order to return to his home on Kauai. The two Samuels, Whitney and Ruggles, went with him to make what capital they could for the mission out of returning the long-absent son to his kingly father.

Meanwhile Bingham kept after Boki who seemed in no hurry to supply the dwellings the king had ordered him to build. New to his job, easygoing and pleasure-loving, Boki let one day after another slip by without action. Hiram Bingham, calm but persistent, kept prodding him. Undisputed leader and only minister of the Oahu group, he would run the mission's affairs with a strong hand and a courageous heart for the next twenty years. That long firm jaw correctly told his character. Though young, he was as solid as rock, never wavering from the principles he believed in no matter what the risk.

By the fifth of May the mission family was well enough set up to entertain some of the foreigners who had been so helpful to them. Half a dozen of these gentlemen including Captains Pigot and Star-buck came to the Bingham-Ruggles-Loomis house for supper and the evening. "Civilized society" had made its debut in the islands. The grateful captains sent gifts and supplies.

Five days later Bingham, who was tired of waiting for Boki, called a public meeting to explain why the group had come to Hawaii, and to see whether any resident foreigners would volunteer to help put their houses up. But Boki persisted that he had orders from the king to put up the buildings and he alone must do it. Something, at least, was accomplished by the meeting—the first of its kind ever held in the islands. A fund was started for the education of "orphans"— euphemistic name for the children resulting from the union between haole sailors and Hawaiian maidens.

While they waited for their houses, the mission family were not idle. On the twenty-third of May they opened a small school which the women prepared to teach. Men like Marin and Holmes were glad of the chance to have their hapahaole children or their Hawaiian wives learn English. Others came of their own will. A woman named Pulunu brought two charming little daughters—apparently also hapa-haole. It was Pulunu who first learned to write a whole English sen-tence on her slate. "I cannot see God, but God can see me," she wrote. Delightedly, she explained it to the class in Hawaiian.

A few days later, towards evening, a bright-looking lad came and stood by the fence surrounding the cookstove. He was young and small, but with exceptionally pleasing features.

"Would you like to live with us, and learn to work and read?" Bingham asked him, evidently through William Kanui, the only in-terpreter now remaining with them.

"*Ae,*" said the lad, smiling his warm and winning smile. So Wil-liam Beals, son of a seaman who had died at Canton, became the first "orphan" of the mission. The ladies took him in, found clothes for him, gave him food, made a place for him to sleep. He learned Eng-lish so quickly that he was soon in demand as an interpreter, and even as a teacher of adult Hawaiians. A warm attachment grew up between him and Sybil Bingham—Sybil whom everyone seemed to fall in love with.

On the sixth of June Captain Starbuck, one of the men who had befriended the mission, sailed into port in his ship, *L'Aigle,* with good news. On a brief whaling voyage of only nineteen days he had made £2500. "Thus he who hath pity on the poor is rewarded," reasoned the mission journal.

Perhaps some of the residents reasoned likewise, for during this honeymoon period they showered the mission with kind attentions and acceptable gifts. James Hunnewell, the ship's mate, setting up shop with five casks of rum and assorted merchandise, led the way with his firm support and open friendship. William J. Pigot, like most of the early residents of Honolulu a combination of sea captain and merchant, not only had suggested the circular which called the first public meeting, but supplied the household, and when he left in July turned over his two-room house, which was assigned to the Loomises and Mercy Whitney—no doubt because Maria Loomis was soon to bear a child. "A pleasant retreat," she found it. As for poor Captain Pigot, he foundered somewhere between Hawaii and Fanning's Island.

Oliver Holmes of Plymouth, Massachusetts, now old, dignified and gray, supplied the mission school with one of its cleverest pupils. The teachers were delighted with the beautiful Hannah's progress until they discovered that her skill in English might in part be due to the fact that she had lived with another resident, Captain William Heath Davis, had borne him a child and was in the way of presenting him with another. As for Davis himself, he became the unelected leader and spokesman of the little group of foreign traders after Pigot left. A great talker, he promised to befriend the mission. But that was before the mission began inquiring into his private life.

Hannah was not the only Holmes daughter. Old Oliver had sired a houseful of buxom, fun-loving girls who combined the soft, languorous Hawaiian qualities with a western vivacity and forwardness that visiting seamen found irresistible. So Polly Holmes, at fourteen, had been carried off unwillingly on a cruise by a captain who apparently had persuaded her father if not herself. Another "orphan" had resulted from this affair. Then there were Mary, Jennie and Charlotte Holmes—all, it would appear, equally attractive.

Many a sea captain who had a respectable family back home in New England found it convenient when in Hawaii to do as the Hawaiians, taking unto himself a companion during the time his ship was in port, living ashore with her in a grass shack that could be put up for a trifling amount in trade goods, and leaving her with a few trinkets when he sailed away—unless he took her along with him on a cruise into the Pacific.

Most interesting of all the American expatriates in Honolulu was Anthony Allen, a Negro from Schenectady who had come ashore in 1810, taken to himself a Hawaiian wife, and become a prosperous farmer through patient industry. As soon as the missionaries arrived he had called on them and daily sent two bottles of goat's milk and other food. Towards the end of June the mission family was invited to visit his place, about two miles from Honolulu towards Waikiki.

It was a neat establishment of a dozen buildings in native style "covered with mud"—apparently a kind of stucco, and surrounded with a high fence of poles set in the ground. Farmers Allen and Chamberlain soon got together, and Allen showed the New England farmer hills of squash which had borne five times in twenty-two months and were now producing a full wagon load. He also had beans which had gone on producing for several years. A flock of three hundred goats supplied milk, butter and cheese.

When the mission family went to dinner, they found spread in front of them a feast which "was not missionary fare"—meat pie, baked pig, pork and fowls, mutton, beef, vegetables, taro pancakes, poi, pudding, watermelon, wine and brandy, and water from an excellent well, perhaps the only one on the island.

That Allen had expected some small return in the commodity the mission presumably supplied became evident when he asked Hiram Bingham to baptize his two children. Patiently Bingham explained that "something else was necessary before his children could thus be given up to God." But they did undertake to put clothes on Allen's wife!

After a cup of coffee served up in good china and a welcome present of pork to carry home, the mission family took their leave as evening came on and a bright moon rose, spilling its tropical light in silver showers upon the waving fingers of the coconut palms.

Those who rode or who could walk faster went on ahead, leaving Sybil and Hiram Bingham to walk slowly together across the empty plain. Sybil, nearly five months pregnant, was grateful for this almost unique chance to be alone with her husband. Married in haste and then rushed off to Boston, onto a crowded ship where there was seldom a moment's privacy, and then into Hawaiian huts with several other couples where there was less privacy still, it is a wonder that these proper New England young women did not end with shattered nerves and short tempers.

Now, as they walked under the full moon with the soft evening breeze blowing in across the moon-drenched ocean, they could talk without fear of being overheard. No wonder Sybil felt that "the walk home was pleasant."

Meanwhile, just a few days before the trip to Allen's, Boki had finally got around to building one of the three houses he had promised on a site about half a mile from the village towards Waikiki—an open, treeless plain with the sea in front and the mountains behind. (The place is now in the heart of downtown Honolulu.) The timbers had to be carried from fifteen to twenty miles on the shoulders of those conscripted for the work, then grass had to be brought several miles. But once the work was begun, it went quickly. By June twenty-sixth the men of the mission were fitting doors and window frames to the building. Soon they moved in, four couples in two rooms, together with furniture which had been made or contributed—two beds, two tables, three portable desks, chairs, cupboard, washstand—15 chests and trunks, looking glass, and a large library.

Hiram Bingham got together enough wood—always a scarce commodity—to make Sybil a rocking chair. He had to make it of what bits and pieces he could gather, but he must have built some of his own sturdiness into it, for Sybil used it constantly thereafter, carrying it to church with her when a church was built, having it lashed to poles and carried by bearers when she traveled, and then taking it round the Horn when she returned to the United States twenty years later. "When God sends the summons for my entrance into heavenly rest, I hope I may be waiting in that chair," she said. And so she was.

Meanwhile she went on with her teaching of the class of little girls she had gathered around her.

As well as they could, the women established a proper New England household. But in spite of their efforts, Hawaiianisms crept in. When they baked on Saturday, it was not only bread and pie they put into the oven, but breadfruit, taro, bananas, sometimes even a suckling pig. Shocked by what they learned of Hawaiian life—its easygoing sexual mores, the cheerful acceptance of vermin, the disgusting skin diseases, the lack of clothes or indeed of material goods of any kind, and the corresponding lack of industriousness—seeing all this, they determined to convert the Hawaiians to "civilized" manners.

Yet here was the paradox. These devoted men and women had come to bring the message of Christianity. And the Christian message was not materialistic. It placed no accent upon possessions, it counseled living for salvation rather than for the things of the material world. Yet the first thing the mission required of the Hawaiians was that they wear clothes, build larger houses, use furniture, and work harder to earn material things instead of living simply and thus having more time for religion.

From a purely Christian point of view, it would probably have been better for the mission to accept the material culture as they found it, putting their emphasis on the teachings of Jesus which conformed with Hawaiian life. But Bingham and all the rest firmly believed that their clothing, their household economy, their sense of decency and privacy were a basic part of Christianity. What would have happened if they had been able to take the other view?

* * *

On June twenty-eighth quizzical Sam Ruggles and sober Sam Whitney sailed in from Kauai after eight weeks away from their wives. They had a remarkable story to tell.

Kauai, at the northwest end of the chain of islands, was and is the scenic gem of Hawaii. Heavy rainfall on the central spine of sharp mountains makes the whole island lush with foliage, an emerald fringed with yellow sand and white surf and set in a deep-blue sea.

On the third of May the *Thaddeus* had anchored at Waimea, Kauai, the king's residence, where a river cutting down through flat land from the mountains left a low brow overlooking the sea. On this bit of raised land an adventurer from Russia, German-born Dr. George Scheffer, after being driven from Honolulu, had built a sizable stone fort only three years before. Over it he had raised the Russian flag. Scheffer had tempted King Kaumualii to revolt against Kamehameha, planning to seize half of Oahu as well as Kauai for Russia. But instead Kaumualii had driven the Scheffer party off the island. Now he had his own residence within the fort.

It was eleven in the morning when the brig anchored opposite the fort. Whitney, Ruggles and Prince George went ashore, landing half a mile west of the king's house on account of the surf. The usual crowd was on the beach to meet them, and attendants cleared the way by beating a path with clubs.

When they came into the king's house, Kaumualii—handsome and noble-looking—rose from his mats and folded George in his arms while they rubbed noses repeatedly, each too overcome to speak. Sam Ruggles, watching them, wept too. When emotions were somewhat more under control George introduced his American friends who in turn endured an affectionate massaging from the royal nose.

"Nui, nui, maikai; nui loa aloha America," the king said when George explained how he had been schooled, fed and transported by the mission. "Very good; great love to America."

The next morning the king and his queen Kapule greeted them with affectionate nosings. When Sam Ruggles told them that the missionaries had come to live out their lives among the Hawaiian people Kapule said, "Good, good—very great love for America," and burst into tears.

"You my son, I you father, my wife you mother," said the king by way of the broken English of his interpreter, a Hawaiian who had once dined in New York with Washington. The king also spoke a little English himself.

For several days Whitney and Ruggles walked around Waimea, visiting the people in friendliness and getting the feel of Hawaiian life. Ruggles already had a nickname, "Neho-pahu—Foreteeth-Knocked-Out." No sooner did he and Whitney step into a house than the host offered his wife or daughter as a token of aloha. It never failed to amaze him when they refused. "All white men before said this was a good thing, but you are not like other white men," said the puzzled host.

When they had been there a week the king told Sam Ruggles: "I love Humehume [George's real Hawaiian name], I love him very much, more than my other children. I thought he was dead; I cry many times because I think he was dead. Some captains tell me he live in America, but I not believe; I say no, he dead, he no more come back. But he live, he come again, my heart very glad. I want my son to help me, he speak English well and can do my business. But he is young, young men sometimes wild, they want advice. I want you stay here and help Humehume, and when vessels come, you and Humehume go on board and trade, so I make you a chief."

Sam declined the offer of chiefhood, explaining that they had not come to engage in trade or politics, but that he would help with advice.

The king showered presents upon his son—two chests of fine clothes the first day, the stone fort the next day, then the rich and fertile valley of Wahiawa. He told the other chiefs to consider George second in command.

The two Samuels had presented the king with a Bible, a gift of the American Bible Society. He appeared delighted with it, asked to have it read to him, and listened for hours. The story of the creation and the life of Jesus appealed to him most of all. He and the queen, Kapule, both wanted to learn to read. They tackled the job so earnestly that they even carried their books with them when they went bathing, and stood there naked in the water, book in hand, while they repeated what they had learned.

Early in June the people began coming into Waimea from all parts of the island and from neighboring Niihau to pay their taxes. They came, sometimes a hundred together, their shoulders loaded with hogs, dogs, mats, tapa, feathers, pearl fishhooks, calabashes, paddles. Much, perhaps all of this, was to be sent on to King Liholiho as a gift, for though Kaumualii and his island had never been conquered by the king of the other isles, he acknowledged sovereignty.

The schooner which was to carry the gifts could also take Ruggles and Whitney back to Honolulu. When they promised to return with their wives, the king showered them with gifts too—thirty mats, a hundred tapas, oranges, coconuts, calabashes, spears, hogs, fans, pineapples, fly brushes. So the two men sailed back to Honolulu and their lonesome wives with the good news.

* * *

Hawaiians and Yankees, from their diverse cultural backgrounds, kept on trying to understand each other with varying results. But there were difficulties on both sides. When Liliha, Governor Boki's handsome, curly-headed wife, came reeling into the mission house at mealtime and, naked to the waist and stinking of liquor, crowded in at the table and threw her arms around Sybil Bingham—well, it was hard for Sybil to interpret this as pure, undefiled love and good will though this is surely what Liliha intended. Liliha had the big dark eyes, the expressive heavy brows and the sensual, bow-shaped lips that went along with Polynesian beauty. But in addition to the pretty round chin there was a shadow of firmness under the mouth and a look in her eyes that showed Liliha to be more than a plaything. Breathing into Sybil's averted face, she took off a wreath of flowers and put it on Sybil's swanlike neck.

Boki now began to take an interest in the *palapala,* the reading, and even in the *pule*—prayer. He and Liliha, suddenly finding delight in this new game, wanted both Binghams to come and teach them every day. This welcome interest on the part of pleasure-loving, rum-drinking Boki was immediately rewarded with a gift of the Scriptures—in English, of course, since the mission was just beginning to learn Hawaiian, had not yet set up the printing press, and first had to figure out what letters should be used to represent Hawaiian sounds.

In this work Bingham and his associates had counted on the help of their three Hawaiian colleagues (Prince George was not a member of the mission). But trouble was now developing in this very quarter where they had expected their greatest help. Ex-privateer William Kanui, led astray by men aboard the *Thaddeus,* had made a right turn from the straight and narrow path once he reached home and had been "walking disorderly" ever since. His mission friends remonstrated with him, begging him to reform. It did no good. The pull

of the relaxed Hawaiian ways after long exile was too much. He took
to drink, to breaking of the Sabbath. He seemed to take delight in
baiting his brothers in Christ. No warnings could sway him. At last
on July 22 he was excommunicated. The sentence was read the next
day in church. Much as the brethren wanted to convert the heathen,
they would tolerate no backsliders.

Meanwhile Ruggles and Whitney with their pretty, pregnant wives
had been getting ready to move permanently to Kauai. On July 24
they sailed away, taking with them young Nathan Chamberlain who
had learned Hawaiian so rapidly that he would be useful as an interpreter. His brother Dexter had done equally well, and was to join
the Thurstons in Kailua at the first opportunity.

On this same day Maria Loomis gave birth to the first white child
born in the islands and named him Levi. "A busy interesting day,"
she noted in her journal. Elisha, she acknowledged, had been "a kind
and affectionate partner . . . attentive nurse . . . tender husband."
The baby engrossed her attention. "I tremble lest I care for him, both
in my heart and with my hands, more than my Divine Master will approve," she wrote. To the dedicated missionary, even mother love
was suspect if it detracted from religious duties.

On August sixth Thomas Hopu arrived in Honolulu bearing the
news of the Holmans' departure to Lahaina without mission approval. But chiefly Hopu had come at the command of King Liholiho, who wanted five ruffled shirts!

Ruffled in spirit, Bingham called the brothers together. Only
Chamberlain and Loomis were left in Honolulu. Chamberlain had
taken charge of the secular affairs and could not be spared. Elisha
Loomis, for whom there was as yet no printing to do, could. So off
he went with Dexter Chamberlain—and presumably with the five
shirts. His assignment was to stop first at Maui to see the Holmans.
He found them bent upon having their own way whatever happened
to their standing in the mission. Suffering from a sense of persecution
which appears to have been unwarranted, both the doctor and Lucia
felt that Bingham, the Thurstons and everyone else had it in for
them. The trouble had begun on shipboard over some oranges and
lemons which Lucia claimed as her own property, a gift of her older
brother. Bingham, insisting that all supplies were held in common,

had accused her of selfishness. She and her husband were also guilty "of practicing and justifying the most sickening familiarity in the cabin and on deck" in the view of the other brothers and sisters, and also of withdrawing themselves from the group and its activities.

When Lucia had gone ashore at Kailua she had said to Bingham, "I shall get away from this place as soon as I can." According to her own account he had answered, "Get away if you can!" And she had. No doubt her pregnancy had something to do with her cantankerousness. Yet the other mission women survived this hazard.

Pleased as the Holmans claimed to be with the groves of banana, breadfruit and coconut trees around their new Lahaina home, they were able to stay there but a month. If they had only been willing to put up with Kailua for another few months, they might have left with honor as the Thurstons were to do. Sam Ruggles, Lucia's brother, apparently thought their conduct inexcusable, for he wrote Lucia a letter to which he received a scorching answer. Lucia, as hot-tempered as her husband, was in no mood for compromise.

Finding that he could accomplish nothing with the Holmans, Elisha Loomis went on to Kailua where Asa and Lucy Thurston received him and young Dexter with delight. Both Asa and his wife were still busy teaching the king, his little brother, and several other members of the royal household. Though the king interrupted his studies for drinking bouts and relaxation, he had managed to learn how to read a little in the New Testament, while the others were working their way through the first lessons of Webster's spelling book. Learning English, however, proved a hard task for most of them. "I feel too lazy," the king would say, throwing down his book. The mission would have to make Hawaiian a written language. But where to begin?

Meanwhile Asa preached every Sunday to such small groups as gathered either at his house or in the schoolroom, with faithful Thomas Hopu interpreting what he said.

* * *

With their tenure established, at least for a year, Chamberlain and Bingham—the only men now left at Honolulu—struggled to complete their establishment. They built a storehouse, Hawaiian fashion, to take some of the goods that were cluttering up their houses. At last, by mid-September, they had three houses in a line in addition to the storehouse. Ten feet apart, the houses were connected by a *lanai,* or open porch, twelve feet wide which served as a dining room and kitchen. At one end was the large house built by Boki in which the Binghams lived. Here also were rooms for school and for worship. Then came the Loomis house, which was smaller, and beyond that a house for the Chamberlain family which, like the Binghams', was twenty by thirty feet. The three families cooked and ate together as one, enjoying the fresh breeze which swept across their long outdoor table. With a dozen children who had been taken into the household, as well as Hawaiian helpers, they had many mouths to feed. It was October before they finished digging and stoning their well. Meanwhile friendly captains continued to bring gifts—Starbuck a washtub filled with crockery to replace the rubble they had been using, the Quaker Captain Allen from Nantucket a book on the Lancasterian system of education.

Sybil Bingham cut into a cheese put up by Mother Bingham back in Bennington. "Finding the mites which had commenced their ravages would dispute us in the consumption of it," she observed with good Yankee economy, "we sent abroad a part." That lively cheese was soon paying dividends in return presents.

Sybil had also had principal charge of the school, and by the middle of September was ready to let the public see what her pupils could do. The quarterly examination to which the public was invited was an old New England institution. Now, along with cheese, clothing, Bibles and the ban against sexual promiscuity, it made its appearance in easygoing Hawaii.

Officers from ships in port, foreign residents and curious Hawaiians attended the first examination of forty scholars who, though most of them had not been able to take more than an hour of school a day, now stood up with that special shine on their faces which goes with the demonstration of new wisdom and read a few words from Webster's spelling book. Sally Jackson, the star pupil, read several English sentences. At the end, the pupils rose and recited in concert a number of edifying maxims, such as "God loves good men and good men love God." They had already gone about the village teach-

ing these bits of wisdom to their neighbors—children like Mary
Marin and William Beals and the five children of Oliver Holmes.
Oliver, present at the examination, had beamed with satisfaction over
their performance.

Some of the foreign teaching, however, seemed downright silly to
them—for instance, the idea that the earth was round. But the chief
Hoapili was not so hasty to condemn. "Do not be so quick with your
objections," he said. "Let us look at it. This is what I have always
seen. When I have been far out at sea on fishing excursions, I at first
lost sight of the beach, then of the houses and trees, then of the
hills, and last of the high mountains. So when I returned, the first ob-
jects which I saw were the high mountains, then the hills, then the
trees and houses, and last of all the beach. I think, therefore, that
these foreigners are right, and that the earth is round."

There was fear of these strange foreigners too. When churches
began to go up, the common people feared that men would be killed
to bury at each door, as in the old heathen temples. They thought
their brains would explode if they read too much. They thought the
wine served at communion was the blood of men killed for their
livers—or so they whispered to each other. They thought the missionaries wanted them to pray with their eyes closed only so that
they might kill them.

But out of curiosity they came anyway, first in small numbers
and then in larger. The chiefs always reached church a little late,
like self-important people everywhere, settling down after they had
created a deal of commotion, often spitting and coughing, or having
their backs and shoulders massaged by attendants. Sometimes, in
good Christian fashion, they slept through Bingham's long sermons.
Anyway, they came; that was something. In time, some of them became church members, though the mission admitted only those whose
lives it considered blameless.

But there were signs that the new religion was becoming fashionable. Hannah Holmes, the belle of Honolulu, began holding religious
meetings in her home on Sunday evenings. It was not hard to find
residents who looked with pleasure on an evening of prayer with
Hannah. So they came to her house, sitting on the floor or on a bench
according to their preference, in their midst a table with a lighted

lamp and a Bible, a chair for the leader beside it. There were prayers, a reading and expounding of Scripture, a hymn—and who could say that the attendants were not edified as much by what they heard as by basking in the pleasant warmth of Hannah's charm?

Against these firm accomplishments in school and church had to be set *l'affaire* Holman. Summoned to Oahu when a ship arrived from Manila with a sick captain and crew, Dr. Holman and Lucia had to leave Maui. The captain pulled through, the crew recovered, but Dr. Holman felt a cool welcome from Bingham and consequently boarded with the grateful captain. Soon he learned that he had been suspended from the privileges of the church.

Relations between Bingham and the doctor—both strong-willed men—worsened with each contact. When Bingham requested medicine, Holman insulted him. When Bingham tried to learn why the doctor had left Kailua, Holman broke out in a passion of abuse. Affairs grew beyond patching. Bingham was not the only one, as Dr. Holman tried to pretend, who was "against" him. Chamberlain, Whitney, Loomis, Lucia Holman's own brother Sam Ruggles felt that the Holmans had not lived up to expectations. The whole issue died down for the time being when the Holmans, on October eleventh, sailed off for the island of Kauai where Mercy Whitney would soon be needing the doctor's services. Her baby—Maria—came just a week after his arrival. The Holmans found beautful Kauai a congenial place, and with Nancy Ruggles' baby as an excuse—it was due towards the end of the year—they stayed on. So Sybil Bingham had to have her first-born on November 9 without benefit of surgeon. But Hiram, who could make a chair, lay up a stone wall, or assist at an amputation as well as preach and pray—Hiram proved equal to the occasion.

Kauai was indeed a pleasant place. Under King Kaumualii it was somewhat like an independent kingdom. The mission had been warmly welcomed from the first, and now a flourishing school of children in addition to the royal pupils was struggling with the pala-pala, spurred on by "the discipline of the district schools in New England" which, with the king's sanction, meant the use of the rod. What wood was substituted for New England birch the record does not disclose.

As the year 1820 drew to an end it looked as though the brethren, except for those on Kauai, might be drawn together at Honolulu again. Elisha Loomis came back (November 10) from Kailua and Lahaina bringing with him several of the favorite boys of Prime Minister Kalanimoku to continue their studies. Brother Chamberlain returned from a three weeks' stay on Kauai. And the Thurstons gave up their barren station at Kailua, arriving just before Christmas on the king's handsome ship, *Cleopatra's Barge*. The king was coming soon to live at Honolulu, and he wanted them there too.

They arrived in the midst of a hula marathon, which had already gone on for eight or ten days and was just getting warmed up. Bingham had been to see it, describing it minutely in the mission journal. When the dance was over he noticed that the dancers cast their wreaths into a small enclosure near the gate.

"What is this?" he asked.

"*Akua*—god."

"What god?"

"The hula-hula god."

"Where is he?"

"There in that little yard."

"You say he is in this little yard, that these leaves are given to him; but I do not see him."

"We cannot see your god Jehovah," said one of the chiefs.

"True, but He can see us, and He made the heavens and the earth. But does the god of the hula-hula know anything?"

"No."

"Can he see?"

"No."

"Can he hear?"

"No."

"Can he speak?"

"No."

"Can he do anything?"

"No."

"What is he good for? And why do you have such a god?"

The answer, though simple, was one Hiram Bingham could not, with all his learning, understand.

"For play," they told him.

There it was—the gentle, life-loving Hawaiian way and the practical, hard-working, what-is-it-good-for Yankee way. The twain had met, but there seemed to be no way for them to fuse.

CHAPTER 5

PRODIGAL SONS
1821

LATE AT NIGHT, TOWARDS THE BEGINNING OF FEBRUARY in 1821, when their first year was drawing to its close, the mission family were startled by the firing of guns out towards Waikiki. They were accustomed to disturbances from Honolulu when drunken sailors or reveling natives were carrying on, but that was in the opposite direction.

The shots seemed to echo across the water. Jumping out of bed and lifting the shutter which closed the open window hole, Hiram Bingham saw flame spurt from a ship's cannon. Almost immediately there was thunder on his right, from the cannon of the fort. Then the cannon atop Punchbowl behind the town let go. Bright wedges of flame lit up the dark night. From the steep mountain sides and the narrow valleys between them the booming echoed back and forth.

In the village dogs began yapping while the people, always ready for any new diversion, ran out of their houses and down to the shore and the fort. Some of those dogs were doing their last yapping, for the crier now went through the streets demanding dogs, hogs and poi. The king was arriving in *Cleopatra's Barge,* the beautiful new ship he had just bought for eighty thousand dollars in sandalwood, and he and his retinue must be fed.

The next morning the king came ashore and, amidst the bedlam of yelping dogs being carted in on poles, went to the grass house which had recently been built for him. He had been drunk at sea, and was drunk when he came ashore. He was drunk that evening when Hiram Bingham and Asa Thurston called on him—dead drunk. Queen Kamamalu, unwilling that the gentlemen should have to leave without some acknowledgment from his majesty, raised his lifeless hand from the mat so that they might shake it.

The next day Bingham and Thurston visited the king again. Early in January a house frame had been landed from America. The mission family was eager to raise it, but of course they must have the king's permission. There had been rumors that the king was being urged to send them home. His reaction to the raising of the house would show which way he intended to move.

This time Liholiho was awake. Cheerful and friendly, he gave them a warm aloha. But when they asked permission to raise their house, his pleasant face darkened into a brown scowl, wrinkling like a rotten apple. Hiram argued that American women were not accustomed to earthen floors beneath their feet, but this argument failed to move the king.

The next day the mission family made an attack in force, taking wives and infants along to see whether his majesty could be swayed by compassion if not by argument. The king overcame this assault by the simple expedient of being asleep. But Hiram Bingham was not a man who easily gave up anything he had set his mind on. He had now learned enough Hawaiian to use it in his relations with the chiefs, and on this very day had spoken to Governor Boki in Hawaiian, apparently for the first time at any length. It was characteristc of Bingham, and prophetic of the future, that he used the occasion to lecture Boki on the benefits of the Gospel and against loading his people with "unnecessary labor."

Now that the king was planning to make Honolulu his permanent home, a swarm of chiefs and chiefesses together with their hangers-on and retainers poured into the town. Among them, of course, was Prime Minister Kalanimoku—Billy Pitt—and his attractive young wife, Likelike (prounced Leekay-leekay). She had once been the wife of Governor Boki, Billy Pitt's younger brother. But Billy had taken a fancy to her, and in the easygoing Hawaiian way had added her to his harem, whereupon Boki had snatched the lovely Liliha from his nephew Kahaalaia.

When Elisha Loomis had gone over to Hawaii the previous year, Kalanimoku had persuaded him to open a school at Kawaihae. Likelike had turned out to be one of his most promising pupils, and she was eager to continue her studies in Honolulu. She visited the mission houses, threw herself on one of the beds, and with a "sedate countenance" which apparently impressed Maria Loomis because it was so un-Hawaiian, spoke of her love for the palapala.

But since Likelike was within a few weeks of childbirth, the studies had to be deferred. On the night of February twenty-fifth her child was born. Billy Pitt, elated at having a son, began setting off salutes by cannon and musket, even at the mother's door. The celebration was premature, for the poor baby lived only a few hours. Hiram thought the firing had something to do with it.

Within a few days Likelike was taken sick. When the people of her household set up a wailing, Bingham and one other—probably Elisha Loomis who knew her best—went to see what could be done. Poor Likelike was writhing in pain upon her pile of mats and shrieking with fear. But the missionaries had arrived too late. For four days her attendants had been carrying her to the ocean to cool her fever. The disease and the cure together were more than she could stand.

Governor Boki, her former husband, was sitting with her when the missionaries came in, his usually handsome face sagging with sorrow. It was he who shortly discovered that Likelike had stopped breathing. Tilting his head back, he let out a wail which chilled the spines of the mission brothers. Almost at once a wailing arose all around the house and then spread throughout the village, for Likelike was young and greatly beloved. As Bingham and his companion left, they passed through a crowd of weeping, moaning people whose antics the missionaries thought shocking.

When Hiram went back to the house to see what Christian comfort he might give, he found a crowd of friends and retainers, some of whom were cutting off each other's hair in token of mourning. Yet in the very act they shrieked with laughter as they saw the effect on the appearance of the victim. Others lay on their faces wailing and crying floods of tears while still others sat on the mats playing a cheerful game of cards, or lay senseless with drink. A few, using pieces of burning bark, scarred themselves with deep semicircular burns.

Bingham, distressed over all these carryings-on, earnestly tried to persuade the chiefs to have a Christian funeral. But Keopuolani, the queen mother, firmly announced, "I will have no praying." The rest of the chiefs backed her up. When Bingham begged the king to call off the hulas which had been going on ever since his arrival in February, he said, "This is the Hawaiian custom, and must not be hindered." Well then, said Bingham, will you at least excuse from dancing on Sunday the dancers who attend our Sunday School.

"I wish to see them dance today," said the king. And dance they did. Persisting, Bingham got the king to call off the dancing for the following Sunday when he planned, having at length got Kalanimoku's permission, to preach a funeral sermon. But when Boki heard this, even in the face of the king's word, he said: "We will dance —no tabu."

Bingham was deeply concerned over the fact that Laka, the hula god, was competing with Jehovah. True, the stick which had been set up to represent him had been removed at the plea of the mission, but the king had decreed that it was all right for hula dancers to acknowledge Laka in sport. Even the Sunday School pupils ate to Laka, smoked to Laka and danced to Laka, hoping to perfect their skill in dancing.

"There is but one God," Bingham told Boki. To worship Laka, even in play, was idolatry and would lead to disaster.

In any case the sermon was preached, in front of the house where poor Likelike had died and to a large audience. For Bingham this amounted to a triumph. Keopuolani's objection to praying and Boki's to prohibitions showed clearly enough that they were still thinking of the old days when priests had controlled their lives, when death *had* resulted from priestly praying, when men and women could not eat together, and when their lives had been hemmed about by a thousand restrictions.

Now the mission wanted to keep men and women from sleeping together—and was not this merely another form of priestly dictatorship? Or from drinking rum, the dispensing of which was highly profitable to some chiefs. The Hawaiians did not need much in the way of trade goods—a state of things highly exasperating to Yankee merchants. But they could be taught to drink. Liquor became an important item of barter in the profitable sandalwood trade, which in

1821 was having its biggest year. Consequently, there were plenty of captains willing to supply it. In Honolulu, also, were haole merchants whose livelihood depended upon the new industry of whaling which was just beginning to affect Hawaii. Here again the chief commodity was liquor, since sailors coming ashore wanted that more than anything else—except women. And since women were often supplied through contact with the chiefs who had to be paid off, liquor again became useful as a medium of exchange. The chiefs, says the historian Kamakau, almost bathed in it.

Not all merchants were abettors of this evil. There was James Hunnewell, as friendly to the mission as ever. But even he had set up shop with rum as one of his staples. There were the friendly captains from New England who called more and more frequently at the mission, happy to find a touch of home in these distant islands. Bingham, fully realizing their importance to the success of the mission, wrote in the official journal: "The king and chiefs who generally respect such men will be more or less influenced by their treatment of us, in forming an opinion of the missionaries as *men.*" A number of these captains from Nantucket and New Bedford were Friends—Quakers—"and friendly indeed they are," remarked Maria Loomis.

Captain Joseph Allen of the *Maro* was a great favorite with the mission. A teetotaller, maintaining order aboard his ship without recourse to weapons or profanity, he was one of the most prosperous merchant-captains in the whaling trade. When the mission family dined aboard his ship in March, he showed them a thirty-pound lump of ambergris worth its weight in gold which he had recently taken from a whale. "The same power which brought the fish with a piece of money to Peter's hook can as easily reward those who make sacrifices for the cause of charity," concluded the mission journal in grateful tone. "Captain Allen, when he called here a few months since made a donation to this mission of about $60, and he has received his hundred fold in special prosperity."

In general, however, mission and merchant had come to Hawaii for very different purposes. To save souls, the mission felt that it had to remake the whole of Hawaiian culture. To make money, the merchants encouraged all that was pleasure-loving in the Hawaiian.

A head-on collision was inevitable. Yankeeism had come to Hawaii in two guises. The Hawaiians found the sailors and merchants far more congenial and easier to understand, yet there was something about the missionaries, strange as it was, which they knew was good. Having overthrown their old ways, they now saw a new drama of good and evil unfolding before their eyes, a struggle in which they were bound to be the victims no matter who won. Unless—and there were chiefs who favored it—they should throw them all out, missionaries and sailors and traders alike, while there was still time.

* * *

The mission lost no opportunity to build up influence wherever it would do the most good. With the Spanish Marin, the king's interpreter, they felt a bond of sympathy because of his industrious and orderly nature. They had given him seeds for his garden, invited him to dinner, and welcomed his occasional visits. When he dropped in while they were in the midst of the campaign to raise their house, they took him into the schoolroom where he was treated to a piping of childish voices singing a Hawaiian version of "Come Holy Spirit." He refused a warm invitation to breakfast because, he said, he was afraid the king would take advantage of his absence to drink rum. (His journal during this period is full of references to the king's drinking. Finally, by the middle of March, he found it easier to note the sober days: "King not very drunk today.")

Marin, then, was on the side of the angels, or at least of those whose nectar was non-alcoholic. He had influence with the king. At least one of his children, Mary, went to the mission school. It seems likely that Bingham asked him to say a favorable word for the mission house.

The king was, meanwhile, making some inquiries of his own, for on this same day he had a talk with an intelligent young Hawaiian just returned from America. Would America be sending frigates to take over the islands?

"No," said the youth, "America no want your island. Rich enough —no come here for that."

According to Lucy Thurston it was a mission wife—apparently herself, though she was too modest to say so—who finally brought the king around. The Binghams and Thurstons called again on the king. As they were leaving, Lucy in her halting Hawaiian begged him to preserve her life and that of the other women by letting them live in the kind of house they had been used to.

"Yes, build," said the king with one of his sudden, intuitive decisions. Lucy had spoken while everyone else was busy with farewells to the queens, and she told no one of her request or his answer. It would be better for the king to announce his decision as if he had made it without her prompting, and better for Hiram and Asa not to know that what the king had refused them he had granted at her suit.

And so it turned out. A few days later the king called, sat down at the long dining table on the porch, and announced that they might build their house, only waiting until he returned from a brief trip to Maui.

On Sunday, March eighteenth, Bingham and some of the other brethren called on the king to see whether he would not like to have a religious meeting and sermon, since there seemed to be too much of a head wind to take him to Maui.

"If there should be a head wind I could beat this way and that and go up quick," he said, apparently preferring an adverse wind to a Bingham sermon.

"I hope that by and by King Liholiho will drink very little rum," Bingham said.

"By and by—by and by—not now," said the king.

"I go now to my house to attend on the worship of God," said Hiram.

"You must pray Jehovah to give me a good wind, and that I may go to Maui and by and by come back. I do not like to have it blow from this quarter, but from this."

"Tomorrow, if you will wait for it, perhaps you will have a good wind. We will pray to Jehovah for this, and I hope that he will give you a good heart, a good kingdom, good chiefs and people and great prosperity."

That evening the king sailed with a fleet of four ships, one of which was the dear old *Thaddeus* which had been purchased by Boki.

Returning from Maui, the king called again at the mission on April fourth. Followed by his five queens, his men to carry spittoons, fly-brushes, shawls, guns and other royal regalia, he stepped into each of the rooms, visited the school and the cookhouse, and even stuck his head into the well. To his old friends the Thurstons he was particularly friendly, examining each item in their little room—the one chair which Asa had converted into a rocker, the settee he had hacked out with broad-ax, jackknife and saw, the shelves of books, the looking glass, and the first piece of window glass in Hawaii. Liho-liho, a connoisseur of reclining surfaces, felt the bed. When it turned out to have nothing but a mattress on it, he continued his tour until he found one with a feather bed. Into the midst of this he threw himself, rolling from side to side like a puppy with an itch in his back, his quizzical but good-natured face cracked across the middle in a broad grin. He kept up his rolling for a full fifteen minutes.

A few minutes later, as he was about to leave, he saw the mission hand cart. It was an essential piece of equipment, since the missionaries had no beasts of burden and had to do all their hauling with this small vehicle. Plopping himself down in the back of it, Liholiho ordered his men to pull him home on the double. Behind him streamed a long line of wives and attendants, their scanty clothes flapping in the strong trade wind.

By May the brothers had nearly finished digging the cellar hole of their new house. The Hawaiians, who had abandoned their institutional superstitions but still kept a healthy supply for personal use, began to say that the cellar was going to be an arsenal and the missionaries would murder them all. Hawaiian houses needed no cellars, so what other purpose could a cellar have?

Despite the rumors, the brothers kept on with their building. Raised, most of them, on farms where a man was his own carpenter and mason, they had no fear of pitching in and doing the job themselves. Only as they got on with the work they found that many parts of the house frame had been lost or stolen. The roof boards had apparently not been sent at all, while Captain Blanchard who was now ashore had borrowed some lumber while building a small ship and had returned it split and broken.

Nevertheless, by the tenth of May the frame was up. Chamberlain and Loomis were shingling the roof when the scaffold fell, dumping them both to the ground. They were shaken up some, but not badly hurt. A bout of sickness then slowed the work for a while, but at last in August it was near completion. For lack of plaster, the inside was covered first with tapa and then with paper—stuck on with a very good substitute for paperhanger's paste, the Hawaiian staff of life, poi. Studs and braces had to be papered, their shapes showing through. For siding to keep out the weather there was nothing but rough, feather-edged boards. When a sudden squall came up, rain soaked through everything—boards, tapa and paper. Thurston and Loomis soaked strips of cloth in tar and covered the cracks. On August twenty-third the Chamberlains, their family increased by a new baby, moved in. Then the Thurstons and Loomises. To Lucy Thurston the house seemed like a mansion after the damp and flimsy thatch. It had solid board floors—painted floors, and windows with glass in them. It had doors which could be closed and locked against intruders. The wallpaper—pink, with twining vines of tinsel —was gay and cheerful, a present from one of the ever-thoughtful captains.

While the house was going up, Daniel Chamberlain had been trying to raise some American crops. Towards the end of the previous year he had put in most of the common garden vegetables and then a quarter acre of corn. But worms had destroyed everything. Taro, sweet potatoes, sugar cane and bananas were immune to pests, noted Farmer Chamberlain. But as for Christian vegetables, they appeared to be doomed. Even before this disappointment Daniel had confided to his journal: "I regret that I feel so much coldness and indifference to this glorious cause." What enthusiasm he retained must have withered away with that corn.

But he dared not speak out, for the Holmans had gained the censure of the whole mission, himself included, for leaving their post of duty. He could not follow their footsteps. Yet, when he looked at that dying corn and remembered his own rich fields of waving grain, he shook his head and made a firm mouth. Near by, the taro fields sent up their huge leaves, dark green and full of health. Daniel Chamberlain must have wondered whether a land that could not raise corn and peas could raise churches and Christians. And how could he raise six children?

As for Holman, after nearly seven months on Kauai where he had brought the Whitney and Ruggles babies into the world and then his own, the doctor took both wife and baby with him to Honolulu, planning to return to the United States with a whaler in the fall. He had already been excommunicated by the church and his wife suspended. His crimes were "walking disorderly, slander, railing and covetousness." There must have been a strong feeling against the Holmans, far outweighing the desire for medical care, for of course once Holman left it would be a long time before another doctor could arrive.

Bingham, in a hundred and fifteen pages of foolscap, gave the whole "History of the Defection of Dr. Thomas Holman" to the board at home, complete with verbatim conversations. When Bingham tried to learn why Holman had left Kailua, the doctor told him: "Christians should not be lawyers. I have done everything I could for the good of the mission, but instead of receiving any gratitude, I am cursed for it."

"Who has cursed you?" Bingham inquired.

"You."

"How and when have I cursed you?"

"You have acted so as to bring a curse upon me."

"What did I do to you while at Kailua?"

"Nothing—but I don't want you to give me any more cants."

Chamberlain mildly interjected· "Mr. Bingham has given you no cants."

"He has," said the doctor.

"When?"

"This morning—more than five hundred."

"No, Doctor," said Chamberlain, "Mr. Bingham wishes to reason fairly with you; he gives you no cant."

"Mr. Chamberlain," the doctor exploded, "I'd have you know that the blood that runs in my veins was born free and I'm determined it shall never be bound by any man."

Holman and Bingham were clearly incompatible personalities—both of them stubborn and tenacious. The doctor felt that with his profession went the right to certain privileges and decisions the mission insisted upon sharing. The breach was now beyond healing.

When Holman came to church in Honolulu, he left without saluting the brethren.

But if he failed to find friends among his former brethren, he was soon finding them in the town. On May twenty-second John C. Jones arrived in Honolulu as U. S. commercial agent. He and the doctor took a liking to each other at once, and Jones was soon forming his picture of the mission through Holman's eyes. When he invited the mission family to dinner to celebrate the Fourth of July, they refused when they learned that he had invited the Holmans too. The seeds of wider discord were being sown. Soon there would be a crop of nettles and briars which was to plague the mission for years, continuing even to this day. The mission thought Jones a "pleasant, agreeable young man." They had no idea how soon and how drastically they would have to change their minds.

Any direct clash between Bingham and Holman was averted when the Bingham family, together with the Ruggleses who had been visiting in Honolulu and a new assistant missionary fresh from the United States, a Hawaiian called George Sandwich, departed for Kauai on the eighth of July.

King Kaumualii had decided to send a ship to the Society Islands and was willing to let two of the mission families go along. For months the mission had been trying to settle upon a plan for writing the Hawaiian language. They knew that in the Society Islands were missionaries from England who had already solved this problem for a language very like Hawaiian, and they were eager to follow the same orthography. Not only in language, but in many other respects the Tahitians were like the Hawaiians. It might save years of error, therefore, if the experience in Tahiti could be turned to the benefit of Hawaii.

To make sure that he was stepping on no toes, Bingham first told King Liholiho, Prime Minister Kalanimoku and the premier, Kaahumanu, of his plan. None of them objected, but Kaahumanu seemed to take the greatest interest. Next to the king himself, the mission now knew, Kaahumanu was the strongest public figure in the kingdom. In rank she was if anything higher than the king. She was *kuhina-nui,* an office for which there is no English word. She was the king's counselor, practically a co-ruler, since her approval was required in all important business and much of the actual administration fell to her. When Liholiho had come forth from the temple in his scarlet feather mantle to be pronounced king, Kaahumanu had stepped forward and said:

"I make known to your highness, Liholiho, the will of your father. Here are the chiefs. There are the guns and this is your land, but you and I will share the realm together." Thus Liholiho became king and Kaahumanu premier—a plan formed by the great Kamehameha who knew that his favorite wife was strong and his son weak. But Kaahumanu had not stopped there. Splendid in her feather cloak and leaning upon the spear of her dead husband, she said, "We intend to be free from the tabus. We intend that the husband's food and the wife's food shall be cooked in the same oven, and that they shall be permitted to eat out of the same calabash. . . . If you think differently, you are at liberty to do so; but as for me and my people we are resolved to be free." It was only after this brave act of Kaahumanu that Liholiho finally, and with his courage fueled with liquor, dared to break the eating tabu. "If no liquor had arrived here in Hawaii," says an unpublished account in Hawaiian, "the tabu would not have been broken, but in this thing is the hand of God."

Now in her middle forties, Kaahumanu was as intelligent as she was huge. Her tremendous breasts and limbs suggested a promise of fertility which had never been fulfilled. Haughty towards the missionaries in the first contacts, she seemed to warm to them when they suggested the trip to Tahiti. With Marin as her interpreter, she told them to take her greetings to King Pomare, sending along one of the beautiful feather war cloaks and other presents. She also sent one of her men, and gave permission for John Ii, a promising student of the palapala, to go as well. Both she and Kalanimoku were at the wharf to bid the Binghams farewell when they left for Kauai—an unexpected and highly encouraging honor.

At the other end, King Kaumualii came down to the beach to receive the Binghams in person—tall, handsome, a slight stoop giving him an air of dignity and majesty. The two men greeted each other with a hearty aloha, a Hawaiian kiss and a shake of the hand.

"I very glad to see you," said the king.

The same afternoon Kalakua, Kaahumanu's sister, arrived with her attendants. The king and his wife met her at the beach, embraced, and then sat down on the sand and wept together as etiquette required. For several days thereafter royalty amused itself with surfing, making necklaces, and feasting.

The Binghams found the Kauai mission well off—located in a big house with glass windows and a good floor, close to the king's house on the river bank. They had two hundred acres of land, twenty goats, and fifty men to work for them. No longer was Sam Ruggles called Neho-pahu—Foreteeth-Knocked-Out—but Keiki, Child. Such was the royal decree, for Kaumualii had a liking for Samuel. This of course delighted the Binghams, who had always felt a particularly warm affection for Sam and Nancy. The defection of Sam's sister Lucia Holman never got in the way of this relationship.

With church and school flourishing, only one dark spot appeared upon the lovely Kauai scene. Prince George had not lived up to expectations. Shortly after his return he had married Betty Davis, hapa-haole daughter of Isaac Davis who had come ashore at about the same time as John Young. But then, with everything before him, George had failed to merit the honors his father had heaped upon him. Retiring into the valley his father had given him, he was seen less and less at Waimea, while his handsome seven-foot brother, Kealiiahonui, took his place at court.

While the *Becket* was being prepared for the departure to Tahiti, John C. Jones arrived from Honolulu. The American traders in Honolulu didn't like the idea of this voyage, he said. It would diminish the honor of the young American republic for its missionaries to go begging to Englishmen in Tahiti for help. Furthermore, the mission ought not to obligate itself so heavily to Kaumualii. Anyway, the two languages were so unlike that the trip would be a waste of time. (He was wrong about this.) Though these were the reasons given, it was clear that the merchants to whom Kaumualii owed money were not happy at the thought of having his brig leave the islands. Jones also had other ideas as to how Kaumualii should spend his money. Plying him with gifts and elegant dinners, he finally persuaded him to buy another brig, complete with cargo.

Faced with this opposition, the king gave up the voyage, much to the disappointment of Hiram Bingham. It is more than likely that he had words with Jones which were not forgotten, for the two men were at loggerheads most of the time from then on.

All this was forgotten, however, in the face of the astounding event which took place on July twenty-second. An open sailboat anchored off the fort at Waimea with King Liholiho aboard. With the bravery of the weakling he had pretended to the chiefs that he was only going for a sail along the coast of Oahu. Rounding the southern tip of the island, he had then ordered the helmsman to steer for Kauai. With him were Boki, the high chief Naihe and his wife Kapiolani, one of the finest personalities among the alii—the chiefly class. They had all begged the king to turn back, but he was sufficiently fortified with rum to be stubborn. Living always in the shadow of his great father, he had found in drink an escape from the greatness that had been thrust upon him. Clearly he counted on this desperate trip to put him on a par with his father who had never succeeded in subjugating Kauai.

Three times close to capsizing, it was a miracle that Liholiho had arrived at all. Having only thirty men and three chiefs with him, he was wholly at the mercy of Kaumualii, who went out to meet him in a canoe. They greeted each other in a friendly fashion and came ashore.

Not long after, as if to outdo the king, Boki's handsome, sultry-looking wife Liliha arrived from Oahu in an outrigger canoe, carried by a small sail and four rowers.

Kaumualii, knowing that he could not, in the long run, hold out against Liholiho, offered his country, his ships, his fort and guns. But Liholiho, who now seemed bent upon being as magnanimous as he had been foolhardly, said: "I did not come to dispossess you. Keep your country and take care of it as before, and do what you please with your vessels." The chiefs greeted this grand response with a shout. Then they settled down to feasting on a chiefly scale.

Two days later Liholiho's five wives arrived on *Cleopatra's Barge.* Then the whole party went on a forty-day tour of Kauai—one of those progresses which the chiefs dearly loved and which the commoners feared, since it led to a great slaughter of their hogs and dogs and a great drain upon all their slender resources.

On September sixteenth the two kings, back in Waimea and declining an invitation to church, went sailing in their brigs. At evening when they came back to anchor before Waimea, and Kaumualii went aboard *Cleopatra's Barge* for a friendly call, Liholiho ordered the brig to sail for Oahu, leaving Kauai without a king.

"Farewell to our king—we shall see him no more," said one of the Kauai chiefs. To foolhardiness and magnanimity Liholiho had now added treachery as one of his grand characteristics. The reign of Kaumualii was ended.

When Liholiho got back to Honolulu, he found a thatched church already built on ground close to the mission houses. Chiefs and foreign residents had raised the funds for it, and the first Sabbath meeting had been held in it the day Liholiho sailed from Kauai. Within two weeks the attendance had picked up in a manner most gratifying to the mission.

Kaumualii, now a virtual prisoner in Honolulu, came to the mission house with Premier Kaahumanu, inspected every one of its rooms with interest, then went out and lay in its shade. Apparently the two had something of importance to talk about, for that night they settled down on the same pile of woven mats, a piece of black tapa was thrown over them, and they thus became man and wife. Then, to make sure that the succession of Kauai was in her hands, and also perhaps because he was the handsomest chief in the islands, Kaahumanu also married her new husband's son, Kealiiahonui.

Meanwhile the Holmans, after many delays, sailed for home by way of China. They had gained the sympathy of a number of foreign residents, for they were young, handsome, sociable—far more congenial with the foreign community than with the mission. Captain William Heath Davis and John C. Jones, taking up the cudgels for them, were to carry on a battle with the mission that would last for years. A few weeks later Jones launched a bitter complaint against the mission when Daniel Chamberlain happened to meet him in the village. Bingham was a complete tyrant, he said, whose purpose was to get all the trade of the islands into his own hands. Everyone in the mission except the Holmans had been duped by him, but Dr. Holman had too much sense, integrity and independence to be fooled. Why, those fellows Hopu and Honolii had spoiled more than three million dollars of trade with the United States (method not specified). Writing home to Josiah Marshall, whose firm he represented, he fumed: "The natives are now too much enlightened. They know well the value of every article . . . and if they do not there are plenty of canting, hypocritical missionaries to inform them." Jones saw an enemy in everyone who did not fall in with his own plans. So much from the "pleasant, agreeable young man!"

With the large numbers they had to feed, the brothers now begged of Kaahumanu a piece of farmland. In addition to the babies who were being born with a regularity which indicated a close attention to the marital relationship, the mission was augmented by the numerous children taken in with the hope that they might lose their "heathen" habits and become fully clothed, knife-and-fork-wielding Christians.

These youngsters came and went in a steady stream, bumping up against the Yankee family discipline and finding it far less comfortable than the lax and sometimes negligent Hawaiian way. Young Charlotte Holmes, for instance, had gone into the Loomis household, where she began to be saucy and refuse to do as she was told. To punish her, Maria tied her with a small string to a chest and ordered her to stay there. When she untied the string, Maria punished her mildly and tied her again. Soon Charlotte's mother came angrily into the house and carried her daughter away.

Isaac Lewis, one of the most promising scholars, stayed in bed through divine service, giving as an excuse the fact that his clothes were torn and he was ashamed to come. He had, however, been trained to mend his own clothes. When dinnertime came, Elisha asked him if he were not ashamed to come in torn clothes. "No," he said. When darkness came, he disappeared.

But with all these defeats, the mission could claim one important victory. Haughty Kaahumanu was drawing towards them.

Returning from Kauai on November tenth, the Binghams found her sick. When they visited her on the sixteenth, Hiram—always willing to use a God-given opportunity for God's work—said to her: "I hope you think seriously of the great God and our Savior."

"I think more about Him since I have been sick," she admitted.

"Is it your desire that I shall engage in prayer to God for you?"

"*Maikai*—good."

Thereafter the Binghams were frequent visitors. The strong-willed dowager queen knew a strong man when she saw one. In Hiram Bingham she recognized a sturdiness and resoluteness like her own. He was a man who knew where he was going. Hawaii, having overthrown the principles which had controlled and given meaning to its culture, was rudderless. If this strong man could supply the rudder, she was disposed to take him aboard.

But Kaahumanu had her soft and loving side too, and to this Sybil Bingham made an irresistible appeal. A true Christian—charitable in the best sense of the word, self-denying, firm in her conception of goodness and in her devotion to it, Sybil drew affection because she gave it, unsparingly. She sat down by Kaahumanu, bathing and stroking her aching head, healing by love—the heart and secret of Christian healing.

Returning health restored to Kaahumanu some of her old haughtiness. She, a great chiefess, was still far from wanting to be a humble Christian. But a start had been made. Whether by accident or design, Bingham had picked out the one person in Hawaii who held the keys to the kingdom—which Hiram intended that she should exchange, in due time, for the keys to the kingdom of heaven.

CHAPTER 6

PLURAL MARRIAGE AND SINGULAR PEOPLE

1822

SOMETHING WAS GOING ON IN ONE OF THE SMALL thatched houses on the mission premises this Monday morning of January 7, 1822. James Hunnewell came walking across the barren plain from Honolulu and stepped in. A couple of sea captains in dark blue coats with brass buttons followed, their gait still rolling to the rhythm of a six-month voyage. Butler from Lahaina, once host to the Holmans, was there, and all the mission brethren.

But the handsomest, most imposing person in the place was a brother of the dowager Kaahumanu and of Governor Kuakini (Adams)—Keeaumoku, or Cox as the foreigners called him, governor of the island of Maui. (Each large island had a chief who served as governor.) Tall and muscular, with an open and good-humored face, he towered over the other men in the room as he watched every move of Elisha Loomis. The mission printer, his face stiffened into solemnity by the occasion, moved back and forth between the little Ramage press and the composing stone, transferring type and furniture. The first printing ever done in the islands was about to take place. It would be the first printing of a text in Hawaiian too. Cox, keenly interested, was eager to have a part in it.

For nearly two years the mission brethren had struggled with a language whose grammar had never been described and for which no way of writing existed. To their consternation, they found that Hawaiians not only lacked many of the English sounds but used some sounds interchangeably—as for instance *t* and *k, l* and *r, v* and *w*. All the sounds in Hawaiian, they finally decided, could be represented by twelve letters.

But this truncated alphabet would make it impossible for Hawaiians to speak such Bible names as Ruth, David, Joseph—or even Christ. Another nine consonants were therefore added which could be learned at a later date after the Hawaiian had mastered the letters necessary to reading his own language.

As Elisha Loomis transferred to the press the Hawaiian syllables which were to make up the first reading lesson for the schools, Cox reached out a hand to help him. Elisha passed him the composing stick, led him to the font, and showed him how to pick out and set a line of type. Then, locking up the page form and carefully laying a clean sheet of paper over it, Elisha lifted Cox's big hand to the lever and let him make the first impression.

A murmur of congratulation went round the room as the first printed sheet was passed from hand to hand. Cox, delighted with his task, went on pulling more impressions. The mission had not only printed a lesson; it had won a friend.

Interest in the palapala had a wonderful effect on church attendance for the moment. On January twentieth more than sixty Hawaiians and fifty haoles gathered together, Cox and his brother Adams among them. Their sister Kaahumanu, however, having enjoyed an improvement in health had suffered a relapse in spirit, so she was not present.

Encouraged nevertheless by the attendance, the brethren tried to do even better the next week. But when they went to invite the king, he told them: "I am tipsy, and it is not right to go to church drunk; when I have got through I will come." He did not name a date. Adams said: "When the king attends, I will attend." Kalanimoku, the prime minister, was busy gambling. Courteously explaining this previous engagement, he said, "I have business and cannot go. My heart will be with you though my body is here."

The next Sunday it was much the same. Even Kaumualii, ex-king of Kauai and a warm friend to the mission, had to regret. "Kaahumanu is ill," he said. "I cannot leave her to go to church, lest she should be angry with me." Poor king, he was now under the thumb of a stern mistress. When he bowed his head in blessing before a meal one day, Kaahumanu threw a heavy dish at his head. The aim was good, but a friend diverted the calabash. Kaumualii went on praying, as he did at every meal thereafter. Perhaps Kaahumanu's anger was really directed against Kapule, the wife from whom she had taken Kaumualii and for whom he apparently retained a strong affection, or against his other young wife whom Liholiho had taken from him.

When Bingham went out to Waikiki to preach to Kaahumanu, he found Kaumualii looking feeble, though calm and apparently resigned to his fate. He listened to the sermon—interpreted sentence for sentence by the faithful Thomas Hopu—with apparent satisfaction. What Kaahumanu thought of the sermon—it dealt with the command of Jesus to go into all nations and teach all men—was not set down. Having just taken on two husbands, however, it was clear that she could not afford to give in to this foreign teaching with its parsimonious rule of one man to one woman.

Her brothers, Cox and Adams, were getting well ahead of her in their mastery of the palapala and the pule (prayer). After hearing a sermon on the text, "Be wise now, therefore, O ye kings, and be instructed, ye judges of the earth," Adams sent for the printed lessons, mastered them in a few days, and wrote a letter to Bingham (apparently actually penned by a Tahitian retainer) which Hiram promptly answered on February eighth. Before long the chiefs were sending notes and letters back and forth at a great rate, delighted with this miraculous new way of keeping in touch with each other. Who could tell but what a people who possessed such a way of touching each other from a distance might truly be in touch with God?

On the first of March a messenger came running from Waikiki with news that the king was dying. He had, of course, been drinking. Bingham and Hopu hurried to the coconut grove where the king's grass house stood, close to the sound of the breakers where the Royal Hawaiian Hotel now stands. Already a crowd had assembled around the house, their wailings and weepings no doubt greatly encouraging the unhappy man. Around the house stood the king's guard, each with a sword or musket and at least one piece of a uniform, whether trousers, coat with bright buttons, or cocked hat.

Inside Bingham found the king surrounded by his family—his own mother, Keopuolani, his stepmother Kaahumanu, his wives and friends—all gathered around his mat and crying freely. He had had a "fit"—had turned red and then pale, stiffened with spasm and then gone into convulsions. He was breathing with difficulty. After vomiting, he had begun to sweat and then to bleed at the mouth—apparently from a lacerated tongue. Hiram Bingham, the nearest thing to a doctor the mission had, gave him medicine and stayed with him throughout the night. The next morning he returned with the king to Honolulu aboard a double canoe crowded with thirty-five people. A few days later Maria Loomis reported: "The king is partially deranged. He is in quite a pleasant mood and amuses himself in picking up straws and presenting them with a great deal of dignity to those around him." Recovering after a few weeks, he invited Bingham to supper, asked him to say a blessing, and shortly afterwards turned up at church with a large retinue. Sickness had succeeded in evoking an interest in religion where persuasion had failed.

In the midst of this, the *Mermaid* sailed into Honolulu Harbor, bringing three passengers of special interest to the mission. William Ellis, a poor London gardener who had felt the call to preach to the heathen, had been sent out to Tahiti by the London Missionary Society and had labored there for about five years. With him came two agents of the London Society, Daniel Tyerman and George Bennet, and nine Tahitians. The brothers gladly took them off to call on the king, whom they found looking vacantly about him, humming a monotonous air and obviously having nothing to do. Two of his queens were playing on a rolled-up leaf, out of which they managed to get a strident squeaking tone which seemed to amuse them.

When the deputation went to call on dowager queen Kaahumanu in her one-room house with its pile of mats covered with black velvet, a real surprise awaited them. With William Ellis were a faithful converted chief, Auna, and his wife. With Kaahumanu was a confidential Tahitian attendant who discovered in Auna's wife his own sister! Having left home as a boy, he had not heard from her in thirty years.

Auna, tall, straight and handsome, with a look about him that was both dignified and loving, was able not only to impart Christian doctrine, but also to tell how this new religion had triumphed in his own land. He and his wife agreed to stay on for a year to help with the work. When Kaahumanu decided to tour the windward islands with her husband, she took Auna and his wife along. Auna Wahine, as she was called, was a beautiful woman—her full round face and black sparkling eyes having a look of vivacity and intelligence which pleased the brethren and sisters almost as much as her "civilized" costume of gown, shawl and bonnet made by her own hands. When she and Auna sang together some of the "songs of Zion" Ellis had translated, the brethren felt moved almost to tears, seeing their own hopes for Hawaii substantiated.

Just when the mission felt once again that they were making progress—the king with his five wives all decked out in green dresses had come to church at the end of April—their hopes were upset by the king's determination to celebrate the anniversary of his accession to power on Sunday, May sixth. The brethren urged him without success to put it off until the next day. The court togged itself out in finery which combined new and old. Uniforms blazing with gold lace appeared, while the women put on satins, silk stockings, jewelry. But there were feather cloaks too, and women naked from the waist up though rolled in yards of tapa. The commoners, lacking all such finery, celebrated with "excesses of the vilest description"—missionary language for sexual activity.

Though the Yankee preachers considered such an affair an affront to Christianity, the king had no such intention. When they asked if Ellis might bring his wife and settle in the country to help them, he gave a cordial consent. "But you may find it hard to get food," he warned them. "This is a poor country. My subjects are given up to drunkenness, and what will be the use of trying to teach such a people?"

The drunkenness of which the king spoke, and in which he was a leader, was doubtless the result of anomie resulting from the breakdown of the old culture. The tabu system, with all its faults, had unified and directed every department of life from the irrigation of the fields to curing the sick, from taxation to family relations. It had taken the place of law courts, schools, churches, theater, police. The culture which had produced it had also produced splendid physical types, generous happy natures, a vast body of poetry, fine dancing, an effective herbology, good crafts, expertness in fishing, a highly developed irrigation system.

The order, the sense of security and organization, arose out of the tabu. When the system was overthrown, life became rudderless, and drink with its oblivion offered a way out.

Most of the men from the west who came ashore at Hawaii had also escaped their tabus—the confinements and prohibitions of the society to which they belonged. They were making the most of it. So they were drunkards too. They knew well enough, when the mission arrived, that if these preachers from home once got a toehold, Hawaii would be like any New England village with all its social restraints. So they fought the mission with any weapon that was handy—when they were not busy fighting each other.

Their methods were often ingenious. Just a month after giving permission to Ellis to live in Hawaii, the king was having his hair cut before going to the mission house to help the preachers with their Hawaiian. He had recently been leaving the bottle alone—a situation which the non-missionary foreign residents viewed with alarm. So the barber, a foreigner, told the king he ought to have his head rubbed with spirits to keep him from catching cold. One smell of liquor, and the king had to drink. Then he wanted a hula, and when the missionaries came to see why he had failed to visit them, they found him beating time with two sticks while his wives danced. That same day Marin noted in his journal that the king was drunk and passing blood.

It was Cox, however, who had the dream the king should have had. He saw the whole island on fire about him, and all the water in the ocean could not quench the flame. He sought a place to hide, but there was none. Awaking in horror, he sent for the missionaries. Two of them—presumably Bingham and Thurston—answered the call. They found him surrounded by chiefs. Cox told his dream; the young bearers of the Gospel—impressed no doubt with the biblical nature of the occasion—interpreted his dream and preached to him of the Savior. Cox asked them to come again at daylight to lead family prayers.

This was the opening they had been waiting for. Morning and evening they called at Cox's house, finding sometimes as many as sixty chiefs and their attendants. He opened his own house for a school. Queen Kamamalu had meanwhile opened another. Soon the king took to reading again, going through his ABC's like a child with the help of Bingham or Ellis.

The palapala had really taken hold with a vengeance. There were not enough teachers to go around. When three chiefs of lofty bearing came to the mission house for help, they found that everyone was already employed, down to a six-year-old Hawaiian boy named George who under Lucy Thurston had already become perfect in his Hawaiian lessons. One of the chiefs settled George on his shoulder and walked off with him, saying, "This is my teacher!"

When Kaahumanu, her husband, and her brother Cox departed with a thousand people on a tour to Kauai, they carried the enthusiasm for the new learning along with them. Little William Beals, also Auna and his wife went along as teachers, and the Thurstons would have gone too, except that the king and queen were not willing to spare their personal instructors.

How much the royal family now valued their teachers became clear when Ellis, Tyerman and Bennet sailed for Tahiti on August 22. Queen Kamamalu, having missed their parting call, came out into the harbor in a canoe, dived into the water and climbed up the ship's side, gave her aloha and then jumped back into the sea.

It had been a most welcome visit. But the already crowded mission house with its four bedrooms had been occupied almost beyond decency. The Chamberlains and Binghams had taken to the unfinished second floor—eight Chamberlains (the boys were back home now) and three Binghams with three Hawaiian children, and only a few mats tacked up between them. "All together called for patience and prudence to sustain the character of good neighbors," Sybil remarked with her genius for minimizing the painful.

Daniel Chamberlain now grew so helpless with rheumatism that his wife, Jerusha, had to give up the care of the household to tend him, leaving Sybil to cook three times a day for a household of fifty. The Whitneys turned up for a visit from Kauai, with two babies who cried all the time. After thirteen days of this, Hiram insisted that Sybil must give up before she collapsed. Lucy Thurston then tried it for five days and announced that some other way must be devised.

Sybil was happy to return to her own chamber with its shelf of books between the two windows, its fluffy white curtains, its beautiful little mahogany work table—a gift from the queen—and the sofa where she could now and then snatch a moment's rest.

Yet she had found time to write her beloved William Beals while he was on Kauai.

"My dear William," she wrote, "I feel as if I was writing to my little son as I take up my pen and say dear William. I hope you are a good child. . . . And William, you will not forget, that you have one Master, one friend, one father in Heaven that you must love & obey continually. . . . We pray that He will keep you from every danger—that He will keep you from every sin and bring you back safely to us, that we may love you and do you good as before. . . . Little Sophia talks of you a great deal. Every night when I put her down in her cradle, before she goes to sleep she calls your name many times. She says, Mama, mama, where is William. . . . Sometimes she makes the tears come in my eyes."

And William, who had apparently found in Sybil's love what he had not had from the woman who gave him birth, wrote back: "I long very much to see you . . . and little Sophia. I think about her every day, and how she used to play with me. I wish [sic] kiss her for me. You might be pleased to hear I have a school twice a day. I have thirty-five scholars, boys and girls, and the remainder of the time I teach the king and queen, so I have no time to write my journal. . . . King Kaumualii give his love to Mr. B. and to you, and Queen Kaahumanu too. They say they like the palapala. Do not forget to pray for me—I am your child."

So successful was the palapala on Kauai that Kaahumanu wrote back to Queen Kamamalu:

"This is my communication to you. Tell the whole heap of *Longnecks* to send more books down here. Many are the people, few are the books. I desire 800 Hawaiian books to be sent hither. We are much pleased to learn the palapala. By and by perhaps we shall be wise. Give our love to Mr. Bingham and Mrs. Bingham & the whole company of *Longnecks*."

The palapala had not solved all problems, however. The king, who could not stick to anything long, locked up his desk and unlocked his liquor case. Foreign residents took to carrying arms as disorders, arising from the increase of ships and sailors in port, grew worse. Sometimes as many as sixty whalers were in port at one time.

"Oahu is becoming one of the vilest places on the globe," wrote John C. Jones, who was in a position to know. There were seventeen grogshops kept by haoles and over a hundred deserters from whaleships causing trouble ashore, he noted. Yet at the same time he could write of the missionaries, who alone were doing anything to bring about social stability and good order, "O that providence would put a whip in every honest hand to lash these rascals through the world."

Jones had a more personal reason for hating the preachers. Although all had been sweetness and light between them at first, and even as late as the fourth of July the whole mission had attended Jones' grand dinner of turtle soup, beef, kid, poultry, pork and various kinds of fish, by fall there was a new issue between them. On November 26 Captain Davis had finally died from excessive drinking. Jones, who had had his eye on the bewitching Hannah, took her and her two boys in charge—naturally without benefit of clergy.

As men of God, Bingham and Thurston thought it their duty to speak their minds on such alliances. Having come eighteen thousand miles to preach a way of life they offered as Christian, they found it highly irritating to have self-styled Christians from home setting the Hawaiian people an example which was far from exemplary. One day Jones and two merchant captains were taking tea with the mission when Captain D—— twitted Captain E—— with being a deacon at home but being no better than the rest in the islands.

"When I see a man at home, on sacramental occasions, carrying around a silver platter, then, in coming round here, I say he has no right to live like us poor sinners."

Captain E—— blushed, rose, and departed. The missionaries now felt it their duty to send him a letter of admonition, hinting that they planned to tell his home church about his domestic arrangements in the islands.

This time the captain did more than blush.

Bringing a friend, he forced his way into the private bedroom of one of the missionaries, brandishing his heavy cane like a madman and shouting:

"Apologize for that letter, or I'll kill you. I have a family at home that I respect, and I am not a-going to have information conveyed to the ears of my church."

The interview lasted two hours, but the missionaries made no apology and no promises. The incident made it clear enough what lay ahead—a struggle with no holds barred for control of the mores of the islands and for the souls of its inhabitants. Neither side proposed to give an inch.

* * *

In the midst of this resistance to the spokesmen for God, the faithful adherence of gentle, rather melancholy Thomas Hopu was a blessing. Yet when he asked the brethren to grant him his dearest wish, a license to preach the Gospel, they refused. Others of the mission brethren, better qualified than he, had not been licensed to preach, they argued. It would not be fair to license him and not Whitney, Ruggles and the rest. And such a thing Bingham and Thurston had no intention of doing at present. As yet they had not even found a single Hawaiian worthy of membership in their church.

Hopu's other request was a wife. Picking a girl from Maui, he had brought her to the Thurstons to learn Christian ways.

"As the Almighty has excited in my heart such strong yearnings for her," he told them, "I think it is His will that I marry her."

Near the Thurstons a little cottage was put up for Delia. Only eighteen, she soon showed good intelligence, a warm heart, and a great willingness to learn. Lucy fell in love with her. A prim and proper housekeeper, Lucy instilled the same love of order in Delia. After a long season of training, Delia was led to the altar one Sunday after church. The king and his queens and all the principal chiefs were present on this August eleventh to see the first Christian marriage in the islands between Hawaiians. Hopu, dignified as always in his black suit, stood up with a girl who but a few months before had owned nothing but a piece of bark cloth to wind around her midriff. Now she stood proudly beside him in a fashionable white dress and trimmed straw bonnet—the first ever to crown a Hawaiian woman's head.

A few months later they settled down in Kailua where Hopu, the favorite of Governor Adams, was teaching and holding Sabbath meetings for the powerful and interested chief.

As the year ended Daniel Chamberlain, recently returned from Kauai where (apparently recovered from his rheumatic attack) he had helped build stone houses for the Whitney and Ruggles families, began to put up a small stone building for a printing office. He built well, for the building still stands.

As the third year of the mission drew toward a close, it was hard to say whether the power of the palapala would win the Hawaiians over to order and moderation, or whether liquor and the easy flow of sailor money would combine with habits of the past to defeat the mission and its aims. In the persons of Jones and Bingham the struggle was clearly shaping toward climax.

CHAPTER 7

THE BELOVED COMMUNITY

1823

SYBIL BINGHAM, WORN DOWN WITH THE CARE OF THE HOUSE-hold, her teaching, and all her other tasks, gave birth on the last day of 1822 to a little boy who lived only sixteen days. Grief-stricken, she did not waver in her faith in God. "I have no sorrow in His employ but this, that I do not serve Him with more fidelity," she wrote.

Hiram saw a way to turn their bereavement to the advantage of the cause. When Kaahumanu and the other high chiefs called to express their aloha, he asked for a piece of ground near the church to be set aside as a cemetery, and then invited them to attend the funeral and the first mission burial. From the king on down, all the chiefs were on hand to see how the Yankees managed these matters. They joined the procession from house to church, they listened to Thurston's sermon, and they walked to the little grave, chopped out of lava and coral.

When a half sister of the king died a few days later, his majesty asked the same rites for her. Kaahumanu requested prayers for the departed soul. "We had yet to teach them that probation ceases when the soul leaves the body," Hiram commented. There were many intricacies of Calvinist truth still, apparently, to be revealed. Convinced that their first duty was to inculcate Christian ethics and faith in Christ, the brethren had avoided theology. In any case the girl had her coffin, her procession, her funeral sermon, and her burial near the flagstaff within the fort. The solemnity of it all made an impression. "For a few days there were indications of seriousness among the rulers," noted Bingham.

Restless as ever, the king soon hurried off to a spot near the entrance to what is now known as Pearl Harbor. With the king's permission Bingham went along to keep the king sober and was even permitted a three-by-six-foot corner of the king's own dwelling. Not all to himself, however, for every foot of it was "stoutly disputed by the *ukulele*"—that is, fleas. One night, tortured more than usual by the ukulele, Bingham woke and saw that the king was also sleepless. "Feeling my heart inclined to win his soul," says Bingham, "I urged the necessity of immediate repentance."

"I cannot repent at once," said the king. "My wickedness is very great; but in five years I will turn and forsake sin." Beyond this Bingham could not move him. But one step the king did take—he commanded a proper observance of the Sabbath, with a dollar's fine for anyone caught working. Perhaps there had been more progress than anyone realized, if it was now necessary to fine a Hawaiian to keep him from working!

The king had also made progress in another way. When the Yankee teachers first tried to convince him that the earth revolved, he had picked up a leaf and, placing it on the globe, had then twirled the globe. "That's what would happen to us all if your notion were true," he told them, or words to that effect. But at last he decided they must be right. "Take care of your calabashes as the earth turns over," he told his people with a humorous wrinkling of his heavy brow.

On the fourth of February William Ellis, having gone to fetch his family, returned to Hawaii with his wife, four children, three Tahitian converts with their wives, and an unmarried Tahitian woman. He went immediately to work—preaching, teaching, helping to prepare the translations from the Bible, the hymns, the lessons which had begun to issue from Elisha Loomis's little press.

While the king returned to his drinking, and in the midst of it took Governor Boki's Liliha to his bed, the other chiefs thronged the mission house. "It was breakfast time in all the rooms," wrote Sybil, sufficiently recovered by mid-February to see the humor in it. "The queens, who are always all over the house, found a cup of coffee here, & a cake there as it happened." It speaks well for Sybil's gentle, enduring spirit that she never complained of this prying into the household affairs. Even if she realized that it was only in this way that the chiefs could acquire the graces the mission hoped for, it would have been no more than human for her to relieve her feelings in writing. But her journal shows only a determination to do what is right, a cheerful acceptance of all burdens, a moral earnestness that never seemed to tire.

The ordained brothers—Bingham, Thurston and Ellis—now formed themselves (February 28) into the Hawaiian Clerical Association and procedeed to examine and license Sam Whitney as a preacher.

They had hardly gained Whitney as a preacher when they at last lost Daniel Chamberlain, their farmer, and all his tribe. There seemed to be no prospect of establishing such a farm as had originally been thought of, Christian crops languished, and meanwhile six children were growing up—learning Hawaiian with astonishing virtuosity and along with it the facts of life which no Hawaiian thought of hiding. So with the concurrence of the mission, they sailed for home March twenty-first.

Meanwhile the second company was sailing towards Hawaii, where they arrived off Honolulu on April 27. This group, with seven married couples, a baby, a bachelor and a Negro girl, together with three Hawaiians and a Tahitian from Cornwall, was even larger than the pioneer group. Among them Lucy Thurston was rejoiced to find her dearest friend, Elizabeth Edwards, now Mrs. Artemas Bishop. They had grown up in the same town and lived together as roommates at Bradford Academy. Lucy, who had just borne her second daughter, sent off a loving letter to the ship.

Two days later the whole group came ashore after the *Thames* was towed into port by 108 men in two rows of boats. As they landed, Queen Kamamalu came out of the grass palace in a pink satin dress and feather wreath, asking them to land nearer shore because that part of the quay was tabu. The newcomers admired her fine black eyes and hair and her look of intelligence, though they thought her somewhat tall and muscular for a woman.

They were shocked at the appearance of the pioneers. Loomis was so emaciated they did not recognize him. The women appeared "almost worn out."

Led into the presence of the king, the new arrivals found him naked but for a strip of chintz about his waist and looking stupid. He "kept tossing," they noted—perhaps a warning touch of delirium tremens. They were more impressed with his new palace than with him. It was a handsome room fifty by thirty feet and rising thirty feet high at the peak with beautifully hewn timbers and neatly woven sides. As the chiefs gathered, Nahienaena, the seven-year-old princess, was borne in on the shoulder of a large man, her feet resting upon his folded arms and her arm around his head. The new company gave her an opera glass which she soberly regarded with big black eyes. To the young ten-year-old prince, Kauikeaouli, they gave a spyglass, and to all the principal chiefs some such gift as a silver pen, a glass inkstand or a finely bound book.

The new company was on hand May eighth to see the climax of a festival commemorating the death of Kamehameha and the accession of Liholiho—a parade the like of which had never been seen even in Hawaii and was never to be seen again. One whole side of the fort was overhung with cloth, while women armed with muskets paraded the walls. The king rode a pony he could not manage, forcing his guard to pant after him in great disorder. The two royal children had been plumped into the middle of a huge platform made of four field bedsteads lashed together, decked with cloth, and lifted to the shoulders of willing subjects. Behind them, walking like humble servants, came two great chiefs bearing calabashes of poi, fish and dog.

But it was the queens who made the most of the occasion. Kamamalu had arranged herself in a whaleboat which, supported by a wickerwork scaffold of poles, was born on the shoulders of seventy men. A scarlet silk pa'u wrapped around her waist and a coronet of brilliant feathers on her head, she sat in regal splendor under an immense Chinese umbrella of scarlet silk. Towering even above the umbrella waved two thirty-foot kahilis, held in the hands of two leading chiefs, Kalanimoku and Naihe, dressed in scarlet malos and lofty feather helmets. Queens Kinau and Kekauonohi were almost as grand as Kamamalu, though their platforms were double canoes instead of a whaleboat. The dowager queens wore yards of rich materials.

But it was another of Liholiho's wives, Pauahi, who stole the show. Riding on a couch richly decorated with fine fabrics, she was herself richly togged out. Where the crowd was thickest, she ordered the couch to be set down. Then, to commemorate her narrow escape from death by fire as an infant, she set fire to the couch and watched all its rich fabrics go up in smoke. Item by item, she then pulled off her clothes and cast them into the fire, her attendants doing the same. Saving only one tiny handkerchief, and all unconscious of having anticipated an American institution, the strip tease, Pauahi completed the parade with her handkerchief taking the place of Eve's fig leaf. Hulahulas "with the filthiness of their songs" completed the celebration.

The magnificence of the festival only accented the need for Christian nurture. Yet something in the outburst of the ancient glories suggested the high leap of a mortally wounded animal. The chiefs of Hawaii were to supplant their own ways with those of the west—but whether the west of Hiram Bingham or of John C. Jones was still in doubt.

*   *   *

The brethren took their time deciding about the permanent stations to which each should be assigned, and it was not until October that all the newcomers were finally disposed. But the need for a mission on the island of Maui was so evident that it was taken care of at once, and on May 27 six of the new group sailed with the king's mother for the town of Lahaina—two preachers, William Richards and Charles Stewart, their wives, the Stewart baby who had been born on the voyage, and the Negress Betsey Stockton. William Kamooula from the Cornwall school went along too.

William Richards, from the little hill town of Plainfield, Massachusetts, had gone to Williams College where his older brother, James, had been a member of the Haystack group out of which the foreign mission movement had grown. Like all the other married men of the group, he had taken a wife—Clarissa Lyman of Northampton—on the eve of his departure from the United States. Tall, and with muscles hardened by farm work, Richards had a pleasantly ugly face, a great reservoir of energy and rocklike integrity. His colleague, Charles Stewart, had been born to the expectation of wealth which had not materialized. An aristocrat in appearance, with a commanding nose and a confidently poised head, he had an optimistic, cheerful temper. He had studied law and was ready to go to the bar when a religious awakening led him to study theology at Princeton. A year before leaving the United States he was studying medicine and other subjects at Columbia, and in June of 1822 he married an equally aristocratic-looking girl, Harriet Bradford Tiffany, in Albany.

With the Stewarts had come Betsey Stockton—"a mulatto, pious, intelligent, a skillful domestic, apt to teach." Wild and thoughtless until her teens, she had got religion, educated herself, and become an authority on Mosaic institutions, Jewish antiquities and sacred geography. Raised in Nassau Hall at Princeton under the eye of the reverend president, Ashbel Green, she had at least had the proper exposure to religion, and had ended as a Sunday School teacher and superintendent. The day before the *Thames* sailed for Hawaii from New Haven, she had signed a carefully worded agreement with the Stewarts and the board which specified that she was to be treated neither as an equal nor as a servant, but as "a humble Christian friend." She was not to be given menial tasks in other households than the Stewarts', could leave their home if she wished, and was expected to teach.

After a trying four days spent in voyaging only seventy miles, the group was put ashore at Lahaina, a little village of thatch houses with a view across open water to the moundlike island of Lanai. Lahaina looked like Eden after the dreary plain of Honolulu, even though no house was ready for them. But Butler, who had once come to the aid of the Holmans, invited the group to use a house in the luxuriant grounds of his plantation. Shaded by the dense greenery of breadfruit trees and listening to the breeze rustle through the bananas and the sugar cane while a mountain brook tumbled near by, the Richards and Stewart households felt grateful for the fate which had sent them here. But they were seeing Lahaina in only one of its moods.

It was Keopuolani, the king's mother and highest-born chief in the islands, who had urged the mission to send them and who, with Prime Minister Kalanimoku as captain, had carried them there in *Cleopatra's Barge*. For some time Keopuolani had been impressed by the message the missionaries had brought, hoping perhaps that it would reform her son the king. When one of her chiefly friends had proposed that they send the missionaries away and get on with their serious drinking, she had demurred.

"It does no good to sing and pray," her tempter insisted. "Let us, I say, do as we formerly did, and drink a little rum together."

"I will follow their instructions, and you had better go with me," she had answered, "for I will never again take my dark heart."

She was the first of the Hawaiian chiefs to accept the strange missionary notion of one woman to one man. Having only a modest two husbands at the time the mission had arrived, she dropped one of these after learning about monogamy, and named Hoapili her sole spouse. Keopuolani had one other peculiarity in addition to monogamy—she was not overweight.

The morning after their arrival in Lahaina the mission group was summoned to the beach where the dowager queen had taken up her residence in a tent surrounded by a grove of koa trees. Here they found her with the little princess, Nahienaena, her chiefs and attendants—altogether a company of three hundred and fifty waiting for morning devotions. Thereafter they visited her morning and evening to conduct her family worship.

The next day Kalanimoku walked them around the boundaries of a piece of land on the beach which was to be theirs. Before sailing away a few days later, he took each in turn by both hands and pressed them to his breast. After his departure Keopuolani continued to look out for their welfare. Sending for their Hawaiian helper, William, she asked: "Have they hog still?"

"Yes."

"And dog?"

"No eat dog."

"And potatoes—melons?"

"No."

Immediately two men loaded down with melons and potatoes appeared at the mission quarters. Soon two Hawaiian houses were put up and then a church. Bingham came over for its dedication on August twenty-fourth. "I had never more freedom or pleasure in attempting to address the throne of grace in the unaccustomed accents of the Hawaiian language, than in offering the dedicatory prayer in opening this house of worship," he wrote. The king and all the great chiefs were there, having come over to Maui to visit the queen mother on one of their many peregrinations.

Keopuolani, who had done so much to aid the mission, now began to grow steadily weaker though she was only forty-five. On his arrival, Liholiho had gone to his mother's tent and fallen on his knees before her, gazing at her silently and then pressing her to his breast. Then he placed a hand on each of her cheeks and kissed her tenderly while the mother's heart seemed to float in her eyes. But if she thought her boy had reformed, she soon learned better. Taking over her tent, he soon began carousing. Moving to the princess's house, she pointed back to the tent when the missionaries came to visit her and cried, "Shameful, shameful." While Taua, her Tahitian teacher, prayed for the king, she threw herself in tears onto the mats, the missionaries also feeling "constrained to mingle our tears with those of the afflicted parent."

Abraham Blatchely, M.D., a new arrival replacing Dr. Holman, was sent for. But there was little he could do. Determined that there should be no heathen rites after her death, the queen mother commanded Kalanimoku to see that she had a Christian burial, urging him to follow the new religion himself. She then turned to her son the king.

"Take care of these lands and the people," she said. "Kindly protect the missionaries. Walk the straight path. Observe the Sabbath. Serve God. Love Jesus Christ. . . . If the people go wrong, follow them not, but lead them yourself in the right way, when your mother is gone."

The king begged Ellis to baptize her, which he did at five o'clock in the afternoon. *"Aloha ino iau i ke Akua*—Great indeed is my love to God," she said. An hour later she died.

When the wailing began, the common people fled in all directions —through ponds and wet taro patches, bearing what goods they could carry. For they knew that in the past the death of a chief meant the end of all restraints. But this time the wishes of the dead queen were honored for the most part. There was no violence—only the dreadful wailing, in tones that varied from a groan to a hair-raising shriek and in attitudes that varied from standing up with faces aimed at the sky to bending forward almost to the ground. When Adams arrived, he and the chiefs wailed at each other for fifteen minutes, standing eight or ten yards apart.

As for Liholiho, he swore off drink for a while but was finally seduced by the usual foreign tempters and was soon sitting with Pauahi on a mat in front of the tent, both of them drunk as they watched a drunk and near-naked woman dance suggestively before them. It was the start of a frightful revel in which twenty or thirty took part, garrisoned with cases full of liquor.

After Keopuolani had been buried, her husband, Hoapili, came to ask the mission whether it would be all right for him to take a new wife. Always before the chiefs had remarried immediately. There were five candidates eagerly pursuing him, he explained, but he would like to be married like the people in America. After a long wait—for a Hawaiian—of one month, he was married after Sunday service by William Richards to Kalakua, mother of two of the king's wives. This made him a second time the king's stepfather. All the chiefs of first grade were closely related. Keopuolani had been cousin, niece and wife to Kamehameha I. King Liholiho was married to several half sisters. The closer the blood ties, the higher a marriage was thought to be, since rank depended on the number of high blood lines that could be brought together. Naturally, the missionaries were horrified by these incestuous ties.

Settling in at Lahaina, Richards and Stewart began their work of carrying the gospel to the people of Maui, aided by Betsey Stockton who soon saved two Hawaiian children—one from a bad case of croup, the other from a nasty cut. It was harder to save them from moral illnesses. One day Richards noticed that one of the many Hawaiians who visited the house took some handkerchiefs from a trunk and slipped them under his mantle. Following him to the gate, Richards grabbed him. Out dropped a whole pile of stuff. Stewart had already missed a silk gown and nine yards of fine flannel, so Richards marched the man off to the local chief, demanding that he be prosecuted. Not only did the chief refuse to do anything, but the townspeople were so angry at Richards that they stopped bringing food gifts to the mission, refused to sell them any, and stopped talking to the Hawaiian boys of the household.

Instead of trying to understand this behavior, the mission set it down to depravity and redoubled their efforts to create a Christian respect for private property. Even the chiefs were not above lifting items that took their fancy in the mission houses. The sin, to them, was not in taking but in getting caught.

*   *   *

While the Stewart and Richard families were getting established on Maui, Ellis and Thurston together with two of the new men, Joseph Goodrich and Artemas Bishop, went off to Hawaii, touring the whole island in order to preach and decide where to place new mission stations. Like the disciples of old, they walked through the country, stopping at little villages where the naked inhabitants had never seen a white man, visiting the decaying temples of the old gods, urging the people to learn reading in order that they might know the true God.

"If we were to spend the time at our books," argued one of the men they talked with, "there would be nobody to cultivate the ground, to provide food, or fetch sandalwood for the king." Ellis examined them closely on the amount of time it took them to do these things, and then pressed them to say what they did with the rest of their time. "Ate poi, lay down to sleep, or just talked for amusement," they told him. Ellis, pressing his advantage, asked them whether they would not do better to learn the word of God than to waste their time in idleness. When they tried to turn the subject by saying that England must be a very great country to send such large bales of fine cloth, Ellis said the difference was not in the country but in the people; that the English had also once been poor savages but that in becoming Christians they had become wise and wealthy. Cautiously his hearers promised that if the chiefs approved of their studying, "by and by they would attend to it."

Winding up their tour at Kailua, the travelers were delighted to learn that Governor Adams had already begun to build a church. On Sunday more than eight hundred people assembled at the governor's for worship. Adams had made the day tabu—not a canoe passed across the calm surface of the bay, no tapa mallets were heard, not even the noise of playful children. "Truly gratifying," Ellis found it.

When Ellis described to Adams the resurrection of the body, the last judgment and the existence of heaven and hell, Adams said, "How do you know these things?" Ellis simply reached for his Bible and translated. Then the governor wanted to know if most of the people in America and England were acquainted with the Bible. Yes, said Ellis.

"How then is it so many of them swear, get intoxicated and do other evil things?"

As to the heaven Ellis described, one of his listeners inquired, "If there is no eating and drinking, or wearing of clothes in heaven, wherein does its goodness consist?"

Though the chiefs had followed the advice of the missionaries and forbidden work on the Sabbath, the people were not convinced. Ellis, coming upon a man working on a Sunday, asked him if he didn't know it was improper.

"Yes, but I am just working secretly," he said. "The chiefs will not see me as it is some distance from the beach."

"God will see you," said Ellis.

"I did not know that before," said the worker, "and will leave off when I finish this row of plants I am weeding."

The brethren now returned to Honolulu where all but Stewart and Whitney assembled to make a final decision about the opening of new stations and the placing of the second company. For over a month they maneuvered, trying to satisfy everyone. James Ely, chosen by ballot to go to Hawaii, held out for Kauai and was finally allowed to have his choice. Bishop, Goodrich and Thurston were assigned to Hawaii but could not agree among themselves as to their stations. When the deadlock was broken by balloting, Bishop got Waiakea, Thurston and Goodrich Kailua. Thurston did not like the arrangement and said so. No doubt Lucy had set her heart upon having her old friend Elizabeth Bishop with her as some compensation for returning to dreary Kailua. The brothers wrote a letter urging Thurston to accept the decision.

"If the brethren should all say he ought to go to Kailua with no other aid but that which they had assigned," he answered, "he would not say he would not go, but if he should go it would be with a heavy heart and with little hope of comfort or usefulness." After deliberating over this unthreatening threat, the brothers relented and put the Bishops and Thurstons together. In the midst of this Mrs. Bishop gave birth to a dead child after a night of agony. "I think it would be impossible to suffer much more and live," wrote Maria Loomis.

After assigning the bachelor Levi Chamberlain (no relation to Daniel) to the job of secular agent and allowing Dr. Blatchely to choose Kailua, Lahaina or Honolulu (the choice was academic, as he spent most of his time traveling), the brothers broke up and scattered to their posts.

The Thurstons, with their little daughters, Persis and Lucy, set out for Kailua on October twenty-fourth, a few days ahead of the Bishops. Here they found Adams, who had gone farther than any of the chiefs in accepting western ways, living in a frame house brought all the way from the United States, taking tea and coffee at his own table, and speaking passable English. The church he was building was finished and dedicated in December. Soon a thousand people were crowding in and around it to hear Thurston preach.

Often Kapiolani and her husband, Naihe, came the sixteen miles from their home at Kaawaloa. Attracted towards the missionaries from her first contact with them, Kapiolani had seemed attuned to the Christian message. She had dismissed all her husbands but Naihe, had learned the palapala, and had found in the Gospel a promise and a comfort which spoke to her naturally calm, dignified and noble spirit. When Prime Minister Kalanimoku wrote to inquire whether she was not lonely at Kaawaloa, she had answered, "Lonely! No. If I am separated from my friends, here is God; and with him I have communion."

With twenty thousand inhabitants living within thirty miles of Kailua, Asa Thurston and his partner, Artemas Bishop, had plenty to do. Until Bishop could learn Hawaiian, most of the mission work fell upon Thurston and his ever-faithful assistant Thomas Hopu, now happy in the arrival of the brethren.

Back in Honolulu Levi Chamberlain, a Vermonter who had just turned thirty-one, settled into the task of ordering all the mission's secular affairs. In business until he was "converted," after which he had spent a year at Andover Theological School, Levi had already proved his business competence by laying aside $3,500 which he had pledged to the mission he was sent to. Offering himself first as a missionary to the Indians, he had worked a year in the offices of the board before sailing for Hawaii.

One of his early achievements in Honolulu was to win five very important converts to the mission—two cows, two calves and a horse, purchased for $220 from a sea captain. Patient and conscientious to an almost painful degree, the rather melancholy-looking Levi was a mainstay of all the brethren for many years to come. Taking over from Loomis, he may have pondered the relative importance of these items in the mission accounts: $83 for rum, gin, brandy and wine; $80 for soap, $79 for sugar.

On the second of December the stone printing house was finished, the press set up, and two thousand copies of the first Hawaiian hymn-book struck off in the following weeks—the product of translations and original verses by Bingham and Ellis. The mission house was thronged with people wanting books; the supply—thanks in part to the wrong sizes of type sent out with the second company—could not keep up with the demand.

The tide was once again running strongly in favor of the mission, and a great deal had been accomplished in a short time. Yet Bingham was not satisfied. A true New Englander, he had never lost the dream of a City of God, a land in which spiritual values would be the controlling ones. The Pilgrims had tried to establish it, exactly three hundred years before the pioneers had landed on Hawaii, and they had failed. Over and again the experiment had been made—in Boston, along the Connecticut, in Narragansett Bay. Always it had failed, and yet not entirely. In another place, with a fresh start, it might succeed—a beloved community of the faithful, bound together in Christian faith and brotherly love. Yes, it might happen—here in Hawaii.

Chief obstacle was the king—weak, shifting, never to be relied upon, a bad example to his people. His sudden announcement that he was going off to England and America was, therefore, not entirely upsetting. Not to the mission, and not even to his chiefs. His behavior after his mother's death was worse than ever, according to Kamakau, the contemporary Hawaiian historian. Liquor flowed like water at the court, he says, while the king gambled, wasted money, and chased after women.

When Liholiho had chosen his traveling party—his wife Kamamalu, Governor Boki and his wife Liliha, a son of John Young and several others—the mission suggested that William Ellis and his

family go too. Unwilling to wait until a ship of his own could be
made ready, the king insisted on leaving at once in Captain Starbuck's ship. But Starbuck refused to take Ellis, even when the king
requested it. Starbuck had apparently listened to some of the local
merchants who, intent upon breaking the mission's influence, wanted
to prevent the king from appearing in England as a mission protégé.
Even Boki, no great friend to the mission, told Bingham, "I feel just
like being sick at Mr. Ellis's staying here."

The departure on November twenty-seventh provided a fine opportunity for a session of Hawaiian weeping. That the tears may have
been more formal than real, however, is implied by Kamakau's story
that one chief who suggested they keep the king from going nearly
had his clothes torn off his back.

Kamamalu, handsome and queenly in her going-away dress,
paused on the stone quay to render up the meaning and temper of
the moment in an impromptu poem which began:

> O skies, O plains, O mountains and oceans,
> O guardians and people, kind affection for you all.
> Farewell to thee, the soil,
> O country for which my father suffered; alas for thee!

The travelers stepped down into the boat, the wailing rose higher,
and cannon boomed from the fort near by.

Even until the last moment Liholiho was apparently hoping that
he would be drawn back by the love of his people. "Is there no ship
coming to take us back?" he asked when they had cleared the harbor.
There was none. "Ah," he said, "they have long despised us."

Secretly conveyed aboard, Jean Rives—the king's evil genius and
of late a grogshop keeper as well—took the place that had been
denied Ellis.

The king's departure, by placing the dowager queen Kaahumanu
and Kalanimoku in charge of government, opened a new era for
Hawaii. All the leading chiefs were now pro-mission. What had
failed in New England might succeed in Hawaii, and the City of God,
the beloved community find an earthly location in the Pacific paradise.

CHAPTER 8

REBELLION

1824

BUSINESS WAS POOR FOR THE YANKEE TRADERS IN HONO-
lulu. For years they had been pressing all kinds of goods upon Hawaiian chiefs in exchange for promises of future payment in sandalwood. But now, with the price of the wood rising from six to fourteen dollars a picul (about 130 pounds) at Canton, they found it
almost impossible to get the sandalwood that was due them. The fact
that two of the ships they had sold in Hawaii had soon proved too
rotten to sail did not help any. Nor the fact that they had charged
mighty fancy prices.

Disgusted, John C. Jones headed for home in January. Not even
the charms of Hannah Holmes could hold him any longer. The
"cursed missionaries," he was certain, had ruined the trade by cor-
rupting the innocent natives with a knowledge of what was and was
not fair business practice. Even James Hunnewell, ablest of all the
traders, could not tell when he would be able to get home. Writing
to his brother Joseph, James confessed: "My hopes of realizing
something handsome from the *Thaddeus* concern has vanished." The
bride he had left behind in Boston was appalled at the length of his
stay. When he promised her that, once home, he never intended to
go to sea again, she wrote, "I hardly believe it." The Chamberlains
had returned with news of him. "May you return to me," wrote
Susan, "not only almost a Christian but altogether a Christian."

"Go home and make your wife happy," wrote a friend. But James
could see no chance of getting away until the year's end—if then.

Meanwhile, in the course of becoming altogether a Christian, he
aided the mission in every way he could. Early in January, 1824, he
loaded his little schooner, the *Waterwitch,* with a full cargo of mis-

sionaries and supplies and pointed her prow toward "the big island" (Hawaii) where the Ruggles and Goodrich families were to set up a new station in the district of Hilo. Ellis, Chamberlain, the Blatchelys and Elys also went along on one errand or another. Stopping for a day at Lahaina, they were ten days on the way, the distance two hundred miles.

It was sunset when they sailed into Hilo Bay with its fine sand beach bordered by coconut and breadfruit trees, the snowy peak of Mauna Kea and the huge dome of Mauna Loa rising in the distance. Almost enclosed by reef and bar, the harbor was an excellent one, with good holding ground for anchorage and depth enough so that ships could lie close in.

By Kaahumanu's order a thatched building seventy by thirty, intended as a shelter for canoes, was turned over to them. "They were allowed, without annoyance or assistance from the stupid inhabitants," wrote Bingham, "to take care of themselves as well as they could." None of the usual Hawaiian aloha was visible here. The Hilo folk showed no enthusiasm at all over the arrival of the pule and the palapala. They grudgingly surrendered one old fowl from which the mission wives, with stores from the ship, made a supper over a little open fire in the middle of the house. Seventeen people—for there were also Hawaiians in the group—had to be fed. Meanwhile the men brought in beds, strung up partitions of tapa, and made a long table of two rough boards.

The next day was Sunday. For a church, Kaahumanu had given the use of another canoe house. In the midst of William Ellis's sermon the congregation suddenly rose and fled. Ellis found himself facing a huge black hog with evil-looking tusks. With martyrdom staring him in the face, Ellis was saved by the arrival of the hog's attendant. For, it turned out, this was a tabu pet of Queen Kaahumanu and even bore her name. The keeper, by rubbing the beast's bristly back, put it to sleep. The sermon went on. For years hogs and dogs were familiar attendants at church services, which was natural enough since they shared quarters with their families at home.

The mission at Hilo (Waiakea) thus met resistance, human and animal, from the very first. The Hilo people, as Bingham sourly noted, "in their self-complacency, questioned or doubted whether any benefit equal to the trouble, could be obtained by attention to missionary instructions." Hilo had no strong and willing chief to tell his people to learn the palapala.

Nevertheless, Goodrich and Ruggles opened a school, got a house built and then a church—there were now nine churches in the islands —and gradually made inroads upon the indifference of the people. The beginning may have been hard, but it was also firm. Fifteen years hence Hilo was to be the scene of the most remarkable religious phenomenon in the islands.

When the little *Waterwitch* sailed out of the harbor of Hilo, the Ruggles and Goodrich families were on their own, with not another "civilized" neighbor closer than a hundred miles. The Thurstons and Bishops were on the other side of the island at Kailua, but it was an arduous journey by foot, across lava beds and deep ravines, to get there. Rarely did a ship call at Hilo. Within a few months the families marooned there were writing to Levi Chamberlain that they had neither food nor any trading goods to buy it with. Twice Chamberlain tried to get a supply to them, and twice he failed. Finally he had to go himself. Fortunately Goodrich, like most Yankees of that day, was handy with tools and understood farming.

The *Waterwitch* carried the Elys around to Kailua where they began to get the hang of the language. Two schools were flourishing here—one in the king's house next to the mission, with fifty scholars taught by the Bishops; the other in Governor Adams's grounds where the chiefs themselves studied under Asa Thurston and John Honolii.

The Elys had hardly got settled here when Kapiolani, perhaps the most devotedly religious of all the chiefly group, begged them to come to her home at Kaawaloa sixteen miles down the coast. Hopefully she had built a church with neatly plaited walls. She and her husband, Naihe, promised a house and maintenance. Although the Elys had been assigned to the island of Kauai where they were to join the Whitneys, the mission recognized the importance of Kapiolani's influence. So James and Louisa Ely went off to Kaawaloa, within sight of the place where Captain Cook had been killed forty-five years before.

Although Governor Adams was eager to take advantage of missionary instruction, he soon turned out to be taking advantage in

other ways. Adams, shrewd as he was huge, was seeing to it that the
missionaries bought all their supplies for cash, and at prices he fixed.
He put a man in their yard when whalers were in port to prevent
them from buying anything at less than Oahu prices. When Hopu
found some goats for sale several miles out in the country, the brethren sent him back with trade goods to buy them. The governor sent
a man forbidding the sale, except for cash and at the fixed price.

A great impetus to the palapala was given early in the year when
the chiefs, meeting at Lahaina, decided that it would be safe to let
the common people study. When the mission had first proposed
schools the chiefs had said: "If the palapala is good, we wish to
possess it first ourselves. If it is bad, we do not intend our subjects
to know the evil of it." Now they had decided.

In April Kaahumanu herself performed at the school examination
in Honolulu, submitting a piece of her own writing. "This is my word
and hand," she wrote. "I am making myself strong—I declare in the
presence of God that I repent of my sins, and believe in God our
Father." Five hundred pupils were on hand to celebrate the fourth
anniversary of the Honolulu mission. When they all in unison
shouted, *"Hoolea ia Iehova—Praise the Lord,"* Kaahumanu said it
felt as though God were coming down upon them.

Uplifted by the experience, Kaahumanu assembled the high chiefs
and missionaries. When Bingham asked why they had been brought
together, Prime Minister Kalanimoku turned to Kaahumanu and
said, "Is it not to make known our resolution concerning the palapala
and the law of God?"

"It is," she said. Then she explained that as she intended to follow
God's laws herself, she wished the people to receive the palapala and
the pule. Kalanimoku—Billy Pitt—now made a stirring speech in
favor of the new religion. When he asked the chiefs if they agreed,
they shouted back a loud *ae*–aye.

Kaahumanu was busy with other affairs too. Eager for the com-
forts as well as the spiritual consolations of the Yankee way, she had
a frame house built near the landing place in Honolulu, inviting the
missionaries to christen it. When Captain Dixey Wildes introduced
a carriage, she harnessed a dozen men to it, ordered her handsome
young seven-foot husband to the footman's place, put ex-king Kaumu-

alii inside, and then mounted the driver's seat herself. The mission children were delighted when Captain Wildes took them and their mothers for a ride—pulled, however, not by men but by the mission horses. Kaahumanu eventually had horses broken to the bridle, and when one died in service, she economically ate it.

*   *   *

On the thirteenth of February young William Beals, Sybil Bingham's foster son, fell sick. Three days later the poor little fellow was dead. A month after William's departure, the governor of Maui, Cox or Keeaumoku, died. Brother to Kaahumanu, he was a great chief and merited great honors. Flags in the harbor were dropped to half mast, while throughout the day cannon boomed from the fort. He had, of course, a Christian funeral with a sermon by Bingham. But if the historian Kamakau is right, the sermon was preached over an empty coffin. Cox's brother Adams had removed the body "to see whether the foreign God would know the difference." With a squadron of vessels to attend it, the coffin—with or without Cox—was taken to Kailua.

Two months later, on May 26, the dignified, noble-looking ex-king Kaumualii died in Honolulu and people began to whisper that the chiefs were dying because they had accepted the new religion. Laid out in state with his beautiful feather war cloak at his head, a short cape at his feet, a wreath of feathers across his eyes and folds of rich green velvet and yellow satin leaving his chest bare according to custom, Kaumualii, noble to the last, had escaped his imperious wife just as she was beginning to show signs of gentleness. "King Kaumualii, he have but one heart," said one of his admirers, "and that was a good one. Some chiefs have two hearts—one good and one bad."

Four days later the church was burned down, probably by a Hawaiian who had created a drunken disturbance at the afternoon service, and, when admonished, had threatened to burn the place. Bible, lamps, pulpit, seats, doors and window frames were saved. The chiefs began to build a new church immediately, gathering and bringing grass and rushes with their own hands. Prime Minister Kalani-moku, who was building a two-and-a-half-story stone house soon to be the showplace of Honolulu, sent his carpenters to hasten the church. On July 18 the first service was held, complete with bass viol and flute to aid the singing. Two days later Billy Pitt's fine house was dedicated with prayers. Whatever effect the mission was having on morality, it was in large part responsible for the building boom.

Hiram and Sybil Bingham had missed the excitement of these events. Taking along their four-year-old Sophia and their newborn baby, Jeremiah, they had sailed on May second for Kauai to be with the Whitneys for a while and to help them in their labors. Little Maria Whitney was the same age as Sophia, while young Sam, now two, had been born the same year as the Bingham child who had died. On June fifth Mercy presented Sober Sam with a third to match Jeremiah Bingham. They called him Henry.

The Whitney house stood between the sparkling river and a steep cliff, a fine grove of coconut trees behind and a clump of kou trees in front which provided a delightful shade from the tropic sun. Sitting under the trees while the little girls ran tirelessly back and forth in the excitement of their new and delicious friendship, the grown-ups exchanged their long budgets of news. In the evening Hiram took Sybil out to walk along the bank of the gentle river while the moon spilled its light down along the palm fronds and into the moving water where a silver image of the trees and houses on the other side shone bright and clean. It was rarely that they could be alone like this. Sybil's mind must surely have jumped back to that moonlit evening walk from Waikiki four years ago. How much had been won and lost since then!—William and little Levi gone, Kaahumanu turned towards the light, the king departed, the mission firmly rooted, as firm as these fine kou trees, in Hawaiian soil.

But these idyllic moments could not last. Hiram was soon off on a preaching tour of the island. He was back in Waimea when the news of Kaumualii's death disrupted the mission schools and put the whole island in an uproar of grief and anxiety. Although the ex-king had left all his possessions in the hands of Kaahumanu and Kalanimoku for Liholiho, it was an important question with the chiefs of Kauai as to who would be their next governor. With all his advantages, it should have been Prince George. But he had turned out to be good for nothing.

When Kalanimoku appointed a nephew, Kahaalaia, as governor of Kauai, George showed signs of resistance. If he had moved quickly, he might have got control of Kauai. There was widespread dissatisfaction with Kahaalaia the governor—stupid, tall, weighing three hundred and fifty pounds, and with a full face, protruding eyes and a covetous, superstitious nature according to Sam Whitney. The chiefs of Kauai, who had wanted the customary redistribution of lands at the ex-king's death, resented him and the power which had sent him. A strong current of self-determination still flowed in Kauai hearts.

"You shall not pay him homage," said one of the chiefs to George. "Neither will we. Come with us—you shall be our king."

Before daylight on August eighth, the Binghams and Whitneys were wakened by sounds of firing at the fort. Some of the balls came whistling over the house, and soon there was a running back and forth at their very door. Next came a shout from the walls of the fort addressed to the people on the two sides of the river:

"*Ho Waimea! Ho Makawele!* Come on—the Hawaiians are beaten —the Kauaians have the fort!"

Kalanimoku, who had recently arrived on the island to look into complaints against his nephew, sent for Bingham and Whitney. As they passed the fort on their way to him, the firing broke out again. Sybil and Mercy listened prayerfully, hoping their men were safe.

Crossing the river, the men found Billy Pitt. "What is all this?" they asked.

"This is war," said Billy Pitt.

In a few moments word came that George and his insurgents had been driven from the fort. Hiram and Samuel crossed over again to bind up the wounds of the injured and to bury the dead. Before long the chiefs—Kalanimoku, Kaumualii's former wife Kapule and others —marched into the fort, the women as of old armed for war like the men. Kalanimoku, sending a schooner to Oahu for help, advised the mission families to sail on it. Though they were almost swamped in their efforts to get aboard, they left that evening, drenched to the skin.

When the news from Kauai reached Honolulu, thousands rushed to offer themselves as soldiers. Excitement such as had not been

known since the days of the old warrior Kamehameha I swept through
the town. Government reinforcements soon flowed in to Kauai from
Oahu and Maui.

On the eighteenth of August a force under the chief Hoapili moved
towards Hanapepe where the rebels had dug in behind a wall with a
small fieldpiece. Resting on the Sabbath, Hoapili attacked the next
day. It was not much of a fight. The rebels were routed, forty or fifty
were killed, and the rest ran off into the mountains, George and his
family with them. His wife and daughter were soon taken, but George
went deep into the mountains. At last, weeks later, they found him
without food, without a stitch of clothing, half drunk, his only possession a joint of bamboo with a little rum in it. When he was
brought before Kalanimoku, the old chief took off his mantle and
threw it over him, saying simply, "Live." To keep him from stirring
up any further mischief he was sent with his family to Oahu, where
he lived, thoroughly undistinguished, until his death in 1826. Poor
George! He had learned either too much or too little of Yankee ways
—enough to spoil him for his native culture, not enough to enable
him to lead the way to the inevitable fusion of Hawaiian with New
England ways. Writing before the battle in an attempt to persuade
Kalanimoku to let none but Kauai men—and women—take the field
against him, he had tried to express himself in Hawaiian, but then
had given up and written his message on the other side of the paper
in English. Even at the moment when he was trying to assert his
leadership, homelessness in his own culture had defeated him.

Despite the instruction of the missionaries, who had advised the
inquiring chiefs that they should love their enemies, some women
and children and old people were slain in the course of wiping out
the revolt. Bodies, left unburied, were eaten by dogs and swine. A
period of license followed during which the game of *pili*—at first only
the kissing of boy and girl meeting in the dark—became "an assembly of wanton lewdness" which met almost nightly. Two flourishing
mission schools were nearly broken up by it. The chiefs assigned a
new governor, Kaikioewa, to Kauai—a man dedicated to the palapala and the pule. But the disturbances had shown how deep and
strong were the currents of the old culture beneath.

The currents appeared in another way alarming to the mission when the chiefs discussed the propriety of a marriage between the young prince, Kauikeaouli, and Princess Nahienaena; "this prince and princess having lived in a state of incest though the boy is ten and the girl about seven," according to Elisha Loomis. The chiefs argued that the offspring of this brother-sister marriage would be a very great chief, the missionaries that any offspring of so ungodly a union would be sick and weakly—a proposition hardly borne out by the evidence of the hulky, healthy chiefs all around them. The subject was to be debated many times until its dramatic solution years later.

Meanwhile the mission did as much as it could to influence the princess, who became a constant visitor and almost a ward of the Stewarts in their home at Lahaina.

*   *   *

Spread around the four principal islands, the mission stations now began to develop a life, a rhythm, a pattern of their own. Lucy Thurston's house at Kailua, though most systematic of all, with a daily schedule regulating every half hour, was typical. The yard, walled around with stone, contained buildings for three purposes. Asa's study served as reception room, and no visitors were to go beyond it without invitation. Next was the dining room which also served as the family living room and as a school. Within this sphere, and the near-by cookhouse, the household helpers functioned. Beyond this was the sleeping area, with an enclosed play yard for the children, to which no one could have access without Lucy's permission. The children hated being cooped up, but on one thing every member of the mission agreed—Hawaiian talk was altogether too free about sexual matters for Yankee children to learn.

The day began early, starting at four and with breakfast soon after five. Every day was a busy one for the overworked missionaries. They had not only to teach, preach, and maintain their households. They had to deal with a constant stream of visitors, they had to see to their food supply, and often the men made long and arduous preaching trips on foot in an attempt to reach the thousands of people living too far off to come to church. Sometimes they took their families along. Then a cradle or a chair might be lashed to a pole borne on the shoulders of two men. Up and down deep gulches and across busy streams they went, where often no passage seemed possible. Or they might go by sea, in a double canoe with many paddlers, the steersman slapping his paddle against the bulwark as a signal to change sides.

Supplies—enough to feed not only the mission family but the several Hawaiian workers and children in the household—were a constant worry. The native foods—sweet potatoes, taro, roast bananas, fish, arrowroot, taro tops—came to be mission staples. Fresh beef was rare, bread a luxury. Usually a goat or two was relied upon for milk. Flour, shipped around the Horn from Boston, was so hard that the only way Thurston and Bishop could divide their barrel was to saw it in half. The solid cake was then mouldy two inches in and well occupied by worms throughout.

From America Levi Chamberlain also ordered the mission's bread (ship's biscuit), Indian meal, pork, beef, molasses, coffee and sugar. Pearl ash was needed for soap-making; for trading goods, calico, broadcloth, gay prints, knives and scissors, and fishhooks. As for spirits, Levi wrote that the amount must be left to the board, though more rather than less would be desirable. Elisha Loomis was doing a little experimenting on his own, and in November succeeded in making beer from the root of the ti plant whose juice, he reported, was as sweet as molasses.

As fall approached, William Ellis felt that his wife was too ill to remain any longer in Hawaii. With his whole family, therefore, he sailed for the United States and England, leaving his rooms to the Binghams, who found them more comfortable than anything they or any of the mission had hitherto enjoyed. Sybil, like all the mission women, was wearing herself out—teaching school, caring for her own children and two Hawaiian lads, cooking and washing and cleaning. Bingham wrote the board that it was to save expense she endured this labor, though it was a questionable economy. For a hundred dollars a year each of the families could have a Hawaiian couple to help them. Meanwhile men like Jones spread the story that the missionaries were living in luxury.

The best and most intelligent of the Hawaiian chiefs, however, saw in the mission program the one hope of salvation for their country and people, fast being eaten up by drink and venereal disease. These powerful evils, they saw, only the strong medicine of the Gospel could heal, or at least palliate. Most earnest of them all at this time was Kapiolani—keen-eyed, intelligent, able. She now dressed like the mission ladies, had chairs and tables in her home, put up her long black hair on a comb, and devoted herself to the task of saving her people, by the pule and the palapala, from destruction.

To encourage the mission at Hilo, where Goodrich and Ruggles were still having a hard time opening the hearts of the heathen, she decided to make the long trip—over a hundred miles—by foot. This, for a person of her size, was in itself a brave undertaking. But there was more. She proposed to stop on her way at Kilauea, the crater where Pele, the volcano goddess, was supposed to live. By violating the tabus of the crater, she hoped to destroy the belief in this last and most tenacious of the old gods.

On her way a woman claiming to be *ke akua,* one in whom the god dwells, stopped her, warning her to go no farther.

"If God dwells in you, then you are wise and can teach me," said Kapiolani, offering her food.

"I am a god. I will not eat," she said. Then, holding up a piece of tapa, she pretended to read a message from Pele. It was incomprehensible stuff.

Kapiolani took up one of the mission books with its biblical passages. "I have a palapala as well as you," she said, "and will read you a message from our God which you can understand."

After the reading the prophetess said that ke akua had left her; she could make no reply.

As Kapiolani started up towards the volcano, Joseph Goodrich met her. Hearing of her trip, he had come over from Hilo to join her. Ruggles would have come, too, but he had been for six months without shoes. Goodrich had learned to travel barefoot—a martyr's fate in that land of lava. So together, with about eighty followers, they climbed to the rim of the huge crater and then down inside to the black ledge. Below them hot lava boiled and bubbled; steam hissed and rose in columns from the uneasy holes in the crust. Kapiolani turned and spoke to her people.

"Jehovah is my God," she said. "He kindled these fires. I fear not

Pele. . . . If I trust in Jehovah, and He shall save me from the wrath of Pele when I break through her tabus, then you must fear and serve the Lord Jehovah."

While the volcano wheezed and roared, the company raised their voices in a hymn of praise to the true God. No harm came to them.

The old gods had fallen on hard times. No longer were the red berries sacred to Pele, or the filaments spun by the crater which were called her hair. Pele was as dead as Zeus, and the isles were Jehovah's.

CHAPTER 9

THE KING IS DEAD
1824–1825

IN THE MIDDLE OF MAY, 1824, KING LIHOLIHO AND HIS party reached London. The king's arrival was promptly reported in English newspapers, which announced that he had come to place his islands under the protection of the British king. "He went to Britain to seek a landlord," the regent, Kaahumanu, scornfully said of him. The British government arranged lodgings for the whole party in the fashionable Adelphi area and assigned the Honorable Frederick Byng to attend them. Under Byng's guidance they saw the sights of London, impressed beyond words by the vastness and solidity of the city. Walking through Westminster Abbey, the king did little but stare at the lofty ceiling, staggering up and down the aisles until he made his exit.

The king, in turn, was also an object of curiosity and—sometimes— of ridicule. The queen, on her arrival in London, was wearing what a contemporary observer described as trousers and a long bedgown of colored velveteen. She lacked the regal dignity the British expected, complained constantly of the cold, and played cards a good deal of the time with a dirty pack. The party ate frequently, Hawaiian fashion, and were particularly fond of oysters. The only time they drank too much was after they had fired Jean Rives for his repeated ill behavior. Rives, apparently, had grown too big for his boots and was pretending to an authority he did not possess. Returning to his native France, he promised all sorts of special privileges in the islands to French traders, and actually succeeded in getting up a voyage, with effects that were to keep Hawaii upset for years.

Entertained by the famous foreign minister George Canning, and then by many of the great and near-great, the royal couple were shown "like rare animals," drawn out by journalists, and apparently laughed at behind their backs.

Before Liholiho had the interview with King George which he had come so far to seek, he fell ignominiously ill of the measles. Queen Kamamalu caught them too. This was no laughing matter to people who had never before been exposed. The Hawaiian islands, until the arrival of westerners, had been entirely free of germ-borne diseases. Hawaiians, therefore, lacked all the immunity and resistance of the haole and the inroads made by disease multiplied with every increase of commerce and contact.

Soon the whole party was stricken. King George sent his own physicians. Boki, Kekuanaoa and the others recovered. But Kamamalu grew steadily worse. On the eighth of July Liholiho had to be told the truth—Kamamalu was dying. He insisted that he be carried into her room and laid by her side. They clasped each other in a warm Hawaiian embrace, then the king ordered all his attendants to leave the room. What passed between them remains their secret. At last Liholiho was carried away, and an hour later sweet-featured, dark-eyed Kamamalu was dead. Liliha prepared the body Hawaiian style—with naked breasts, ankles and feet, the hair adorned with flowers. Stricken at his loss, the king grew steadily worse. Calling in Boki, he said: "This is my death in the time of my youth; great love to my country." On July fourteenth, 1824, he followed his favorite wife. He was only thirty-two, his wife twenty-six.

On the eleventh of September Boki, now leader of the party, had an interview with King George, James Young serving as interpreter. The king promised to protect the islands from any aggressor and not to annex them himself. On September 23 Richard Charlton, a sea captain who had voyaged and traded in the Pacific, was appointed British consul for Hawaii and other Pacific islands. On the twenty-eighth the whole party boarded the 46-gun frigate *Blonde* at Portsmouth. The bodies of the king and queen, encased in heavy caskets, were placed aboard and with George Anson, Lord Byron—cousin and successor to the poet—as commander, his majesty's ship hoisted sail and set out on the long voyage.

News of the king's death reached Honolulu with the American whaler *Almira* on March 9, 1825—two months ahead of the *Blonde*.

Prime Minister Kalanimoku immediately sent the news by letter to Kaahumanu who was resting at her cottage in cool, showery Manoa Valley behind Honolulu. Quick to realize that if religion was to reform the lives of the people, it must take a prominent part in their national crises, the mission held services both at Honolulu and Manoa on the same day. Fortunately the groundwork had by now been well laid. So far as the high chiefs were concerned, the palapala and the pule had become their guides. The nation was therefore well braced against the shock of the news from London.

When Bingham ended his sermon, therefore, on the theme, "The Lord gave; the Lord hath taken away, and blessed be the name of the Lord," Kalanimoku rose in church and suggested that prayers be offered morning and evening for twelve days in succession. He and Kaahumanu, acting for little Kauikeaouli, sent the news to the other islands, instructing the chiefs to follow the word of God and keep the people quiet. Levi Chamberlain went with Namahana, one of the queens of Kamehameha I, to carry the news to Maui and Hawaii.

In the old days the death of a king had been the signal for a wild debauch. Now, except for a few outbreaks here and there, the country was quiet.

When the *Blonde* reached Lahaina, Boki went ashore with his wife Liliha and was met on the beach by her father Hoapili, governor of the island of Maui. Throwing his head back, Hoapili let out a roar of anguish. Behind him a thousand people began a wailing which wiped out the sounding of the surf. After embracing his daughter, Hoapili fell to his knees and began scouring his face in the sand. The crowd followed him. But Boki, who had seen England, said: "Where shall we pray?"

William Richards was ready to lead them. The crying died away, the prayer began. Then Boki and Liliha spoke of the good things they had seen in England.

Among their listeners was the young princess, Nahienaena, sister of the dead king. Somewhat heavy-featured, with a deeply incised upper lip and sober, dark eyes, she had been fought over by those who favored the palapala and those who wanted to maintain the old ways. Recognizing how great a stake they had in Nahienaena, the missionaries had done their best to shape her mind and heart in the knowledge and love of God. They had wanted to have entire charge of her so that she might by living in a Christian household acquire all its habits. But she was too high a chief to be given over to them. Both the Stewart and the Richards families had, however, done their utmost to influence her. But whether they had won her away from the pagan forces that would marry her to her brother, the missionaries did not yet know.

The *Blonde* sailed for Honolulu the next day, taking along most of the principal chiefs. She appeared off Diamond Point (also called Diamond Hill) at sunrise on the sixth. By nine she had reached the mouth of the harbor where she fired a salute of fourteen guns which was promptly answered from the fort and from the Punchbowl. At midmorning barges came ashore with the members of the Hawaiian party. Chamberlain, Loomis, Stewart, and of course Bingham walked to the wharf to meet them. Kaahumanu was there with her sisters and the surviving wives of the dead king, all of them dressed in sober black though not all wore shoes. Standing in a row, they began to weep in concert as soon as the barges approached.

When the barge touched the wharf, Bingham gave his hand to big-eyed Liliha. Then the rest of the chiefs climbed out of the barge, forming a line opposite to the one waiting to receive them. Approaching very slowly, the two lines loudly wailed their "Au-e." The crowd behind them joined in, while the minute guns booming from the near-by fort shook the ground under their feet. Now friends who had been parted fell into each other's arms and wept some more. The chiefs went off to Kaahumanu's new house for a brief exchange of news and then to church. Here, after prayers, Boki—the once-profligate Boki—stood up and told the whole people that they must learn the palapala and worship the true God.

The next day Lord Byron and the officers of the *Blonde* came ashore, accompanied by the new British consul, Richard Charlton, who with his wife and her sister had arrived in April. It was a colorful procession in full uniform, with Byron at its head. Charming in manner and conversation, tall and slender with fine dark eyes and hair, lively, intelligent and warm-hearted, Byron gained an immediate popularity. Led by Boki and Charlton, he walked to an audience room recently built in Hawaiian style. It was fifty feet long, with high-peaked roof and neatly woven walls, its floor strewn with the best mats. The smell of the fresh grasses was sweet and clean.

On a platform at the end of the hall sat the little king Kauikeaouli and Princess Nahienaena on a Chinese sofa. Ranged around the end of the hall were the principal chiefs, the women on one side, the men on the other, with Prime Minister Kalanimoku and his Christian teachers in the middle. All the chiefs wore western clothes, but the princess also wore wrapped around her waist a wonderful pa'u of yellow feathers. Behind her and her brother rose the tall kahilis, feathered symbols of their high rank.

As Byron entered the room, everyone but the two royal children stood up. The party were presented, and then Byron handed around gifts. To the boy king he gave a splendid royal Windsor uniform, complete with yards of gold braid, sword, epaulets and hat. His dark eyes lighting with pleasure, the little boy with the big name—Kauike-aouli—longed to put it on. When Byron, who evidently knew something about children, suggested that he do so, the formal proceedings halted while the twelve-year-old youngster got into the brilliant coat, donned the hat, and had the sword strapped about his slim little waist.

"I am made very happy by your coming to this country and by your kindness towards us," said Kalanimoku.

"I am very happy to have this service to perform for my king and country," Byron answered, "and only desire to show kindness to you and your nation." The meeting closed with prayer and refreshments.

On the tenth of May Adams, Kapiolani and a dozen missionaries from outlying stations reached Honolulu. The next day the bodies of the king and queen in their triple coffins of lead, oak and mahogany, and covered with richly ornamented crimson velvet, were brought ashore while minute guns boomed from the fort. Here the procession formed—first twenty men bearing tall kahilis, then a company of marines from the *Blonde* in white jackets and trousers carrying their arms reversed, then the ship's band, the men of the mission, the two hearses pulled by chiefs, and then the chief mourners, each supported by a British officer. Moving slowly along Honolulu's one street, the procession worked its way past the crowds to the thatched church. Here the chaplain from the *Blonde* read the burial service and Bingham preached a brief sermon. Then the coffins were borne to the audience hall near Kalanimoku's house, now converted with hangings of black tapa into a temporary mausoleum. Here the heavy coffins rested until a plain stone mausoleum was built.

Only six years earlier the old king Kamehameha had been dissected and his bones hidden in traditional Hawaiian fashion. Only the previous year Cox had been stolen out of his coffin and his body handled after the old custom. But no one would break through the heavy boxes in which poor Liholiho was encased. Even in death he was imprisoned by the new customs which seemed destined to take possession of his country.

This Christian funeral service gave new drive to the move towards Christianity. On the first Sunday in June ten leading Hawaiians rose in church to describe their religious feelings and announce their desire to be Christians. Among these were Kalanimoku and Kaahumanu, Kapiolani, the defier of Pele, and seven-foot Kealiiahonui, once Kaahumanu's husband. Always cautious, the mission decreed a probationary period. But it was clear now that the tide had turned. The effective forces in the islands stood on the side of the mission. Palapala and pule would be the foundation upon which a new Hawaii would rise.

Yet there would never be an end to the struggle, for there were always interests which profited from a freer way of life. So when the mission held its monthly concert of prayer on the first Monday of each month, foreign residents staged a horserace to tempt the young king, precocious in his pleasures.

"See," said Kaahumanu on one such occasion when the king rode by just as the prayer meeting ended, "there is the king—he has yielded to the foreigners."

On the seventh of June Byron departed for the island of Hawaii, taking along Kaahumanu and the Stewarts, to see whether a voyage would restore Harriet Stewart's rapidly failing health. As for Kaahumanu, she thoroughly enjoyed the voyage, sitting on deck and saluted with volleys from the ship's guns, infinitely gratified by the quantity of gunpowder expended and the smell and smoke created in her honor.

As soon as the *Blonde* anchored at Hilo, Kaahumanu sent word to Sam Ruggles to come and see her. Sam declined the honor. He had

seen something of Kaahumanu at Kauai, at the time when she had
lorded it over Kapule, the wife of King Kaumualii whose place she
had usurped. Kaahumanu sent again, humbly begging him to come.
When he arrived, she threw her arms around his neck and, weeping,
told him she had submitted herself to the Lord Jesus and would try to
do his will.

"When I formerly saw you I disliked you, I hated you," she told
him. "But now I love and respect your character." And she plunged
into the work of encouraging schools and churchgoing. Amazed, the
people of Hilo called her the new Kaahumanu. The old imperious-
ness, the little finger extended in haughty greeting, were gone.

After erecting a memorial to Captain Cook near the spot where he
had been killed at Kealakekua Bay, Lord Byron sailed for home,
leaving in Hawaii an abiding respect and trust for his country.

The mission, too, had its departures. Harriet Stewart had not been
improved by the voyage, and in the hope that she would live to reach
home, the mission assented to the departure of the Stewart family
and Betsey Stockton. Too ill to walk, Harriet was carried in to say
farewell to Sybil Bingham, who was herself so ill that she was not expected to live. On June eleventh she had lost her second son, golden-
haired little Jeremiah Evarts, only sixteen months old. Most of the
women were ailing—Bingham says from climate, overwork and unaccustomed modes of living. He might have added a stubborn in-
ability to alter their own habits to fit the climate. It was a shortsight-
edness of the whole mission movement that it insisted upon trans-
planting its material as well as its spiritual culture complete.

Yet the mission prospered. At Honolulu over three thousand people now came to church. Catechisms and spelling books and hymnals
poured from the little press as fast as the supply of paper would permit. The people came with melons, bananas, or whatever they could
spare in order to buy a palapala. No self-respecting house was without some product of the mission press. The demand grew so great
that the mission could and did regularly get six times the cost of these
pamphlets—a form of profiteering which it considered, as perhaps it
was, a legitimate way of getting the people to support it.

So great was the demand now for the new religion that the Yankee
preachers found themselves flooded with work. Artemas Bishop one

day preached six sermons to a total of 2,500 people. The effort was too much. He fell into a fever, suffered a relapse, and did not preach again for ten weeks.

Hawaiian enthusiasts were quite ready to step into the breach. A chief of Maui named Ti harangued his people: "Jehovah made the owl. He made the shark. He made the lizard, and all our gods. He loves all His creatures, and He has sent His son into the world to save them. This we never knew, till our foreign teachers came and told us." Then to Richards Ti said: "I think my words went into their ears, then turned and went down their throat, entered the heart, and there stuck fast."

One of the most effective Hawaiian converts was a blind man known as Bartimeus who had once danced and sung for the amusement of the king. With his shaggy black hair, ruined eyes, and black chin beard tired in a knot, he was strange to look at. But he had a wonderful memory, an eloquent tongue, and a love of the Gospel. Stationed on Maui with the governor, Hoapili, he led devotions with fervor.

While the Yankee preachers prospered in their labors though their wives wilted, the Yankee merchants and sailors continued manfully to shoulder the responsibility of demonstrating in Hawaii another facet of New England life. Old Oliver Holmes, father of all the pretty daughters who were both willing and available, went on a last drunken frolic which ended in his death on the sixth of August. With touching sentiment, the grogshops of Honolulu lowered their flags to half mast! Several of the missionaries attended his funeral the next day, but abandoned the idea of going to the grave with him because they found themselves surrounded by notorious prostitutes—each on the arm of a Yankee or English trader.

The traditional attitude towards island women was carried on by an Englishman named Buckle, captain of the *Daniel*, who gave a chief $160, in return for which he was allowed to take a girl with him on a whaling cruise. To add insult to injury, the girl, Leoiki, had been a promising mission pupil. When the ship put in at Lahaina in October and its crew went ashore as usual to get women, the situation had changed. Women were tabu; no longer were they to visit the ships, staying aboard for days or weeks as they had used to do. Two men called on Richards, threatening him and demanding that he have the law repealed—which naturally enough he refused to do.

Richards then appealed to the captain. But Buckle, with his $160 girl still aboard, was hardly the man to back up the mission. Enraged at their inability to get girls, the sailors left their ship in three boats under a black flag, armed with knives. They surrounded Richards' house, demanding females—or his life. William and Clarissa Richards stepped out to meet them.

"If you are determined to take our lives, here we are," they said, "but our principles we will never give up. We came hither with our lives in our hands, and we are ready to sacrifice them in the cause of our religion." Hawaiian protectors quietly gathered about, standing ready with stones and clubs to defend their teacher. A sailor made a pass at a Hawaiian with his knife.

"The play is over," said a chief. "We must be serious now." The cannon in the Lahaina fort were loaded, the matches lighted. If necessary, the ship would be seized. Looking at the stalwart Hawaiians, the sailors made an inglorious retreat.

Soon the *Daniel* weighed for Honolulu, to see if luck was any better there. Forewarned, Honolulu had a guard ready to prevent trouble. A year later the whole *Daniel* affair was to blow up with a bang when Buckle, returning from a voyage, learned that Richards' account of his behavior had appeared in print in the United States.

In view of the conversion of the chiefs to Christianity, the *Daniel* affair was small potatoes. For on December fifth most of the leading chiefs of the nation were finally admitted to membership in the church which had been established in the good old Congregational way at Boston, back in 1819. Always cautious, the brethren had kept them for six months on probation. If any of them "slept mischievously," in Hawaiian phrase, during that time, the brethren did not find it out. Their conduct had been exemplary. Among them were Kaahumanu; Kalanimoku (Billy Pitt); Kapule, the former wife of the king of Kauai, seven-foot Kealiiahonui; Kapiolani, the defier of Pele, and several of the ex-queens of Kamehameha I or II.

Hiram Bingham, having made a translation of the Ten Commandments, presented it to the chiefs who decided that, since Hawaii was in need of laws, these would do very well indeed. At the close of the

church service on December 11 a meeting of the chiefs was announced
for the following day at the rear of Kalanimoku's house. Thus alerted,
and fearing a mission plot to impose rigid blue laws upon the islands,
the foreign residents attended in a crowd. Two or three missionaries
were also present. The issue between Yankee preachers and Yankee
traders was now forced into the open. In the course of a long dispute,
during which the traders accused the preachers of trying to control
the Hawaiian government, one trader said, regarding the evils known
to exist there:

"You think to stop these things, but you never can."

"I learned long ago that wicked men and seducers wax worse and
worse," said Bingham. "We do not expect to stop them wholly."

Despite the opposition of the traders, Billy Pitt and Kaahumanu
proposed the adoption of the Commandments as the law of the land.
Boki opposed them. The young king decided that "they did not know
enough yet and must stop a little longer before they did it."

That was the end of making the Decalogue the law of the land.
But it was the beginning of an increasingly bitter conflict between the
two groups from Yankeeland.

"The most impudent puppy I have seen in many a day," wrote
trader Stephen Reynolds of Bingham in his confidential journal. The
old drama of good and evil, fought out these many years on New
England soil, was now transferred to the Pacific paradise. Unfortunately for the Hawaiians, they stood helpless and exposed on the no
man's land between the two relentless, advancing forces.

CHAPTER 10

ENTER SAILORS, DEMANDING WOMEN
1826

JACK PERCIVAL, COMMANDER OF THE U. S. NAVAL SCHOONER *Dolphin,* was a bold, daredevil sort of fellow who had gone to sea with only nine months' schooling and a clean shirt. Sent into the Pacific to pick up the survivors from a mutinied whaleship, he stopped at Honolulu on his way back home on January 23.

Percival—or Mad Jack as he was fond of calling himself—was soon comfortably supplied with a Hawaiian girl. But his men did not fare so well. The chiefs, though they had failed to establish the Ten Commandments as the law of the land, had put a tabu on drunkenness, debauchery, theft, murder and other crimes. In August, 1825, the public crier had gone through the streets of Honolulu calling out a tabu against lewdness, and on September 13 the chiefs had decreed that women were no longer to go aboard ships in the harbor.

Until this time it had been a constant offense to the Yankee preachers, whenever they sailed in or out of Honolulu, to see Yankee ships crowded with half-naked girls who lounged on the windlass, leaned against the rail, or came laughing out of forecastle or steerage —always surrounded by a group of admiring and eager males who had been long at sea. When the ship had to sail, the girls would often sail with it into the open sea, and after taking a lingering and suitable leave of their friends, would plunge into the ocean, swimming about the ship like mermaids until at last they struck out for shore.

Mad Jack Percival must have sensed immediately the change that had taken place in the islands, for when he proposed an exchange of salutes on Sunday, the chiefs sent back word: "We keep sacred the Sabbath, and observe the word of God." When he learned that women were tabu, his fiery disposition burst into flame. An insult to the honor of the United States, he called it. For had not Byron been allowed to have women? The chiefs said no, the *Blonde* had been a tabu ship. Mildly, they urged that they had a right to rule their own subjects as they saw fit.

Percival demanded an audience with the chiefs, which was arranged for February twenty-second at Kaahumanu's house.

"If Mr. Bingham comes, I'll shoot him," Percival fumed.

Standing before the council of chiefs, Mad Jack demanded: "Who is the king of the country?"

Kaahumanu pointed to the boy at her side, whom she had called from his studies with Hiram Bingham.

"Who is his guardian?" asked Percival.

"I," said Kaahumanu.

"Who has the charge of his country?"

"I and my brother, he being under me," Kaahumanu told him.

"By whom are the women tabued? Is it by you?"

"It is by me."

"Who is your teacher that has told you that the women must be tabu by the law?"

"It is God," said Kaahumanu.

Percival gave her a scornful laugh. "It was not by you; it was by Bingham," he said.

"It was by me," Kaahumanu insisted. "By Bingham the word of God is made known to us."

Warning them to let his men have women, Percival said, "You formerly attended properly with Kamehameha to the ships, both American and English."

"In former time, before the Word of God had arrived here, we were darkminded, lewd and murderous. At the present time we are seeking a better way," said Kaahumanu with dignity.

Failing to move Kaahumanu, Percival next tried to get Boki to break the tabu. When this failed he went back to Kaahumanu and snapping his fingers in a rage, said: "If the women are not released from the tabu tomorrow, my people will come and pull down the houses of the missionaries."

There were other crews in port, all thirsting for women and intent upon the outcome of Percival's battle with the chiefs and the mission.

On Sunday afternoon, February twenty-sixth, they came ashore determined to "knock off the tabu." Upstairs in the large hall of Prime Minister Kalanimoku's house a number of the chiefs had assembled with Bingham for a prayer meeting.

In rushed a band of seamen, brandishing clubs and shouting, "Where are the women? Take off this tabu and let us have women on board our vessels, or we will pull down your houses. There are a hundred and fifty of us—the tabu must come off."

A crowd of sailors now began milling around Kalanimoku's house and forcing their way in, smashing the glass along the veranda until they had broken sixty-seven panes.

Sybil Bingham, hearing the crash of glass, sent a message begging Hiram to come home. At first he thought it safer to stay where he was, for if he were followed, his family might be endangered too. But when he saw a party of seamen make for his house, he went off by another path, hoping to get there before they did. He reached his door only a few steps ahead of the mob. But the door would not open. Sybil, seeing the sailors but not her husband, had locked it.

"Here he is," shouted an excited sailor, grabbing Hiram by the shoulder. "I have got him—come on."

Another grabbed the tails of his clawhammer coat. Someone smashed a window with a club. Hiram found himself hemmed in by shillelaghs. Calling for help, he started towards Kalanimoku's.

"Why can we not have women?" said a sailor.

"Because it is prohibited in the word of God," said Bingham.

"It is damned hard that we can't have our wives on board," the man answered—meaning, apparently, Hawaiian girls.

"You can have your wives aboard provided you are married."

Would Bingham marry him? the man wanted to know. Yes, under proper circumstances.

"I will come tomorrow and be married," said the fellow.

The crowd now pressed in upon Bingham again. An Irishman passed a knife under Hiram's nose.

"Do you see that knife?" Bingham said to Lydia Namahana, dowager queen and sister of Kaahumanu, who stood near by. Then, seeing loyal John Ii and some of his other men students, he said to them in Hawaiian: "Do you not take care of me?"

"We do take care," they said.

At that moment a *Dolphin* man aimed a heavy blow at Bingham's head with his club. Queen Lydia sprang to Hiram's side, helping to ward off the blow which Hiram parried with his umbrella.

This was the overt act Ii and the others had waited for. They sprang upon the rioters, tore knife and club from the two who had threatened Bingham, knocked down two others with clubs and stones, and with Hawaiian skill and muscle overpowered any who resisted. A zealous Hawaiian jumped to the side of one of the rioters now lying senseless on the ground, and raising a stone over him was about to deliver a blow that would probably have been fatal. Loomis and Chamberlain arrived just in time to save the fellow.

Hiram now retreated to his house. Pursued by a growing mob, he slammed and locked the door in their faces. When a window came crashing in, he took Sybil and the two children upstairs to the bedroom. A club now began thumping on the door. Men put their shoulders to it and tried to force it in. Looking down from the room above, Hiram saw one of these men suddenly turn and strike down his fellow with a club. At this point Percival arrived, waving a heavy cane which he landed on the heads and shoulders of the rioters as he ordered them to break it up. Carrying their wounded off the field, the men departed.

But in the evening Percival made another call on the chiefs. Though he admitted that his men had gone too far, he implied that they were right in resenting the tabu as a slur upon the honor of the American Navy! Rather than submit to such an insult, he told the chiefs, he would have his hands and feet cut off and go home mutilated. "I wish to Christ they had murdered the damned rascal [Bingham] and torn his house down," Mad Jack privately told Captain Edwards of the *London*. He did, however, repair the damage done and threw into the brig the men who had assaulted Bingham. Though willing to intimidate the chiefs and curse the missionaries, he apparently feared the consequences of violence.

Two days later Governor Boki and Manuia, commander of the fort, gave in to the sailors' demand though without permission from Kalanimoku. Girls poured out to the ships in boatloads, or swam out and climbed up the chains. A shout of victory and anticipation greeted the first load of women to reach the *Dolphin*. During the remainder of its three-month stay, the *Dolphin* men made up for time lost. The girls went back and forth from ship to shore, happy with the trinkets their admirers showered upon them, or the dollars with which they could buy bits of finery in the shops of Honolulu. Since the chiefs no longer collected a fee for the girls, convinced that the wages of sin did not make acceptable taxes, these damsels had so much more to spend. "What's good for business is good for Hawaii," concluded the merchants, among whom were the United States consul Jones, now back in the islands, and the beefy-faced British consul Richard Charlton. Two girls' schools were entirely broken up by the ending of the tabu. Sadly the missionaries had to conclude that improving "native females" in manners and dress and then teaching them English only made them more attractive to foreigners who were all the more eager to "ruin" them.

On April first the chiefs sent a crier through the town to say that the tabu was on again. Perhaps they felt that the round of illnesses and the wet season which made the cellar wall of the mission house fall in were somehow connected with their weakness in dropping the tabu. Kalanimoku, long ailing, was tapped by Dr. Blatchely about the middle of the month, and gave up two gallons of liquid. Prince George, outcast and nearly forgotten, died on the third of May. Pauahi, the strip-tease queen, succumbed in June after giving birth to a little daughter who became the ward of Kaahumanu.

The rising tide of religious fervor seems to have had its effect upon lovely Hannah Holmes, "companion" of John C. Jones. When Jones left the islands she had placed herself again under the mission, and now at his return she refused to live with him unless he would marry her. This rupture in the accustomed etiquette of the islands was infuriating to Jones, and in his letters home he was soon railing at the missionaries again. Everything was their fault—the slump in business, the lack of potatoes, the distress of the country, the distracted state of the government, and apparently the widespread sickness and the rainy weather as well. "Nothing but the sound of the church going bell is heard from the rising to the setting sun," he wrote, "and religion is crammed down the throats of these poor simple natives whilst certain famine and destruction are staring them in the face."

The Yankee preachers were guilty of conduct "infamous, degrading, revolting . . . trampling on men's rights on the pretense of saving souls."

Though Hannah relented and was shortly living in a house Jones built and furnished for her, he never forgave the missionaries. Around him, the English consul Charlton and Boki an anti-missionary party began to form. It included most of the foreign residents of the ports, and the rumors and attitudes it gave birth to still float about the islands under the guise of fact.

In midsummer Kaahumanu decided to make a complete circuit of Oahu in order to recommend the new religion to all the inhabitants. Armed with slates or books, nearly three hundred people went along with Kaahumanu, her sister Lydia Namahana and Bingham. Since there were only a few horses, most of the company traveled the whole 130 miles on foot. Bingham preached and examined schools. Kaahumanu exhorted the people to turn to the true religion. Her tour was so successful that she visited other islands as well, encouraging the people to give up their heathen customs, go to school, and obey the commands of Jehovah. Schools went up everywhere. Soon there were twenty-five thousand students and four hundred native teachers. Seventy-four thousand small books had been printed. Congregations, numbered in the thousands, gathered wherever there was a preacher. In spite of Jones, Percival and Charlton, the mission was forging ahead.

In September the missionaries met together at Kailua to help dedicate the handsome new church and to hold their annual business meeting. Many of the great chiefs were present at the dedication, and in the presence of four or five thousand people declared their determination to rule according to God's word.

As for the business meeting, Bingham dominated it as usual with his ready tongue and his quick mind. Thurston, diligent and patient but far less facile, could not match him. While the pioneers had grown accustomed to Bingham, the members of the second company felt that he assumed too much. Except for Bishop who was "wholly wanting in common prudence" and might say anything, most of the brethren kept their own counsel. Dr. Blatchely was opposed to Bingham, but though rough-mannered he managed to keep quiet in meetings. Ely, unsocial and disagreeable, had no influence with the brethren. About the only man who could come near to matching Bingham was William Richards, whose heavy mouth and chin disguised a quick and perceptive mind.

While the brothers were still at Kailua a swarm of sailors from English and American whaleships descended upon Lahaina looking for Richards, the man who had (in their view) been responsible for the tabu on women there. Failing to find Richards, they seized his hogs and fowls—obligingly pointed out to them by Butler, the man who had once befriended the Holmans and other early arrivals but was now bitterly anti-mission. But in seizing the hogs they lost the women, all of whom fled to the mountains along with Kekauonohi, the chiefess left in charge while Hoapili was at Kailua. For several days the sailors ransacked the town, breaking into houses, stealing the property of the poor inhabitants, but finding no women. At last they went back to their ships and asked the captains to take them to Honolulu.

A few days later, on November 12, trouble developed in another quarter in Honolulu when Boki, rising up in church, began a bitter attack on the mission. The Yankee teachers had called him a thief, he said, though he was guilty of no fault. What was more, they had called the king a thief too.

"This is the last time that either the king or myself will come to this meeting," he said, and then stalked out of meeting, taking the king with him.

Lydia Namahana told the brethren not to worry too much about Boki. "He is like a calabash of poi which has been fermenting till it becomes sour and pushes the cover off, gushing over the top."

The growing tendency of Boki and the anti-mission party to challenge the mission's motives and policies had been met by the publication of a circular in which the mission's aims were set forth, and the anti-mission party called upon to investigate the facts instead of circulating unfounded complaints.

At this point arrived Lieutenant Thomas ap Catesby Jones of the U. S. Navy, in command of the sloop-of-war *Peacock*. Jones had come in response to the request of a group of Nantucket whalers that something be done about the swarm of deserters prowling the Ha-

waiian Islands, many of them naked and destitute. The Nantucket
men feared that this group might turn the islands into a pirate headquarters.

Jones went to work in systematic fashion, and with the full co-
operation of the Hawaiian government. Every American who had
ever been a sailor was rounded up by Hawaiian soldiers and "penned
like sheep" until Consul Jones and Lieutenant Jones could look them
over. Runaways and stragglers were put to work loading ships, with
Hawaiian taskmasters to urge them on with a cat-o'-nine-tails.
Others were chained to carts which they were forced to haul through
the streets. Sailors could not come ashore without liberty tickets, and
anyone who fed a man lacking such a ticket could be fined fifty
dollars.

Having thus cleaned up the deserter situation, the able young officer—a veteran of the war of 1812—turned his attention to the bitter
complaints he heard on every side against the mission. The anti-mission party had had plenty of opportunity to prejudice him, for he had
arrived in Honolulu when the missionaries were holding their general
meeting at Kailua.

Learning that the challenge to investigate the mission had been
accepted, a group which included Bingham and Richards set sail for
Honolulu in their own little schooner, the *Missionary Packet,* which
the board had sent out with no other than James Hunnewell in command. Hunnewell, after returning home to his Susan for a few brief
months, had set sail again for the islands, his little ship so loaded that
she took in water with every wave. After a miserable voyage—it took
him nearly eight months to reach Valparaiso from Boston—Hunnewell set up shop again in Honolulu on October 25.

It was December eighth before the meeting of the two parties was
convened. Meanwhile both sides had been doing their best to build
up a case. The mission had asked the chiefs to express themselves in
writing and had collected an impressive set of testimonials. "I know
of no faults in you," Kalanimoku had written. "If I knew of any I
would mention them to you. . . . It is on our own account you are
blamed; it is not yourselves."

And old John Young: "The great and radical change already
made for the better, in the manners and customs of this people, has

far surpassed my most sanguine expectations. . . . I rejoice that true religion is taking place of superstition and idolatry; that good morals are superseding the reign of crime; and that a code of Christian laws is about to take the place of tyranny and oppression. These things are what I have long wished for, but have never seen till now. I thank God that in my old age I see them, and humbly trust I feel them too."

Twelve Honolulu residents, including the British and American consuls, the merchant Stephen Reynolds, and Captains Eliab Grimes, John Meek, John Dominis and Dixey Wildes, had signed the letter taking up the mission challenge to investigate its conduct. When the meeting opened at Boki's house forty residents filed in. Beefy-faced Consul Charlton opened the meeting with a blast against the mission schools. All this book learning was leading people to neglect their fields, he said. People were starving, fields were going to waste, and there was no way to victual visiting ships. Why, in one of these mission schools he had with his own eyes seen four couples fornicating during prayers!

William Richards, spokesman for the mission, jumped up to demand that these vague charges be made specific, and that they be put in writing. Instead, he was met with another barrage of questions, this time from the once friendly Captain Ebbets. "Who supports you?" he cried. "Who gives you your bread? Who gives you your meat? Answer me that!" He ended by threatening to prosecute any one of them whom he ever managed to catch in the United States.

Now Captain Grimes pitched in. "What have you called us here for?" he demanded. Since the mission circular and the response to the challenge were well known, this query seemed superfluous. But Richards patiently replied: "From you, gentlemen, we have asked an investigation of our conduct—we have challenged it. Now as you have accepted the challenge, let your charges be stated definitely, and bring your evidence in support of them. Then, and not till then, will there be anything for us to do, either offensive or defensive."

"There's not a chief in the islands who dares testify against a missionary," shouted Charlton, his red face glowing brighter until it ignited his neck. Reynolds said the evidence against the mission was of a kind impossible to bring forward.

When it was obvious that the meeting was getting nowhere, Lieutenant Jones proposed that the circular be read again, to be sure that everyone understood it. Richards read it out. Then Jones stood up again. Obviously, he said, it was up to the men who had answered the circular to bring specific charges backed up by evidence, since the mission would not arraign, try and condemn themselves. If no one was prepared to do this, they might as well adjourn.

Stephen Reynolds moved adjournment and the meeting broke up. When he got home, Reynolds wrote in his journal: "As no one went there to make charges the meeting was dissolved."

"The Lord turned their counsels into foolishness!" Kaahumanu said, overjoyed when the news of the meeting reached her. "I told Boki if the missionaries were found bad and sent off the islands, I should go with them."

The meeting had turned into a victory, not only for the mission, but for the United States. For Thomas ap Catesby Jones had appeared as a champion of the American mission, no matter what his intentions, while Charlton as spokesman for the opposition had only succeeded in losing prestige for Great Britain. From this time on the lieutenant paid the kindest attention to the mission family. He entertained the whole group aboard ship, asked Hiram Bingham to preach every Sunday aboard the *Peacock,* and invited all the men of the Honolulu mission to a meeting to discuss the debts of the chiefs.

These debts, having dragged along for five or six years, were a source of irritation to the haole traders. The accounts were so confused that no one knew their amount. Jones, "the kind-eyed chief," as the Hawaiians were beginning to call him, patiently plowed his way through all the evidence, whittled the sum down to half a million, and worked out with the chiefs a plan by which the people would be sent to cut sandalwood and the proceeds carefully segregated until the debt was paid off.

Finally, on December 23, he met with the chiefs at ailing Kalanimoku's house to sign a treaty of commerce and friendship—the first treaty ever to be signed by the chiefs of Hawaii. To honor the occasion the chiefs dressed in dove-colored satin and brocaded silks. Jones and his officers wore their navy blue uniforms, splendid with bright buttons and gold braid, while the mission brothers appeared in their black suits with white stocks clutching their necks.

Kaahumanu suggested prayer. With Jones's approval Bingham prayed.

Just as the quills were being taken up for signing, Richard Charlton rose to protest. The Hawaiian Islands were under the protection of Great Britain, he said, and its citizens "subjects of Great Britain, without power to treat with any other State or Prince."

The chiefs, powerless to deal with this sudden twist of haole subtlety, looked at Jones. Handsome and straight in his well-hung uniform, Jones turned to the consul and inquired what sort of commission he had from the British king.

"Consul General to the Sandwich Islands," said Charlton. Jones kept his face steady, but there must have been a gleam in his eye.

"What are your duties or functions?" he inquired politely.

Annoyed, the short-tempered consul replied that they were "in accordance with the acknowledged international understanding of the office."

Now Jones had Charlton where he wanted him. Did a king ever send a consul to any place within his own dominions?

Charlton had confounded himself. And American prestige took another leap forward. Kaahumanu, as regent, picked up the quill and wrote her name in her large, clear hand, beginning with her Christian name Elizabeta. Then Kalanimoku as prime minister and several other chiefs, followed by Thomas ap Catesby Jones for the United States. Ironically, the treaty he had so skillfully saved from wreckage by Great Britain's representative was never ratified by the Senate, though for years it was regarded as operative in Hawaii.

During his stay at the islands Jones had performed the remarkable feat of pleasing chiefs, foreign residents and missionaries alike. The amiable officer had a high opinion of the mission. "Not one jot or tittle —not one iota derogatory to their character as men, as ministers of the Gospel of the strictest order, or as missionaries—could be made to appear by the united efforts of all conspired against them," he wrote in his official report.

The effort to undermine the mission had failed. But it had not been given up. The affront to Charlton's self-esteem would influence the course of events in Hawaii for many years to come.

CHAPTER 11

GOD SEND US A SPEEDY DELIVERY

1827

AT THE VERY MOMENT WHEN THERE WAS SO MUCH WORK TO be done and Hawaiians were pouring into the schools and churches, demanding more and more books, and crowding the doorstep and study of every mission home—at this ripest of moments when more and more teachers and doctors and preachers were needed, two of the most valuable members and their families had to be released.

Dr. Blatchely, rough-mannered, brusque, and no admirer of Hiram Bingham, decided that he was ruining his health by staying in the islands. Pronouncing sentence on himself, and in spite of strong reluctance on the part of the mission, he sailed away with his wife November 6, 1826, bound for New London on the whaleship *Connecticut*. With them went sweet little Maria Whitney. She was only six. Though it wrung their hearts to part with her, Samuel and Mercy did not see how they could keep her on Kauai where she had no age mates to play with. Better to part with her than to expose her to the wicked knowledge, the uninhibited talk and sex play of Hawaiian children.

Kauai was still a fairly primitive place. Though it no longer happened that the queen came into the mission house fresh, naked and dripping from her morning plunge and followed by twenty naked attendants, there was still a rugged strain of heathenism underneath the surface. On at least one occasion Whitney's life had been in the balance when two men whom he had refused to admit to church membership had planned to murder him according to an ancient Kauai art of the noose. The Whitneys had endured much and accomplished much on Kauai. They had seen war at their very doorstep. They had lived through a flood which forced them to take to canoes. As for

Sam's effectiveness as a missionary, had he not persuaded a chief with seven wives to limit himself to one?

The way he had gone about this shows that behind his solemn, rather melancholy eyes there lived an acute knowledge of human nature.

Don't you feel anxiety over so many wives? Sam had asked the chief.

"Yes—I can't sleep for fear some other man will get them."

So Sam pointed out that to be relieved of anxiety, all he had to do was to part with all but the first one, who had borne him a child.

Should he keep the rest of them in the house and care for them?

Sam knew enough of Hawaiian susceptibilities to answer quickly: "No, send them back to their parents." And so it was.

Despite its drawbacks, the Whitneys must have loved Kauai, for, with the exception of a few visits to other islands, they lived out their lives there, sending their children off to the United States in their tender years. Young Sam and Henry went off together when they were eight and six. "That day my heart broke," Maria said. Nothing they asked of their converts ever equaled the demands the mission people made on themselves.

*   *   *

Early in January, 1827, Elisha Loomis, the printer, regretfully gave up his struggle with the Hawaiian climate and took his family back to America to see whether he could get well enough to return. He was also to supervise the printing of three of the Gospels in Hawaiian—a task far beyond the resources of the little press at Honolulu. Elisha finished the job. But he never grew well enough to return to Hawaii. After serving two years as missionary to the Indians, he died in 1836.

From all parts of the islands the cry continued for more teachers, more doctors, more preachers. Richards was trying to serve the islands of Maui, Molokai and Lanai—preaching, translating, directing schools with Hawaiian teachers which served six thousand pupils, overseeing the construction of a stone house for his family just behind the thatched house at Lahaina with its coconut, breadfruit and banana trees. The new house was to have a sort of turret on top to serve as a lookout for ships and a retreat from hostile sailors.

Richards was also doing a land office business in marriages. Christian marriage had suddenly become the rage, and on Wednesdays after the public lecture he joined all those who came before him—sometimes as many as fifty-nine couples.

Of all the islands Hawaii was the best supplied with mission stations. Ruggles and Goodrich were well established in thatched houses at Hilo; the once-recalcitrant people reduced to complaisant good order both in church and in a flourishing school. James Ely was with Kapiolani at Kaawaloa while Thurston and Bishop labored at Kailua. The Hawaiians had a special admiration for Bishop, for he was a big man—six feet three and weighing two hundred and fifty pounds. When he toured his district the people came running to talk with him and crowds followed along in his wake. One of the services that became traditional was for Hawaiians to carry the missionaries across the many streams that poured down from the central mountains. When they picked Bishop up they always remarked, *"Kanaka nui—great man."* When he reached a village, the people would spread mats for him and then rub his tired legs and shoulders according to their special art of *lomilomi.* Piles of food were heaped up for him, and what he could not eat he could carry away, or give in payment for his guides.

Bishop had no great love for his nearest colleague, Brother Ely. "He has swept off the greater part of our *waiwai* [trading goods] in getting his house built," Bishop wrote Levi Chamberlain. So when Ely asked for his watering pot, Bishop gave back the answer Ely had given when he had asked for one of his planks: "Write for one where they are plenty."

If the brothers thought their numbers too small, however, there were those who would say that in numbers and influence they were already too great. Stephen Reynolds, a Honolulu merchant who had begun by being friendly towards the mission but was now skeptical if not hostile, on January sixteenth watched men and women come into Honolulu from all over the island for the school examination. Some of them might be away from home as much as eight or ten days "to accomplish a few hours' examination before the great Hiram Bingham." Many grew hungry, unable to carry enough food to see them through the ordeal. Yet they seemed to enjoy it, standing up, group after group, to display their skill before the head teacher. On January nineteenth, according to Reynolds, they were at it from three in the morning until eleven at night. It never occurred to Reynolds to feel sorry for Bingham!

Just a few days before, on January eleventh, the mission's stalwart supporter and Hawaii's prime minister, Kalanimoku, feeling that he could not live much longer, had said farewell to his friends and set out for the island of Hawaii. Stopping at Lahaina, he had the pleasure of seeing the princess admitted to the church there. The poor child felt herself strongly pulled in two directions. She wanted to be a good Christian. Yet she would like to be a good Hawaiian too. Raised in intimate—the missionaries said incestuous—relationship to her brother the king, she did not know how to break this union without giving him and the chiefs offense. Recently, when they had parted, she had embraced all the other chiefly members of his party and had then come to stand in front of the king, tears pouring down her face, without daring to touch him.

Good old Billy Pitt lived only a few days after reaching Kailua, dying on February 8. Kaahumanu hurried over from Oahu to do him honor. As regent she would miss her first minister and strongest supporter beyond telling. Alive, Kalanimoku had exerted some influence upon his brother Boki. But Boki was coming more and more under the influence of Charlton and the Honolulu traders while his influence on the king was growing. Kaahumanu's control of the islands might, therefore, be in danger.

Indeed the events which now followed in Honolulu seemed to say so. Kalanimoku's death was apparently taken as a signal by those Hawaiians and haoles who felt that the paradise of the Pacific was exempt from the sexual restrictions laid down in the Bible. The chiefs got out their cards and dice. Maika stones appeared and the old bowling game began. Worst of all, the young king was being drawn into the middle of all this idle or sinful carrying-on. At Charlton's urging, he ordered a hula just as the nation was mourning the death of Billy Pitt. He was also rolling ninepins daily "with a complete rabble." According to Reynolds, this thirteen-year-old boy had a

number of favored ladies. "His favorite is Kinau to sleep with. Haalilio's wife in the day time, with many others."

Meanwhile Chamberlain was reporting that Kinau—half sister of
the present king, half sister and widow of the previous one—was
guilty of sleeping with Kekuanaoa. Kekuanaoa, later to distinguish
himself as governor of Oahu, had previously yearned after another of
Liholiho's wives, Pauahi, had slept with her and later married her.
Then she had died in childbirth. Now he and his new inamorata, together with Boki and his wife and—worst of all—Kaomi, a mission
teacher, were fined by the chiefs for drunkenness and intemperance.

Kinau and Kekuanaoa refused to separate, but finally hit upon the
happy solution of legalizing their relationship by marriage, which
they did before an immense crowd on October seventh.

Kaahumanu too, pillar of the church, had relapsed into Hawaiian
custom, according to Stephen Reynolds. He heard that she was sick
"from sleeping with a young man." When the doctor gave this news
to Bingham, Hiram said it had better not be mentioned since she belonged to the church. "I do not know what religion you teach," the
doctor is supposed to have said. "The religion I have been taught
directs me to tell the truth." True or not, the fact that this piece of
gossip was making the rounds is significant.

Encouraged by these doings of the great, lesser people strove to
keep up. Stephen Reynolds confided to his journal in February that
his woman had been delivered of a fine boy. Jones, the American consul, moved to his country seat with Hannah Holmes in May. But she
does not seem to have felt happy about it. Chamberlain met her on
the road a few weeks later, coming back from Bingham's where she
had found no one at home. When he spoke to her, she burst into
tears. He urged her to forsake her sin. Maybe she did, for a month
later Jones was making an alliance with a "handsome daughter" of
Marin called Lahilahi. Early in the next year handsome Hannah
broke with him completely.

As summer came on, Hiram Bingham began to wonder how much
longer he could live if he remained in the dust and clamor of Honolulu. Levi Chamberlain insisted that Hiram take his family over to
Hawaii and see what altitude and cool air would do. When the Whitneys arrived for a stay at Honolulu, ready to take on some of Hiram's

duties, he decided to go. Sybil needed the change perhaps more than he did. Sick on and off a good deal of the time, too weak even to write a letter, she pulled herself together now and with six-year-old Sophia and the baby, Lucy, embarked on the little *Missionary Packet*. For Sophia the trip was an adventure, a chance to see a girl nearly her own age—Persis Thurston. But for Sybil, the voyage was another cross to bear. "I am too gloomy for her," Sybil had confided to Nancy Ruggles. "It makes the tears drop as I pen it."

As usual, the voyage was frightful. In the channel between Maui and Hawaii waves dashed over the little schooner, knocked off the scuttle, damaged the boat.

"What shall we do?" the Hawaiian skipper asked Bingham. "We cannot reach Hilo."

"Whither, then, can we go?"

"Whither, then, indeed?" came the characteristic Hawaiian response.

"Can you run for Kailua?" Bingham asked.

"Ae, maikai—yes, good." The sea calmed when they altered their course. The next morning they reached Kailua, and soon were established in a cottage belonging to Governor Adams five miles behind Kailua and about fifteen hundred feet above sea level. Around it grew bananas, potatoes, squashes, sugar cane. Behind stretched the forest, rich and green, a welcome contrast from Kailua and Honolulu. By day a breeze blew in from the sea, by night from land.

Writing to America about Bingham's illness, Jones reported cheerfully: "There is some hope that he will not survive the climate long. With all my heart I say God send us a speedy delivery." But his letters snarl also at Kaahumanu, "the old woman," at the chiefs, at Charlton, always finding someone to blame for something. His wish that Bingham would drop dead was not to be gratified. Early in August Hiram wrote Levi Chamberlain that he had a good appetite, his bowels were regular, and the pain in his side had lessened. Unhappily the climate that suited Hiram was bad for Sybil. The air and the earthen floor were too damp for her, he wrote. Perhaps the real trouble arose from the fact that she was just then weaning Nancy. As for young Sophia, she was busily employed sewing a shirt for Levi whom all the Binghams loved.

After two months of rest, the Binghams returned to Honolulu to confront an alarming situation. Jean Rives, who had gone to London with Liholiho, had found plenty of backing in France when he represented himself as a man of influence in the islands. Two commercial expeditions and a religious mission had been organized and sent out. Rives, sailing with one, got as far as California where he apparently learned that he would find no welcome in Hawaii. Here he disappeared from the scene. The other ship, carrying half a dozen Catholic missionaries (lay brothers and two priests) and several farmers headed by a young lawyer, reached Honolulu July seventh.

Within two weeks of their arrival, Levi met a French gentleman in Hunnewell's store. He could speak no English and was eager to learn Hawaiian. "I suspect he is an ecclesiastic," Levi reported.

The Catholic mission quietly awaited developments, making no effort to get converts. But Bingham and his colleagues recognized the threat to their hard-won success. Kaahumanu saw a threat to her administration, as if she had not already trouble enough with Boki and the mischief-making foreign residents and a young king who was being tempted to follow his brother's footsteps. After a brief stay, most of the Catholic party left. The two priests quietly remained, though Kaahumanu had ordered them to leave.

While this new situation was agitating the missionaries and the chiefs, word reached Honolulu that William Richards' account of Buckle's carrying off Leoiki on his ship had been published at home. Now the foreign community really got its back up. If the mission was going to publish at home every illicit affair going on in the islands, who would be safe? Charlton, his face glowing with anger, told Chamberlain that Buckle ought to sue the mission for libel. After working himself into a lather, over a period of about two months, Charlton announced that he was going to Lahaina to seize Richards and destroy the town.

At this point another incident exploded in Richards' face at Lahaina. A British whaler, the *John Palmer,* had anchored off Lahaina and several girls had gone aboard in defiance of the tabu. When Governor Hoapili asked the captain to send them ashore, he denied having any knowledge of them. Hoapili, reminding Captain Clark that he had always co-operated in returning deserters to foreign ships, argued that by the same rule the girls should be brought ashore. Hoapili continued to ask for the girls for several days without result.

On October 23 the *John Palmer* was ready to sail and still the girls were aboard. Clark, however, was on shore.

"What shall we do?" Hoapili asked.

"The boat!" said one of his followers. In a moment Clark's boat was lifted out of the water and hauled up on shore, leaving the captain stranded. Clark called at the mission house, and Richards promised to intercede for him on his promise that the girls would be returned the next day. Richards then got the chiefs to release Clark's boat. But word had already reached the ship that her captain was being held. The ship's doctor threatened to shell the town. Five minutes after Clark had started for his ship the firing began. The balls came whistling right over the mission house, plowing into the ground behind. The Binghams, stopping there on the way back to Honolulu, were with the Richards family. Together they herded their children into the cellar with a prayer that the house would not tumble down on top of them.

After five or six shots, the firing ended. Clark had reached the ship and called it off. He sailed without setting the women on shore or inquiring whether the firing had done any damage.

Hoapili, hurrying an account off to Kaahumanu in Honolulu, said that Clark had threatened: "I shall sail to Oahu; Boki and the Consul will come and fight you." Sure enough, news soon reached Lahaina that Charlton was readying a fleet of whaling ships to avenge Clark and had warned the government to remove the young princess from the town.

Buckle himself, the man in whose behalf Charlton had begun all the bluster, now reached Hawaii again. Rumor said that he would lead the expedition against Lahaina, would force the removal of the hated tabu and liquidate Richards. To make matters worse for the mission, Leoiki now said that she had not been forced to voyage with Buckle but had gone quite willingly.

An anxious lookout was kept on the approaches to Lahaina, but when a ship arrived it was with a message from Kaahumanu, asking the Maui chiefs and the missionaries to come to Honolulu for an investigation. Another investigation! The Bingham and Richards families, finding a ship about to sail for Honolulu, left at once. As they came ashore Kaahumanu herself was waiting to receive them with a warm embrace and motherly tears. Leading them through the fort, she walked all the way to the mission house with them after a brief stop to greet the king at his new residence in Kalanimoku's house.

"I have seen you safe to your own house," she said. Then she went back to talk with the chiefs from Maui.

Charlton now summoned Richards to appear before him, whereupon he treated the poor man to a ranting attack on everything and everyone. "At one moment he attacked me, then the mission generally, then the chiefs, then the Society Islands, then the English missionaries, then the London Missionary Society, then the A.B.C.F.M., and all these being too small for him to attack, he included the whole Christian Publick," Richards recalled with a touch of wry humor.

A few days later, on November twenty-sixth and after the chiefs had arrived from Hawaii, Hoapili told Richards that all the foreigners in the village were coming to the king's house for a council with the chiefs regarding the Richards letter. They intended to claim that Richards had lied in saying that Buckle purchased the woman Leoiki.

"If I have been guilty of that crime, it is right you should punish me," said Richards.

"We all know he did purchase her," said Hoapili. "It cannot be denied."

Richards sent a message requesting of the council that if the foreign residents had any charges to bring against him, they do so in writing so that they could be properly translated into Hawaiian and everyone would know what the issue was. Then he would make his reply in writing.

"He has already written—that is his crime," said Charlton when this news reached the meeting. Then he demanded that Richards be punished.

Captain Buckle announced that he would attend to Richards himself and warned the chiefs against attempting to defend him. The chiefs, nevertheless, saw to it that Richards was surrounded by stout

men. The next day Buckle's ship moved to the mouth of the harbor.
Richards, willing to pacify Buckle so far as his conscience would permit, wrote him a letter to say that he had not expected the board
to publish his account of Buckle and Leoiki, and that he did not
say or intend to say that Buckle had enslaved her. The *Daniel* sailed
without any further demonstration against Richards. The mission
had survived another investigation.

But it could not hope to quell the rumors. Now it was being said
that the missionaries were competing with the merchants in trade—
a crime even more heinous than telling the truth about their sleeping
companions. Richards, wrote Reynolds, was carrying on all the trade
at Lahaina, selling inferior calico at seventy-five cents a yard. "People will believe anything against us," Levi Chamberlain sadly concluded.

It was true, however, that the missionaries were in business. Bishop
sent Hunnewell 7,100 cigars which he had had the natives roll from
their own leaf, requesting Hunnewell to sell them at ten dollars a
thousand, or less. The proceeding apparently shocked Hunnewell,
always a loyal friend to the mission. But Bishop explained that the
Hawaiians yearned for books and slates. Some of the people had
nothing to offer for them except tobacco, so Bishop got two of them
to make cigars. The proceeds would be used to build his house.
Thurston had already been seven years in the islands, said Bishop,
and yet when it rains his house "leaks like a riddle." Others were also
in need of houses, and why should he, therefore, not ease the demand on the limited mission funds when a little Yankee enterprise
would raise him a building fund?

The chiefs were at work, during these closing weeks of the year,
on drawing up a code of laws to control the always-threatening erup-
tions of what was essentially a frontier community. In their council
on December seventh they agreed to outlaw murder, theft, rum-
selling, prostitution and gambling. The king signed the code. The
laws were about to be promulgated. But when the foreign residents
got wind of this, they hit the ceiling. Outlaw rum, prostitution and
gambling—cornerstones of prosperity? Preposterous! Again Charlton arose as the champion of free men who would not have their
liberties interfered with. No laws could be passed here, he asserted,

until the British king had approved them. Boki, now reaping profits from rum, gambling, and possibly from prostitution, was quick to take Charlton's view. Kaahumanu said she would send Adams to England with the laws. "Such as are suitable let the king of England select & such as are not good let him reject." Adams would never get to see the king, said Boki.

"Why not?"

"Oh, he may be sick perhaps. Something will prevent. Liholiho did not see him."

When Kaahumanu persisted that they would have their king send a letter of introduction, Boki shifted his ground. "Let the consul write," he suggested.

"Do you not know that the consul is a liar and that no confidence is to be placed in anything that he says?" asked Kaahumanu.

Up spoke Adams. "I can read a little English and I can understand some," he said. "If England gives us laws she will send men to see that they are executed. Our harbors will be filled with ships of war and our vessels cannot go out or come in without their permission. We shall not be visited by American ships without leave from Great Britain and we shall forever be their servants."

Adams was right, the chiefs decided. They must make their own laws.

But the foreign influence was too strong to be ignored. The laws finally boiled down to three—against murder, theft and adultery. Three other laws, against rum-selling, prostitution and gambling, were to be drawn up and explained to the people but not immediately adopted.

On December 14 the several thousand people of Honolulu were called together in a coconut grove near the fort for the reading of the laws. The chiefs invited Bingham to open the meeting with prayer—if he was not afraid the foreigners would be angry with him.

"Why should I be afraid of the anger of the foreigners while I am engaged in my own proper duties?" said Bingham.

While the huge crowd waited, Kaahumanu put a hymnbook into his hand. He sang a few verses, prayed, and then departed without waiting for the laws to be read—thus indicating that while the mission was ever ready to ask the blessing of God upon the commonwealth, it would not meddle with the laws.

"To defeat the mission will require something more than rant, and riots, and clubs, and cannon balls from lawless anti-reformers," Bingham promised the board. In Bingham the brawlers had found a man they could not intimidate. No wonder they hated him so devotedly.

Early in 1827 the people of Lahaina had begun to be annoyed by a new kind of pest which sang in their ears and then dived in for the kill. Richards investigated, and his fears were confirmed. The mosquito had arrived! Investigation showed that it had been carelessly—though not viciously as some believed—brought by the ship *Wellington* which had dumped its casks, alive with wigglers, before filling them at a pure stream of water near Lahaina. The vicious insects soon spread through the islands, adding to the misery of life and to the list of things—rum, syphilis, infectious diseases—for which Hawaii stood indebted to the haole.

CHAPTER 12

THE CONSUL'S COW

1828–1829

THE SHIP *Parthian,* ONE HUNDRED FORTY-EIGHT DAYS
from Boston, dropped anchor in Honolulu Harbor on the last Sunday morning in March. Despite the strict Sabbath observance, someone must have paddled out to see whether the ship was in need of
provisions—or women, for shortly the news reached Hiram Bingham
that a whole new crop of Longnecks had arrived for the mission.

Caught in his own Sabbatarian mesh, Hiram would not have been
able to visit the ship out of mere sociability, but he was about to hold
a service on another ship in the harbor. Taking Levi Chamberlain
and Joseph Goodrich along, therefore, he stopped briefly to greet the
new arrivals.

As the three men climbed up over the side, Laura Judd, wife of
the new doctor aboard, noted that they looked careworn and feeble.
Bingham, on the other hand, was delighted to find a fresh, young and
eager group of twenty—four of them ordained men with their wives,
then a physician Gerrit Judd with his lively, keen-eyed wife, a printer,
Stephen Shepard, who also had a wife with him, and four unmarried
ladies. "Single women!" exclaimed Stephen Reynolds. "Decency art
thou lost? Shame art thou fled the female breast?" But Levi Chamberlain, who had been sending plaintive letters back to the board
to remind them that he was "not indifferent to matrimony," found
their presence interesting indeed. Then there were four Polynesian
youths—three Hawaiians and one Tahitian, all intended as helpers.

The haole group was young, most of them in their twenties, a few
just over the line into the thirties. As usual they had been recently
married and the married women were mostly pregnant. About half
the group were from New England, but of the remainder many were

153

from western New York, their families having moved there from Yankeeland.

The next morning, March 31, they were rowed ashore to the fort where the commander Manuia, full of that innate Hawaiian dignity which at once gained the Judds' respect, received them. The usual crowds followed them across the plain to the mission house. Laura was embarrassed to note that one man wore only an umbrella and a pair of shoes, while many of the women were naked to the waist. Laura's quick eye also noted that Honolulu was a sadly dilapidated town. It might have been a garden, but Marin who could have made it one by giving away his cuttings, burned them instead. There was hardly a vine or a fig tree outside his garden, although Levi had begun to put in plants and trees around the mission area. Still he could not do much to hide the big, ragged-looking thatched church, browsed all the way around as high up as wandering goats and cows could reach.

Kaahumanu, happy at the arrival of new teachers, looked the group over with the candid, expert eye of a horse trader. She examined their hair and eyes if not their teeth, felt the arms of the girls to see if they had enough flesh on them, appraised no doubt the swelling middles of Mary Andrews and Fanny Gulick, and made critical comments on their dress. When they left, she kissed them all Hawaiian style, putting her nose against their cheeks and "giving a sniff as if inhaling the fragrance of flowers," as Laura described it.

Somehow room was found in the little mission houses for all the new arrivals. A few days later Kaahumanu dined with them, after sending one thing after another to be added to the feast. Still she asked if there was something else the newcomers would like. "You have been very thoughtful today," Bingham told her.

"Ah, is it only today?" the big woman parried, with an archness that seemed strangely out of proportion to her size. For Laura, celebrating her twenty-fourth birthday, it was a happy occasion. After the miserable voyage under a captain who did his best to make the missionaries uncomfortable, even dusty and dingy Honolulu seemed, as its name promised, a fair haven.

On this same eventful day the newcomers were presented to Governor Boki, just back from an island tour. Unexpectedly friendly,

Boki handed them a letter full of loving phrases, as did Kaahumanu who hoped that "you and we may dwell together in the shade of His salvation." The young king, off on an inter-island tour, also sent affectionate greetings. The new arrivals gave a Bible to Boki, a Bible and an engraving of the Lord's Supper to faithful Kaahumanu.

A week later the little *Missionary Packet* sailed away to gather the mission families from the windward islands for a general meeting at Honolulu. By the twenty-third of April they had all reached Honolulu and were sitting down together to get acquainted and to assign stations. To the newcomers most of the old hands looked worn out. Why this should have been so, when Hawaii has as healthy a climate as any in the world, can only be explained by the stubborn Yankee insistence on continuing ways of life—dress, diet and household chores—which were well adapted to survival in cold New England but ruinous in a warm climate.

Four days later came the emotional climax of the meeting, when the newcomers became members of the mission church.

"Mr. Bingham addressed us tenderly and affectionately," wrote Theodosia Green, adding that he was so affected he could hardly proceed. "I think I never heard a man speak so well."

One of the things that had moved Bingham to tears was the death of Elizabeth Edwards Bishop, Lucy Thurston's friend. Elizabeth had reached Hawaii with rosy cheeks and a radiance about her that compelled admiration; no one could have appeared more healthy. She became the mother of two healthy children. But then, attacked by a strange disease, she had grown feeble, emaciated, excessively nervous. Even the rustling of leaves or the running of a mouse would waken her. Lucy had to take over the care of her children. A special house was built so that she could have quiet. The illness grew worse. After weeks of agony and delirium, she grew suddenly quiet one midnight. "Let me depart in peace," she said, and died.

While the preachers and teachers now scattered to their posts to step up the religious activity of the islands, the unregenerate citizens of Honolulu did their best to balance the account. John Jones, having set up housekeeping with Lahilahi, felt that he could not do without Hannah either, and made arrangements which apparently satisfied all three. Reynolds had a second child by a woman he calls Winship

—apparently a hapahaole daughter of one of the Yankee captains of that name. After her death he married Susan Jackson on August 11, 1829. One after another the Yankee merchants—Dana, Mitchener, Alexander Adams—were marrying the girls they lived with. Whatever they thought of it, the mission influence was having its effect on them.

* * *

Laura and Gerrit Judd set up housekeeping in two little rooms and a chamber at the Binghams', emptying quarts of dust from their bedcovers after a night's sleep. The young doctor, destined to become one of the most influential men in the history of the islands, had been born of Yankee parents in western New York. When he had offered himself to the board and begun to look about for a wife, his glance had fallen on Laura Fish. He didn't know her well and hadn't the nerve to ask her. So he persuaded his Uncle Hastings to act as go-between. After thinking it over for nine days, Laura consented to marry and go.

While the doctor now plunged into medical practice, Laura and Sybil commenced a school for native women, including many of the chiefs. The schoolroom had no floor or desks, but it did have a flag which was raised in that clockless community as a sign for school to begin. Retrieved from a ship named *Superb,* it had that word in white on a red background. "Superb schoolmistresses," Hiram called the two teachers.

Levi Chamberlain, meanwhile, following Maria Patton (one of the new arrivals) to Lahaina, proposed and was married to her the first of September (1828), in the presence of a number of chiefs and members of the mission and with cakes and wine to celebrate.

Wily, ponderous Governor Adams (Kuakini) also caught the marrying fever. Having lived with a succession of wives, he asked Bingham to marry him to the current favorite. But when Hiram went to question him about his former women, he found the big chief drunk. When he refused to marry him in that state, Adams in a fury ordered him to get out. Always on the edge of skepticism, Adams had kept the missionaries guessing. He was the last of the really big chiefs to hold out—except, of course, Boki. To gain his favor would have been an important triumph for the mission. But they would not curry favor where a matter of principle was involved, not with Adams or with the king himself. At last, after years of skepticism, though he had meanwhile supported schools and churches, he did decide to accept Christianity for himself as well as for his people. On October 25, 1829, he was admitted to the church.

The Binghams were now called upon to part regretfully with the Elys, who hoped to regain their health by returning home. With them went little Sophia Bingham, now eight years old. Much as it tore their hearts to part with her, Sybil and Hiram dared not keep her longer in the islands.

"We fled with our first born from the war at Kauai," Bingham wrote the board, "we carried her asleep into Mr. Richards' cellar when Lahaina was fired on—but we could not easily hush her cries, when I and my house were mob'd at Honolulu, nor will she soon lose the impression that we are here in continual danger from the assaults of wicked men." Clearly, they did not want Sophia to grow up where sex so often reared its ugly head, and where some ineligible man might some day take a fancy to her. Sophia must go home in order to form "a suitable connexion."

When the *Enterprise* sailed, Sophia stood with tender, melting gaze at the head of the companionway, looking heart-rendingly small and alone. "I turned away my face from you," Sybil later wrote her daughter, "and soon had my seat in the boat, but my heart was with you. I wanted to comfort you, but that could not be."

After parting from their daughter, the Binghams moved for a while to a little one-room cottage in cool Manoa Valley, where Hiram worked on his translation of Luke with the help of Keku-anaoa.

While Hiram and other members of the mission worked to build a Hawaiian Bible, the chiefs built churches. Lahaina had the first stone church, built in this year of 1828. Honolulu also began a new meeting house, but it needed one so huge that building with stone seemed out of the question. Nearly two hundred feet long and sixty-three wide, it would seat four thousand people—if they squatted all at once and in tight rows upon mats. It took forty-four great pillars set in three rows to hold up the roof. A large pulpit window, New

England style, was set incongruously in the middle of the long wall behind an uncompromisingly Yankee pulpit.

The young king, handsome in Windsor uniform, took part in dedicating the church on July 3, 1829. Rising from a sofa covered with crimson satin—no seat on the floor for him—he said: "Chiefs, teachers and commons, hear: We have assembled here to dedicate to Jehovah, my God, this house of prayer which I have built for Him." Then he stepped over to join the choir, where he sang a good bass. The princess, a soprano, also spoke to the people. At the end, much to everyone's surprise, the king rose again and prayed. He offered to God not only the house of prayer, but his kingdom. He acknowledged his own sins—no mere formality, this—and prayed for deliverance from them. Hiram was amazed and delighted with his pupil, while Kaahumanu, looking prematurely old, was moved to tears of joy.

Though it was easy for the king to order a church built, the labor falling on the people had been backbreaking. They had to drag the huge timbers from forests miles away. Some of the pillars were so huge that four ropes—each three quarters of an inch thick—snapped at the first pull. If stone was used, they had to dive for coral which could be burned for lime. But burning the lime called for a pile of wood of equal size. So men and women walked into the forests to bring out the firewood. They trudged back and forth hauling coral and sand and water. Such expense of human effort had not been seen since the building of the vast pagan temples. Perhaps the missionaries felt that the energy burned up this way would not be available for more dangerous activities.

It did seem to the brothers that the people were growing more attuned to Christian ethics. Chiefs who had formerly got the best of the whaling captains whenever they could, now scrupulously returned a few cents' overpayment or made restitution to captains they had cheated with equanimity before the advent of the Gospel.

While the chiefs were learning to do what Christian ethics required of them, some nominal Christians were setting them a very poor example. Consul Charlton, for instance. His cows had strayed many times into the taro fields, destroying the young crops. Charlton had, without warning, shot native cattle that strayed into his enclosures, so now he was warned and warned repeatedly to keep his cattle out of Hawaiian fields. At last a Hawaiian who had seen a particular cow of the consul's ravage his field once too often took up his gun and fired. The cow escaped. The man ran out onto the common and shot her again. This time he killed her.

Charlton, whose florid face always took fire at the slightest incident, went fuming to the chiefs. Sputtering with anger so that he could hardly be understood, he demanded that they authorize him to punish the man. They replied that they would investigate, and if the man were guilty they would award damages.

Charlton stormed off, got John C. Jones to help him, found and seized the man at pistol point and tied a rope around his neck. Mounting a horse, Charlton pulled the man after him into the village, forcing him to run until he was exhausted. When he fell, Charlton kept going, the man dragging behind in the dust and dung. Sam Mills, a Hawaiian who had come out from America with the third company and who had married one of the handsome Holmeses, cut the poor fellow loose. Otherwise he might have died.

Determined to make a major issue of the affair, Charlton called all British subjects together and had them sign a petition asking him to get the Hawaiian government to guarantee the safety of their lives and property.

The chiefs replied with the facts. The cow had broken into an enclosed field. Cattle had broken in many times before and their owners had refused to heed warnings. But even if the owner of the field had done wrong, it was for government to punish, not for Charlton to take the law in his own hands.

"Have compassion on a nation of little children, very small and young, who are yet in mental darkness," said the chiefs, "and help us to do right, and follow with us that which will be for the best good of our country."

But Charlton was not built that way. He wrote several letters home to Lord Aberdeen about his cow, as if it were a major affair of state. Yet he was hardly able to compose a clear, intelligible sentence. "They cannot be dealt with as civilized people as they act upon every occasion on the impulse of the moment without for a moment considering or thinking on future consequences," he wrote. He could hardly have hit upon a closer description of himself.

It was a stroke of good fortune for the chiefs that just at this time an American sloop-of-war, sent out by government on a mission of good will, reached Honolulu. She was the *Vincennes,* under the command of a sensible and diplomatic officer, Captain William Bolton Finch. Not only had Finch been instructed to show kindness to the chiefs, but the letter he bore from Samuel Southard, Secretary of the Navy, made it clear that President John Quincy Adams approved of their progress in Christianity as "the only means by which the prosperity and happiness of nations can be advanced."

Especially timely and heartening to the chiefs was the President's dictum that if American citizens violated Hawaiian laws, the Hawaiian government had a right to punish them—an attitude very different from that of Charlton, who considered British citizens above Hawaiian law.

Chaplain aboard the *Vincennes* was none other than Charles Stewart, former missionary to the islands and a friend of Secretary Southard. Stewart was delighted with the evidences of progress since his departure four years before. Regard for the Sabbath was so strict that sailors could buy nothing from the people. No nation was more temperate or less given to gambling. The language had been reduced to writing, at least thirty thousand were studying in the schools, and seven million printed pages had been issued. Commerce had vastly increased, Stewart found, morals were improved, religion firmly established, old habits of evil broken up—and, he might have added, the extinction of the Hawaiian race was in sight, thanks to contact with foreign diseases and vices. Congenitally optimistic, Stewart saw all that was good. His enthusiastic account was to make it difficult for the missionaries to explain why, if Hawaii had become a Christian nation, the churches at home had to go on supporting them.

There were material evidences of improvement too. Stewart noted the several stone quays along the Honolulu waterfront where there had been only a sand beach. He cocked an eye at Boki's hotel, the Blonde, with its green blinds, flagstaff and ship's lookout. He was delighted by the king's guard of two hundred in their white uniforms with scarlet cuffs and collars and black caps, all neatly drawn up around the palace square at the formal reception of Captain Finch. The king's house also pleased him, with its fine woods lashed together with coconut fibers in a beautiful pattern, its chestnut-colored wall lining made of mountain vines.

But most of all his former ward, the Princess Nahienaena, delighted him. She had been so close to the Stewarts that she had taken Mrs. Stewart's Christian name, Harriet. She had been a child of eight then. Now fourteen, and with the precocious ripeness of a girl of the tropics, she was a different person. The Reverend Charles Stewart obviously fell in love with her. Amply formed as befitted a Hawaiian chief, Nahienaena responded warmly to Stewart's adoration. He found her charming—amiable, playful, her fine teeth and brilliant eyes accenting a beautiful smile and a lively intelligence.

Stewart described every costume she wore—her straw-colored satin with its handsome pelerine, her elegant walking dress of purple silk-velvet richly trimmed with satin and with blond ruffles at cuff and collar; her white Italian crape with bindings of white satin worn with a light silk bonnet and French scarf.

In his report to the Navy, Captain Finch frankly admitted that he could not see why the foreign residents were complaining about the mission. "The constant complaining against the Missionaries is irksome in the extreme, and in such contrast with the conduct of the Missionaries themselves," he reported, "that I could not but remark their circumspection and reserve with admiration." The trouble with the foreign residents, said Finch, was that they preferred to have the Hawaiians remain ignorant so as to take advantage of them. They preferred to have them without laws so that they might make their own. They resented the fact that the work of the mission was placing the Hawaiians on a footing of equality with the men from the west. These same Hawaiians had once taken an abject and slavish attitude towards the haoles, but they did so no more. If anyone in the islands were to exert undue power, he concluded, it would come much better from the missionaries than from the merchants.

Before Finch left, the chiefs addressed a letter to him complaining about the many injuries they had received from French and Jones, one of which was their circulating the story about Nahienaena. "Our hearts are broken by the scandal, and we can bear it no longer," they concluded.

Yet it was Boki, one of the signers, who only a few months before had met the princess on her arrival from Lahaina and said: "Do you kill Kaahumanu and all her family and take your brother for a husband, or you will not be ruler of these islands." Though he was drunk at the time, as sober an observer as Chamberlain thought he was speaking what he really thought. "If you and your brother marry and have a child he will be the rightful heir to the kingdom," he had continued.

"What you say is foolish," said the princess, trying to pull away from him. But Boki grabbed her by the ear and led her along, saying, "What did you come down here for? Did you come down as a god to be worshipped?" And he tried unsuccessfully to separate her from her attendants and get her into his house along with the king.

Though the threat against Kaahumanu sounds fantastic, the Hawaiian historian and statesman, John Ii, confirms it. King Kauikeaouli himself told Kaahumanu that Boki wanted her killed. "I did not agree to his wish because I love you," he told her.

That Boki had grown desperate is clear enough in what he now undertook. Hearing that large amounts of sandalwood could be had in the New Hebrides, Boki quickly fitted out two brigs, got together more than four hundred men, and sailed away on December second. Boki went ahead with one ship after arranging for a rendezvous at Eromanga. That was the last anyone ever saw of him and his ship— whether accidentally blown up by gunpowder, or wrecked, or lost in a storm no one knows. The other ship got into a fight with the people of Eromanga, fled, was attacked by disease and then by starvation. On August 3, 1830, it finally reached Honolulu with twenty gaunt men, the only survivors out of the four hundred.

Handsome, ambitious, restless Boki was gone. The foreign merchants had lost their only supporter among the high chiefs. The mission saw the hand of God in it.

CHAPTER 13

THE FIRST DECADE
1830–1831

AFTER TEN YEARS, HONOLULU WAS BECOMING AS YANKEE as a New England village. An exaggeration, of course, since the sharp, emerald-green range behind Honolulu could never be mistaken for the Berkshires or the Green Mountains, nor could the little grass houses that accommodated the five thousand inhabitants ever be mistaken for trim Yankee houses or even barns, though they might pass for haystacks.

But on the streets and in the shops the nasal twang of Yankee English was at home. The ships in the harbor, stoutly built in Salem or Boston of New England timbers, spent more time here than in their home ports. John C. Jones's two-storied wooden house with its verandas and Venetian blinds would have looked at home under the elms of any New England village, and more of these Yankee houses were springing up all the time, with their queer-looking boxes or cupolas perched near the ridgepole where a man could fix his spyglass on whatever ship hove into view.

Honolulu had its face towards the sea. From the ocean came news, commerce, much of its food, new faces and personalities, trouble. Honolulu was a small community, and the foreign community was even smaller—hardly three hundred on the whole island of Oahu. It was consequently full of gossip—a commodity in which Stephen Reynolds dealt quite as often as in the assorted merchandise with which his shop was littered. Thanks to his Susan, he had first-hand access to gossip about the court; in fact he was in a position to originate it. Since Susan's father, Jackson the carpenter, was a neighbor of the mission, Stephen could keep an eye cocked in that direction too. Susan was thinking that she would like to join the church. But

Reynolds, whose mind could not separate that "impudent puppy" Bingham from the Christian faith, was not so sure. Still, she was pregnant now and had to be humored.

It must have struck Stephen Reynolds that, whether you liked it or not, the mission had gone a long way in ten years. They had reached all the principal islands with their churches, their schools, their missionaries. The chiefs would hardly stir without first taking mission advice, and had even let "King" Bingham tell them what laws to make—so thought Stephen Reynolds.

Then here was the "Old Bitch," as he privately called Kaahumanu, making a tour of the whole island to visit schools and encourage Christianity. Surrounded by her female attendants, and followed by a train of men loaded down with supplies, she had set out on the third of February from Honolulu, riding in a low green cart drawn by two shaggy gray donkeys in tandem. Settling her vast bulk in the rear of the cart, the regent let her legs hang down behind as the caravan moved out across the dusty plain.

At her side and mounted on a horse was the Reverend Ephraim Clark, her pastor for the journey. Bingham, who always regarded Kaahumanu as his special charge, was too unwell to make the tour. Ephraim Clark, a New Hampshire man who had been educated at Dartmouth and Andover Theological Seminary, was small and earnest-looking, with an acute sensitivity to religious experience slightly tinged with melancholy. On his entrance into Dartmouth he had feared that he would be "subject to new temptations and more exposure to the baleful influence of an unhallowed ambition." Within four days he had already begun to feel "the deadening influence of College," a condition which he measured by having remained unmoved throughout an impressive sermon.

Forced like many a young New Englander to earn his way, Clark had spent the winter of 1822 "very pleasantly at Bennington, Vermont, as an assistant in an academy." Entering Andover in 1824, he made sufficient progress to satisfy even his rigid requirements ("sat under the droppings of the sanctuary with some delight,") graduated in 1827, and was soon married, ordained, and on his way to Hawaii.

He and Kaahumanu now stopped wherever there was a school to

examine. Field bedsteads were set up in a grass hut from which some poor family was turned out, and with nothing but a cloth partition between them, he and the regent lay down to sleep. Though the accommodation was primitive, the crowd of retainers carried somewhere among their innumerable bundles everything that might possibly be wanted. So Clark and Kaahumanu drank from silver goblets. But the road was rough, the hills steep, and sometimes Clark found himself in water up to his saddle. Yet he managed to complete the tour, examining four thousand scholars, who were delighted with their new raiment of learning, and marrying twenty-four presumably happy couples. To be married by the preacher was all the rage now. Many a smiling damsel who stood before him showed in the ripeness of her figure that he had not come a moment too soon.

Not satisfied to stop with this tour, which must have been fatiguing to a woman of Kaahumanu's bulk, jolted and tilted and dunked as she was in her little cart, the tireless woman now prepared to make the circuit of the other islands with the young king. On June 16 they called a public meeting in the grove of palms beyond the fort, committed Oahu to the care of Kinau and Boki's widow Liliha, told the people to behave themselves, and the next day set sail to windward.

Their first stop was at Lahaina on Maui where heavy-featured William Richards was in command, assisted by the two single ladies (the other two having married), Maria Ogden and Mary Ward. Richards had at last finished his stone house, forty-two by seventeen with four good rooms and a kitchen on the first floor. His associate, Jonathan Green, a young man with a gleam in his eye and an unfailing sense of humor, was about to leave Lahaina for a season to go to Honolulu "and stammer a little in Mr. Clark's pulpit and to assist in correcting matter for the press." Lorrin Andrews, a man with a quick bright manner and a passion for getting things done, had already gone to Hilo to assist Goodrich. In the presence of the king, Richards baptized thirty-three "hopeful converts from heathenism."

For three months Kaahumanu and the king toured Maui, Molokai and Lanai, exhorting the people and examining schools. As there were now nine hundred schools and fifty thousand scholars spread through the islands as a whole, they had their work cut out.

The schoolhouse was always of grass, usually with nothing on the dirt floor except dry grass. There were no seats, no table, no equipment, though Honolulu had hit upon the idea of making seats out of sun-dried mud bricks. The scholars—most of them, even ten years after the arrival of the mission, largely adults—usually assembled in the late afternoon. About three o'clock the teacher began blowing on his conch shell to let his clockless people know that it was time to gather. By four school was in session. It only lasted for about two hours—long enough, however, for a people who had to become literate in their maturity or even in old age.

It would have been impossible, of course, for the missionaries to teach all these schools. The system they had to adopt was to give promising pupils the best training they could, and then send them out to instruct people from whom again promising pupils might be selected as teachers. No vast amount of learning was lodged in the noggins of men so hastily prepared. Yet they did teach enough so that many a Hawaiian could read his Bible.

In this very year of 1830 Hiram Bingham finally got around to making a little primer for children. The response was immediate. As soon as Shepard began pulling copies off the press, children came trooping in. Within two months, more than a thousand youngsters were cheerfully turning these magic pages with the dark smudgy little cuts, the songs and lessons from the catechism. As the books became more widely available children began going to school throughout the islands, thus putting an end to that perpetual holiday which had been until then the birthright of Hawaiian youngsters and the envy of all properly brought up mission children.

As the youngsters began coming to school, they brought with them the high spirits and wild disorder which belong to youth—running, climbing, yelling, quarreling, laughing, while the poor teacher tried to impose a discipline to which they had never been accustomed. He did accomplish something never achieved in more literate nations; his pupils learned to read upside down and sideways. Books were so scarce that children had to gather around them in circles. Some never could read a book afterwards without rotating it to the angle they had grown used to!

In September the king and his train moved on to Hawaii, landing at Kawaihae where ten years before the mission had first come ashore. Bingham, who had come over to Hawaii again in search of health, readily accepted an invitation to preach there. Three thousand people assembled in the open air "and listened to the unfolding of the doctrine of God our Savior."

Thereafter, the king and Kaahumanu, their party swelled by a number of chiefs, went back up into the hills to the place where Bingham was staying and paid a family visit which lasted several weeks. This place was Waimea, a site selected by Dr. Judd who had been requested by the mission to locate a permanent station where missionaries who had been worn down by the warm climate might also come to recuperate. Picking up Sam Ruggles at Kaawaloa, Judd had tramped about the uplands of Hawaii until he was satisfied as to the location—a place about twelve miles inland at an elevation of two thousand feet. Then the men returned and brought the ladies up for a stay. Sam Ruggles needed to do some recuperating too.

They were still on the ground, therefore, when the Bingham family arrived in search of health—Hiram, Sybil, Lucy, and one-and-a-half-year-old Elizabeth who had been born on the very same day as the oldest Judd child, Gerrit Junior. Together with the Ruggles family, they made a sizable party. Judd and Ruggles had already got some buildings put up, thanks to the orders of Kapiolani and the now pious Governor Adams, yet not nearly enough to take care of the crowd that poured in with the king. He and Kaahumanu moved in with the Binghams, while simple shelters were soon thrown up for the rest. The mission families, refreshed by the cool air and soft showers, the bright green foliage and the sound of falling water from a near-by cataract, climbed the hills to gather wild strawberries, ate fresh beef supplied from the thousands of wild cattle roaming the neighborhood, and put on needed weight and color.

"It does one's liver good to look out from my study window upon the snows of Mauna Kea and Mauna Loa," wrote Bingham, "and to feel the New England air while the mercury stands at 60."

When the chiefs moved on to Hilo, Bingham went with them. There had been rumors that Brother Goodrich spent too much time "in fishing, bullock hunting, mechanical work." Goodrich was also raising cane, had built his own sugar mill and was boiling his own sugar. In his spare time he made scientific observations! Even so, he was not the only missionary to apply his Yankee ingenuity to Hawaiian needs and opportunities. Sam Ruggles had recently begun to raise coffee in the Kona district, and Jonathan Green was to conduct some important experiments in agriculture. But Goodrich went ahead of them all. The brethren were not above making use of his talents, though they censured him for being too secular.

In the king's presence Hilo's big new church, built by Governor Adams who had sat in an armchair in the shade commanding four hundred conscripted laborers, was dedicated in October. Then the chiefs continued their circuit of Hawaii.

At Kailua, first of all mission stations, the Thurstons and Bishops still labored. Lucy Thurston, bright and methodical, continued to manage her home with the precision of a drill sergeant, but the precision was softened with love. Big Mr. Bishop, left with two small children when his first wife died, had within a few months found a new partner in Delia Stone, one of the four "unmarried females." The children had fallen in love with her too. "I feel like one in a happy dream," wrote Artemas.

The only island the king did not visit on this long-extended tour was Kauai where the Whitneys and Gulicks continued their busy but isolated lives. Having been the only missionary on the island for several years, and the first to arrive, sober Sam Whitney had grown somewhat dictatorial in manner. Peter Gulick, who was quick-tempered, found him hard to get on with. Mercy Whitney, though her eyes still had that deep, brooding look, had lost the perfect, youthful roundness of chin. She had four children, the Gulicks two.

In these country mission stations—and with the exception of Honolulu they were all in mere villages or less—life took on a rhythm of its own. The days were full, very full, and therefore short. Families rose before daylight, began the day with worship, and then tackled the many tasks that awaited them. The parents had to tutor their own children, run schools for teachers, see a constant stream of visitors who wanted to tell their thoughts or get a pill, conduct prayer meetings, make translations—the mission was trying to get the whole Bible into Hawaiian—prepare sermons, build needed furniture, care for cattle and fowl, farm, sew, wash, and carry on all the other household chores. Often the family took several Hawaiian children in to live with them, and usually a Hawaiian family was settled in a near-by grass house, fed and clothed by the mission in return for help with cooking, washing and tending the animals.

Isolated as they were, their biggest thrill was letters and packages from America. Sometimes the messenger came at midnight, but no matter—the whole family roused up to open the precious envelopes or boxes. Children crowded around the wonderful mysterious packages from which were drawn out dolls or dresses or jackknives from uncles and grandfathers, aunts and cousins they had never seen. Meanwhile the grownups hastily ran through their letters to see whether all their distant loved ones were still alive, and then, when the children were in bed, read them again slowly and lovingly, their minds carried back to the scenes and scents and seasons of childhood.

In Honolulu sober, earnest Levi Chamberlain, a married man now with a son who had arrived promptly yet decorously ten months after the marriage, was building a big stone house to accommodate his family and the mission supplies. It rose, tall and angular and with a look of everlasting solidity, within three feet of the little stone printing house, which in turn crowded up against the first framed house. These three remain today in the heart of downtown Honolulu.

In this year of 1830 the Honolulu station lost one of its most loyal supporters. James Hunnewell, having spent four more years in Honolulu since his arrival in the *Missionary Packet* and having parlayed an investment of $5,000 into $67,000, now sailed for home and his Susan. "We think you are one of few who have stayed honest in those parts," wrote the firm of Bryant and Sturgis to him from Boston. He had served as their agent, and when he left he put his affairs in the hands of Henry Pierce. Hunnewell's concern later evolved into C. Brewer & Company, one of today's "Big Five."

Hunnewell's departure marked the end of the sandalwood boom. The wood was now of inferior quality and almost worthless when delivered at Canton. All the big Yankee firms which had dealt in it were closing their Honolulu offices. But the loss of revenue at least had the virtue of releasing the Hawaiian people from a backbreaking chore. For years, at the command of their chiefs, they had climbed the mountains, working almost naked in cold and rainy regions, often running out of food, hauling the sticks out in great loads on their backs. Not only men, but women and children had also been conscripted to meet the debts the chiefs had run up. Now they could turn to raising produce for the whaling ships, always a good market for meat, potatoes, garden stuff. Unless, of course, they preferred to supply the commodity that was even more in demand. But tabus were making this ever more difficult.

There was no doubt about it—the mission had in ten years brought about a remarkable change. From a warring, pleasure-loving, superstition-ridden, naked, illiterate and concupiscent people the mission had changed them into—well, into a warless, pleasure-loving, superstition-ridden, partly clothed, somewhat literate and concupiscent people.

But they were mighty eager to get into the church. All the important chiefs were in, so the commoners were naturally eager to join the same lodge. They could attend, of course, but they could not be admitted until they had convinced the Yankee preacher that their conversion was sincere.

Usually it began this way. A man would go to the mission house with a present of a fowl or even a pig. He would tell his *manao*—his thought, shed a few tears for his sins, and keep coming back until after a period of probation the preacher decided that he was a sincere candidate and would admit him. But sincerity was hard to judge; the Hawaiians wept easily anyhow and were good actors. One man confessed that he had not only gotten in by feigning the whole business, but had thereafter counseled a whole procession of his friends and neighbors through the ordeal. Since each of these candidates had to grease his palm, he had found piety a profitable affair. "This man was called Peter, and in a sense he truly held the keys," wrote a friend of the mission.

Hawaiian ideas of religion were, to put it mildly, different from those of New England Calvinism. When Bingham asked one of them who made the earth, he answered truthfully enough, "I do not know."

"Who made the sun?"

"I do not know, but we believe there is somebody up there who made it."

"Who made the moon and the stars?"

"There must be somebody up there that made them."

"I can tell you. It is Jehovah, the great God who made all things. He is a wise and good God and we must worship him."

"Well, you know all about it—we do not know anything about it." The Hawaiians were like that usually—ready to believe what the teachers told them. Yet occasionally there was a skeptic.

"If this God will bring my father back to life then I will believe and worship Him," said one of these.

"At the last day all that are dead will be brought to life," answered the missionary. The doubter said he would be glad to see that.

The communion service came to be greatly loved by Hawaiian congregations. But it took strong men to qualify as deacons. Somehow the word had got around that salvation depended upon the amount of wine drunk. Deacons often had to wrench the two-handled cup away from eager lips and strong hands.

In some villages where there were no missionaries, the people kept track of the days and when Sunday came they washed themselves, put on their best clothes, and then lay down in their huts and went to sleep—to the glory of Jehovah!

When it came to church government, the mission brothers carefully kept it from getting into Hawaiian hands at all. "It is not expedient on account of the ignorance of God's word . . . to admit Hawaiians to partake in the government of the particular churches," the ministerial association voted in this same year 1830. The original church—that is, the one formed at Park Street and taking in all the missionaries as they reached the islands—was to have the power of review and control over the particular churches, a system far removed from the plain New England Congregational way.

As the church gathered strength, the missionaries exerted their influence upon every aspect of life, for in every department they could see a moral issue and usually a vice which needed correcting. To wipe out indolence, source of gambling and other evils, they encouraged and promoted western household arts, agriculture, clothing, bigger and better buildings. They preached against stealing, gaming, desecrating the Sabbath. To wipe out sexual freedom they backed the laws against fornication and adultery. They used the churches to enforce discipline in this regard. When Kealiiahonui, the seven-foot chief, confessed to adultery, a committee was appointed to labor with him and bring him back to the fold. Even faithful Hopu was disciplined for the same sin. Others were suspended for lying, assault, theft, selling liquor. Even royalty itself was not immune to church discipline. Fourteen-year-old Princess Nahienaena stood up in church and confessed to having been drunk. Richards labored with her until she repented. When the church members voted that her repentance was sincere, she was again allowed to take communion. When commoners could vote on a princess, there had been a change indeed!

*   *   *

Early in 1831 while the chiefs were still on Hawaii they made two important decisions. The Catholic priests must leave the islands and Liliha, Boki's widow, must be displaced from the governing of Oahu. The two matters were interconnected.

In opposing the chiefs, the Yankee and British merchants naturally opposed the missionaries whom they regarded as the responsible source of the irksome laws. When the Catholic priests arrived, the merchants saw a chance to attack the Yankee mission behind a cloak of religious tolerance. For if they could destroy the influence of the Yankee Puritans, they were sure that the Catholic yoke would be milder.

The New Englanders knew well enough what was going on, and they were worried. At their general meeting in 1830 they had appointed a standing committee on the "Jesuits," composed of Bingham, Clark and Chamberlain, charged with the duty of deciding what course to follow regarding "this dangerous sect."

"Though I feel afraid of open resistance," Bingham wrote Chamberlain, "yet I cannot, with my present views, adopt the policy of one of our number who sought them out, extended his right hand, saying 'There is room enough for us all.' Should Regal power however, resist, expel or imprison, this is not the act of our church nor can our church forbid it."

When Liliha got word of the chiefs' decision to remove her, she prepared to resist, collecting arms and ammunition and readying an army of a thousand men. There is no doubt that she was encouraged by the foreign residents who opposed law, order and missionaries. The chiefs were at Lahaina when word of the incipient rebellion reached them. At first they thought of landing forces at several points to seize Oahu. But Hoapili, governor of Maui and Liliha's father, thought he could persuade her to give up her rash plan. The chiefs agreed to let him try.

He left immediately, his arrival causing a great stir among the people of Honolulu who knew well enough how trigger-poised affairs were. The next morning Paki, Liliha's lover and chief captain, came into Hunnewell's store where Henry A. Pierce was now in charge. He was trembling with passion in every joint, the sweat rolling down his cheeks like water. After a long moment of silence he exploded.

"Wrong is the woman," he said, meaning Liliha and her revolt.

But then Hoapili's words persuaded his daughter and she gave up the fort to him. Her power was broken, never to revive. Hoapili took her back to Maui with him, allowing her perhaps as a consolation prize to take her man Paki along.

On April first the grove below the fort was again crowded with people when young King Kauikeaouli rose to announce that Oahu was now in the hands of Kaahumanu. She in turn placed it in the hands of her huge, shrewd brother Adams who had come over from Hawaii, leaving Naihe in charge there.

Adams, rising ponderously, made no bones about his policy.

"My thought for you white men, especially those who sell rum, is this," he said. "If you sell any more rum I will strip you of your property and tear down your houses."

Righteousness was firmly in the saddle. "The blue laws of Connecticut are the laws of Hawaii," Pierce wrote Hunnewell.

An English merchant trying to dissuade Kaahumanu from enforcing the laws regarding the Sabbath said: "They do not prohibit these things in England or America."

"We do not rule there," said the regent. "But these islands are ours, and we wish to obey the law of God."

"I don't know that there is any law against riding on the Sabbath. Where is it?"

"Yes, you do know there is a law against it. 'Remember the Sabbath day to keep it holy.'"

Now that government had taken an active hand in putting down drunkenness, the mission encouraged the formation of a temperance society headed by the four governors: Adams, Hoapili, Kaikioewa and Naihe. (Naihe, however, died at the end of 1831.) The year before, the brethren had voted to give up the use of spirits themselves, but they had not dared tell the chiefs how widespread the temperance movement was in the United States because they did not want them to know how much drinking went on there!

When the merchants, pushed to the wall, begged Adams to let them sell rum at least to white men, he told them: "To horses, cattle and hogs you may sell rum, but to real men you must not on these shores."

With Liliha deposed and temperance enforced by law, the islands were in spick-and-span condition to receive the next company of missionaries who arrived from New England, four couples of them, on June sixth.

*   *   *

One of the decisions reached at the general meeting of 1831 was to open a seminary at Lahaina where young men might be trained as teachers and religious leaders. The job was handed over to Lorrin Andrews, a Connecticut Yankee who had emigrated to Ohio and Kentucky before coming to Hawaii. Picking a site about two miles up the hill where the air was cooler, Andrews started his school early in September with practically nothing in the way of buildings, equipment or books. It was the first thing of its kind in the whole Pacific Ocean. Since the first students were grown men who brought their whole families along, each scholar built a house for himself. Then they started to build the school. They laid up mud walls and then went off into the hills for timber. The chiefs had ordered the people there to feed the scholars while they cut trees. The students ate so well that they stayed five weeks. When they got back to Lahainaluna, as their spot was called, they found that rains had crumbled the walls. Meeting in the open air, they often had to hold their slates at a sharp angle to keep them from being washed clean. Still they would not quit. Some fainted from hunger, for they had to supply their own food. But they kept at it. They raised another school, this time with stones which had to be carried by hand to the site. Their number grew from twenty-five to sixty-seven during that first year.

The mission could hardly have picked a better man for this job than Lorrin Andrews, for he could not stand to see things going undone that needed doing. Yet at the beginning of his second term he wrote in discouragement to Levi Chamberlain:

"I am displeased with myself at my want of skill in managing such a school, I am displeased with the mission for not having more sense than to start such an institution without any means of carrying it on. And I am also displeased with the scholars for their never ending awkwardness."

In Honolulu, meanwhile, the matter of the Catholic priests had reached a crisis. In April Kaahumanu had ordered Fathers Alexis Bachelot and Patrick Short to leave the islands. In the chiefs' minds, no matter how unjustly, Catholicism had become identified with resistance to their authority, with attempts to promote factions, and the old idolatry which had been put down after the death of Kamehameha I. Kinau, explaining the attitude of the chiefs, said: "When the Roman Catholic priests came they sought out the ignorant, those who despised learning, and those who favored idolatry, and found them ready to join their party. They suspended images about their necks and practiced foolish things." She went on to say that to permit such things would be to encourage the return of the old idolatry and to bring on civil war.

In spite of the fact that the missionaries had warned the chiefs against persecution, Hawaiian Catholics were put in the fort and were forced to perform filthy tasks. Others were made to labor on the wall separating the dry plain from the plantations in the rear, with the hope of keeping cattle out of the cultivated fields. But Catholics were not the only ones required to do this.

Bachelot and Short professed that they could not leave the islands since no ship would take them. This was perfectly true for, as they themselves reported, they wrote to each captain about to depart, requesting free passage. The captains, knowing well enough that the priests wished to stay and being disposed to follow the views of the Honolulu merchants, refused to take them. The chiefs at length grew tired of the game, prepared their own ship, and on December 24 sent the two men off to California where they were safely landed at San Pedro near Los Angeles. They stayed in California, working at the missions there and awaiting a chance to return to the islands. For they had by no means given up. The "Methodists," as Bachelot called the missionaries, had only seen the first round of this match. Stronger by far were the wallops yet to be delivered.

CHAPTER 14

THE PRINCESS MISBEHAVES
1832–1834

KAAHUMANU, FIRM CORNER POST OF THE FAITH, WAS DAN-
gerously ill. Both state and church, though scrupulously separate,
had found in her their chief support. No one knew what would happen if this sturdy pillar were withdrawn.

Naturally the mission brought forward its best medical advice
which now consisted not only of the very able Dr. Judd, but also
Alonzo Chapin, who had studied at Amherst and taken his medical
degree from the University of Pennsylvania. He had arrived on May
17, 1832, with the fifth company—the largest mission group yet sent
out. The previous company had also contained a doctor, the Reverend Dwight Baldwin, who had been assigned to the health station
at Waimea, Hawaii.

Judd and Chapin tried everything known to them without halting
the progress of Kaahumanu's disease. So they did what every physician of that day did when he hadn't the faintest idea how to effect a
cure—they prescribed a change of air.

Too feeble now to ride even in her jouncing little donkey cart,
Kaahumanu was lifted up, bed and all, and carried on the shoulders
of her attendants all the way into Manoa Valley, a distance of about
five miles. A village of two hundred grass houses sprang up like
mushrooms around Kaahumanu's cottage, to shelter from the frequent Manoa showers the crowd of servants and chiefs who now, in
Hawaiian fashion, gathered about their stricken leader. Someone
from the mission—usually the Binghams or Judds—stayed in the
cottage she had built for them next to her own.

When the last pages of the Hawaiian New Testament came off the
press in Honolulu, Bingham got the reverend jack-of-all-trades, Jo-

seph Goodrich, to bind the first copy in red morocco and sent it to the stricken regent by the hand of Dr. Judd. Kaahumanu, though too weak to read, turned it over and over in her hands—unusually delicate ones for a Hawaiian—and riffled through its pages. *"Maikai—* good," she said. Then she wrapped it in her handkerchief, laid it on her ample bosom, and rested her clasped hands upon it.

Though too weak to read herself, she listened eagerly when Hiram Bingham read from the sacred palapala or prayed with her. Even the tough and skeptical Yankee traders in Honolulu, impressed by her piety, began to admit that her conversion must be real.

On the third of June, a Sunday, Dr. Judd sent a midnight messenger down to Honolulu to fetch Bingham. Kaahumanu, thought the doctor, was approaching her end. Hiram hurried to her side.

"The way that I am going . . . the house is prepared . . . send the thoughts thither with rejoicing," she said to him the evening of the second day.

"This perhaps is your departure," he told her presently. "Stay yourself on Jesus. He is your physician, your helper, your savior. Trust in Him."

With a wraith of her old playfulness Kaahumanu said, "Perhaps you are tired of me."

"Oh no," Bingham said, concerned lest she mistake Christian resignation for unseemly anticipation. "We wish you to stay with us; in that we should rejoice. But we think the Lord will soon take you away from us."

"I will go to Him, and shall be comforted."

When Bingham had watched over her nearly forty-eight hours, she insisted that he lie down on a large field bedstead near her side and get some rest.

Just before dawn of June 5 she called him. Springing to her side, Hiram took her hand. It was cold. With a great effort she raised her heavy lids and fixed her dark, languid-looking eyes on the man who had changed her life.

"Is this Bingham?" she asked.

"It is I."

"I am going now," she said.

"Aloha," said Bingham, finding in this alien word a depth of affection which could not be expressed in the colder Yankee tongue. "Go in peace, leaning on your savior, and dwell with Him forever. May He receive your soul."

The dark eyes closed, the big bosom ceased to heave, the breath grew fainter and then stopped. Around her the king, the princess, her brother Kuakini (Adams) and the other principal chiefs wept freely. Tears coursed down Bingham's face when, preaching the funeral sermon three days later, he told how Kaahumanu had renounced idolatry and become a believing Christian.

Kaahumanu had willed her authority and her lands to Kinau, half sister of the king and a wife of the former king, Liholiho. Married next to Kahaalaia and then, after a period of trial, to Kekuanaoa, Kinau seemed to lack Kaahumanu's strength. After becoming a Christian, however, she had learned to combine modesty with firmness, courtesy with high rank. She had a good figure, was "comely but not handsome" in Bingham's eyes, though Hawaiians thought her beautiful, and was somewhat smaller than Hawaiian female chiefs in general.

On the fifth day of July Kinau and the king issued proclamations which made it clear that she was not only prime minister (*kuhinanui*), but regent during the king's minority—he was now eighteen. She was also governor of Oahu. Upon her, rather than upon the king, fell most of the responsibility of governing.

Kauikeaouli—to call the king by his proper but unfortunately difficult name—was apparently content to have it so. A handsome youth, with curly hair and a wide nose, but with a look of impatience and weakness in place of the boldness and decision his rank required, Kauikeaouli was more interested in playing than in governing. He had taken a fancy to a girl named Kalama—daughter of Naihekukui, "Captain Jack"—and had even been willing to marry her. But the chiefs would not permit it, for any children this couple might have would rank below Kinau's children (she already had three), or any born to Nahienaena, thus throwing the succession into confusion. The king took Kalama anyway.

Gathering around him a group of like-minded young men who took the name of Hulumanu—Bird-Feathers, the king took to the pursuit of pleasure in a thoroughgoing way. Leader of the gang was the apostate Kaomi, the half Tahitian who had once been a favored mission protégé. When Kinau refused to approve the king's plan of buying a brig for his pleasure trips, he responded by stepping up the tempo of his debauch. The old games were revived. In March, 1833, the king sent a crier through the streets to say that all laws were abrogated except those against theft and murder. Hulas, gambling, games ending in sexual favors—all the pastimes of the pre-mission days sprang up throughout the islands in response to the king's leading. Schools were deserted while "parents, brothers, sisters, and relatives united like beasts in common prostitution."

Perhaps the young man was searching for a way to assert the leadership of his people. Since he could not outshine the mission-influenced chiefs in sobriety, he would rally his people around the symbols of their own culture, depreciated and discarded through mission influence. The response showed a lively belief that what gave pleasure must be good, and that the delights of the flesh justified themselves. Encouraged, Kauikeaouli commanded an assembly of the people on March 15 in the meeting place below the fort, towards what is now Fort Armstrong. The chiefs feared that he wanted to set Kinau aside and bring back Liliha, under whose governance Oahu had already had its bath of rum.

Kinau, walking through the crowd, approached her half brother. "We cannot war with the word of God between us," she said.

The king arose and announced that he considered himself of age (he was about nineteen, his exact birth date unknown) and that he was assuming full sovereignty. Then he raised his hand to show who would be the next highest officer. Kaomi and Liliha were near him as well as Kinau. The future course of the islands depended upon the fall of his hand.

Much to the disgust of his feathered friends and the foreign traders, it fell upon Kinau. When his companions later remonstrated with him, he said: "Very strong is the kingdom of God."

Kinau spoke to the people, declared that she was ready to undertake the duties of her office and that no acts of government would be constitutional without her approval. This was a point the king fought against for a while. But in the end he gave in.

The next day Hiram Bingham sought out his former pupil and urged him to look to God for guidance. The following day the young king came to church and asked that two hundred copies of the New Testament be sent him for his Bird-Feathers. Confident that the Feathers might yet be nested in the church, Bingham complied.

However strong the kingdom of God might be, it was not yet strong enough to control the king. Though eager to be an absolute ruler, he would not buckle down to the hard labor this would have required. So he went on in his own way.

Then in July came the awful truth the mission had been dreading. The princess had taken to bed with her brother, the old Hawaiian custom of incest had been resumed. "Last night at 3 o'clock the criminal act was done in the house of Paki," Levi Chamberlain confided to his journal on July 22. Since the king had a child by Kalama which was born and died the following March, he was obviously not reserving his favors for his sister exclusively.

When John Ii brought the horrid news to Lahaina, Richards was heartbroken. The princess had been his prize pupil. Her piety and conformity had been a great support, for in birth she was an equal of the king. Not only was she living in incest with her brother, said Ii, but she was also drinking, attending hulas, listening to vile songs. When Richards wrote a remonstrating letter, the princess acknowledged her guilt and admitted that she had destroyed her soul. She hoped, however, that he would continue his instructions to the people and not forsake them.

Here was a situation the missionaries simply could not understand. Ignorance of God was one thing. They had come and brought the knowledge of God to the heathen. But how could a rational being, having known God, fall open-eyed into sin?

So Nahienaena of the sad eyes, a child no longer—though she carried herself gracefully she weighed two hundred pounds now, still not very much for a chiefess—Nahienaena returned to the ways of her people, but burdened with a conscience. Kinau, her half sister, must have felt the shame.

While attendance was falling off at the Hawaiian schools, the foreign residents of Honolulu began to talk about setting up one of their own. The number of hapahaole youngsters was growing daily, thanks to the alliances of various sorts between haole men and Hawaiian women. There was not a school in the islands where these youngsters could study in English. As for the Hawaiian schools, they were coasting into their worst slump since the mission had first begun teaching, and no wonder. Since the use of books required some effort, many teachers preferred to teach without them, simply calling out the alphabet and letting their scholars parrot them in chorus. Ill-trained or untrained teachers, taking advantage of the prestige their positions gave them, had forced the people to labor for them or deviated into sin and thus lost prestige. For though the people were mighty fond of sinning themselves, they associated the teachers with the mission and expected exemplary behavior of them.

Attendance had dropped to a third of what it was, schoolhouses were falling to pieces and even the one at Honolulu under the care of the mission had blown down in a high wind, its "furniture" of mud brick seats and rough board desks crushed in the debris. "Not fit for a barn anyway," remarked the disgusted Dr. Judd, who felt that it would be better to teach eighty-five boys well than three thousand haphazardly.

The mission was therefore happy to see the movement in Honolulu for a proper school. Where mission and merchants had disagreed on so many things, here surely was a common interest through which they might deviate into harmony. That was what they thought.

The beginning was full of promise. Andrew Johnstone, a member of the mission who had arrived in 1831, one day met a lad of twelve years or so who was the hapahaole son of an English sea captain named Cutter. Johnstone, a Scot who had left home for the West Indies at the age of ten and therefore had a feeling for lonely boys, invited this one to his home. When he came, he brought a friend. Soon more asked to come. Johnstone, whose mission duties as assistant to Chamberlain were apparently not too heavy, began to teach them. His wife, an able teacher and a native of Nantucket, helped out.

Encouraged by this beginning, the merchants and captains of the town now proposed to raise money for a school if the mission would allow Johnstone to teach it. The agreement reached, a subscription was taken up on August 9, 1832. The king granted a piece of land between King and Queen streets (as they are now called), and a meeting was called at the Oahu Hotel to make plans for building. Charlton, who considered himself spokesman and leader of the foreign community, presided. The residents, still a little uneasy at being even thus remotely yoked to the mission, voted (at a later meeting) that no religion was to be taught beyond that of reading the Bible without note or comment.

By the end of the year $2,000 had been raised and so had the building—a coral stone affair entered through a vestibule over which rose a tower and a cupola equipped with a bell—gift of John C. Jones. Inside was a handsome desk for the teacher and benches for the pupils. The grand opening took place on the tenth of January, 1833. A procession formed in front of William French's—first a band, then the boys, then the missionaries, the school committee, the king himself, the subscribers and strangers. Off they marched to the new schoolhouse where the ladies of the town awaited them—those of the mission and the few other haole women. The mothers who had produced the scholars do not seem to have been invited.

Bingham opened with prayer. Four months later the school's trustees voted that he was to be debarred from the school—also used for church services in English—because of his libels against foreign residents. But on this day, at any rate, harmony was preserved. Jones made a speech and Reuben Tinker, another recently arrived missionary, gave the concluding prayer.

"The day was fine and everyone appeared much gratified," wrote Stephen Reynolds, permanent treasurer of the school board and one of its staunchest supporters. Reynolds had first come to the islands from Massachusetts in 1811 on the *New Hazard*. After a number of trips, he had settled at Honolulu about 1823, first as a clerk for William French and then in business for himself. His store (at the corner of the present Nuuanu and Merchant streets), cluttered with heaps of goods in perfect disorder, became a favorite loitering place for the town's male scandalmongers. Reynolds, "a little, short, dried up sort of man," dark, and given to epileptic fits, listened carefully to what was said. Much of what he heard he set down in his journals.

Many a Yankee merchant or skipper stumped across the half-dozen well-worn planks leading to the rickety veranda of Reynolds' store in order to consult the proprietor on a legal matter, for Reynolds, though no lawyer, had a reputation for skill in the law. Customers always found him dressed the same way, in a costume of his own invention—unbleached cotton shirt buttoned at the throat but with no stock or linen bosom, the wide collar turned over a light-colored nankeen jacket. Trousers of the same material, white stockings and low shoes, and a Panama hat without a ribbon finished off his garb—a far more sensible one for the Hawaiian climate than the stiff dark clothes of the missionaries or the heavy coats of the sailing captains. His wife Susan had by now borne him several children whom she presented at the mission church for baptism.

The Oahu Charity School was scarcely launched when the Reverend John Diell, sent out by the American Seamen's Friend Society, arrived to do religious work among the many sailors who prowled Honolulu with time on their hands. Twenty-five years old, John Diell plunged into his job with enthusiasm—much to the relief of the mission brothers, who had done what they could for the seamen though lacking time, materials, and perhaps inclination. Diell came supplied with the materials for his own chapel and with a carpenter, Charles Burnham, to put it up for him. The king and Kinau gave land in the part of town most frequented by sailors, and on November 28, 1833, John Diell proudly invited the community to the dedication ceremonies. His two-story building had a library and reading room downstairs, a meeting hall above. Church services in English were now moved here from the school and Diell took charge of them too. The singing became quite a feature of the service, and many a sea captain and merchant who cared little about the subtleties of Calvinist doctrine came to stretch his lungs in song.

With the Bethel flag flying over the cupola of his boxlike haven for seamen, John Diell went right into the saloons to get his men, inviting them to make his reading room their headquarters. Since many a sailor did not know how to read, however, the use of the reading room had a limited appeal.

At Lahainaluna, meanwhile, that beautiful site on the mountainside with its view of the sparkling ocean and the moundlike island of Lanai, Lorrin Andrews struggled to get his school in order. The students had labored hard to put up a coral schoolhouse. They worked best when hungry, were quarrelsome and lazy when fed, Lorrin discovered. So he did not worry too much about their bellies. With a roof over his head at last Andrews began to teach his students—Greek! He also looked forward to giving them Hebrew. Soon he was joined by Brothers Clark and Dibble. Charles Burnham, the carpenter, came over to put up houses for the three teachers and their families, and stayed to become secular agent.

Always full of ideas, Andrews set up a printing press and soon began to publish Hawaii's first newspaper—*Lama Hawaii* (*The Hawaiian Luminary*). Thus he could provide reading material for his students, an incentive to write for publication, and a trade they could learn. His pupils were soon not only printing, but engraving cuts for his press. Andrews was well ahead of the rest of the world in his scheme of teaching the practical arts as part of the school curriculum. In the United States industrial training was unheard of at this time.

The students soon discovered that the training they were getting in agriculture had more than a purely academic advantage—had even a value beyond that of filling their own bellies. Their surpluses of yams, beans, potatoes, could be sold at fancy prices to the whaling ships putting in at Lahaina. Within one six-week period they took in $300. Where Andrews had hardly been able to drive them to the fields before, he could now hardly get them away from their hoes and into the schoolroom.

Whether or not it was this which brought about the change, the mission soon decided to change the makeup of the student body. Until now they had mostly been married men, bringing their families along and thus introducing other problems—such as the tempting proximity of males and females who had been raised in the notion that the free dispensation of sexual favors was the basis of polite society. The erring princess had in fact ridden into the school grounds with a train of her debauchees, spreading about a contempt for learning and a lust for the good old days which Andrews had found most unsettling. So it was decided that Lahainaluna would become a boarding school for boys from eight to twenty. Never noted for letting well enough alone, the brothers also decided to open a girl's school at Wailuku—near enough so that boys and girls could get acquainted and ultimately find suitable mates, but not so close that a lovesick Leander could swim to his Hero.

As for the mission family itself, the arrivals and departures now grow too numerous to keep up with. (The curious may consult the

Appendix of names and dates.) Sam Ruggles gave up on account of ill health. With his once-pretty, now peaked-looking Nancy, half a dozen children of their own, and two seven-year-olds—Lucy Bingham and Emily Whitney, they sailed for home early in 1834. Lucy, despite her upbringing, had turned out to be a volatile, impulsive, somewhat giddy and no doubt thoroughly lovable child. But Sybil, anxious over her lack of seriousness, authorized Nancy and Sam to punish her by depriving her of meals or privileges when they thought it necessary—or to spank her if she was "guilty at the bar of Scripture."

Little Hiram, now three, missed his playful sister. When the family went to their Punahou cottage in Manoa Valley where Hiram senior did most of his translating of the Bible, the youngster ran into the room calling, "Lucy! Lucy!" Then he stopped, remembering. "Lucy gone—gone over to America in the great ship." Whenever he saw a ship entering the harbor, he came running to Sybil. "Mama, ship— Lucy coming," he said.

The arrivals, both by ship and by stork, far outnumbered the departures. With more than thirty families, each of whom had from one to half a dozen children, the numbers were truly impressive, while a general meeting with its swarms of children was a three-ring circus. There were far too many youngsters for the mothers, burdened with babies and with cooking for the whole mob, to attend to. So in the midst of deliberations, fathers patiently walked their children up and down the room, or dandled them on their knees.

The rural mission stations—and there were more and more of them now—had a quiet charm of their own. The Emersons, for instance, had settled at Waialua, at the other end of the island from Honolulu. They were handsome young people—Ursula with big blue eyes full of vivacity and fringed with long dark eyelashes, her nose, chin and mouth deliciously small and delicate. Shortly after their arrival at Waialua their thatched church near the house of the chief Laanui was finished. A vast attendance poured in at the first service. Truly, the spirit of God is at work, thought earnest John Emerson. Later he learned that Laanui had commanded every person in the district to attend. A woman with but one foot had obediently hopped four miles. Emerson gently explained to the chief that it might be better not to demand attendance. All right, said the chief's right-hand man. Then he stood up and told the people that no one would make them come again. But now they had proved they could come, they might as well continue!

*   *   *

When the Baldwins went for a season to Kohala from Waimea on the "big island" of Hawaii, the chiefess sent twenty men to bear their belongings. On arrival the family found a new grass cottage awaiting them. The people thronged the meeting for worship and the Sabbath school. Nearly two hundred children came trooping along behind the Baldwins when they returned to their cottage, still charmed with the novelty of a white woman in their midst. Charlotte, though no beauty, had a warm and friendly smile. So did her husband, for that matter, with his eyes bright under deep brows, his wide, friendly-looking mouth with dimples at the corners and two creases of geniality extending from below his cheekbones to his chin. That he was a frank and outspoken and even contentious man time would show— he had already gotten into a minor spat with Bishop over some articles in the mission house at Waimea which Charlotte had used without Mrs. Bishop's permission. But if he threw off sparks occasionally, he could also sparkle.

Somewhat more serious was the disagreement between Bingham and Andrews. Andrews had been asked by the general meeting to draw up a Hawaiian vocabulary. When the manuscript was sent over to Honolulu, Bingham began to alter and amend it. Like any writer, Andrews was furious over this tampering with his product. There are "too many fingers in the pie," he complained to Chamberlain. "Every brother knows that, for the purpose of distinguishing sounds, I have the longest pair of ears in the mission except Brother Bingham." In a long and humorously legalistic statement, he warned all parties to keep clear of altering his work. He wrote Rogers, the printer, to stop the press at once if his work could not be put through without being altered by the Printing Committee. He then wrote to Bingham, firmly telling him to lay off. "Our opinions on the principles of the language differ," he told him. "When you publish your grammar you may set straight everything you suppose to be crooked, and I will vote for its publication." But leave the vocabulary alone!

Poor Andrews—he was still trying to get out his vocabulary several months later. After a three-month delay he had got only the first sheet from the printer. It would take five years at this rate to get the book out, he complained to Judd. "Let us *do* something—let us *do something,* let us *do it.* Let us do it *now;* by and by we shall die."

* * *

After years of struggling with inadequate numbers, the mission was now richly supplied. But instead of using all its members to best advantage, the brothers now hit upon the crazy notion (approved by the board) of sending three couples off to the Marquesas to work among the cannibals there. The Alexanders, Armstrongs and Tinkers were ticked off for this duty. They reached Nukuhiva in August, 1833. The Marquesans were a handsome, proud, fierce people. Lacking the soft, easygoing nature of the Hawaiians, they did not take readily to the mission, though they were eager enough to exchange bedfellows with the brothers. When they tried to hold services, the people soon stretched out and slept, mimicked the preacher, smoked their pipes and made such a chatter that the preacher could hardly hear himself. After eight months, finding the island far from the paradise Melville was to make it in *Typee,* the three couples gave up in despair and returned to Honolulu.

The missionary brothers, treating them as deserters, sent them off to new and isolated rural stations. William Alexander, "5' 10¾", high forehead, eyes gray, nose Grecian, mouth large, chin common, hair dark brown, complexion light, face oval" according to his passport, went with his lovely-looking wife, Mary Ann, to Waioli, a beautiful mountain-walled valley opening out into a long bay on the rainy side of Kauai.

Less fortunate were the Armstrongs, close friends of the Alexanders, whose exile took them to Haiku on the slopes of the great extinct crater Haleakala (House of the Sun) on Maui. They lacked the necessary clothes and bed covers to keep warm at this cool spot, even though they used their trading goods to cover their beds. Both their children became ill, Richard Armstrong himself had a high fever, and Clarissa was momentarily expecting her third child. A desperate message brought William Richards who, when he saw their condition, stood speechless at the door with tears running down his cheeks. He moved the family twelve miles down the hill to a warmer climate, but even so one child died.

Reuben Tinker, the third member of the team, was sent first to Wailuku on Maui. "Preached in the A.M.," he wrote in his diary soon after his arrival there. "Walked to Hamakua Poko 5 miles and preached again—walked to Manoni and preached again—walked three more home, and Mr. Green conducted the English service as I was very weary." Weakling! After a few months he was called to Honolulu to edit another Hawaiian paper, *Ke Kumu Hawaii—The Hawaiian Teacher*. A loving, genial man with a rich fund of humor, he made a good editor and a wonderful father. He never did learn to preach well in Hawaiian, and even in English was awkward, jerky, full of inverted inflections and odd mannerisms. But his sermons had punch, which was perhaps more important.

* * *

Those who had prayed that the princess might repent and return to the church gave up all hope when, towards the end of 1834, the word began to be whispered about, or written by the brethren to each other in Hawaiian rather than in English: "Shame! The word is that she is pregnant by her own brother."

CHAPTER 15

PARADISE INDEED

1835–1837

IF THERE WAS ONE THING MORE THAN ANY OTHER WHICH led the brethren to despair of making Hawaii a Christian nation, it was the case of the Princess Harieta Nahienaena. Early in January, 1835, she came to church at Lahaina when keen-eyed (Do-It-Now) Lorrin Andrews was preaching. She sauntered into the church in a provokingly casual manner, talked while the service was going on, and laughed into Andrews' face when he preached, "God is Love." The princess, apparently, had other ideas. Before the sermon was much more than half finished she walked out.

This was serious, because the people of Lahaina loved their princess and were likely to follow her lead. She was very friendly and agreeable towards them, not at all stand-offish and proud as chiefs were likely to be. As she strolled down to the rickety old stone fort at the landing place, or to the row of chiefs' houses that lined the shore, or to the grove of great kou trees where the chiefs spent their time in sports and storytelling, she was greeted everywhere, not as a drunkard and an incestuous apostate, but as a heroine. The missionaries could not understand it.

In February they sent the great chief Hoapili, Kalaikoa and a dependable convert named David Malo to reclaim her for the church if they could. The deputation called on her at her house next to the grove of kou trees—the finest straw house in the village, its interior lined with dry banana stalks. Their efforts must have been vain, for a letter of excommunication was prepared. Then the poor princess, torn between the two cultures whose ways she was attempting to reconcile, sent messengers promising to reform. But when she sailed over to Hawaii in April she slid back into transgression. When she

returned to Lahaina in May, Richards called the church together and
proposed to cut her off. The vote passed on the twenty-third while
she was in the midst of a drinking bout aboard a foreign vessel in the
roads. Not long afterwards she was carousing with the king at Wailuku on the other side of Maui. Then came confirmation of the word
that she would be having a baby by her brother.

No matter how hard they tried, the Hawaiians simply could not
get this sex business straight in their minds, the way the mission
would have them. They listened every Sunday to sermons which told
them it was their Christian duty to love one another. Didn't the Bible,
therefore, teach that it was the business of Christians to have one another's person in common? And hadn't they been doing just that?

Patiently the brethren tried to explain the seventh commandment.
But in rendering it into Hawaiian they learned to their horror that
there were about twenty ways of committing adultery Hawaiian-
style. If they used any one of the twenty names, that left all the other
avenues to pleasure wide open. They ended with the vague phrase,
"Thou shalt not sleep mischievously," thus making the whole thing
a state of mind.

But Lorrin Andrews, up the hill at his seminary, had to deal with
realities. "If other vices bear any proportion to that of lewdness," he
sadly noted, "the High School has no claim to the epithet of moral.
. . . Adultery has been the crying sin of native teachers from the
commencement of the school system," he concluded. "It was viewed
in prospect by the scholars of the High School as a part of the per-
quisites of office."

"Most teachers have lain with many or all of their scholars,"
Dibble concurred. No wonder teaching had been so popular!

Genially eager to tell Andrews of their past sins, the students must
have given him more of an education than he gave them. In fact,
such confessions, required of candidates for admission to the church,
backfired like almost everything else the mission undertook in an
effort to enforce its ideas of morality upon the Hawaiians. The candidates were so fond of having something to tell that they went out
and sinned some more, in order to have the pleasure of telling the
preacher about it. Andrews found that one of his men had slept
frequently with various women while he was seeking admission, and

"even was guilty of adultery the night before he entered the church!!!"

Shocked by his discoveries, Andrews hastily canceled plans for a public examination of his scholars, knowing that it would have drawn "a host of females in the attire of harlots from Lahaina, who would probably have allured more victims into their toils." And here was another source of bewilderment to the mission. They had insisted upon clothing the heathen, only to discover that the clothes the girls put on became a source of allurement to men who all their lives had taken nudity for granted!

Defeated on this front, the mission tried again to see what it could do against the demon rum. With mission encouragement, several of the high chiefs including Kinau, Kaahumanu's successor, begged the king to put a stop to all distilling and rum-selling throughout the islands. Nearly three thousand plain citizens added their names to the petition. At last he signed a brief code of laws which imposed punishments for drunkenness and offenses committed by the intoxicated.

"Kamehameha III was entirely conquered by the spirit," wrote one wit, "partly that of religion through the missionaries and partly that of cognac through the French."

No one as yet thought of total abstinence. Mission wives went on brewing their barrels of beer while their husbands administered wine at the communion table or took a glass for refreshment.

But they did try to do something about smoking, which had become so prevalent a habit that the smallest children indulged in it. Hawaiians soon discovered that by persistent inhaling they could get almost as good a jag on as if they had imbibed the rum which the brethren frowned upon. Regretfully, the missionaries decided that they would have to give up their own pipes and cigars and impose a strict prohibition upon the churches. Smoking now became as great a sin as "sleeping mischievously"—perhaps it should have been called "breathing mischievously"—and a member could be excommunicated for indulging. Many did, and were. Before the mission legislated against smoking, however, many a Yankee preacher was enjoying his fragrant pipeful while not far away at another station one

of his stricter brothers was reading a poor Hawaiian out of church
for the same act.

* * *

On June sixth, 1835, the *Hellespont* sailed into Honolulu Harbor
with the seventh company of missionaries. "Truly a mouldy set,"
remarked Juliette Cooke. One of the eight members was Lydia
Brown, a spinster from New Hampshire, sent out in response to the
mission's appeal for someone to teach Hawaiian girls how to spin
and weave; the theory being that such employments would keep their
minds off carnal things. Lydia looked like one who could do this, if
anyone could. Already fifty-five and therefore a proven spinster in
both senses of the word, she had a long, sagging face with a death's-
head look about it, except that it lacked the grin. She was promptly
assigned to Wailuku on Maui where Jonathan Green, the pastor with
the sense of humor, had begun two years ago to build up a mission.
With them also went the Armstrongs who had but recently been
rescued by William Richards from the cold slopes of Haleakala.

Wailuku, situated where a gradual rise from the distant ocean
changes to an abrupt background of creased and towering lava hills
carpeted with green, was a fine location. Cool Iao Valley with its
frequent rains was always available as a refuge from heat or sun.
The broad and gentle slope to the sea provided almost limitless opportunities for farming. Cotton already grew wild, and if Lydia
Brown succeeded in her efforts, a whole industry might grow up.

Half a dozen schools were already in operation—for adult men,
adult women, for two hundred children, two select classes of girls,
eighteen lads who were being prepared to enter the seminary or high
school, a Sunday School of five hundred. Lydia began with a small
group of about eight young women whom she taught to card, spin,
knit and weave. In five months they produced ninety yards of cloth,
most of it woven by Lydia since the girls had only mastered the art
of spinning and had yet to conquer the loom. It was a noble experiment, but it was doomed to failure.

* * *

General meeting, usually held in June and lasting for three weeks
or more, had become the great event of the year. For adults as well

as for the children it was a wonderful time of social renewal. (At most of the rural stations there were at most two mission families and often only one. Calls from haoles were infrequent.) The influx of guests created a critical housing shortage. Every available grass house was pressed into service, and the mission houses simply overflowed with guests. Meals were taken picnic-style at long tables on the porches or under the trees. For the older children there were daily classes under a wife who could be spared from other tasks. Even so there were hours when they all came together in the adobe school-house with its rows of desks and benches made of unpainted boards. The fathers carried on their deliberations in the front of the room. Behind them sat the women with their babies and near the door the boys and girls. Fathers often made speeches with little ones in their arms, and infants frequently interrupted the proceedings "by ex-pressing independent ideas on foreign subjects."

Numerous as the children were, many had already been sent off to the United States for their education and in order to form "suit-able connections," either for a livelihood or a life partner. Only the Thurstons of all the mission families had kept their daughters in Hawaii into their teens. Now Lucy and Persis came forward and joined the mission church—the first of the children to do so. And the mothers of the mission, impressed with the visible fact that they were vastly outnumbered by their children, joined together in a Maternal Association which discussed such subjects as whether to take children to church to hear a Hawaiian sermon or stay at home with them, what duties were proper for a mission wife, and all the questions of child care which occupy mothers everywhere. Sooner or later, of course, sex was bound to rear its ugly head. How should they pre-pare their children for it? How could they explain its rather ob-trusive presence in the sacred Book? Should they skip over such parts? (As if the children wouldn't find them!)

"The subject of their origin was felt to be the most difficult of management to the satisfaction of the child," they concluded. When and how to tell them? Bravely they accepted this as a mother's duty. They went on to reach a very sensible conclusion: handle the sub-ject with delicacy but without disguise or mystery. If only they could have persuaded themselves to let the youngsters learn Hawaiian, the

matter would have taken care of itself! Yet it was exactly on this
point that they had shut their children off from Hawaiian life with
its frank, uninhibited acceptance of the body and its functions. One
result was that when a mission child was taken to visit the prison
at Charlestown, Massachusetts, he remarked, "They have as much
liberty as we had at the Sandwich Islands."

The mission ladies, when they returned to their own stations,
formed branches of the Maternal Association among Hawaiian
mothers, who may have wondered what all the fuss was about when
the same delicate questions were raised.

*   *   *

As the brothers got on with the important meeting of 1836, they
had to face the fact that the Hawaiian population was decreasing at a
fearful rate. In the past four years (during which they had kept a
census) it had dropped from 130,000 to 108,000. If this trend continued, there would be no Hawaiians within twenty years. Meanwhile
only a thousand had been received as church members in the mission's sixteen years, although nearly 15,000—more than an eighth of
the population—went to church on Sunday.

Knowing that the mission must some day be converted into a self-
supporting church, the brethren were vitally concerned in the matter
of Hawaiian industry. At this general meeting, therefore, they drew
up a memorial on the arts in which they stressed to the American
Board the need for artisans of all kinds—a blacksmith, wheelwright,
millwright, papermaker, cooper—to be sent out to practice their
trades and to train Hawaiians up in them. Men who knew cotton and
sugar should be sent out to establish plantations, also a merchant
and a superintendent, the whole to be formed into a separate society
or company if the board was unwilling to employ such people the
way it now hired printers and bookbinders. When the document was
shown to the chiefs, they not only approved it but wrote a letter to
the board urging its adoption in full.

Still another major document was drawn at this general meeting,
and after four or five days of earnest discussion was adopted. Usually called "the circular," but in its printed form *The Duty of the
Present Generation to Evangelize the World,* its fifty-five closely

printed pages were to prove strong medicine for the board. With six hundred million heathen perishing for the word of life, it said, the board had sent out only one hundred missionaries throughout the world. This was fewer than the number of men preaching in New York. As for the $200,000 the board spent on missions, this was "a sum so worthless," in view of the need, as to be ridiculous. Go yourselves, the circular said to ministers sitting in their comfortable studies at home. It's your fault that the world remains heathen.

"Brethren, I am going down into the well, now you hold on to the rope." That was the way to reach the Christian public with an irresistible appeal. Yes, and let the members of the board also go out —why, such a move would advance the cause of conversion five hundred years. Forget narrow controversy among the churches—there is no need or place for such futile disagreement in mission fields. Spend your energy instead upon the main thing.

"Your situation is by no means enviable," the circular concluded. Tackle the main task, or expect the displeasure and punishment of God.

To be certain that it would not be brushed aside, the brethren appointed William Richards a committee of one "to go with our circular containing our views in his hand." In November he arranged passage for himself, his wife and six of his eight children on the *Daniel Webster,* reaching New England in May, 1837. The eldest Bishop daughter went with them.

Richards could hardly have reached the United States at a worse time. A financial depression was sweeping the country. Far from planning an expansion of missions, the board was wondering where to get the money to meet its current obligations and had already ordered the Hawaiian mission to cut its expenditures in half. They refused to receive Richards as an agent of the mission, denying the mission's right to appoint or send an agent to them.

"A cloud rests at present both on the agency of the Sandwich Island Mission and also on the cause of missions generally," Richards regretfully wrote back to his colleagues. Yet he traveled around the country lecturing on Hawaii, went to his old home in the Berkshires and saw his father, found homes for his children, and after being handsomely received by President Van Buren at the White House headed back to the islands.

Before Richards left, his former charge, the Princess Nahienaena, had given birth to the king's child. For form's sake, apparently, she had married Leleihoku, son of old Billy Pitt, towards the end of 1835. In August, according to an old Hawaiian custom, the chiefs began gathering to see her bring forth her first born. Girl or boy, it would be a great chief and there would be none—not even Kinau's children—who could approach its high rank. It was a son, but it lived only six hours.

Poor Nahienaena never recovered from the doubt and confusion into which her struggle with two worlds had cast her. Perhaps the death of her little son convinced her that the missionaries had been right after all.

"There is no mercy for an apostate," she said to Laura Judd one day towards the end of the year. "I am one. I have crucified the Lord afresh."

"Jesus spoke to the dying penitent on the cross," Laura told her.

"Do you say so?" She clasped Laura's hand. "Can there be hope for one who has sinned as I have?" And she began to pray.

She died on the next to the last day of the year. While the coffin still stood in his house, the king took his favorite girl, Kalama, to wife. She lacked high birth, but perhaps she could give him an heir.

* * *

On the ninth of April, 1837, two months after the king had married Kalama, the largest group of missionaries ever to reach the islands (dispatched before the depression hit the board) floated into the harbor aboard the *Mary Frazier* after the happiest voyage any company had ever made. Captain Charles Sumner had grown so impressed with his crowd of earnest, attractive young people that towards the end of the voyage he had begun to lead prayers himself.

"I did not love them when we started," he confessed, "but now I feel a deep interest in them."

On the first Sunday ashore half a dozen of the crew marched up to the mourners' bench in church, confessed their sins, and requested admission.

One of the missionary newcomers was Mrs. Emily Curtis Bliss, a young lady with an impish look about her mouth whose sister Betsey Lyons had already come out as a missionary five years before with her husband, the Reverend Lorenzo Lyons.

Betsey Lyons was so attractive that when she had called to say farewell to friends before leaving home, the hired man on the place had said, "That one oughter not go. She's too purty. Them savages'll eat her." The Hawaiians had been as much impressed by her youth —she was only eighteen—as by her beauty. "The very children are coming to teach us," they said.

The "savages" had loved her. But the climate had not. As soon as she heard of her sister Emily's arrival, she hurried from the lonely upland station of Waimea on Hawaii to Honolulu. They met on the twenty-fifth of April. Two weeks later poor, tiny, charming Betsey faded into death after giving her husband and her sister a parting kiss. Dead at twenty-four, she left two children to be cared for.

The parting must have been a bitter one for Emily, who had looked forward to reunion with her beloved younger sister. She and Isaac Bliss stayed only four years, for Isaac turned out to be an eccentric. "It won't do to settle him alone," Sam Ruggles wrote the brethren after meeting Bliss in the United States, "and he will know so much more than all his brethren put together" that he could hardly be placed with anyone else. After a brief trial the brethren had agreed. A man of moods, Bliss had appeared cheerful—even too merry for a minister—on the way out. Established in his church at Kohala, he had proved "an itinerant preacher"—walking about the house as he talked, grabbing the heads of men and women indiscriminately and shaking them to compel attention. The people were somewhat afraid of him, with his long face and his thin sandy hair. Nor were they the only ones. He beat his poor wife, Emily, while they were on a visit to widowed Lorenzo Lyons. He extracted heavy gifts from his people, turning church discipline against those who would not accept his low valuation of their offerings. "Wild, indiscreet and fickle," he turned out to be wholly unfitted for the ministry or for missionary life. The mission sent him home.

At the general meeting in June, 1837, the greatly augmented mission went about the usual tasks of assigning stations and deliberating on things of the spirit. Honolulu was split into two areas, partly as a response to renewed Catholic activity. Lowell Smith, another young Williams graduate from a Berkshire hill town, took charge at the new station, Kaumakapili. More circulars went forth to the United States, urging the necessity of converting the world.

The home board had already had enough of the circulars. They now severely censured the Hawaiian Mission for presuming to tell them how to convert the world, forbade them to send home any such communications in future or to come home themselves without prior permission.

"Are we to be made slaves of?" Lorrin Andrews indignantly wrote to his father. "Are we to be refused the use of the press, our bodies and our minds confined? Thus you are now paying your money to the A.B.C.F.M. to keep your son in bondage to the Prudential Committee." Far better if each congregation in America would support a missionary directly, and do away with the dictatorial board, argued Lorrin.

The brethren had been prepared to fight lust, rum, indifference, Catholicism, heathenism, rioting sailors and backsliding Hawaiians. But now to find themselves opposed by their own board! It was hard to take.

Nevertheless they went on with their work. A handsome stone meeting house had been completed (January 31) at Kailua thanks to the efforts of Governor Adams. With bell and steeple, it looked mighty like New England. After a town meeting had been called in Honolulu in 1836—the first of its kind in the islands—the people voted to build a stone church there too. The work began on a wave of enthusiasm and on a grand scale, with basement walls forty-four inches thick and huge sills and posts that had to be pulled by hand as much as ten miles. But the enthusiasm dampened as the scope of the work grew clearer.

"As it has cost the natives so much labor and oppression," wrote Amos Cooke to Sam Ruggles, "some of the brethren seem to think they shall be unwilling to preach in it."

The cutback in mission funds to a mere $30,000 for the whole year—to support more than forty families with their horde of children, carry on the mission press, provide medicine and school supplies and travel—now threatened disaster. True, the chiefs and the people did a great deal for the mission. They paid in kind for their books, contributed labor and materials to the building of churches and schools. But they would have to do still more, or the brethren would have to launch out on secular ventures of their own to support themselves. Farm-raised Yankees for the most part, they were quite capable of doing this if they had to.

Meanwhile they were getting shabby. Hiram Bingham, his one coat in rags, went to Peter Brinsmade's store for a replacement but refused to take it when he learned that the price was $27. After a while one came from the board, at a charge against his account of $17. "This is the only coat furnished me by the board in eighteen years," he remarked.

* * *

Far more than he minded his shabby coat, Hiram Bingham was troubled by the renewed attempt of the Catholic priests to get a toehold on Hawaii.

On April 17 (1837) Bachelot and Short returned aboard the *Clementine.* While Bachelot went ashore openly, Short tried to get in under the disguise of a long beard and a broad hat. Recognized, he nevertheless managed to get to his old quarters. Kekuanaoa as governor ordered both men to depart. The king, then at Maui, issued an edict to say that the expulsion order of Kaahumanu was still in force. But they refused to re-embark.

"If you can force a residence here against the will of the king, then *you* are the sovereign," Haalilio told Bachelot.

When Kekuanaoa led them back to the ship, the owner, French consul Jules Dudoit, carried the ship's flag ashore to Charlton's house since the vessel was under British registry. Charlton bore it out into the street and burned it publicly. The Hawaiian government had in effect seized the ship, he argued, in an act of piracy. At this point a British man-of-war, the *Sulphur,* arrived in command of Captain Belcher who immediately took Charlton's part. The argument was in mid-course when a French ship, *La Venus,* sailed in under Captain A. Du Petit Thouars. When Bingham, as interpreter, tried to explain the facts to him, Charlton interposed, saying, "The chiefs were well disposed. Mr. Bingham is to blame. He is the chief dictator in all these transactions."

"That is not correct," Bingham said.

Charlton's face flamed with anger. "Mr. Bingham, if you insult me again I'll horsewhip you," he shouted. Belcher, too, began to "rave like a chained tiger," shaking his fist in Kinau's face until her husband stepped between them.

"You ought to be sent off from the islands," Charlton yelled, continuing his attack on Bingham.

And Dudoit, joining the pack, "Mr. Bachelot shall serve you as you have served him, and land you on a desolate island."

"I was quite cool, and undisturbed—for me," Hiram recalled later.

There followed an exchange of letters between the Hawaiian government, Belcher and Thouars, the upshot of which was that Short and Bachelot were permitted to remain ashore until they had a suitable opportunity to leave. This amounted to an acknowledgment that the government had the right to send them away. Short finally left in November for Valparaiso, Bachelot a few weeks later with another priest, Maigret, who had meanwhile arrived and been invited to leave. The king then issued an edict forbidding the teaching of the Roman Catholic religion in the islands. The priests were certain that Bingham was at the bottom of all this, and so was Charlton.

In the midst of this hubbub John C. Jones sailed off to California, leaving behind him his two women—Hannah and Lahilahi—and their children.

Surveying the record of these crowded, troublesome three years—the defection of the princess, the continuing warfare with the foreign residents, with evil in all its forms whether liquid, vaporous or sexual, the bout with the Catholics and with their own board—Hiram Bingham and his brethren must have wondered which side of paradise they had settled in. Yet even now, in the midst of all their troubles, a wave was making up which would lift them higher than they had ever been raised before.

CHAPTER 16

A YEAR OF THE RIGHT HAND
OF THE MOST HIGH

1838

"THE SANDWICH ISLANDS, BUT ESPECIALLY HAWAII, ARE the scene of wonders," wrote Abner Wilcox, a thin, ascetic-looking Yankee from Connecticut who had reached the islands with that largest of all the companies. "Till within a year past all that Missionaries had witnessed of the outpouring of the Spirit was but as a few drops before a shower. Since that time God has poured floods upon the dry ground. I never yet in the most interesting part of a revival saw any thing which would at all compare with it in power. The most hardened sinners seem to melt like wax before the fire. . . .

"I finally believe that no scenes have been witnessed equal to it since the day of Pentecost," Abner concluded. "The work has been so powerful, the most hardened have been so convicted of the sin that they have literally roared out with anguish of spirit."

With his plump, pretty, almost Hawaiian-looking wife, Abner had been sent to Hilo on the island of Hawaii where he was placed in charge of the schools. Two Yankee preachers were already there—David Lyman and Titus Coan (pronounced Co-an), both like Abner Wilcox from small Connecticut towns which provided the majority of Hawaii's missionaries. Abner never went to college, but David Lyman was a Williams man who had gone on to Andover, met Sarah Joiner at a meeting of the American Board in her home town of Royalton, Vermont, married her and carried her off to Hawaii. Rather stern-looking, David was given to a good deal of soul-searching and worrying over his own state of grace. His character can hardly better be described than through his bout with the banana. David hated bananas, but knowing that they were an island staple, he got a bunch in South America on the way out, hung it in his room, and ate one every morning before breakfast. By the time the ship reached Cape Horn he had learned to like them.

Of the three missionaries stationed at once-inhospitable Hilo, however, Titus Coan was the firebrand. He was a fine-looking man, with deep-set, kindly eyes, long hair brushed back and falling over his collar, a strong mouth and a look of Christian love in the whole cast of his features. After a healthy, happy New England childhood he had followed his brothers into western New York. There, at a schoolhouse in Riga, he had seen a teacher "with a face like an angel." She was Fidelia Church of Churchville, another of the Yankee settlements in western New York. Though Titus often saw her in the choir, it was months before he met her. Then he went off on an exploring trip to Patagonia for the American Board. Returning in 1834, he hurried up to Middlebury, Vermont, where Fidelia was teaching in the Female Seminary. He took her back to Churchville, married her, and at the end of the year sailed with her for Hawaii.

Assigned to Hilo, the Coans took over the snug little Yankee house which Joseph Goodrich had built. (Goodrich had been sent home for paying too much attention to temporal affairs.) Two storied but low, it was painted red with white sills and casements to set off its double rows of small windows. Neat, snug and prim, it was famed all over the islands as the perfect reproduction of a New England farmhouse. Sailors far from their native towns grew homesick at the sight of it. It was the only frame house in all of Hilo. Near it the Lymans had a small stone house. Thanks to Goodrich's energy and skill, the mission buildings made a pretty cluster, their paths lined with pineapples and set off by fruit trees. Coan loved the place from the start, adding other trees to those Goodrich had planted. If, like a peach tree he set out, they failed to produce fruit they supplied a sermon. Coan also loved the spacious harbor with its crescent of fine volcanic sand, the broad blue ocean with its quiet surface of molten silver or its gentle throbbing as with life, the living green of the sloping land, the limpid streams and plunging water-falls.

Coan plunged into his work with almost frightening zest. Three months after his arrival he preached his first sermon in Hawaiian.

"Must be doctor, schoolmaster, lawyer, minister, carpenter, mason and a few other things in the same day," he wrote.

Leaving the schoolwork to Lyman, he dashed off on long tours of his big missionary district, his clothes and provisions packed into two big calabashes which a bearer carried slung from a pole. A complete tour of the Hilo district called for the crossing of sixty-three ravines whose depths varied from twenty to a thousand feet. Sometimes Coan leaped across with the help of a ten-foot pole and sometimes he mounted the shoulders of a stout Hawaiian, grabbing on to his hair while they struggled across a fast-flowing stream only a few feet above a plunging cataract.

Sometimes Coan tried to save time by taking to a canoe, but this, too, had its hazards. On one such trip the canoe was caught in a storm which filled it with water. Throughout the night the storm continued. At dawn, the travelers found themselves off a rock-bound shore where the surf still pounded. Men crawled out of the few huts along the beach. The travelers waved frantically at them. At last four men on shore, risking their lives, plunged into the huge waves and swam out. Ordering the tired crew to swim ashore, they took charge of the canoe while other men standing on high cliffs with signal cloths of tapa stood ready to tell the new crew when to strike for the mouth of a near-by river.

At last the signal came, the paddles were thrust into the water, the canoe rose upon a wave and running just ahead of its boiling crest, sped safely into the river's mouth.

As he traveled, Titus Coan sent a messenger thirty to sixty miles ahead to give word of his coming, so that the people could assemble. Usually they came in crowds, pressing him so that he had no time to eat, staying about him until midnight and returning at cockcrow. They were eager for the "Word of Life," and they liked his fiery way of bringing it. Fresh from the revivals of the famous Charles Grandison Finney, Coan was a spirited speaker, full of the warm, vibrant emotionalism which the Hawaiians loved because it was part of their own natures. He seized upon their minds with his pithy aphorisms couched in familiar language—no windy, abstract doctrine for him. Sometimes he shot a question at his congregation. From thousands of throats came the roared yea or nay the preacher expected of them.

At an outdoor meeting in the Puna district Coan was preaching repentance when a man burst into fervent prayer. The sword of the spirit, he said, was thrusting him through and through. Tears streamed down his face as he said, "Lord, have mercy on me; I am dead in sin."

He trembled. Others began to weep aloud, to tremble and to pray. For twenty minutes the preacher could not make himself heard. Then he tried to calm them.

Like the diseases the white man had brought, religion now swept across the islands. The Hawaiians, who had, naturally enough, remained cold to the doctrines of Calvin, took religion to their breasts when it offered an emotional substitute for the things mission influence had forced them to abandon—the hula, the *mele* (poetic chant), the games.

"The presence of the spirit was indicated by the fixed eye, the gushing tear, the quivering lip, the deep sigh, and the heavy groan," noted Coan, as attentive to symptoms as a good doctor. The response at first surprised, then startled and finally scared some of the missionaries.

But not Titus Coan. He was delighted.

"The word fell with power," he wrote, "and sometimes as the feeling deepened, the vast audience was moved and swayed like a forest in a mighty wind." People poured into Hilo from the countryside in order to be near their pastor. Whole families came, building little cabins that stretched up from the shore like the tents of an army. The little village of Hilo grew to ten thousand. People stayed long enough to plant potatoes and taro. The church grew crowded to suffocation with thousands still outside. Without telling Coan, the people went up into the forest, cut timbers and dragged them with ropes made of vine and bark through mud, streams and jungle down to the town.

"We will build a second house of worship so that the people may be all sheltered from sun and rain on the Sabbath," they explained when Coan asked what the piles of timber were for. "And this is our thought: all the people of Hilo shall meet in the larger house, where you will preach to them in the morning, during which time the people of Puna and Kau will meet for prayer in the smaller house, and in the afternoon these congregations shall exchange places, and you will preach to Puna and Kau people; thus all will hear the minister."

Only one village in all Coan's vast territory remained inhospitable. When the pastor stopped there they refused to feed him, saying they had no food for themselves. Yet they ate when they thought he was sleeping. At last, after several fruitless visits, he said he would not come again until he was sent for. Soon afterwards a crater erupted, wiping out the town. Those who managed to flee the crater were stricken with smallpox, and the few who crawled off into the jungle in their illness were eaten by swine. No wonder the people felt that "the word fell with power!"

"I hear some praying," wrote Abner Wilcox, "as if they would do violence to heaven." Abner estimated that of the twelve thousand souls in Hilo and Puna hardly a thousand above the age of eight could be found who did not think themselves to have experienced a change of heart.

Coan always preached six or seven sermons a week, and on his tours as many as thirty. Wherever he went, talking to the people personally as well as in church, he noted those whom he thought sincere converts. He entered their names, unobserved, in a notebook. The list rose to three thousand. Vigilantly he kept track of these people for several months or a year. Those who stood fast were invited to come to Hilo where they were watched over and instructed from week to week and from day to day, still under close scrutiny. Any who knew anything against them were urged to testify.

Coan selected 1,705 who had stood the test. At last, on July 7, 1838, the immense crowd marched into church. Row after row, they were lined up the whole length of the building with only room enough between the lines for Coan to pass. Every name was called, every individual recognized and seated. Then all the members of the church were called in and seated on the opposite side. After singing and prayer, Coan with a basin of water and a whisk broom passed back and forth between the lines until all had been sprinkled.

"I baptize you all into [*sic*] the name of the Father, and of the Son, and of the Holy Ghost. Amen," he said.

"All heads were bowed, and tears fell. All was hushed except sobs and breathing." He then administered communion to twenty-four hundred. During 1838 Titus Coan admitted more than five thousand. To give communion to such a crowd, he had to gather them in a grove.

Some of the brethren frowned upon Coan's methods, his enthusiasm, his way of dispensing religion wholesale. Others, however, felt it was about time the mission—the largest in the world—began to show results. The board at home was growing critical; the financial panic was cutting funds to a dribble. It was a providence of God, thought Bingham, that at this critical moment "these heavenly showers" should fall upon the islands. Meanwhile, he concluded, God had deflated prices at home to punish those who had hitherto failed to give generously to missions. This interesting explanation of the Panic of 1837 has somehow failed to work its way into standard histories of the era.

While Titus preached, his wife, Fidelia, taught. "In the female Boarding School of Mrs. Coan was heard the voice of supplication and long weeping," wrote Abner Wilcox with satisfaction. "In the boarding school for boys also there was a very great weeping."

This was the school David Lyman had started in 1836, in a couple of thatched buildings between his house and Coan's. Starting with eight boys, Lyman had thirty-one by year's end. After several years' trial, he decided that he could do best with boys from ages seven to fourteen. Promising students were sent on to Lahainaluna where further education, it was hoped, would fit them as church, business and government leaders.

Though Lyman got up at four every morning to read the Bible in Hebrew, he let the boys dawdle in bed until five. After prayers they worked at raising their own food until seven o'clock breakfast. School hours were from nine to twelve and two to four. Then they worked another hour in the fields. In the evening there was music and prayer. The gift of a few musical instruments—flute, accordion and cello— aroused a real interest in instrumental music. Mrs. Lyman showed the boys how to make bamboo flutes. When a visiting ship gave a brass band concert, the urge to make music overleapt all bounds. Homemade flutes, fifes, violins, clarinets, even slide trombones flourished. Finally enough real instruments were collected for a real band. Sarah Lyman taught the boys to play instruments she had never played herself. To the accompaniment of flute and viol they also sang every Sunday in Coan's church.

It was a remarkable school in many ways. A pioneer in vocational training, it taught the boys farming, tailoring and dairying as well as the three R's. Hygiene, astronomy, anatomy, geography and Bible were also in its curriculum. Games and recreation found a place too. Although the boys got an occasional thrashing, or had their food rationed in punishment for trying to steal food for midnight feasts, they thrived on the regime. Visitors found them healthy and robust, even if they did occasionally run short of poi and have to climb for breadfruit. Even after the enrollment had reached sixty, the Lymans managed to run the school on $500 a year—thanks in part to the fact that Sarah made up the whole lot of pantaloons for the student body! Of course in Hawaii's climate they would have been better off without any, but no Yankee was going to teach boys whose bottoms were unswathed in pants.

The Reverend Lorenzo Lyons, who had lost his beautiful Betsey the year before, came to Hilo to marry one of the "single females," Lucia Smith, in July of 1838. Whether or not he carried the enthusiasm of his "beloved Brother Coan" back to his upland station of Waimea, it is a fact that he produced the most converts next to Coan —so many that even Hawaiians at other places were skeptical. Lyons seemed to take to the Hawaiian language from the start. He thought like a Hawaiian, absorbed the poetry of their language and gave it back to them in Christian hymns which they learned and loved. His influence in shaping Hawaiian as a written language was second only to the Bible.

In spite of his many converts and the love his people bore for him, Lyons had his troubles. A rigid disciplinarian, he would allow none of his church members to smoke or plant tobacco or to waste the daylight hours in sleeping. They must build good houses, cultivate the soil, avoid quarreling and love one another.

His early visits through the country districts met with ridicule, dirty gestures, obstruction. The people refused to tell him their names, or answered in derisive singsong. They were sure he was going to kill their children and put them in barrels, or serve their blood and brains at communion. One night he went to sleep in a house with a few tapa curtains for privacy. Suddenly the curtains were thrown up exposing a crowd of men, women and children.

"What do you wish?" he asked, starting up.

"We wish to see a white man's body, after it is undressed."

But as the people perceived his skill with words, his untiring labor for them and his love, they responded with true Hawaiian warmth. One man, seeing Lyons on the road, ran into his house and got out his Testament, then began to read very loud while he pretended not to have seen the preacher. And this, too, was a testimony of love.

Richard and Clarissa Armstrong, earnest, big-eyed and still young-looking, were now well established at Wailuku (Maui) in a low, sturdy stone house which Richard himself had helped to build. It was beautifully located at the top of a long, slow rise from the sea with sudden green mountains behind and a rushing brook near by.

"My work is pleasant but arduous," Richard wrote home. "I attend a meeting every morning at dawn of day and speak to an audience of about two hundred, visit my schools from eight to nine, then attend the sick, bleed, blister, cup, poultice, dress wounds, give doses and all with the air of a notorious quack. Then go to my study, till some one calls for books, advice, etc., which is often in five minutes and repeated constantly till ten o'clock at night. I am cumbered with many cares. In the afternoon I teach singing and lecture again. On the Sabbath I preach at sunrise, speak to the children at ten, a sermon at eleven to the people, Bible class at one, lecture at four, and on Mondays am somewhat blue. I spend every third Sabbath at the out station where the labor is greater than at home."

Throughout the islands the revival swept. People who had never been seen before appeared in the churches—the blind led by children, cripples crawling on hands and feet. Children gathered together in little groups and prayed and wept together in the cane fields and banana groves—imitating like children everywhere what they saw in their elders. A wave of aloha for the missionaries arose in Hawaiian breasts. The very faces of the people, thought Ephraim Clark, had changed from a stupid expression to one of lively intelligence. Although fewer than thirteen hundred Hawaiians had been admitted to church membership before the revival, twenty thousand were taken in during the years of awakening. Congregations of three, four and even five thousand were common.

Even the king, chastened by the death of his beloved sister, was now on the side of the *pono,* the good. Living at Lahaina since Nahienaena's death, where the ocean sparkled under a cruel sun and the lovely mountains thrust their bright greens against a cloud-studded blue sky, King Kauikeaouli supervised the building of his coral palace near the beach or sported with moon-faced, squinty-eyed Kalama. The king himself was now a handsome young man of twenty-four, with heavy brows and deep, dark eyes. A moustache which joined a fringe of trimmed beard gave him a rather patriarchal look. In later years he got rid of the beard but kept a moustache.

To show the earnestness of his conversion, Kauikeaouli gave up drink, shut down his distilleries and outlawed the importing of spirits. Then he chose William Richards, now back from America, to be his chaplain, teacher and translator. Richards severed his connection with the mission and went to work translating books on the science of government and lecturing to the king, chiefs, and Lahainaluna scholars on political economy.

As confidential adviser to the king, Richards was now the most influential foreigner in the islands. Though no specialist in government, he had had as good a college education as any of the brothers. He also had, behind his heavy eighteenth century features and domed forehead, strong principles and driving energy. The heavy pouches under his eyes, the heavy black eyebrows and incongruously dimpled chin, the deep hollow in the middle of his upper lip gave him more the look of a country squire than that of a minister of government. Armed with a text written by President Wayland of Brown, Richards plunged into the sea of politics amid howls from the foreign residents that the mission was usurping the throne.

The government Richards undertook to serve had evolved from absolute monarchy under wily old Kamehameha I into one with powers divided among three agencies—the king, the kuhina-nui or premier, and the council of chiefs. The common people still had no rights beyond that of leaving a chief who bore down too hard on them. But Richards entered the government with the assurance that the king wanted to make changes in favor of the people.

When he left the mission to become the king's adviser, William Richards had translated seventeen books of the Bible, fourteen of them single-handed. His skill in Hawaiian was but one of the reasons why the chiefs trusted him implicitly.

Another mission brother chose this year to leave the fold. Reuben Tinker, coming to a slow boil as he pondered the new rules of the board against writing to home newspapers, leaving the islands without permission, and acquiring private property, sent in his resignation to Boston in April.

The whole problem of relations between board and mission was aired at the yearly meeting—now no longer a general one since funds were lacking, but an assemblage of representatives from each island. The brethren discussed abandoning the common stock system for one of salaries—a question that had been raised as early as 1831. A missionary and his wife would have an annual salary of $400, with allowances for children. A single woman would get $150.

But they came to no final decision. How, for instance, could they do without the commissary run by patient Levi Chamberlain who dispensed their flour (complete with mold and maggots), their sugar (cockroaches), their chamber pots with and without covers, their writing paper, gingham (pink, buff, stripe and plaid), printed goods (nice, small, and large figure), green silk for bonnets, bed cords, ox bows, shoe blacking, tools? For trade with the Hawaiians he also supplied brown, bleached and blue cottons, soap, slates, pocket knives, scissors and fishhooks. Without these supplies, the economy of the mission stations would collapse.

Feeling that they had a good deal to be grateful for, on December 6 the families in Honolulu gathered together to celebrate the first Thanksgiving in the islands "in imitation of New England custom" as Levi wrote. From then on Thanksgiving was an island institution, though celebrated usually in December. By 1850 cross-cultural currents had reached the stage where at a Thanksgiving feast Hawaiians ate their poi with spoons while the Americans were dipping it out with their fingers.

The mission, in 1838, was *not* thankful for the establishment of the first English newspaper in the islands. Started two years before, the *Sandwich Island Gazette* had jumped on the mission with both feet. Strongly pro-Catholic—many of its articles were by the Reverend Robert A. Walsh who had managed to get a foothold in the islands despite government opposition—it lambasted the mission for "black cloth, long faces," for backbiting, deception and inconsiderate interference in their neighbors' affairs. To its editor, Stephen Mackintosh, Bingham was "the great ventriloquist" who "was at the elbow of power, to throw his poisoning voice between the lips of government." In long-winded articles unadorned with fact the editor claimed that the mission was a complete failure. With all his tub-thumping, however, Mackintosh could not make a go of the paper. He quit and left for home at the end of 1838, leaving the paper in the hands of a group of local men including Father Walsh, John C. Jones and Stephen Reynolds.

To round out the year, Jones had returned from California on December 4 with a señorita who had managed to lead him to the altar. The premier, Kinau, called him to account for this, but he refused her summons. At last on December 20 he was haled to the fort with Hannah and Lahilahi. Kinau reminded him that a dozen years before when Christian marriage had been established, Kaahumanu had told him to choose from his many women the one wanted. He had pointed to Hannah, saying, "This one." Yet he had lived with Lahilahi after that and now here he came with still another woman whom he claimed as a wife. This was bigamy—at least. What did he propose to do about it?

Jones apparently refused to do anything. Angered both by his behavior and his manner, Kinau wrote to President Van Buren, requesting his recall.

Recalled forever, in this eventful year, was faithful John Honolii who had come out from the United States with the pioneers after a schooling at Cornwall, and who like Thomas Hopu had remained a good and faithful servant, having "walked irreproachably with this church" as Titus Coan noted in the church record at Hilo. Though he died in February, before the great influx of July, John had lived long enough to see the groundswell of the oncoming wave of repentance and salvation which made 1838 a peak as high as Mauna Loa in the annals of the Hawaiian mission—in Hiram Bingham's phrase "a year of the right hand of the Most High."

CHAPTER 17

UNDER FIRE
1839

WHEN THE JUDDS' SECOND CHILD, A GIRL, HAD BEEN BORN IN
1831, the great chiefess Kinau had come to see her. Hawaiian fashion, she had announced that she wished to adopt the child. Laura
Judd, too weak and fearful to say no, sent for her husband.

"We don't give away our children," said Dr. Judd, who feared
nobody.

"But you are poor, I am rich. I give you much money."

"You can't have her," said the young doctor, his iron jaw rusting
into firmness.

Kinau, herself young and iron-willed, tossed the baby onto the bed
and walked away. But at the christening she appeared, elbowed the
doctor aside and with a haughty glance at him said, "Call the little
baby Kinau."

Christened Elizabeth Kinau, the child grew up under the eye of
the large but beautiful chiefess. Many an afternoon she spent at the
palace near the fort, or riding with the premier in her light blue hand-
cart lined with red velvet, watching the ground rush out from under
her feet as she rode with her legs dangling from the cart's tail. Elizabeth loved to look at all the wonderful things Kinau owned—her
Chinese shawls, her rich clothing, brought to her in exchange for
sandalwood, from all parts of the world. For the mission people
"lived very poor," as Elizabeth's mother had confided to a friend,
with very little milk and no butter. Even bread was too great a luxury
for them. The board, decreeing that American flour was too ex-
pensive, had advised them to eat the locally produced arrowroot.
Made into a kind of pudding, it was fed to the children with molasses three times a day. One pious mother made her children eat a

213

pint of it before each meal so they would not hunger for the scarce, imported supplies.

In 1836, when Elizabeth was five, the Judds had moved across the street from the old mission house to a new one built for the doctor. Of one story (a second was added later), it had a high cellar where Dr. Judd kept his office—one side lined with shelves and drawers full of medicines and instruments, the other with benches for his patients. Three deep casement windows built into the corral walls formed little wells into which the mission children loved to creep, watching the doctor while he bled his patients, making a swift, sharp incision and letting the blood trickle down the victim's arm into a basin.

By 1839 the Judds had six children. So Laura, after eight years of teaching with the youngest baby in a cradle by her side, decided that her family needed her full attention, even though she had Polly Holmes to help her.

Now Dr. Judd was called to take care of Kinau who, herself the mother of five, was suffering from—mumps! These childhood diseases could be fatal to Hawaiians—thousands had been swept off by measles—but Kinau was making a good recovery when a tidal wave left thousands of fish on the shore and stranded inside the reef. The temptation was too great. Excited as a child over this rare stroke of fortune, Kinau joined her people in gathering the harvest. On the thirtieth of March she suffered a stroke. When Stephen Reynolds called on her the next day he found her unable to speak. Two days later she appeared to be half asleep, and could neither hear nor see. On the fourth of April she died, still young and unwrinkled. The missionaries, as Reynolds noted with some satisfaction, had again lost their mainstay.

After the funeral, King Kauikeaouli proclaimed Kekauluohi premier. Like Kinau, Kekauluohi had been a wife of King Liholiho and before that, a wife of Kamehameha I. Her father had been a half brother to Kamehameha I. She was therefore the king's sister-in-law and cousin. Living in a two-storied foreign-style house surrounded by the thatched houses of her retainers, Kekauluohi was called "the big-mouth queen" by the foreign residents—a reference to physical size rather than talkativeness. Six feet tall and weighing three hundred pounds as became an important chief, Kekauluohi was vastly impressive in her yellow silk with huge gigot sleeves, her tiara of rare golden feathers surmounted by a large tortoise-shell comb. Yet there was a sweetness and good nature in her round face which tempered the regality. Receiving foreign visitors, she sat in a large arm chair draped with a feather mantle, her man's shoes sticking boldly out from under the hem of her dress.

To balance the loss of Kinau the mission completed an achievement towards which it had been striving for nearly twenty years— the translation of the whole Bible into Hawaiian. To hurry it along, Hiram Bingham rode up to his little cottage at Punahou every day. In this retreat—now being enclosed with a stone wall—he could get a few hours alone. Always when he returned to town his house was thronged with people waiting to see him. But each day he came closer to his goal.

At last on May 10 the final sheet was pulled at the enlarged print shop across the street from the little coral building where Elisha Loomis had set up the first mission press. The mission printers had trained a whole shopful of Hawaiians in the work, every stage of which they now performed under the general supervision of one or two haoles.

Far ahead of their time, the mission brethren had cast the Hawaiian Bible into poetic form wherever the original called for poetry, thus producing a text which captured the genius of the Hawaiian language as expressed in the now-forbidden meles—chants. Also Hawaiian in style were the "begats" with their resemblance to Hawaiian genealogical verses. If the mission had done nothing else, its work in establishing a written language and preserving the beauty of the old Hawaiian poetry have entitled it to first place among cultural influences in modern Hawaii.

It was with this achievement to strengthen them that the brethren came to their yearly meeting at Honolulu in June, where they had to deal with a complaint from Kekauluohi herself (also known as Auhea) that church regulations were getting altogether too strict. Good people were being excommunicated, she complained, for wearing wreaths of flowers, eating dog, planting tobacco, or even for failing to attend every church meeting.

There was no doubt about it—some pastors were enforcing a discipline no American congregation would have submitted to. The brethren deliberated a long time before they were able to answer Kekauluohi, and their answer shows clearly enough that they still did not agree among themselves. About wearing flowers, all agreed that "they are foolish and cause pride. We command all churches to forsake beautiful and childish things which decorate their own selves." As for eating dog, church members were guilty of the sin of falsehood when, having given it up, they returned to it. Not that it's fatal, argued the brethren, but it's disgusting and unwise. Here again they were unable in their minds to separate the essentials of Christianity from all the other aspects of their own European-Calvinist-Yankee culture. Tobacco was clearly an evil since it caused intoxication and even death. "We wish you would give it up. This is our word of love and exhortation."

The brethren also had to grapple with the problem of church government. Most of them were Congregationalists. In the Congregational church, power resides in the people, in the members. Historically Congregationalism stressed the priesthood of all believers, the right and duty of the individual Christian to choose his own form of worship and to join together with others in a covenant with God, thus forming his church and thereafter choosing his pastor and elders. But in Hawaii the church could hardly develop in that way since the Hawaiians lacked any tradition of self-government. The brethren had improvised various means of dealing with the situation, but chiefly had kept control of the church to themselves. Now they decreed that ruling elders should be elected and set apart and that these together with the pastors should be a committee for governing the church. Those churches which preferred a congregational form of government should be at liberty to adopt it, but would still be under the control of a presbytery, in which they would be represented by their pastor and a delegate. Each island was to form a presbytery, and these acting together would constitute a general council.

"Congregationalism as such does not properly exist among you," complained Rufus Anderson, secretary of the board, "yet two-thirds of our support is from Congregationalists. . . . They do not yet know this."

Even more urgent was the problem of salaries. As the voluminous correspondence between Levi Chamberlain and the outstations clearly shows, the common stock system was growing impossibly cumbersome. Items interchanged among the various stations had to be credited or debited to various accounts. Shipments arrived in poor condition or failed to arrive at all. Dr. Baldwin, for example, who seems to have possessed as hot a temper as any of the brothers—his correspondence is full of controversies—gave Chamberlain a dressing down for sending sugar which had been "damaged" by cockroaches. Patiently Levi explained that he sent out nothing he was unwilling to use himself.

Many of the brethren were now in favor of arranging for their own support by investing small sums in a sugar mill or other work, employing Hawaiian labor and thus teaching industry as well as finding their own keep. It would also be far better for the people, they argued, to support their own ministers.

But the board, having decreed that missionaries had no right to private property, forbade this logical next step. "The right to acquire, hold and dispose of property furnishes the great and commanding motive to industry and economy," argued the brothers, "gives life to enterprise and allows the full development of the benevolent feelings of the soul." Here was good Calvinist doctrine! Yet the brethren had said, three years previously: "No man can point to private property to the value of a single dollar, which any member of the mission has acquired at the Sandwich Islands." Obviously an important shift was taking place in the thinking of the mission, forced by the sudden and drastic cutting down of funds from home, but also by the realization that if the declining population was to be saved and taught to thrive, the mission brothers would have to lead the way.

While the mission struggled with the problem of church government, William Richards was leading the chiefs towards the declaration of rights which came out on June 7.

"God hath made of one blood all nations of men," it began, "to dwell on the face of the earth in unity and blessedness. God has also bestowed certain rights alike on all men, and all chiefs, and all people of all lands.

"These are some of the rights which he has given alike to every man and every chief, life, limb, liberty, the labor of his hands, and productions of his mind."

Clearly the hand of William Richards, and of the faith which had sent him to Hawaii, informs these lines—even to the careful omission of "the pursuit of happiness" as a right Hawaiians had exercised with altogether too much enthusiasm!

After tracing the origin of governments to God, the declaration went on to establish a sort of civil code covering taxes, inheritance, fishing and water rights and the governing of the individual islands.

Built into the declaration, which was incorporated into the constitution of the following year, was the idea that government is a contract between God, the rulers and the people—a concept central to the thinking of the first American Congregationalists, the Pilgrims.

* * *

The chiefs had no sooner proclaimed these shiny new rights than an incident took place which to the foreign residents seemed to deny their existence.

On June 24 two women, one about fifty and the other thirty, were dragged to the house of Premier Kekauluohi by a mob who accused them of idolatry and following the religion of the Pope. In the evening they were moved to the fort where, in the absence of Governor Kekuanaoa, they were fastened in irons. One woman was taken to a tree where her arms were shackled to a limb over her head. The other, her legs in irons, was shackled with her arms over the rafters of a thatched house, her face pressed against the rough ends of the thatch. During the night heavy showers poured down upon the women, and when the sun rose they baked in its rays. No one brought them food or water. "The calls of Nature they were obliged to obey as they stood!!" wrote Stephen Reynolds, who with the rest of the foreign residents went running to the fort to see what was going on.

Thinking that Hiram Bingham could get the women released, William Hooper went in search of him. He found him doing an errand in town. "Perhaps if you inquire, you will find the women are confined for some offence against the laws, not for being Catholics," he said, and drove off, promising, however, to speak to the governor immediately. To Bingham's credit it must be said that only a week before he had received the assurance of Kekauluohi that the punishment of Catholics had been brought to an end. The foreign residents, however, saw in Bingham's refusal to visit the fort an approval of religious persecution.

Artemas Bishop, hearing what was afoot, went to see for himself. "I never expected to see such a thing," he confessed. "I shall put my veto against this today."

Taking the law into their own hands, the foreign merchants released the women, finding their hands cold, their wrists lacerated and swollen, their heads burning with fever. After recovering a little, the prisoners were led away, meeting Governor Kekuanaoa who having spoken with Bingham was headed for the fort.

"Your business is to take care of your stores," said Kekuanaoa, angered at the merchants for taking the law into their own hands. "That is the road to them. The government of the island and fort is mine—this is my path." And he took the women back to the fort, examined them and dismissed them, fining the officer who had tied them up.

The echoes of this affair had hardly died down when into the harbor on July 9 sailed a French frigate of war, *L'Artémise*. The commander, Captain C. P. T. Laplace, after consulting no one but the local French consular agent, Jules Dudoit, issued an ultimatum charging the Hawaiian government with persecuting Catholics and Frenchmen and demanding that Catholic worship be immediately declared free. To make sure that the government would carry out the promise, twenty thousand dollars were to be placed in the captain's hands. The alternative was war. The sixty guns of the *Artémise* were ready to lay Honolulu flat.

Sending the bad news to Brother Baldwin at Lahaina, along with the request that he urge the king to hurry to Honolulu, William Richards ended: "I never felt a sweeter and all pervading confidence in God's good designs for this nation than now."

On the same day Peter Brinsmade, American consul and friend to the mission, put up a public notice for all American citizens. Laplace, he said, had offered asylum aboard his ship to all American citizens in case hostilities should begin—to all, that is, except the American missionaries.

Premier Kekauluohi urged Laplace to put off his threatened war from the twelfth to the fifteenth so that the king would have time to arrive. Meanwhile the local residents came to demand of the chiefs what protection they could expect for themselves and their property in the event of war. The chiefs, who had once prided themselves on their prowess in war, had to advise the residents to "arm themselves against the Natives for the protection of their persons, families & property," and in case of war to arrest or even fire on any Hawaiian attempting to steal, kill or set fires. Having received this unusual authority, the residents requested Laplace, whom they treated as a hero, to furnish them with the arms they might use against the Hawaiians. But Laplace with many polite words refused to supply them. "I have prepared forces sufficiently strong," he boasted, "that in giving a dreadful blow, the French shall be the masters and the protectors of the town at the same time."

None the less, the residents, apparently enjoying the game, formed a vigilance committee, appointed Stephen Reynolds chairman, and gathered up all the lethal weapons they could find.

The *Gazette,* backing them and Laplace to the hilt, praised "the noble and magnanimous king, the beloved and ever-to-be-admired Louis Phillipe" whose name it could not spell, who had sent his "beautiful ship" commanded by the "brave and gallant" officer. Never before had there been so welcome an arrival in Honolulu harbor, drooled the *Gazette.* In the next column stood the peremptory demands of Laplace against a defenseless government.

On Saturday, the thirteenth, Governor Kekuanaoa without waiting for the king to arrive, carried the $20,000—borrowed from the local merchants at high interest—to the frigate. He also gave Laplace the dictated articles signed by Kekauluohi and himself.

The king arrived the next day in time to see Laplace come ashore with 120 marines and 60 seamen under arms. Headed by a military band and with fixed bayonets gleaming, the party paraded through the streets to a mass celebrated in one of the king's houses by the patient but now-triumphant Father Walsh.

Angered at this insult to his sovereignty, the king said of the capitulation of the governor and prime minister: "They ought to have waited till the war-club touched the forehead."

Only three days later, however, the king himself capitulated to a further set of demands which, under the guise of a treaty of perpetual peace and friendship, forced Hawaii to admit French brandy at a duty no higher than five per cent and required that French subjects accused of any crimes whatever should be tried by a jury of foreign residents. The article admitting brandy was clearly opposed to the law passed only the year before. No wonder that when Amos Cooke, one of the more recently arrived missionaries, looked in on Bingham at this time he found him singing and playing the bass viol "to soothe his agitated spirit!"

On the twentieth Laplace sailed away, well satisfied with having cowed the helpless little nation into submission. Thereafter, one word —*palani*—meant both "Frenchman" and "brandy" in Hawaiian.

The brethren did not, however, take the enforced introduction of Catholicism complacently. Lowell Smith, another Williams man from the little Berkshire hill town of Heath, wrote to Dr. Baldwin that Hawaii might expect an influx of Catholics like the locusts of Egypt as a result of the treaty. From his pulpit in Honolulu's Second (Kaumakapili) Church he had preached against them, he boasted, "with direct reference to stamping this 'other gospel' in the dust, and informing my congregation that the teachers of this new gospel are to be accursed of God. (Gal. 1:6-10). Walsh has his apostles all over Oahu, entering into the churches and leading off the goats, and collecting all the chaff, wood, hay and stubble that they can find."

The missionaries wanted to get into print a true account of Laplace's discriminatory acts against them (they had already written to Congress), and looking around for the person to do it, chose James Jackson Jarves. Jarves, a young man who had just reached his majority, had first come to Hawaii in 1837. A guest of Consul Peter Brinsmade and recommended to Laura Judd by her favorite "Aunt Bacon," Jarves' own aunt, the young man was welcomed by the mission. Leasing some land on Kauai, he had gone into silk-raising, and then had returned home for the girl to whom he had become engaged when he was eighteen, she only sixteen. In October, 1838, Elizabeth Russell Swain became Mrs. Jarves and, October 20, sailed with her shy and modest young husband for Honolulu.

The silk plantation was not doing well. Within a year Elizabeth—

Libby—was writing home that all hope of success had been given up and all the money poured into it sure to be lost. So when the mission asked James Jarves to write an account of the *Artémise* visit for a short-lived journal called *The Hawaiian Spectator,* he was glad to comply.

His account rocked the Honolulu community. Jules Dudoit, the excitable French consular agent, ran to the king claiming libel and demanding that Jarves be prosecuted. When the case was referred to arbitrators on August 14, William Richards' testimony so enraged Dudoit that he followed him out of the room with a horsewhip, shook it under his nose and shouted that only his black coat saved him from a drubbing. Jarves refused to apologize for the statements that exasperated Dudoit. Libby Jarves wrote home that Dudoit prowled the streets asking if anyone had seen that rascal Jarves, as he intended to horsewhip him. If told that Jarves had just gone into Brewer's store, Dudoit would then start off in the opposite direction still asking for that rascal.

While Honolulu was still at the boiling point over *L'Artémise* and the Jarves article, the village crier on August 24 went through the town calling from one end to another the news that Liliha, the still handsome widow of Boki, was dead. Almost as quickly ran the rumor that she had been poisoned. If the story was true, there was poetic justice in it, for Liliha, who with her husband had been the protector of the grogshops, had died of drinking poisoned liquor. Suddenly she had fallen down, moaning and foaming at the mouth. According to Reynolds, who never missed a crumb of gossip, it was Kekauluohi herself who had ordered the poison because of jealousy over Governor Kekuanaoa.

There was a good deal of wailing, for Liliha had been loved by many—perhaps too many. Kamakau says in his history that the river of Kikihale was stamped dry by the feet of people coming into Honolulu to express their grief. Whether this be regarded as a symbol of the horror with which Liliha regarded water, or of the drying up of the sparkle and flow of ancient Hawaiian life under missionary influence, it was true enough that Liliha was a symbol of the old ways for which many a Hawaiian still hankered. Had she not stood out against the mission-influenced drive against liquor and sex and hula?

Had she not been deposed for standing up to the whole crowd of chiefs and missionaries? Yes, Liliha was the symbol of a golden past that perhaps had never really existed but that certainly could never— the Hawaiians had to face its now—return. The world had caught up with them with its treaties and trading, its accent on grasping instead of giving. No longer could a woman give herself to a man out of sheer aloha; she had to expect recompense—either pay or marriage. No longer could a whole village while away the days of the Maka- hiki in surfing, dancing, bowling and the hundred pastimes of old. Now a man had to work for a living. Pleasure was frowned on for its own sake. At this very time Lowell Smith was expelling people from his church for wearing the lovely strings of feathers and for smoking pipes.

With Liliha the hope of all this died again, and died forever.

CHAPTER 18

THE CHIEFS' CHILDREN'S SCHOOL
1839–1849

WHEN THE CHIEFS PETITIONED THE MISSION TO OPEN A school for young chiefs, Bingham, Whitney and Armstrong were appointed a committee to consider it. Sturdy republicans, raised in the atmosphere of town meeting and the public school, the Yankee missionaries disliked the idea of making any special arrangements for children of chiefs. Yet they were not going to school—even the inferior schools available. They were growing up ignorant and indolent when the nation had need of young people able to govern. So with some misgivings, and with sturdy objections from some brothers, they decided to go through with it. With the king's example before them, they could see no other way to keep the chiefs of the future on the side of what the mission stood for. Amos and Juliette Cooke were chosen for the job.

"Here is our thought to you, that you become teacher for our royal children," the high chiefs wrote to Amos on June 1 (1839). Reluctantly, Amos and Juliette agreed to take over the ticklish job of training up the future rulers of the islands.

Since their arrival in 1837, the Cookes had had some experience at teaching Hawaiian children, and they knew it was no cinch. Reared under New England schoolmasters who literally believed that sparing the rod meant spoiling the child, they were prepared to teach the young chiefs obedience if nothing else, knowing well enough that the wrath of the chiefs might descend upon them.

They made a good team, even though their marriage had been another of those hasty affairs consummated on the eve of sailing. Amos, whose desire to be a missionary in Hawaii had been aroused by Sam Ruggles, had asked two other girls before Sam suggested Juliette

Montague. She hated to decide so quickly, asked the members of her church to meet together and seek an answer for her in prayer, and with Yankee caution had Amos get the board to send along credentials on his character! The time was getting so short by now that they could not marry in Massachusetts, Juliette's home state, but had to go to Amos' home in Danbury, Connecticut, where the reading of banns was not so lengthy an affair.

Amos had a stern mouth but kind eyes. Juliette, though no beauty, was a pleasant, efficient young woman, skilled in all the household arts and an able teacher.

On June 13 Dr. Judd came to the Cookes' door with word that the governor of Oahu, Kekuanaoa, had brought the children and they had better start their school. They had no building and apparently little of anything. Yet there was nothing to do but begin.

The children were Moses, Lot and Alexander—the sons of Kinau and Governor Kekuanaoa; Bernice Pauahi, the daughter of Konia and Liliha's one-time boy-friend Paki; William Lunalilo, the son of Prime Minister Kekauluohi and her husband Kanaina; and Kelii. In Hawaiian fashion, most of them had been adopted by one high chief or another even though their own parents were high chiefs. That the adoption was more than a legal fiction could be seen by the way they clung to their adoptive parents. Young Moses, when his adoptive father Kaikioewa tried to leave him at Oahu with his real mother, ran to the wharf, held on to the brig that was taking the Kauai governor back to his post, and yelled and howled for two hours. At last Kekuanaoa, his real father, had to send a file of soldiers down from the fort to arrest and convey the lad to the palace near by.

Moses' brother Lot put up a similar struggle when parting with his adoptive father, the governor of Maui, to go to school. His *kahu* (nurse or guardian) brought him bawling into class.

The Cookes tried to make the youngsters feel at home, but they would put up with no nonsense. The first time Amos applied the rod to ten-year-old Moses the boy cried that he was the son of a chief.

"But I am king of the school," said Amos, laying it on.

No chief's child had ever been disciplined before. Each had a string of attendants who followed about, anticipating every need. Alexander, only five years old, had a whole establishment of his own where he lorded it over twenty-five willing slaves. But Alexander had been adopted by the king, which placed him on a pedestal higher than that of his older brothers, as he well knew.

One day when the boys were talking about the future, Moses, the oldest, said, "I shall be governor of Kauai."

"I shall be governor of Maui," said Lot.

Said Alexander: "When you are governors who will be king?"

To take care of these youngsters, and the others who would be coming along, the chiefs began to build an adobe structure in the form of a hollow square with quarters for the Cookes and twenty boarding students, and with a schoolroom, parlor, dining room and bedrooms. In the center courtyard was a well with an iron pump. The *Artémise* affair put a stop to construction for a while, however, and it was not until April, 1840, that the Cookes could move in. By then they had sixteen students—the oldest thirteen, the youngest two!

The opening of the new school was celebrated with a feast, after which Hiram Bingham dedicated the house and several other brothers spoke, and the king shed tears, and the children sang. A few weeks later the children moved in. Governor Kekuanaoa decided to spend the night there with his three boys. He and all the kahus had been weeping at the thought of parting, and some of the children cried themselves to sleep. It was no happy occasion for Juliette either. She dreaded the thought of having these spoiled children in her household where they might corrupt the manners of her own little Joseph or of the child she was now carrying. They were a bunch of little tyrants, she confided to her family at home, and she would prefer to teach the poor and ignorant. Yet she sympathized with them in their homesickness. (She knew well enough what that was like. "You ask what you shall send me," she wrote home. "I would thank you for a snowball.") Too late, she realized that she should have prepared some games for them.

The children seemed to have recovered some of their cheerfulness by morning, yet they kept looking over the fence for their kahus who lurked near by, and some got over the fence to them. Poor Juliette wrote her mother that the confusion was almost more than she could bear. But gradually the children grew accustomed to their new environment. They had been used to loving attendants who did everything for them; now they had to do for themselves. They had been accustomed to eat when they were hungry, sleep when they were tired, and play when they were not merely idle. Now they had to rise early, stay awake all day, study six hours or more, and eat regularly.

They never could get used to eating only three times a day. The three meals provided but Spartan fare to youngsters who had been urged to eat and grow big as became chiefs. A thick slice of bread covered with molasses was all they now got for supper. It seemed to them that they were always hungry. They smuggled in food with the help of their kahus, were punished for it, searched the garden for anything edible and devoured it, and were punished again.

To help the Cookes with their difficult tasks the chiefs had chosen one of the finest men in the islands and his wife—John Ii and Sarai. In spite of his cragged, heavy-featured face, John was as kind as he was able. Brought up in heathen days, he had been religious even as a boy, always reserving some of his fish for the gods. When the mission arrived he was attracted to the palapala and finally to the pule. He was one of those whom Liholiho had lazily turned over to the mission to study in his place. In 1828 John Ii joined Kawaiahao Church, Bingham's big Honolulu congregation. Soon his reverent, beseeching voice in prayer became a familiar sound. Guard of the young king's sleeping, eating, waking, Ii was a temperance man. The king's feathered friends scattered when they saw him coming.

John's wife, Sarai, was small for a Hawaiian—about two hundred pounds. Sweet of face, wavy of hair, she loved children.

In place of the horde of kahus, the children now had only John and Sarai to fall back upon when the Cooke discipline, with its strange, cold, foreign point of view, grew unbearable. It was not that the Cookes were unkind; it was only that their whole world was different, with no place in it for indulgence and ease and lassitude and whim and aloha.

One day, for example, the children got to talking about ghosts. They had heard a good deal on the subject from their kahus who, Amos Cooke thought, made a point of scaring the children so as to gain influence with them and make them think they would not be safe without a host of protectors around them. One of the older girls (which would mean Jane or Abigail or Bernice), having heard of the death of one of her kahus, told the rest of the children that the kahu's spirit was after her. The older children laughed, though a little uneasily. But the youngsters were scared—especially little five-year-old William, Premier Kekauluohi's son. That night William fell out of bed and woke up crying and yelling, *"He akua! He akua!—* A ghost! A ghost!"

Amos ran into the room where he found poor little William rolling around under the bed in a dreadful state. He quieted the boy and put him back to bed. Half an hour later he was screaming again. This time Amos told Moses and Lot to sleep with him. Sarai and John had come running in to see what was the matter, and Sarai stayed too. The three boys were awake at daybreak, talking it all over. This scared William again, setting off another train of cries. Amos, disgusted, ordered the older boys into separate rooms until prayer time.

"At noon I mistrusted Moses & Lot had gone into the rooms of the girls & went there and sure enough—they were there, and had gone to bed," Amos recorded. They were ashamed at being caught in bed with the girls, but Amos was scandalized. Juliette summoned the girls and talked to them while Amos lectured the boys. Thereafter heterosexual sleeping was tabued.

Along with their English, the children were acquiring a respect for the Cookes and a liking for the school.

The children liked nothing better than to be invited into the Cookes' sitting room of an evening. Often they would knock at the door, say, "I thank you walk in," and seat themselves on one of the painted chairs or on the koa settee while Juliette sat sewing near the central table where stood an astral lamp.

While the children studied English by way of Parley's spelling book—soon they were also studying their mathematics and science, their history and theology in English and hardly using Hawaiian at all—they had plenty of opportunity for exercise. The Cookes were not going to make the mistake the mission had made in some of its other schools, confining indoors children who had spent their lives in the sun. So there was sailing and riding, walking, playing ball, rolling hoops, flying kites. Swings and seesaws were put up in the yard. At

Waikiki each of the scholars had a surfboard at the royal bathing place where they often went for a swim.

The four oldest Judd children joined the school and liked it, despite the discipline. Lot and Alexander joined Nelly (Helen) and Elizabeth Judd in an accordion quartet. The music, of course, was hymns. The two future kings were bright lads, and Elizabeth marveled at the skill they displayed in mental arithmetic in school examinations. The king, impressed with the children's affection for each other, suggested that Lot marry Elizabeth and Nelly Alexander. The Judds offended the king by turning down the proposal, but Lot continued to whisper his alohas to Elizabeth in church, and once even saved her life when her horse sank in quicksand.

Everyone thought the scholars a handsome lot as they marched to church of a Sunday morning in pairs—Moses and Jane, Lot and Bernice, Alexander and Abigail, William and Emma, James and Elizabeth Kekaaniau, David and Victoria, and so on down to the little toddlers John Kinau and Lydia (later Queen Liliuokalani).

"A happier group of children than they now are, is seldom found," the Cookes were finally able to report. But, like children anywhere, the young chiefs were always getting into trouble. Alexander and William sneaked out of a window to go and play. On the way back William hit his head and raised a big bump. The doctor came, and immediately the kahus sprang up from nowhere and ran crying to see what was the matter. Moses tried to hang from a crossbar over the gate while letting his horse run out from under him. He missed the crossbar with one hand, fell to the ground and lay stunned for ten minutes. Dr. Judd found that he had broken a hand. Governor and prime minister came on the run, and both slept in the room with him, the governor on the bed, the prime minister on the floor.

The youngsters celebrated the Fourth of July and the New Year with firecrackers. But as they grew older, the fun began to take on a boy-girl slant. One night a group of the older boys sneaked out and went, disguised, to the dancing school Stephen Reynolds held.

Moses, the oldest boy and a big, square-built fellow, was the ringleader. He usually took Lot (later King Kamehameha V) and Alexander (Kamehameha IV) along with him. One evening Sarai woke the Cookes to say that the three were missing. John hurried off to

Moses' kahu and found the boys there. They had been there many times for wine, he learned, and drank it frequently. (At this time Moses was sixteen, Lot fifteen, Alexander only eleven.) The boys promised to stop drinking, but they continued to slip out at night, even after a guard had been posted. And they continued to get hold of wine.

Soon the chance discovery of some letters opened up a fantastic plot. Moses was in touch with a man named Binns through whom he and Lot proposed to escape to a ship and sail off to some place where teachers were not so strict. Scarcely was this affair exposed when Moses admitted that he had been in Jane's room by invitation.

Then the sad truth came out that Lot, at sixteen, had made Abigail pregnant. Richards talked with them; Lot was ashamed, Abigail not. It was out of the question for Lot, a royal child, to marry Abigail, so a marriage with a commoner was arranged for her.

This was bad indeed, but worse was to follow. Moses, who had continued to disappear from the school at night, was detected in an intrigue with the queen. He was expelled from the school and lost control of his property, while Governor Kekuanoa put a notice in the newspaper that he would not be responsible for his debts. Poor Moses died two years later before he was twenty.

Governor Kekuanaoa wanted Bernice Pauahi (daughter of Paki) to marry Lot. But she didn't care for him. She did, however, fall in love with a young man named Charles Bishop from the United States. Her father was angry and refused to come to the wedding, which took place on June 4, 1850, with the Cookes and Armstrongs as witnesses.

By this time most of the chief's children had finished the course and there were no more young ones coming along. The once-noisy buildings had grown so quiet that Amos was able to have a study of his own for the first time. Wondering what to do next, Amos thought of going into business. He had two thousand dollars, left him by his father. Men had done well in the islands with no more than that. But the mission persuaded him to stay on as assistant superintendent of secular affairs, for a while at least.

The school, renamed the Royal School in 1846, lived on in another form and in a new building as an English day school for both Hawaiian and haole children.

Discouraged in his effort to make little Yankees out of Hawaiian chiefs, Amos Cooke concluded that the school had been a failure. Yet when Dr. Judd took Lot and Alexander with him to England, Lady Palmerston herself complimented the boys on their manners, and inquired where they had been taught.

"We have a little court of our own," said the doctor, laconically. What the boys had, they had learned largely from Amos and Juliette who with great reluctance and many misgivings had, out of pure Yankee stubbornness, stuck to the job.

Four kings and a queen—better than a full house—had passed through their hands. No one had had a greater chance to shape the destiny of the nation.

CHAPTER 19

ERUPTION

1840

PEOPLE HAD BEEN MISBEHAVING. NOW IT WAS NATURE'S turn. Looking from the window of his snug little Yankee house in Hilo, Titus Coan saw a glow in the sky one evening towards the end of April. Word soon came that Kilauea crater, about twenty-five miles from Hilo, was belching tons of red-hot lava into the sky.

Pouring over the crater's rim, a river of lava began to burn its course through trees and tree ferns. The river went underground, came out again, and then tunneled another six miles. At last, on the third of June, the vast volume of smoking, flaming stuff seared its way seaward in a river as much as two miles wide. Sometimes it moved five miles an hour, sometimes only half a mile. But it never stopped.

It reached the sea at a point where a sheer cliff rose thirty to fifty feet above the ocean. Here a moving sheet of fire a mile wide poured in a liquid firefall down into the churning ocean. As the cataract thundered down, the sea leaped to meet it, boiling and raging, raising clouds of steam that filled the whole sky. For three weeks the river of fire poured into the salt ocean. When it stopped at last, thousands of acres lay under the deadly blight of the lava—land forever useless.

To the Yankee preachers, some of whom had now spent twenty years in the islands, the event was full of signs and symbols. They saw in the eruption a visible sign of God's might, his displeasure with some of the goings on in Hawaii, and a sample of the eternal fate he had in store for unbelievers and apostates.

The Hawaiians saw things too. Some still believed in Pele, goddess of the volcano. They saw in the eruption a sign of her displeas-

ure that the old ways had been forsaken. Others who had freed themselves of old superstitions and embraced the new learning—men
like David Malo—found in the destroying river of fire an illustration
of what the haoles were doing to Hawaii.

The merchants of Honolulu were not as sensitive to symbolism as
preachers in search of a metaphor or Hawaiians with their love of
poetry. But they were unhappy about the state of things too. While
the new newspaper, *The Polynesian,* was full of their long lists of
goods for sale, Stephen Reynolds complained in his journal:
"$8.37½ cash taken in this week!" and wondered how he was to go
on living. A couple of enterprising Cantonese, Sam and Mow, tried to
lure customers with this singing commercial:

> Good people all—walk in and buy,
> Of Sam and Mow, good cake and pie:
> Bread hard or soft, for land or sea,
> "Celestial" made; come buy of we.

There were a dozen Chinese in the islands now, their long queues
and skull caps and their flowing gowns giving to Honolulu the first
authentic touch of a cosmopolitanism that was to become a major
part of its charm.

So the three principal groups of residents—the original proprie-
tors, their religious counselors, and the merchants—believed, each
in its own way, that the islands were, indeed, on the edge of a volcano and that disaster, either from sinning or sickness or want of
trade, hung over them all.

The mission, to be sure, was not entirely dissatisfied with its
twenty-year effort. A fifth of the total population had been admitted
to church membership after leaping the many hurdles set up by the
missionaries. All the important chiefs except the king himself had
joined the church—which was called simply the Christian church.
The brethren had seen no need to engage in theological hair-splitting,
at least not before the Hawaiian public. Although some of them had
been raised as Presbyterians and most as Congregationalists, they
found that neither the Hawaiian language nor the experience of the
people could cope with doctrinal subtleties. Most of the brothers
seemed happy to have it that way. They preached the basic things—

Jesus Christ as the savior of man, the need to live a blameless life in order to be saved (they did not get into the argument over justification by faith or works), the overruling power of God.

In twenty years the mission influence had placed the stamp of Yankeeland so firmly on the islands that it would never be wiped off. The mission houses and many of the churches had that Yankee look about them—as did the homes of sea captains and merchants with their widow's walk or Nantucket platform. Nearly a hundred million pages of Hawaiian text had been printed, fourteen thousand children went to school, young men were graduating from Lahainaluna who would be able to cope with the weighty problems the islands had to face. Yet the brethren had not seen their way to ordaining a single Hawaiian preacher.

The influx of Catholic priests, after Laplace, gave them their excuse. Church members were being lured away by promises of cures, they reported. Instead of asking for contributions, Catholic priests were giving presents, especially to children who were brought to be baptized. They held short services with no sermons, had no objections to smoking or drinking, promised indulgence to the sinners and willingly received any to membership. Instead of building good Yankee houses, they adopted the Hawaiian style of living.

The Yankee preachers thought this unfair competition. The Catholics might have retorted that they were doing what the Yankees should have done in the first place—accepting as much of the native culture as possible instead of trying to wipe it out root and branch.

This struggle between branches of the Christian religion was symptomatic of a wider struggle. The European powers were beginning to see that Hawaii might be of strategic importance as a point of transfer and refreshment in the potentially vast trade with Asia and the whole Pacific area. But while they maneuvered, the Yankee traders and whalers had already dug in.

The Hawaiian government was in no condition to cope with these converging foreign interests. As Laplace had shown, the islands were helpless in the face of any infringement of their sovereignty. The undeveloped land resources were a constant lure to foreigners. The chiefs had always been reluctant to sell or even lease land to foreigners because control of the land had always been their handle of power. But if they did not use the land themselves, how long could they deny it to others?

The old chiefs, meanwhile, were dying out. Hoapili, governor of Maui, had died on the third of January. A true Christian and loyal supporter of the mission, he had had himself carried to the stone meeting house at Lahaina only ten days before his death, once more to see the building he had been instrumental in raising, the first stone church in the islands. When the king visited him in his last illness, Hoapili begged him to change his ways and live according to God's word. Laying his hand on the king's lap, he had burst into a flood of tears.

King Kauikeaouli, still young and handsome with his dark eyes and clipped moustache, was living at Lahaina now, wasting a mint of money on the big coral palace which was never to be finished. Meanwhile he lived with his retiring, now half-invalid Kalama in a grass house hidden in the trees.

Prime Minister Kekauluohi and Governor Kekuanaoa had struck up an alliance that was more than political. "She is too fond of our governor and her fondness is reciprocated," Lowell Smith wrote to Dr. Baldwin. "They cannot keep apart and I have got tired watching them." Coan was finding that Adams, last of the old group of island governors, was not yet too old to cut up. "You speak of Adams marrying," he wrote Baldwin. "We are overwhelmed—it is adultery of the most unblushing sort."

To offset this bad news, the mission gained an important victory when, through the agency of Brother Richards, the chiefs proclaimed a law for the common schools and took over their support. The schools had been a heavy burden upon the mission, its funds still drastically reduced. Now, following the famous Massachusetts school laws of 1642 and 1647, Hawaii was to have a common school in every community. Where there were fewer than fifteen children, communities were to club together. The fathers were to elect a school committee which together with the local missionary would choose a teacher whose support would come from nine days' labor a year supplied by each member of the community. Each island was to have a school agent, and before long (May 11, 1841) John Ii was chosen for Oahu, David Malo for Maui. Malo, a graduate of Lahainaluna, was also superintendent of the whole. The law had to be amended the following year, the Catholics having naturally objected to its favoring the Protestant mission.

David Malo, with his curly hair, neatly bowed brows, wide upper lip and a quizzical look that promised intelligence as well as curiosity and a sense of humor, was one of the ablest Hawaiians the mission had trained. Born a commoner about 1793, he had been taken into Governor Adams's family as a youth. In 1823 he had moved to Lahaina and in 1828 joined the church there. Arriving in the same year which brought William Richards, he had formed a firm attachment to the preacher. During the thirties David had raised cotton and woven his own cloth, happy to walk about in a truly homemade suit. Then he had started to raise cane—sugar cane, that is—growing modestly prosperous from the sale of molasses. Perhaps it was some of David's that Dr. Judd wrote to Lahaina for and apparently failed to receive. "How is it about my bbl. of molasses? Dear, sweet molasses, when shall I see thee?" he inquired of Baldwin.

With his beloved wife, Bathsheba Pahia, whom he had married in a Christian ceremony, David Malo was one of the leading Christians in the nation. He was one of the first to be lifted by a mission education up to a level of influence equal in some ways to that of a chief.

* * *

On the third of August Honolulu was stirred by an epochal event. The Binghams after twenty years in Hawaii were sailing for home. For years Sybil had been in poor health—"a careworn pilgrim" one of the arriving missionaries had thought her even eight years earlier. For months she had hardly been able to stir from the sturdy rocker in her bedroom—that same chair which the resourceful Hiram had built for her out of bits and pieces years before. Wise, motherly, careful, she still remained the presiding spirit of the household, her eyes and hands still usefully employed. Hiram, now fifty, was none too well himself, though he had never relaxed his grip on the mission or his control over the minds of the chiefs and the people. There was something slightly mesmeric about Hiram. Even the children felt it— they were a little afraid of him yet glad to be in his presence, feeling the emanation of his calm strength. Hiram hated to give up, though the mission "reluctantly but on the whole cheerfully" approved their going home for a visit to their two daughters, one now married, with the hope that they would get well and return.

Crowds came to the house and then to the dock to bid them farewell. The wailing was so great that a missionary had to climb into the rigging to comfort the people.

So goes one version. But Stephen Reynolds thought otherwise.

"Mr. Bingham had been begging besides all the missionaries to help him, in the Desk [pulpit?], in the natives' houses and in the streets for more than two months past of the natives. This morning those who had not found means before went to his House—the street was thronged. Bingham had occasion to cross the street to Doct. Judd's quite often; every time he crossed he stopped, collected money until his pockets were full—then step into his House or the doct., empty them and cross again. All the way up the street he was accosting the natives—receiving money. After he got aboard about an hundred women were on the wharf. Bingham could not let this opportunity pass. Down he goes among them to see what he could get. An eye witness said he took more than twenty dollars—his pocket was 'very full.' He is gone, it is hoped never to return, nor any of the rest of the blood-sucking—cash-sucking—lazy—lying wretches."

There were mission brethren who would have gone at least part way with Reynolds in his criticism of Bingham. Richard Armstrong, who took his place as pastor of Kawaiahao, the First Church of Honolulu, thought him "a compound of vanity, self-importance, forwardness, obstinacy, self-complacency, and at the same time kindness, moderation, conscientiousness, firmness and piety." Clarissa Armstrong wrote her brother that she hoped he could make a teetotaller of Bingham while he was home, and also in smoking. "This is a hard post to labour on account of the former slack management of the church," she confided.

No one, however, had a word to say against patient, kindly, long-suffering Sybil. Behind her self-depreciating manner there hid a rock-like strength, not only to endure suffering, but to direct even King Bingham. "Mrs. B. lays out the work and Mr. B. does it," one of the sisters recorded. Still, Hiram Bingham had a large share in leading

Hawaii into the world of nations and in defending the best interests of Hawaii against the avarice and lust of sailors, traders and would-be imperialists.

With the Binghams went their three youngest children, Lucy Thurston with three of her own and another mission youngster. Lucy, the only one who had kept her children in the islands until they were young ladies, was now taking them home. Persis was now almost nineteen, Lucy seventeen. Mother Lucy had hoped Asa would go with her, but Asa said no, he had engaged to come to Hawaii for life and he proposed to go through with it. So he stayed at Kailua with the other three children, well supplied no doubt with Lucy's rules and regulations. She had finally permitted her daughters at twelve and fourteen, when she considered their characters formed, to learn Hawaiian and then to teach in Sunday School. "They were allowed to come in contact with the natives as teachers, under school regulations, but not as associates." That was Lucy's firm rule, from which she never deviated.

A six-month trip carried the Binghams and Thurstons to New York where Lucy the younger promptly caught a fever and within a week was dead. "The loveliest of my family," lamented her father when the sad news reached him. In his loneliness Asa had meanwhile sent to Honolulu for a bass viol, and was cheered to learn from Levi Chamberlain that it was on its way.

"The special object for which I desired it," he wrote, "is to try to teach some very base singers to sing bass, as my voice is not of sufficient compass as to sound the low bass notes with clearness. It may also assist my thoughts to rise in praise to God. I have no one now to sing with me in the morning and evening hymn."

It was not with any great enthusiasm that Clarissa and Richard Armstrong left the beautiful location and comfortable home at Wailuku on Maui to take the Binghams' place. Slim and dark, with large, earnest eyes, Richard Armstrong nevertheless set energetically to work. He divided the huge congregation into ten schools, each one of which he met every other week. Though he had no enthusiasm for the "outlandish" stone church which Bingham had begun, he saw it through to completion. It was Bingham, however, who had designed it, figured out how the huge walls could be roofed in, and specified every brace and timber. Kawaiahao Church remains his monument to this day.

* * *

The gossipy little town of Honolulu buzzed with news. A great exploring expedition was on its way to the islands under the command of Lieutenant Commander Charles Wilkes. Peter Brinsmade, a pious merchant who had once been a preacher, had been so eager to be on hand for its arrival that he had stayed in Honolulu though his wife was said to be dying on Kauai. He went to her at last, and she obligingly died in plenty of time for him to get back and greet the expedition.

James Jackson Jarves, his silk plantation a failure, had hopefully begun to issue *The Polynesian,* a weekly paper favorable to government and missionaries. It didn't pay him much—Libby wrote home to her parents that they were very poor but happy and in love. She hated being economical, she said, it was such hard work. She and James were living with the Judds. Yet she managed to have a piano on which she played prettily. The Judd children loved to hear her—especially "Woodman, spare that tree."

Jarves had a hard time finding news enough to fill his four pages, even though much of his space was taken up with reprints from home papers and with the long lists of things for sale by Honolulu's merchants. "The stone church is taller, business duller, eggs cheaper, the streets cleaner, the plain greener, news scarcer and the *Polynesian* drier—this is growth in Honolulu," he reported.

Surprisingly, he printed little about the U. S. Exploring Expedition, which arrived in the fall and spent half a year in the islands. It had already been out for two years when it reached the islands, and was to continue two years more before reaching home, its two sloops-of-war, the *Vincennes* and the *Peacock* supported by several smaller ships and equipped to study all forms of natural life as well as to explore and map. When he reached Honolulu, Wilkes had already discovered the Antarctic continent, though he was to be charged with having invented it on his return home. It was not until 1909 that his discovery was verified and Wilkes Land named in his honor.

His ships had hardly cast their anchors when the girls came swimming out, many of them half drunk and smuggling liquor aboard. The grogshops of Honolulu gave Wilkes plenty of trouble, and at one point he had to go into the streets to prevent his men from breaking into the fort where some of their drunken buddies were being held.

Wilkes was not much impressed with the streets of Honolulu. They were of no regular width, he reported, and were ankle-deep in dust. Hogs wallowed in their many sinkholes, rising to shake dust over the pedestrian. Though *The Polynesian* reported that the streets were even then being widened and straightened, there were really only four in the whole town—King, Merchant, Beretania and the one leading to the Punchbowl.

The ever-present dust gave its color to the town, Wilkes noted—to the mud walls drooping with erosion, to the houses like haystacks, even to the skin of the people. No trees lined the streets; there was neither shade nor verdure. Hawaiians padded about in all sorts of dress and undress, many still with nothing but the malo or breech-cloth. Some wore shirt, vest and coat but no pants, and one a pair of white mittens. The women had gone into "long loose garments like bathing dresses"—New England's gift of ugliness to Polynesia, the Mother Hubbard. If a sudden shower came up, you might still see pretty maidens decked out in their best dresses shuck them off and roll them up, heading naked for shelter—to protect not themselves or their modesty, but the dresses. Yet when the governor visited Wilkes aboard his ship, no prince of Europe could have looked nobler. Tall, large, and dignified, Kekuanaoa wore a full dress uniform of blue and gold. Received aboard with manned yards, he behaved as if he were accustomed to such courtesies every day. Such Hawaiians did not have to put on dignity, for it was a part of them. Many of them have it to this day.

If Wilkes found Honolulu drab, he also found it squirming with life. From the thick-walled fort and the neighboring royal enclosure with its handsome native-style palace, on out to the mission buildings with their adobe wall and garden, Honolulu was lively as a hive. Intermarriage, or in any case interbreeding, had produced as much variety in feature and skin color as there was in costume. Windmills turned and creaked. Kites of every size and color filled the sky, including Chinese kites that made music as they soared.

But the big thing was racing on the plain on Saturday afternoon. Bare-headed and bare-breeched, their naked legs gripping the horse, their bodies bent forward, the riders urged their nags forward with waving arms and loud shouts. Girls raced too, hair and ribbons streaming behind them as they sped.

Wilkes went to one of the famous school examinations, this one at Lowell Smith's Kaumakapili Church. Seven hundred children marched to the examination, bearing banners on which such inspiring legends as "Purity" or "Steadfast Faith" had been inscribed. Afterwards came the annual feast for fifteen hundred people—an occasion so popular that parents sent their children to the school in order to be eligible for the feast of poi, raw fish and molasses. The task of seating fifteen hundred hungry customers proving too much for the mild manners of the missionary, Governor Kekuanaoa sailed in, using his fist on men and women impartially, tumbling them amongst calabashes full of sticky poi and stickier molasses until he had seated or felled them all.

The big event of Wilkes's visit to Hawaii, however, was his exploration of the 14,000-foot Mauna Loa and of the crater of Kilauea. To handle the troop of about six hundred Hawaiians who would be needed to carry instruments and supplies, Wilkes needed someone who spoke the language. Having formed a high opinion of Dr. Judd, he asked him to go along. Judd consulted the brethren, who agreed that it was his duty to go. Wilkes was delighted with the doctor—with his efficient management of the large company of Hawaiians, his constant cheerfulness. He made everyone comfortable and happy, Wilkes said.

At Kilauea Dr. Judd went down into the crater to collect some of the hot, molten lava in a frying pan lashed to a long pole. Pausing by a small, apparently inactive crater to collect "Pele's hair," the doctor heard a sudden explosion. A fiery jet leaped into the air and a river of fire rolled towards him. In a moment a sizzling heat surrounded him. He made for the wall but could not get up over the projecting ledge. Trapped, he prayed to God for help. Then he shouted. Kalama, a guide, heard him and came running to the ledge. The heat drove him back.

"Do not forsake me and let me perish," Judd called. Kalama came again, threw himself on the ground, and seized Judd's hand in both of his. Judd pushed himself out and made a desperate upward lunge. It was not a moment too soon. The fire swept under him as he went over the ledge, burning his shirt-sleeves and wrist and blistering brave Kalama's face. In a few minutes the place where Judd had stood was filled with hot lava. With Yankee stubbornness the doctor went back and collected the lava he had failed to get on the first try. Then he had to run for it as the crater began to overflow.

Shortly after Wilkes reached the islands the king signed a constitution which created a representative body, thus giving the common people for the first time a voice in their own government.

"No law shall be enacted which is at variance with the word of the Lord Jehovah or at variance with the general spirit of his word," the constitution stated. The influence of the mission had thus at last been incorporated into the basic law of the land. Freedom of religion, the right to a proper trial, and the duties of king, premier, governors and the council of chiefs were specified. Provisions for courts and taxes were spelled out.

At last the rights of the people had been guaranteed. A community of interest had taken the place of the idea of chiefly supremacy.

Another important step took place while Wilkes was in the islands, and partly through his influence. Once again Hawaiians were prevented by law from making and using liquor. Though American influence took away liquor where France imposed it, at least the squadron, instead of sailing off with $20,000, left $62,000 in the islands.

Perhaps this was what was called balance of power.

CHAPTER 20

DAMN THE MISSIONARIES!

1841–1842

CHARLTON, THE BEEFY-FACED BRITISH CONSUL, WAS ON the warpath again.

The immediate cause of his anger arose out of an order from the governor requiring all Hawaiians to work on the roads—a form of taxation long in effect. He apparently felt that his consular privileges were being trampled on when his own Hawaiian servants were conscripted for the usual government labor.

Perhaps the real source of his irritation went back to a letter he had received from Governor Kekuanaoa in January, complaining that Charlton's cattle had again been eating and trampling the crops of the people, chewing the thatch off their houses and actually destroying the frail houses made of poles and grass.

"That is what I notify you of," said Kekuanaoa. "That is the proper thing to do between us who have the care of the government. They should be accompanied by some person, and return them to your pen this evening."

Ever since 1836 the Hawaiian chiefs had been trying to get the British to remove Charlton. King Kauikeaouli had even written a personal letter to King William IV, complaining that Charlton treated the high chiefs like criminals, threatening to cut off their heads and boasting that he would have the next British man-of-war wipe them out. But the British had not removed him. He had continued not only as consul but as a merchant, cattleman, and self-appointed leader of the foreign community. He had accumulated a comfortable property. According to the king's letter, he had also had a child by a Hawaiian mother though he lived with an English wife.

On the sixth of March Jarves printed in *The Polynesian* a private letter written by Charlton and relating to the labor tax. Charlton claimed he had never written it and that Jarves had invented it. But no one took much stock in Charlton's word. When the foreign congregation of Honolulu had compiled a singing book and were casting about for a suitable title, someone had suggested "The Honolulu Lyre." Objection was immediately made that Charlton already was that. The objection was sustained.

On the night of the sixth Charlton got a man named Starkey to go with him to Jarves' home. The two men walked up onto the veranda where James was sitting with his wife, Libby, and the merchant James F. B. Marshall, one of the predecessors of today's C. Brewer & Co. After treating Jarves to a torrent of abuse, Charlton brandished a horsewhip and brought it down on the young editor's shoulder. Marshall jumped upon Charlton and threw him to the ground. While they were going at it hammer and tongs Starkey engaged Jarves, who had the presence of mind to grab a cane which he broke over Starkey's head.

Charlton had meanwhile broken a finger and bruised his hip when Marshall downed him. When residents stepped in to separate him from the aroused Yankee trader, he retreated to the street, threatening prosecution and vengeance. The governor promptly fined the consul six dollars for assault and the citizens held a protest meeting against Charlton's behavior at which Brinsmade, Reynolds and others spoke up for Jarves. Clearly, the whole community was sick of Charlton.

* * *

As much as all Hawaii hated Charlton, it loved Kapiolani, defier of the volcano. Ever since the first missionary had seen her sitting naked on a rock near the seashore saturating her finely-proportioned body with coconut oil, Kapiolani had seemed especially drawn towards the message of the Yankee preachers. Shorty after her husband's death in 1831 she had suffered a slight stroke. Nancy Ruggles, who like all the mission group believed in facing death rather than avoiding it, told Kapiolani that she might be about to depart in the same fashion as Naihe. "Do you feel ready to go?" she asked.

"When I think of my many sins I am afraid, but when I think of the righteousness of Christ I am comforted," she answered.

Nancy was highly pleased with her answer, and equally pleased when the sensitive, thoughtful, loving chiefess completely recovered.

Eight years had passed since that recovery and Nancy had long since returned to the United States with her Sam. Kapiolani had continued to tour her district on Hawaii Island, caring for her people and leading them in the faith. But now, in the early months of 1841, sickness had caught up with her again. Examining her in Honolulu, Dr. Judd affirmed her fear that it was cancer of the breast and that it should be removed. There were, of course, no anesthetics. Antiseptics were equally unknown.

With the same courage which had led her to defy the volcano goddess Pele, Kapiolani made up her mind to the operation. To assist him, Dr. Judd called in Dr. Fox of the *Vincennes* and Dr. Robert W. Wood, a recent arrival in Honolulu who had already shown himself a good doctor as well as a flutist and a friend to the mission. While the three men prepared their bandages and instruments—including the large knives for the rapid incisions made necessary by the lack of anesthetics—Kapiolani walked about the room somewhat nervously. Excusing herself, she went into the next room where she prayed alone. Then, refreshed and strengthened, she came back, placed herself as directed and bared her large breast.

When the elliptical incisions were made in the brown skin and Dr. Judd was cutting away at the flesh beneath, he asked her whether it was painful.

"It is painful," she said, "but I think of Christ who suffered on the cross for me and I am able to bear it." Throughout the half hour of agony she uttered no cry or groan.

Judd was delighted with the way the wound healed; he was hopeful of her complete recovery. After six weeks he approved her plan to visit Maui. But before leaving Honolulu, Kapiolani took a long walk which brought on a pain in her side. None the less, she called on each of the mission families the following day, including those who were then visiting in Honolulu.

Shortly afterwards a livid red, tender spot appeared and spread in the area of the apparently well-healed wound. Judd recognized erysipelas, though no one in his time knew that it was a streptococcus infection. There was no effective cure. The disease spread rapidly.

After twenty-four delirious hours, gentle, intelligent Kapiolani died on May fifth. The mission had never had a more devoted friend or sincerer convert.

Dr. Judd had also lost another patient—Angeline Castle from Sudbury, Vermont. Juliette Cooke, who had come out on the same ship, thought Angeline and her husband, Samuel, the best of them all. "Himself and wife are such as I should select as favorites if I were to have any such," she confessed. "They apparently possess ardent piety joined to just such spirits as I love. Everything they say and do has a peculiar beauty and propriety in it to my eye." Since Castle & Cooke were destined to be linked names in Hawaiian history, Juliette's words have a prophetic touch.

But Angeline did not live to see the alliance. Wasting away with consumption and feeling herself near death, she called the mission children to her bedside. To each she gave some little token of remembrance, delivered with kind words and affectionate counsel. Frequently members of the mission came in to pray, read the Bible or sing hymns to her—even at the moment when they supposed she was dying.

When it was obvious that she could live but a few moments longer, Samuel said to her: "Having loved His own, He loved them unto the end."

"No doubt of that," said Angeline, and died.

Sam, left with his little three-year-old daughter Mary Tenney, soon took her to the United States where he married his dead wife's younger sister—the one for whom his daughter was named. Eleven years his junior, Mary was not so pretty as her sister. But she was far more rugged, living to be almost ninety and to pour upon Honolulu out of her wealth and affection a great number of benefactions.

*   *   *

Stephen Reynolds was dividing his time these days between cussing out the missionaries and "learning" some young ladies to dance. A fiddler of some skill, Stephen loved to see young misses move with grace and ease. Honolulu was all too backward in this respect, thought Stephen. So, with his fiddle tucked under his arm, he took to calling at Hannah Holmes' house where a crowd of hapahaole girls—

Elizabeth, Helen, Maria, Harriet—gathered to learn of him. In time the sessions moved to his own coral house near the point where Union and Bishop streets now meet. There many a passerby saw Reynolds scraping at his fiddle, nodding his head, or breaking off to correct the motions of one of his pretty young pupils.

Stephen Reynolds hated missionaries as much as he loved young ladies. Now he had new cause to hate them, for had they not persuaded the king to snatch every foreign resident's land from under him? This was the way Stephen interpreted the proclamation of June 18 which said that foreigners who had no written leases on the land they occupied should come to government for them. Long leases up to fifty years could be had at higher rates, short leases at lower.

Damn the missionaries! fumed Reynolds. They already have leases and deeds for their lands. Now they are having laws made to rob us of our holdings. "If ever villains deserved the gallows, they do. The only safety foreigners can hope for is through the French nation."

Stephen had a habit of blaming the missionaries for everything—a habit which was to become almost a reflex in Hawaii. The fact was that the chiefs had always felt that ownership of the land and sovereignty went together. When Richards tried to explain land tenure by fee simple, hoping to gain such titles for the common people and thus to encourage industry, an old chief had said: "If we cannot take away their lands, what will they care for us? They will be as rich as we."

The land always had belonged to the king and the chiefs, and they were not yet willing to give up their title to it. Yet the haoles raised such a howl when the proclamation went out that it was never fully enforced.

The chiefs were faced with an insoluble dilemma. Their own people were rapidly dying off, the foreign population gaining. Industry and productiveness must be raised, the land put to good use, or else control of the islands would fall to the foreigners. Yet foreign aid was needed to establish such industry and productiveness. And once it was accepted, control would again fall to foreigners. Trying to meet this problem, the chiefs again had to turn to foreigners for help—to Richards for advice about government, more and more to Dr. Judd for an additional opinion, and to Ladd & Co.—a Yankee firm operating government-leased land—for a possible way out.

On July 4 Reynolds heard that Ladd had got control of the whole island of Kauai for $4,000—"payable in Ladd & Company's spurious paper—to be paid in merchandise at the Koloa bank." Reynolds, with his keen ear for news, had got wind of discussions which were not completed until the end of the year, and even then the agreement, signed November 24, was supposed to be secret. What Ladd and his associates actually got was the right to use unoccupied and unimproved lands throughout the islands suitable for raising such crops as sugar, indigo and wheat, together with the necessary water power for milling. Joint stock capital would be raised both in the islands and abroad, and profits be distributed to the stockholders. Recognition of the independence of the islands by France, Great Britain and the United States was a condition of the agreement. To get this recognition and the necessary capital, Peter Brinsmade, a Ladd partner, now departed for America and Europe. A definite objective of the plan was to encourage Hawaiians to grow and sell agricultural products for milling, thus raising their standard of living and in time, it was hoped, overcoming the drop in population.

*   *   *

Saddened by the death of a new-born son, the king at last did what he had long been trying to bring himself to. He took the pledge. On April 26 at Lahaina he and thirteen chiefs joined the temperance society of which the king himself became president, with kindly-looking Dr. Baldwin as secretary. Then they all put their names to a paper promising to drink nothing alcoholic and surrendered the stocks on hand, except for seven barrels of rum which the king in a fit of economy returned for credit. Quick to follow the chiefs, the commoners now crowded up to sign the pledge too—fifteen hundred of them. The ceremony had to be carried over to another day.

Thereafter the king was a frequent speaker at temperance meetings, carrying his people with him to sobriety. So strong grew the feeling that Hawaiians looked with contempt at the drunken haole sailors who reeled through their streets. Hawaii became one vast cold-water army. On the anniversary of his temperance pledge the

king broke out a quantity of liquor which had been held in his cellar
and had it poured into the sea. No one seems to have inquired how it
happened that he had held this supply in reserve. Everyone was too
delighted with the change in the young ruler that went along with his
abstinence—his fatherly interest in his people, his good humor and
kindness and attention to affairs of state.

* * *

After years of discussion, the brethren finally went on the salary
system, with the permission of the board, in this year of 1842. The
board, though thinking it too large, granted a salary of $450. But
now a host of new problems arose. Who owned what? When a missionary had built his house with his own means, did it belong to him
or to the mission? What if it was built partly with his own funds?
How about the land it was built on? And how about herds? Granted
that the original cattle belonged to the mission; but what about the
increase?

"We cannot consistently engage in business for private gain," the
brethren concluded at their general meeting, nor could they possess
private herds. They voted to sell off the herds on Kauai that could be
dispensed with, the profit going to the mission.

Brethren in the country, who had put their own sweat into their
homes, gardens and cattle, thought they ought to be able to enjoy
them as their own. City brethren who had no such opportunities did
not see why they should be made the goats. Bishop, who had netted
$144 on the sale of butter and beef during the past year, did not care
for the board's attitude that every penny a man made by his own
good management had to go to the mission. He threatened to quit.

Lorrin Andrews not only threatened—he did quit. The board was
supporting slavery, he said, by taking money from slaveowners. He
wanted none of this tainted money. Leaving the school at Lahainaluna to which he had devoted most of his Hawaiian years, he took
steps to support himself—by serving as seamen's chaplain at Lahaina, by growing his own food, and by carrying on the printing and
engraving he had begun at the school. Actually he had asked for his
dismission (this was the word the brothers used) before the salary

system was voted. The common stock system, he thought, rewarded the lazy and industrious alike.

"My father has left the Board so we haf to work for our living," wrote ten-year-old Sarah Andrews to her grandmother. It was a neat distinction.

Levi Chamberlain thought Andrews ought to go home when he quit, and implied as much in a letter to him.

"I came here of my own free will," replied Andrews, "and accordingly, when I leave the islands it will either be by direct compulsion or under a conviction of duty."

Impatient at the mission's failure after all these years to do anything about the education of its children in the islands, Andrews set up a school of his own at Lahainaluna. The brethren at Honolulu felt that he was endangering their plan for a school at Punahou. They had begged the board to help them establish such a school, but in the end had decided to do it themselves, giving fifty dollars each out of their own pitifully meager funds. On July 11 the school finally opened in a new building two miles from downtown Honolulu where the Binghams had built their small adobe cottage on land originally given to Bingham by Boki.

To run the new school the brothers chose their colleagues, Reverend Daniel and Emily Dole, both from Maine, who had arrived only the year before. Emily was described as beautiful by contemporaries, though no portrait has survived. Daniel was scholarly, with the look of a stern disciplinarian. No beauty was Marcia Smith, now brought over from Maui to assist them. She looked the old maid she was—bony and sad of feature, and quick to punish her charges.

Into the new building poured the first fifteen students—the boarders with their carpetbags and boxes, their calabashes and Hingham buckets (wooden pails with a lid). The boys, wearing their hair rather long, came in long pants and short jackets, the girls in short dresses with pantalettes to the ankles. Within a month seven more arrived, and soon the school was taking care of thirty-four, nineteen of whom were boarders.

Their food was not only plain but scanty. Those who lived at home in Honolulu were better off, for they brought their own lunches and went home at night. One of the boarders grew so hungry that he took to pilfering these lunches. Instead of concluding that the diet might be inadequate, Daniel Dole advised the Honolulu parents to send smaller meals!

Discipline was strict—Marcia Smith apparently got her exercise by using the rod—and there was also work to do. Every student had to hoe in the fields which supplied the table. But they had time for sports too. The boys had twenty minutes a day for swimming. No dancing, cards or marbles were allowed, but ball games were permitted, as well as horse-back riding and occasional trips to the beach. It was a good outdoor life, and they thrived on it. But religion was not forgotten. Besides morning and evening prayers, there was a verse of the Bible to be learned every day. All seven had to be repeated on Sunday before the two-seated carts carried the scholars to church in Honolulu.

Dole did the best he could with his high-spirited students. They found him somewhat shy and retiring, though with a warm sense of humor, an excellent teacher to those who wanted to learn, but not too successful with those who would not or could not. But the mission children were mostly bright anyway—in spite of the fact that Miss Smith kept telling them they lagged far behind children in the States. It was not until they went home to college that they discovered they were far from subnormal; in fact quite the reverse.

Tragedy struck the school when Emily Dole died after giving birth to her second child, Sanford (later Hawaii's first president), in April, 1844. To assist the stricken Daniel, his former shipmates William and Mary Rice now came to Punahou where they remained for ten years until Rice left the mission to become sugar plantation manager at Lihue, Kauai.

With the opening of Punahou, Andrews' school at Lahaina was soon given up. After his departure from the seminary the mission transferred to it the attractive Emersons, Ursula and John. In their ten years at Waialua on Oahu they had built a strong station. Gentle, blue-eyed Ursula had walked hundreds of miles to tend the sick. A teacher, she had also labored to make the Waialua choir one of the best in the islands. The church fairly rang with the singing as the choir of big men and women swayed back and forth, their big chests heaving like bellows, their fine, full voices making the rafters vibrate.

Leaving two of their five children (there were three more to come) at Punahou, the Emersons went to Lahainaluna, horrified by the clouds of red dust which poured down on the schoool out of Kawaula —Red Gorge. The dust had to be shoveled off the verandas. John Emerson, a country boy from Chester, New Hampshire, studied the situation. Then he got the students to help him dig and blast a channel which turned the waters of a stream so that it would run through the school grounds. Lahainaluna changed from a barren dustbowl to a green and fertile hillside.

Meanwhile the school had sent a stream of useful young men into teaching and government. Only eleven "are doing nothing or worse" as the school report put it. With characteristic poetry David Malo, thinking of the influence of the school on the nation and at the same time of that strong wind from Kawaula said: "This is the torch that the winds of Kawaula cannot extinguish." But Waialua remained the Emersons' first love; they returned to it after four years and spent the rest of their lives there.

*   *   *

Among the Hawaiians in whom the mission had put its trust, Blind Bartimeus had finally in 1841 been licensed to preach. An eloquent speaker, he frequently seemed to light up from within, his rapid delivery, simple earnestness and poetic imagination holding his audience spell-bound. In 1843 he was given a station of his own at Honuaula on Maui, but sickness overtook his always feeble frame so that he soon had to move back to Wailuku. He died September 17.

At about the same time William Kanui, who had come out with the pioneers and soon been excommunicated for misconduct, returned to the fold. Long a wanderer, he had been in California when he heard a voice telling him to change his ways. Immediately he had returned to Honolulu, given up his sailors' life, and opened a school where he taught English to fifty boys, using the Bible and Webster's spelling book. Pleased over the one sinner who repenteth, the mission welcomed him back into the arms of the church.

And in Honolulu the great stone church was finished at last after five years of labor. "Tyranny and exaction laid its foundation," said James Jarves, "but voluntary labor completed it." It stood near the original mission station where seven houses, a printing office, bindery, workshop and storehouse were now necessary to carry on the work. On July 21, 1842, the church was dedicated with suitable ceremonies, packed to the very doors by those whose labors had helped raise it. Only the chief architect—the man who had encouraged the king and chiefs to support it, who had drawn the designs, determined the thickness of the walls and the proper size and placing of the roof timbers—was absent.

More than any other man, Hiram Bingham was responsible for the raising of Kawaiahao Church. So it took the shape of the plain, dignified churches he had known in his homeland, with nothing but the four columns in front and the wooden steeple (later altered to stone) to relieve its foursquare boxiness.

Hiram, meanwhile, was getting his children settled at home, preaching and talking about Hawaii, planning to write a book about the mission, and hatching a grandiose plan to Christianize all the heathen. When Lorrin Andrews heard of the scheme, he remarked: "I am glad to see his large mind at work on large things . . . but I should like to see some other man besides Brother Bingham at the helm."

This point of view must have reached the board, for in the fall of 1842 they requested Hiram to embark for Hawaii, apparently trying to force his hand. He replied that Mrs. Bingham needed another winter at home. When their stay was prolonged into the next year, Levi Chamberlain wrote to say that Armstrong wished to continue no longer at the Kawaiahao Church as substitute pastor. He either wanted to be given the post permanently or returned to Wailuku. Bingham, sensing that he was being shoved out, complained to the board that Armstrong was trying to replace pure Congregationalism with Presbyterianism. Nobody had the power to separate him from his church, he concluded.

But at last in 1846 Hiram faced the fact that Sybil would never be able to go back. So he resigned and received an honorable discharge. Sybil grew no better, and at last in 1848 (she was fifty-five now) she felt that her time had come. One evening in February she began panting for breath. Hiram helped her rise from the old rocking chair and led her to the window. Breathing in the clean, biting New England air she looked up at the stars. "How beautiful!" she said. Then with Hiram to support her she went back to the chair. She seemed to be praying.

"Let the Lord be praised," she said. Then, "The Lord cares for me. "Stop, stop, I live!" she cried, after a pause. Then, "Hiram! . . . Almost overcome. . . . Break the bands."

Hiram prayed and sang a hymn, "Go, pilgrim, to thy Savior; on joyful wings ascend."

Years ago, Sybil had prayed that when God sent the summons for her entrance into heavenly rest, she might be waiting in the chair with its firm, supporting arms that Hiram had made for her. And so it was.

Hiram never returned to Hawaii. He married again in 1852, and lived until 1869 without ever finding a permanent post suited to his abilities.

"You will always be distinguished for mediocrity of talents," a classmate had facetiously predicted at Bingham's graduation from Middlebury. "Probably no fortuneteller ever deserved more credit," Hiram remarked when recalling the prophecy twenty-six years later. This was modest in him, for he was a man of great and varied talents, ideally suited to the pioneer's task that had confronted him. If his firmness had amounted often to stubbornness, his fathering care to interference, his determination to dictatorship, these were qualities the first years of the mission had needed in order to survive. Through him the New England mind pressed its qualities so strongly upon Hawaii that other possibilities came to seem alien.

The whalers and merchants also did a good deal to change Hawaiian ways of life. But the mission changed their minds. It made them look at man, God and nature through new eyes. It altered their notions of the physical world, gave them the intellectual tools to grasp the new vision, changed their basic motivations and attitudes. And in the crises that lay immediately ahead, these attitudes were to be of historic importance.

Bingham was gone, but his influence was an inseparable part of Hawaiian life, history and culture. Even the great French and British empires would prove ineffective against the bulwarks Yankeedom had erected in Hawaiian minds.

CHAPTER 21

WITH BENEFIT OF CLERGY
1842–1844

WILLIAM RICHARDS STOOD UP IN THE STONE CHURCH AT LA-
haina which had been built under his care. Dr. Baldwin was in the
pulpit now, and plain, big-featured William Richards a servant of
government.

"Brethren, pray for us," he said.

Beside him was Haalilio, cousin and confidant of the king. The
church was stirred with a feeling of brotherly emotion for these two
men, about to depart on a difficult mission.

The purpose of the long journey on which they were to start went
back to the arrival early in 1842 of Sir George Simpson, governor in
North America of the great and powerful Hudson's Bay Company.
Simpson had shown himself so friendly to the Hawaiian government
that Richards and the chiefs told him about Brinsmade's mission (in
connection with the Ladd & Co. agreement) and asked his advice on
international affairs.

Brinsmade's powers were too limited to succeed, he said. A commissioner should go from Hawaii to America and Europe empow-
ered to negotiate treaties guaranteeing Hawaiian independence. In
the end Simpson himself agreed to serve on such an embassy, and to
meet Richards and Haalilio for that purpose in London around the
end of the year.

So on July 18 William Richards sailed for America with Haalilio,
while Simpson soon left for London in the opposite direction.

But the king and chiefs could not be left without an adviser. For
several years they had been in the habit of talking with Dr. Judd, not
only about their physical ailments but about problems of the ailing
government. They had come to feel a good deal of confidence in their

doctor, who had some of Bingham's rocklike dependability and somewhat more skill in human relations.

For one thing the finances of the kingdom were chaotic and would have to be put in order. Judd suggested a plan, and as a result on May 10 found himself, with John Ii and Haalilio, a member of the treasury board he had recommended. "Dr. Judd General Treasurer of the Government," wrote Reynolds. "What next?" Next, he was made translator and recorder and, in preparation for Richards' departure, was charged also with helping Governor Kekuanaoa in all important business with foreigners. When Richards left, the doctor was made responsible for carrying on the official correspondence with the embassy to London.

These official appointments made it necessary for Judd to resign from the mission, though continuing as mission doctor in return for his house and land. The board frowned on his action even though the mission had approved, for "thus the whole mission might dissolve overnight." But Judd was not a man to waver once he had made up his mind. For the next ten years he was the dominant figure in Hawaiian affairs. Naturally enough, he was soon the butt of all the hatred, ridicule and criticism which had once been aimed at Hiram Bingham.

"You cannot know how much this vexatious business has cost me," he wrote to Dr. Anderson of the board. "My health, my eyesight, my reputation, my family, my hope of a future—all injured."

While Judd was attempting to make order out of financial chaos, Richard Charlton on September 27 departed secretly for London, his bills unpaid, as Reynolds sourly noted. Charlton had convinced himself that the Yankee missionaries were taking over the Hawaiian government with nationalistic purposes in mind. He wanted to scuttle the Richards-Haalilio mission if he could. Opinion in Honolulu was that he wanted to persuade Great Britain to annex the islands. This, in any case, was the outspoken intention of Alexander Simpson, the man Charlton appointed consul in his absence, but whom the Hawaiian government refused to recognize.

A master of intrigue, Simpson now went seriously to work to bring about his purpose while his cousin, Sir George Simpson—whom he bitterly hated—was doing his best to strengthen the native government and gain the support and recognition of Great Britain. By sending a highly-colored account of affairs in the islands, he was able to have Admiral Richard Thomas of the British squadron in the Pacific send Lord George Paulet, commander of the frigate *Carysfort,* to see what all the fuss was about.

Before Paulet had started for the islands, however, William Richards had reached Washington, where he and Haalilio met the great Daniel Webster, Secretary of State, on December 7. Webster seemed to know very little about the Sandwich Islands, but he was cordial enough, and on the evening of the ninth invited his fellow Yankee in for a frank and pleasant talk, the upshot of which was that Richards was to write an official communication to which Daniel promised a reply. Richards' main points were recognition of independence and the settlement of disputes between the Hawaiian government and foreigners.

Richards waited eight days without a reply, called on Webster and waited again. "The fact is that the great Daniel is looking for popularity and he will not do, nor fail to do anything which can affect that without considerable reflection," Richards confided to his journal. On the twenty-seventh, however, Richards and Haalilio were introduced to President Tyler and the whole Cabinet. Richards hinted quite broadly that if the United States would not recognize Hawaiian independence, he intended to place the islands under the protection of Great Britain.

Tyler did not miss the point. After questioning Richards closely, he inquired where he was from. "Yankees are shrewd negociators [*sic*]," he said. Three days later he sent the Richards-Webster correspondence to Congress, together with a message which stressed the importance of the islands to American shipping and the American interest in the welfare of the island government.

"Far remote from the dominions of European powers," he said, "its growth and prosperity as an independent state may yet be in a high degree useful to all whose trade is extended to those regions; while its near approach to this continent and the intercourse which American vessels have with it, such vessels constituting five-sixths of all which annually visit it, could not but create dissatisfaction on the part of the United States at any attempt by another power, should such attempt be threatened or feared, to take possession of the islands, colonize them, and subvert the native Government."

Tyler had in effect extended the Monroe Doctrine to the islands.

Well pleased, Richards and Haalilio sailed for England in February, 1843. But on the eighteenth, the day they reached London, Lord Paulet had delivered an ultimatum at Honolulu, threatening to attack the town unless a number of peremptory demands were complied with. Paulet had swallowed, hook, line and sinker, Alexander Simpson's account of things, and had taken a supercilious, insulting attitude towards the local government.

An English ship was towed out of the harbor to serve as a refuge for British residents. "Everyone is so excited that decency is out of the question," Reynolds complained. The streets were full of carts bearing valuables to the ships in the harbor. The days of Laplace and the *Artémise* had returned.

There were some who advised the king to let Paulet fire on the town, knowing that if Britain took such a step, the outcry in the United States and the reaction in the islands would hasten the union between the islands and the nation with which they were already in many ways closely associated. But the government decided to yield, though under protest, the king insisting that his emissaries in London were already carrying out any necessary negotiations there.

Simpson was now high in the saddle. With Paulet to back him up, he pressed demands which became more and more impossible.

"Let them take the islands," said the king, after four days of such demands. He considered ceding the islands to France or the United States in order to flout Paulet. But he realized that if he did this, Simpson backed by Paulet's guns would be in control until either of the other powers could send ships. He did not yet know what Richards might have accomplished in Washington. Finally on February 25, after carefully considering and rejecting every alternative, the king provisionally ceded his islands to Paulet, trusting that when the facts were known in London, justice would be done.

"I have given away the life of our lands," said the king in the ceremony at the fort. "I have hope that the life of the land will be restored when my conduct is justified." Plain, noble words which must have made the young lord feel a little cheap if he had any sensibilities, as the aggressor must always feel humbled and inferior before his victim.

The Hawaiian flag came down the staff and the British flag went up to the salute of twenty-one guns. A proclamation of Paulet's was read, specifying the way the government would be run. A commission, to which the king named Judd as his representative, was to be in charge of all but purely native affairs.

But the doctor was not happy on the commission, for Paulet ran things to suit himself. He seized the three government schooners and changed their names, preparing one of them to carry the story of his brave exploits to San Blas from which dispatches could be sent to London. Entrusted with this mission was none other than Alexander Simpson, the villain in the piece.

But now the plot thickened like the veriest melodrama. Ladd & Co. had already arranged to charter this same ship before Paulet seized it. They had surrendered their right only on condition that their agent be allowed to go with the ship on company business. Since they were in close touch with the native government, they offered to have their agent go on to Washington and London, to carry the true story of what was happening in the islands—this, of course, entirely unknown to Paulet and Simpson. The government was quick to make use of this opportunity to smuggle out an ambassador, and appointed young James F. B. Marshall—the man who had knocked Charlton down in the Jarves fray—"envoy extraordinary and minister plenipotentiary" to the queen of Great Britain, to act with Richards in getting a redress of grievances.

Marshall's mission had to be kept an absolute secret, or Paulet would never allow him to sail. So Dr. Judd, in the dark of night, crept into the royal tomb. There, using the coffin of Kaahumanu as his desk, he wrote out the necessary documents. Meanwhile a canoe was sent over to Maui after the king, who made the return voyage in the same frail craft, landed at Waikiki in the dark, signed the documents, and went back to Maui.

It may have been this very night that a British officer came to the Judd door and demanded to know where the doctor was.

Laura Judd drew herself up. "I do not know," she said, "and if I did I would not tell you." According to her daughter, the officer threatened to run her through. "Do it then," said Laura.

The officer departed without learning the whereabouts of Dr. Judd.

When the ship sailed for San Blas on March 11, Marshall had the secret papers with him, unknown to Simpson. By land and sea, the men traveled as companions for months, each charily guarding his papers from the other—papers that were finally to wind up on the same desk in London.

Meanwhile Paulet became more and more a dictator, interfering with the courts and putting an end to any punishments for "sleeping mischievously," much to the satisfaction of the sailors in port. Judd, disgusted, resigned on May 11 and the king refused to replace him.

Soon Paulet was demanding $80,000 "damages," although his original figure had been $3,000. He destroyed every Hawaiian flag in the islands, ordered the land Charlton claimed to be cleared of houses, but at the same time tried to curry favor with the foreign residents. Visiting Hilo, he called on the Coans. Young and jolly, he went out of his way to be pleasant and sociable to them.

"Well," he said, "you are now under the British flag; how do you like it?"

"Well, sir," said Coan, "we choose to be under the Hawaiian."

"No, no! but the English government is strong, and your protection is sure."

"True, but we desire that this weak and small people should be free and independent. It is a right which should not be taken from them without just cause."

Paulet argued that he had saved the islands from being seized by the French. "You ought to thank me," he concluded. No one did.

*   *   *

After his resignation, Dr. Judd secretly carried all the public archives into the royal tomb where he hid them from Paulet, determined that the records should not fall into the conqueror's hands.

Meanwhile the children of the Chiefs' Children's School held indignation meetings, called the British soldiers lobster-backs, and glared at them in the streets. When the U.S.S. *Constellation* sailed into Honolulu harbor in July, Commander Lawrence Kearney invited the chiefs' children aboard. To show Paulet what he thought of

him, he had a Hawaiian flag made. As the children were leaving the
ship he had it broken out at the foremast and saluted "in good style."

*   *   *

On July 26 (1843) Honolulu was rocking with excitement. Admiral Richard Thomas had arrived in port aboard his flagship the
Dublin to look into Paulet's behavior.

In his first communication it was apparent that Thomas was a very
different man from Paulet. Instead of curtly demanding an interview
with the king, he sent a message to Governor Kekuanaoa desiring
"the honor of a personal interview with His Majesty." He told the
king that he would restore the independence of the islands immediately if the rights of British subjects in the islands could be guaranteed. These guarantees turned out to be more than the king approved,
but since the arrangement was subject to whatever agreement might
be reached in London, he signed.

Early Saturday morning, July 31, the parade ground out beyond
the mission was packed with people. (It was afterwards named
Thomas Square in the admiral's honor.) Two pavilions had been put
up—one for ladies, the other for the king, the admiral and their parties. While the ladies sat in their pavilion, the men rode about on
horseback. Well before eight o'clock, four hundred marines from the
Dublin and the *Carysfort* marched onto the field in white, tight-fitting
trousers and scarlet coats, their officers looking half choked in high,
gilded collars and high black caps with tight chin straps and white
plumes.

Soon Admiral Thomas came riding up in the king's carriage.
Though his baldness was hidden by his admiral's hat, it was clear
enough that he was far from handsome. But the Hawaiians did not
mind that, for he was their deliverer.

When the king arrived on horseback, the admiral gave him a salute
of twenty-one guns from the squadron's field artillery, drawn up
across the center of the square where the marines stood at stiff attention. Now the British flag officer marched towards the king and his
guard, dipping his colors as the Hawaiian flag was unfurled. Since all
Hawaiian flags had been destroyed, the admiral had ordered this one
made aboard his own ship. As the broad banner with its crown and

olive branch was caught by the breeze, the guns from the British war vessels roared their royal salute, followed by the other ships in port, including the U.S.S. *Constellation*. Then the guns at the fort and high up on top of Punchbowl responded. The echoes bounced back and forth between the hills and the harbor in a way that would have gladdened the heart of Kaahumanu, if only she could have heard it.

When the firing stopped, a great cheer went up from the crowd. Then the marine band played, and after that the marines fought a mock battle, attacking with volleys of blanks and dismounting their fieldpieces. In the afternoon the king rode to the big new church where a vast crowd gathered for a service of thanksgiving. Rough-featured, reliable John Ii was orator of the day. What he said has not been preserved, but what the king said became the motto of Hawaii: "The life of the land is preserved in righteousness." It was a sound biblical sentiment, the fruit of his Yankee training.

"It is from God," the king told young Gorham Gilman who called upon him that evening. "He has done it."

The next day King Kauikeaouli—or Kamehameha III to give him his formal title on this formal occasion—ordered a ten-day holiday and freed all prisoners who had been jailed during Paulet's tenure. On August 2 he gave a grand public feast at his residence up in cool, rainy Nuuanu Valley. Ti leaves placed on the ground made the tables. Admiral Thomas was affected to tears by the rendering of an anthem composed by missionary E. O. Hall in honor of the restoration.

The Judds also celebrated with a dinner. They had moved now from the mission house into a furnished stone house with high ceilings and large windows which belonged to the prime minister, Kekauluohi. Laura, determined to have a perfect dinner, got hold of a French chef who turned out soup, fish, rice and curry, roast beef, mutton, boned turkey, ham, ducks, chickens, salads, lobster, game, omelets, patties, puddings, pies, almond pastry, fruit, nuts and raisins, and crackers and cheese. Each item was faultless, but the service was painfully slow. To poor Laura it seemed a lifetime between courses as she tried to think of something clever to say to the admiral, who plainly missed the wines that should have gone with such a dinner. The dinner dragged on for three hours. When the cloth was removed before tea and coffee, the admiral rose and fled, pleading as an excuse that the time for his evening walk had come.

While Admiral Thomas lingered on in the islands, awaiting the arrival of news or instructions from London, Gerrit Judd went to work to put the island government in order once more. He recovered the state papers from their hiding place in the royal mausoleum. He worked on the official accounts, struggling to make income balance outgo.

In the midst of these labors the newly appointed commissioner to Hawaii from the United States arrived on October 16. He was George Brown, a friend of Daniel Webster. The board in Boston had written to the mission in his favor, calling him abruptly frank, a teetotaller and a friend of missions. "No one will browbeat missionaries with him on the ground," they were sure. But Bingham was just as certain that he would never do, warning the board that he was "a broken-down shipmaster, of narrow mind and scanty attainments, noisy, coarse and overbearing in manner . . . licentious in principle and practice." Events would soon show which judgment was correct.

Since the king was living at Lahaina, Brown went over there to present his commission, preceded by a letter from the Reverend Lowell Smith to Dr. Baldwin. "I hope the king will put on all his dignity and show he is somebody," said Smith. "The world seems determined that he shall be somebody whether or no." The tragedy of the island culture is hidden in that laconic remark.

When Brown asked whom he was to deal with, the king told him Dr. Judd. Has the doctor the proper authority? Brown wanted to know. Upshot of the query was that Judd became secretary of state, though with some misgivings on his part. But someone had to do the job and Judd was not one to retreat in the face of danger. So he was ready to receive the new British consul general who arrived in February, 1844.

Judd and all the mission were delighted to learn that Charlton had been replaced by General William Miller who had called at Hawaii in 1831, impressing the brethren with the sound advice he had given the young government. Miller, an adventurer with a romantic background, had already lived a full life. At sixteen he had entered the British artillery, serving with Wellington and then taking part in the

British defeat at New Orleans in 1815. Then he had sailed off to South America just as the wars to expel the Spaniards were beginning to flame. First in Chile and then in Peru he fought on the side of liberation, rising to the rank of general and to a post of intimacy with Simón Bolívar. For ten years he filled various high offices in Peru, both military and political, until the turn of events forced him into exile.

"An excellent noblemind [sic] wise man of the world and entitled to much respect for his generous and liberal principles," Judd had thought him on that first visit.

Miller had brought with him a convention or treaty which he now presented for signing. Judd objected to some of its details, but approved its signing if Miller would add an additional article (relating to import duties), subject to final approval in London. A settlement, reached in London, of various claims of British citizens was also signed. Richards, though joined by Brinsmade and Marshall in London, had not been able to get Britain to admit guilt and pay reparations for Paulet's unjustified seizure of the islands, nor had he been able to persuade Lord Aberdeen that Charlton's land claim was spurious. But the main object—the recognition of Hawaii's independence—had been achieved. Great Britain and France had signed a joint declaration to this effect on November 28, 1843. The United States, invited to join the declaration, declined on constitutional and traditional grounds but pointed out that they had already recognized Hawaiian independence.

Two objectionable features remained—the restriction on import duties and the right of foreigners to trial before a jury of foreign residents. Richards kept at Guizot, the French foreign minister, to change these until he was pointedly told that no changes in the agreement Laplace had forced upon Hawaii would be made.

Richards and Haalilio had also had an interview with King Leopold of Belgium, having gone to his country to support Brinsmade's attempt to find capital for Ladd & Co. Having done all that they could in Europe, the two envoys headed back toward the United States.

Beset by legal perplexities, Judd was delighted when a tall, handsome young American lawyer named John Ricord stepped ashore on

February 27, 1844. Rumor soon began to circulate that the young man had left his home in the east for reasons of health, close confinement in jail being uncongenial to his constitution. But whether or not it was true that he had been caught removing a pocketbook from a pair of temporarily unoccupied pantaloons in a Buffalo hotel room, had been dismissed for insolence in Michigan, and had forgetfully left Washington with thirteen thousand dollars belonging to a client, it was true that he had headed west, crossing the plains in a swallow-tail coat and a high plug hat.

Judd immediately had the post of attorney general created, and popped Ricord into it before he could be snapped up by the opposition. The only lawyer in the islands, Ricord was clearly a prize. With his facile knowledge of legal twists and terms, his frightening drive and energy, his charm and his love of battle, Ricord was to keep Honolulu in an uproar during his three-year stay. It was characteristic of him that within a few days of his arrival he signed the temperance pledge, took the oath of allegiance, was made attorney general and dined with the king. Working night and day, he not only undertook a complete revision of the laws but also wrote frequently and lengthily for *The Polynesian.*

On April 8, 1844, Marshall returned from his mission to London and the United States, accompanied by his wife, her sister, and James Jarves unaccompanied by Libby, who was pregnant and who had made up her mind not to live with him as his wife. To honor Marshall the king sent his royal double canoe to bring the party ashore. Jarves was soon publishing *The Polynesian* again, his first issue appearing May 18. In July the paper became the official government organ and Jarves—another Judd protégé—director of government printing.

Honolulu, now a town of nine thousand, had four hotels, nineteen stores, three victualing houses and nine grogshops, according to another new periodical, *The Friend of Temperance and Seamen,* edited by the new Bethel chaplain, Samuel C. Damon who had replaced John Diell, dead several years since while on a voyage for his health. Pastor Damon had his work cut out for him, for the whaling business was booming. Six thousand seamen entered the port of Honolulu every year now, and during the spring and fall the harbor was jammed with ships. Damon was also for ten years the sole Protestant pastor to the foreign population. An Amherst man who had come out to the islands straight from the seminary, Samuel Damon was to hold his post for forty-two years.

Dr. Judd was highly pleased with all these evidences of progress. Never since Captain Cook, he wrote, had the islands been in so prosperous a condition. The Hawaiians were building better houses, wearing better clothes, acquiring furniture and utensils and cattle. Tables, bureaus, sofas and beds had begun to make their appearance in native homes. But perhaps the most impressive sign of triumphant western culture was this: Queen Kalama was suspended from communion at Lahaina for drinking awa (an indigenous drug) in order to get her weight down. No queen in the old days had worried about her weight, except to keep it up. This was progress indeed!

CHAPTER 22

THE POWER BEHIND THE THRONE

1845–1847

WHEN COURT PROTOCOL HAD BEEN ESTABLISHED BY RICORD upon the foundation of Vienna, the king gave his first European-style soirée. The date was February 6, 1845, the place the coral palace which Governor Kekuanaoa had built for his six-year-old daughter, Victoria, but which he had diplomatically turned over to King Kamehameha III when the official seat of government had been moved from Lahaina to Honolulu the previous July.

It was an unpretentious yet adequate coral building, with a large reception room to the right of the hall, two rooms on the left, and a sizable lookout room above, where the king, who was fond of ships, could keep an eye on the harbor. There was plenty to see there nowadays—sometimes over a hundred ships in port, as many as sixty hog-tied to each other in the inner harbor. The palace had a rather nautical look itself, for it was square, low and chunky like a ferry-boat. The king and his wife rarely if ever occupied the huge state bed in the back room. They preferred their little cottages in the yard, where they could live in Hawaiian style.

Since Kalama had little taste for haole housekeeping, Laura Judd had had to come in and arrange the household. Hawaiian custom called for keeping everything packed in bundles and then distributed to attendants who secreted it until it was called for. To furnish the house, Laura asked to have all the bundles brought in. Under the jealous eyes of old attendants, she removed dishes and silverware from yards of tapa, placing them where they would make the barren rooms look occupied.

Then there was Kalama's dress to worry about. Despite her size, she was really rather pretty, but the king had kept her so confined that she had had no chance to develop a discriminating taste. The Judd daughters were delighted to help—especially Elizabeth who had just entered her teens. But prettifying Kalama had political repercussions. Kekauluohi, the old premier, was jealous of the queen with her pretty ringlets, smooth skin and round cheeks. So to avoid a crisis, Laura Judd had to give the premier first choice when buying dress goods. And when Kalama moved into the new palace, Kekauluohi dispossessed the Judds from her stone mansion, though she had promised to leave them in it. No low-born queen was going to outdo *her*. Besides, the Judds had dispelled the ghosts which were supposed to have inhabited the place. So the doctor's family had to take another house which the government fitted up for them and in which they were soon accommodating John Ricord and several other boarders as well as their own large family.

On the evening of February sixth the big frogs of the little community walked up the steep flight of steps to the palace and on into the reception room where they found the king looking handsome in his braided uniform. Rough-faced, erect John Ii was there with his sweet-featured Sarai. Paki, six and a half feet tall and weighing three hundred pounds, lent magnificence to the occasion as chamberlain. Another handsome presence was John Young—Keoni Ana—son of a chiefess and of the Englishman John Young who had welcomed the first missionaries years ago. With his fine sturdy figure and good head, he combined the best features of his Hawaiian and English ancestry. Perhaps David Malo was there, for a short time later he wrote in injured innocence to Dr. Baldwin who had accused him of going to Honolulu from Maui with a woman. She came to visit her child, David told the suspicious doctor, and had never lived in the same house with him. She had, it is true, massaged him four nights when he was ill, but was now gone.

To represent General Miller who was on a voyage there also came the acting British consul, a Scotsman named Wyllie—short, affable and with an engaging Scotch burr, who was to become Judd's partner and then his rival in Hawaiian affairs. Rumor said that he had remained a bachelor because he had fallen in love with a nun in Chile while giving her medical attention. Rumor also said that he had a sizable fortune. Charlton, who had returned to plague the government, may have been present too.

The merchants were there—Stephen Reynolds, the Ladds, Marshall and his new wife. And, of course, the mission folk—gentle, earnest Levi Chamberlain, his hair still fair and eyes still blue; his pious wife, Maria, mother and nurse to everybody; big-eyed, earnest-looking Clarissa Armstrong and her still young-looking husband who impressed one visitor at least as "polite and fawning" but with "something slippery and cunning" about him.

In the midst of all the guests, or more likely at the king's elbow, stood Gerrit Judd himself. He had got Laura to sew two crowns on his coat lapels, and though he was small of stature and at first seemed insignificant as one visitor remarked, a few minutes of his steady gaze and purposeful, firmly set features made anyone forget his height. Laura Judd, her eye alive to social or prandial needs, moved about the room. Along with her social ease, she had a firmness of chin remarkably like the doctor's. Mission sisters thought her frivolous, grasping for power, putting on airs—"a gay, fashionable, supremely selfish woman," Clarissa Armstrong called her; but could it have been jealousy? In keeping with the mission interdiction against dancing, Laura tried to lead the queen away from parties which ended with dancing, though she did not always succeed. Honolulu protocol bent at least this far towards the mission, that parties should begin with a reception and refreshments, and when the orchestra began tuning up for the dance, the mission members could then scuttle away.

Although Hawaiian chiefs mixed freely with foreign merchants and missionaries at the parties which now became ever more frequent in gay, busy, little Honolulu, there was one group the social arbiters would not accept. These were the attractive daughters of Hawaiian mothers and haole fathers. Stephen Reynolds could never get haole women to join his dancing classes along with "his girls" of hapahaole descent. When he invited haole men, a social upheaval took place. If a navy ship arrived in port and invited both groups to a party, the haole women regretted. Although most of the mixed alliances had long since been legitimatized, society was slow to forget or forgive the offhand nature of the first matings in the islands between uninhibited

maidens and lusty young men who had hung up their western con-
sciences on the Horn.

Honolulu society was cracked and crisscrossed with feuds and
alliances which must have made such a party as this one at the palace
an amusing affair to anyone in the know—and out of the storm—who
could watch sworn enemies avoiding each other, as with uneasy glances
they hunted out safe passages through the crowd, or passed with smirk
or stony stare if a meeting could not be avoided. Storm center of the
community was Dr. Gerrit Judd.

"You must know that I am at present the King Bingham of the
Sandwich Islands," he humorously wrote home. The islands are at
last, he said, independent. "This annoys General Miller, works Commissioner Brown into a fury and puts an uncommonly smooth face on
Dudoit" [the French consul]. Brewer & Co. had also found a grievance
and withdrawn their support from the government paper, *The Polynesian*. "If they oppose us we must oppose them," Judd went on. "If
they charge the government with vexing and injuring them—as they
have heretofore done without cause—then the government will give
them cause—will vex—will injure—will oppose them in every lawful
manner." After having their own way for years, the merchants were
bound to cry murder when they bumped their noses against this firm
rock wall.

One of the things that infuriated the haoles against Judd was his
attempt to get Americans and other foreigners to become naturalized
Hawaiians. He had himself taken the oath of allegiance, as had Ricord.
William Paty, builder of the Charity School, who had become collec-
tor of customs and harbormaster under Judd, had also taken the oath.
So had a number of lesser officers.

Dr. Judd thought all the mission brethren ought to take it, and
then throw themselves on their people for support. Thus the church
would become truly Hawaiian and could separate from the American
Board.

Brother Smith, on the other hand, thought the oath a plot of Judd
and Ricord to get everyone under their control. Judd was determined
not to be influenced by the counsels of the mission, Smith wrote Dr.
Baldwin, "but on the other hand to curb, bridle and saddle us, and
reign triumphant from the rising of the sun at Hilo to the going down

thereof at Niihau." When Judd came to his church, Smith labored to set him straight from the pulpit. "I was very glad that Dr. Judd was present to hear my remarks, and was in hopes they might do him some good," said the fearless preacher.

When the subject of the oath came up for discussion at the general meeting of the mission it was debated with some heat. Bishop, Cooke, Armstrong and Gulick were decidedly for it, Lowell Smith, Emerson, Baldwin and Lyman as decidedly against. In the end the matter was left up to individuals.

In March Judd gained a new supporter—Robert Chrichton Wyllie, the amiable Scotsman who had come out with General Miller. Appointed minister of foreign relations, Wyllie was soon at logger-heads with his onetime friend and patron who was still trying to persuade the Hawaiian government to yield on Charlton's land claims. Now in his forties, Wyllie had diligently collected information about the islands while serving as British pro-consul, and had become convinced that Charlton's claims were unjust. Hopefully entering the government with the idea of making peace between Brown and Judd, he was soon deep in controversy himself. A great penpusher, he extruded letters, state papers, newspaper reports and briefs in a stream which seems to have been calculated to engulf the enemy by sheer volume.

Three days before Wyllie received his appointment, William Richards finally returned to the islands, bearing the sad news that Haalilio had died at sea. It could hardly have escaped him that in his absence Judd had replaced him as the kingpin. Though his whispering voice and stealthy walk might give the impression of a man apt for treasons, strategems and spoils, he does not seem to have coveted Judd's position, quite content to turn his attention to reforming the schools as minister of public instruction. The schools needed him. Teachers were going unpaid, the buildings had become homes for hogs, and books were being made into kites.

"Mr. Richards appears to be tamely harnessed," Brother Forbes wrote to Baldwin. "How tamely he draws with the leader and thiller I do not know." He might have felt more certain if he had seen Richards' letter to Baldwin in which he professed himself "root, body and branch a monarchist." This was the position taken by Judd and Wyllie, who felt that only by maintaining the monarchy could Hawaii be preserved for the Hawaiians.

So when the legislature convened on May 20, 1845, the huge stone church was chosen* in order to emphasize the magnitude and dignity of royalty. In the middle a temporary throne was raised. Only two of the stately feather kahilis, symbol of royalty, could be found—one with black feathers on a white ground, the other orange and crimson. Twenty feet high, they were placed so as to tower over the throne, which was covered with a magnificent cloak of yellow and scarlet feathers. Around the platform seats were arranged for the chiefs, officials, diplomatic representatives and guests. When they had been seated the remainder of the space was thrown open to the public. Promptly at twelve the king, queen, and ministers marched in, the king in a splendid new military suit, the ministers with crowns at their lapels and ribbons across their chests. The foreign ladies in the audience were richly dressed, the diplomats in their official uniforms— Miller covered with silver lace and decorations, Brown neat but appropriately plain for a republican.

As the king marched in, a new flag was broken out to a royal salute from the fort. The king read a speech from the throne and listened to a response from a committee of the two houses of nobles and representatives. Constitutional monarchy was thus plainly established.

The old premier Kekauluohi lived only a few weeks beyond this landmark, dying on June seventh. Kinau's daughter Victoria should have succeeded her, but until she should come of age John Young (Keoni Ana) was placed in the post. With the departure of Kekauluohi the last link with the great Kamehameha I was gone. She had been his wife, and his son Liholiho's wife. Governor Adams of Hawaii having died a few months before, there were now none of the leading chiefs left who had been in power at the arrival of the mission.

The departure of these old chiefs and the passing into foreign hands of the administration of government deeply disturbed a good many Hawaiians who saw the islands slipping from their control. In Lahaina Dr. Baldwin held a meeting for prayer and fasting which turned into a movement against foreigners in government and led to a petition to the king. The ringleader, it turned out, was David Malo, long

* Thus Laura Judd. *The Polynesian* says "a large hall near the fort."

convinced that Hawaii was being swamped by the tide of foreigners. He was persuaded to moderate his point of view—part of the persuasion apparently taking the form of depriving him of his land.

"Adultery was the great evil of former years," David said. "Nowadays avarice and seeking for honors are the great sins. Some people are saying that avarice is all right and that Dr. Judd, Richards and Andrews indulge in it."

David was merely voicing a deeply seated discontent among the people, who saw their numbers rapidly diminishing, their lands overrun by haoles, their government helpless without foreign help, their ancient culture ignored or ridiculed. "Plovers were unafraid and mice ran about squeaking openly," wrote Kamakau, by which he meant that the foreigners had everything in their own hands. The laws Ricord drew up made the native people "lick ti leaves like dogs and gnaw bones thrown at the feet of strangers."

In replying to the petition the king said that he used foreign officials only when he could not get qualified Hawaiians, and that as the young chiefs grew up, they would be able to fill posts now filled by foreigners.

Both the king and the petitioners were right, because Hawaii was caught in a web not of its own weaving and from which there was no escape.

To fill the post of judge in cases where foreigners were concerned, Judd now brought in Lorrin Andrews who had been trying to make a living for himself since separating from the board—farming and preaching to foreigners and sailors at Lahaina. Apparently he had not been very successful, for Lowell Smith reported that his family often went hungry, sometimes with nothing but bread and molasses to eat. The pioneers could remember the time, though, when bread was a luxury! Andrews himself, in reporting the offer to his brother at home, said he would probably accept it because the government needed such an officer, because the foreign community seemed to favor him, and because "it will afford something like a support to my family which has been rather slim for several years past."

Meanwhile the tiff between the former bosom companions Miller and Wyllie over the Charlton claim went on and on. The two men could hardly bear to be in the same room together. The temperature rose wherever they met, and sometimes they had to be pulled apart.

At last Charlton left on the nineteenth of February, 1846—"we trust for ever," said The Polynesian—but not before trying to get up a brawl in the street with Wyllie, according to the same biased source.

To celebrate the king's birthday—and perhaps the departure of Charlton—Mr. Wyllie gave a grand ball for two hundred people on March 17. It went on until the late hour of one, but with perfect propriety and no liquor. The missionaries stayed away, since they thought dancing sinful. But Reynolds' young hapahaole ladies were there. After years of instruction under the old master, they danced charmingly. They had already been presented at court that day, leaving samples of their needlework with the king.

A few days later the French frigate Virginia put in at Honolulu, bringing back the $20,000 Laplace had sailed off with seven years before. Close on the heels of this arrival came Peter Brinsmade.

Back in 1843, while Richards and Haalilio were in Europe, he had persuaded them to join in signing a contract with the Belgian Company of Colonization which had in effect made Kamehameha III a party to a scheme by which Ladd & Co. turned over all their properties and rights to the Belgian group. Next a royal community was organized, at least on paper, to carry out the plan. But months went by and no capital was subscribed. At last Brinsmade, giving up hope, tried elsewhere in Belgium and then in England and America with no better luck. Unable even to pay his passage to the islands, he arrived a bitter man, bent upon punishing someone for the failure of his plans.

Meanwhile Ladd & Co., which had apparently been in shaky condition for some time, was forced to close its doors on November 1, 1844, after borrowing large sums from the government. In an attempt to recover the land and the loans, Judd as president of the treasury board had the property attached. On April 18, 1845, all the property at Koloa was offered at a sheriff's sale and bid in by the treasury board. When Brinsmade returned, Ladd & Co. brought a claim against the government for $378,000 on the grounds that the government had deliberately ruined the company.

The Ladd claim, submitted to arbitrators, dragged on for months, pulling most of the community into its interminable arguments and counter-arguments, and piling up mountains of testimony as the hearings went on, day after day, in the vestry room of the Bethel Church.

Brinsmade, starting the *Sandwich Island News* to state his position, argued that the government had forced Ladd to sell its properties while he was still in Europe, thus ruining the chances of completing the Belgian contract. And he tried to show that Ladd & Co. had been the most important contributor in building up Hawaiian industry. There was some truth in this, since they were the first to introduce agricultural operations on a big scale, to set up what became the characteristic Hawaiian system of plantations managed and financed from a central agency in Honolulu, and to show that sugar-producing could make money.

The government tried to prove that Brinsmade, as a friend of the missionaries, had managed to get for Ladd & Co. favors that were easily worth $100,000. Even after the failure of the company, according to witnesses at the hearing, Judd had done his best to save what he could for the Ladd partners and had planned to settle their affairs in such a way that they would not remain saddled with debts. He had also planned to find suitable work for them in the government.

At last, towards the end of May, 1847, Ladd, Brinsmade and Hooper signed a letter breaking off the arbitration because of ruinous expenses which were running $90 to a sitting. Since the government had not yet begun its testimony, it protested that this withdrawal meant the firm and its creditors no longer had any claims against the government.

When Brinsmade tried to get James Marshall, the patient arbitrator in all this haze of testimony and cloud of witnesses, to take issue with government on this point, he blew up. "Mr. Brinsmade," he said, "you ought not to ask me to take any further part in your controversies with the government or government officers. . . . I have been obliged to neglect my own business, and my interests have suffered from it. I have been mixed up too much already in these useless contentions with the government folks, and I am glad to get out of them."

So ended the arbitration, though not the effects of it, which continued for years in broken friendships and bitter memories. Among the bitterest of these was the quarrel between Jarves and Brinsmade, editors of the two papers, one for government, the other for Ladd. Brinsmade sued Jarves for $50,000, charging libel. But while Brinsmade had been making acidulous attacks on Judd, Ricord, Wyllie, *et al.,* Jarves had hardly said anything about Ladd & Co. that was not plain fact—that they owed money to many creditors, that their bills were protested in the United States for non-payment. The libel suit was eventually dismissed.

Brinsmade also lashed out indiscriminately at the mission. "Can it be," Armstrong wrote of him in his journal, "that a man who studied divinity in Andover and New Haven, and preached the Gospel with much acceptance—a man who was one of the founders of the Bethel Church in Honolulu, who has officiated as chaplain on the failure of Mr. Diell—a man who once as one of us often bowed the knee in our monthly concerts and prayer meetings—that he has gone over to the side of the enemy?"

The answer was yes.

The conflict between government and anti-government forces broadened as it went on, attracting every newcomer to one side or the other. When Anthony Ten Eyck arrived in June, 1846, to replace Brown as commissioner, he quickly soaked up his predecessor's views and was soon actually representing Ladd & Co. as counsel before the arbitrators. For this he was firmly reproved by the secretary of state, James Buchanan, but not before he had made himself so obnoxious to the Hawaiian government that it refused to deal with him. Not the least of his indiscretions was composing—or at least submitting in his own easily verified hand—the following piece of verse for publication in the *News*:

Should a monkey wear a crown,
Must we tremble at his frown?
Could we not, thro' all his ermine,
Spy the strutting, chattering vermin?

Should a *Doctor* leave his shop
And mount a throne in one hop:
Could we not, in all he did,
Spy the firm—"Jalap and Phid"?

Should a judge put on a sack
Ne'er designed to fit his back:
Could we not through all the *wool,*
Spy the doctor at the pull?

Should a *Saddler* leave his awl
Must we own a statesman tall:
Could we not, in all his acts,
Smell the stench of cobbler's wax?

Should an *Ass* put on a skin
Nature ne'er designed for him:
Could we not, when he's fed highly,
Spy the fool—as well as Wily?

Should a *Reverend* leave his station
For good of the Kanaka nation:
Could we not, by his leer,
Spy *six hundred pounds a year?*

These scarcely veiled references to all the chief ministers of state, and even to the king himself, angered Judd as much as they delighted his opponents.

To balance the accounts, two energetic and capable young men arrived from the United States in October, one of whom—Charles Bishop—soon established himself in business, the other—a lawyer named William Little Lee—being appointed chief justice. Mild, gentle and self-possessed, Lee was a very different sort of person from the mercurial Ricord. His good judgment began to restore confidence in a government which many had grown to hate. Only twenty-five, he was already in poor health, but the gentle island climate gave him eleven more years of life, all of them devoted to building up respect and a firmly based procedure for the courts and government.

Lee had only been on the bench a few months before Ricord resigned from his government post. Always a wanderer, he had begun to get itchy feet again. But he stayed long enough to face the trial against him for that alleged absconding with funds belonging to a client in Florida. Here was a case made to order for the enemies of government. They were all certain beforehand that he was guilty. The *News* claimed that he had skipped out without accounting for the claim he had successfully collected from the United States government —a claim arising out of damage done by American troops during the War of 1812. At the trial in June, 1847, Ricord astounded Honolulu by admitting that he had collected and kept $14,800. But it was all perfectly proper, he explained with his usual urbanity. His fee had been agreed to as $10,000, and as for the remainder, it was more than eaten up in costs! The jury decided that the plaintiff had no just claim. Exonerated, Ricord left the islands for California in the fall. Too restless to stay anywhere long, he never fulfilled the power and ability that were in him, dying some years later in France. But the skill and energy he gave to organizing the laws and courts of Hawaii are a monument more lasting than marble.

To embarrass Dr. Judd the opposition had meanwhile dug into his wharf rents. According to the *News*, Governor Kekuanaoa had made over to Judd the rights to the wharf which had been rented to Ladd & Co. Judd had also received another wharf lot worth $1,000 a year— twice as valuable as the first. "It was thus, in the days when darkness brooded over the prospects of the Sandwich Islands nation, and the whole Christian world was moved by the tale of Lord George Paulet's outrages, that Dr. Judd secured for himself an income for 33 years of $1500 per annum."

The matter came to trial by way of a case Judd brought for government against Ladd, Brinsmade & Hooper, wherein it appeared that the governor had rented the wharf to Ladd & Co. on February 21, 1843, and had then on April 15 given the rent of it for 33 years to Judd "in consideration of fifteen years service as a missionary." The judge decided that the gift was made after Judd had left the mission and was therefore no longer bound by mission rules against acquiring private property.

Could any missionary, then, by resigning his post receive from government twice the income he would get from the mission? If missionaries were to be rewarded in arrears for their services, were there wharfs enough to go around? Dr. Judd had done nothing dishonest, yet it did not look well. Laura, however, claimed that they had never been so poor as missionaries as they were now—borrowing money to build a house up in Nuuanu Valley and having to mortgage the property. "It is a miserable feeling to be in debt, and yet we are supposed by many people in this community to be rich, very rich," she complained. Perhaps whispers of the oncoming wharf scandal somewhat humbled the good doctor, for when the 1847 legislature convened he appeared without the crowns on his coat lapels which had aroused such a storm.

While Judd and Wyllie fought their loud battles, William Richards toiled to rebuild the educational system and worked at other tasks of government. In July, during a meeting of the privy council, he found that he could not remember what he wanted to say. The general opinion was that he had worn himself out with overwork.

"A heavenly-minded man," Juliette Cooke thought him—generous, kind, disinterested. No one could accuse Richards of profiting from his job. When he returned from Europe he found his family in debt, only a small part of his salary having been paid to them. The chiefs voted $1,500 to help him pay his debts and build a house. But when he died on November 7 he had nothing to leave his family. The chiefs, in gratitude, granted an annuity of $800 and property having an income of $500.

One of the first company had also gone to his reward. Big, melancholy but pleasant Sam Whitney had died two years earlier, December 15, 1845, the first of the pioneers to die in the islands. Devoted to his beloved island of Kauai, he had spent most of his twenty-five island years there, a model missionary. When his time came, three of his children were in the United States, but Maria, his oldest and the first white girl born in the islands, had returned to be a missionary.

Poor Sam was a long time dying. "It is hard work to die," he said, after leaving messages for all his friends and children.

Would he like to have morphine, the doctor asked.

"I do not wish to go intoxicated into the presence of my Maker," Sam replied.

William Alexander bent over him. "Brother, now you are crossing the Jordan, tell me, do you feel the rock?"

"Yes, I am on it. Jesus is the rock!"

As his strength failed he asked Alexander to raise him up. Clasping his brother in his arms, he said: "Can it be that this is death? . . . Here all is peace and light and joy!" And so he died.

*   *   *

With government in the firm hands of Dr. Judd and morals in the firm hand of the church, it might seem that all was well. But human nature, that stubborn thing, had not yet yielded to the desire of the mission brethren to make a little heaven in this near-perfect spot of earth. Young Chester Lyman, another Yankee though no missionary (and no kin to the Reverend David Lyman), decided as he wandered about the islands in this year of 1847 that "the whole nation is rotten with licentiousness. Men hire out their wives and daughters without the least scruple, for the sake of money. It is computed by Dr. [Baldwin] of Lahaina that at that port, during the whaling season there are up-wards of 400 instances of intercourse with sailors daily. Waldo & Ben-son's establishment at that place is a perfect sink of iniquity. They are accustomed to have dances of naked girls for the entertainment of their customers, the whalemen. The most gross licentiousness is practised— & on one occasion the police took 40 women from their house at one time. The roads on the islands are mostly the work of persons convicted of adultery or some like crime." Lyman might have added that the roads were in remarkably good shape.

So long as strict monogamy remained an integral part of the Chris-tian code, there was work, and plenty of it, for the brethren to do. They did not even feel justified in entrusting church posts to Hawai-ians. Armstrong had been delighted with the help of Keikenui and had got him a license to preach. Shortly thereafter he had been found in bed with a woman not his wife. No wonder he had been able to preach "powerful and pointed sermons on licentiousness!"

The board at home kept criticizing the mission for holding all the strings in church and government. "The Hawaiian people are in danger of being excluded from all important offices and responsibilities both in church and state," it warned the mission. "Give them small tasks and then larger; train them up. They must have experience in order to become leaders, and you must not be unwilling to give up your posts to them. Something is wrong—can it be your reluctance to give up your posts?—if you cannot raise native leaders."

Sadly the brethren pointed to the evidence, even to the king him-self. To save Hawaii, the brethren were convinced, they must officer the craft for some time to come.

CHAPTER 23

THE GREAT MAHELE
1848–1849

DURING THE FOUR MONTHS WHEN RICHARDS LAY DYING, the privy council was looking for someone to take his place. Ever since the mission had brought the magic of writing, the palapala had been a central fact in Hawaiian life. First regarded as a mystery, a game, a wonderful toy, it had come to represent the haole's mastery of his surroundings, the secret of his strength and cleverness. Ever since Richards had become the king's "chaplain, teacher and translator"—indeed ever since the arrival of the mission, learning and good government had been closely identified. It had almost been taken for granted that sound knowledge was the basis of sound government. The post of minister of public instruction was therefore a crucial one, for it appeared to educated Hawaiians as well as to the Yankees (and one Scot) in the government that only by learning could the Hawaiian people save themselves from annihilation and their islands from being taken over by foreigners.

Having decided that Richard Armstrong, now pastor of Kawaiahao Church, was the best man for the job, the king himself urged him to accept it. But Richard held back. The brothers were mighty critical of the men who had left the mission for government.

"This is your proper work," the king said to him. "Why do you hesitate?"

The missionaries were being accused of a fondness for riches or honors, Richard replied.

"There is no end to what folks say, but what of that?" said one of the chiefs.

After first turning down the job, Armstrong wrote in his journal on December 6, 1847, that he had accepted it on a temporary basis until general meeting; "then, if the mission will consent, to accept of the office."

When general meeting came around in May, the brethren spent four days discussing Armstrong's case. When the mission refused to approve, Armstrong rose and with tears running down his face, said: "Brethren, I am going to leave you." Though they would not change their minds, the brethren wrote a letter saying they acknowledged the importance of the call and had the fullest confidence in him. On June 7, 1848, he finally became minister of public instruction. He held the post until his death in 1860, growing old and gray in the service and traveling tirelessly from island to island to visit every one of the five hundred schools and to examine personally every one of its students.

In 1848 Richard Armstrong was in his mid-forties, spare and wiry and rather small, full of drive and energy, fluent in Hawaiian, and with an attractive smile. The Hawaiians loved and trusted him.

To take care of his large family of eight children, ranging in age from three to sixteen, Richard moved into a building at the foot of Punchbowl (at the head of Richards Street) which the family named Stonehouse after the English residence of their friend Admiral Thomas. When the battery atop Punchbowl was fired, the windows and dishes rattled, much to the delight of the children—all of whom found the less restricted life outside the mission far more fascinating. Mary Jane wrote in delight to tell her cousin back home about a pet lamb which followed her upstairs and down. Then as now, going barefoot was socially acceptable in Honolulu, at least in the younger set. Begun as a matter of economy by the mission families, the habit remained because it was so sensible. Barefooted the children trotted through the thick dust of the Honolulu streets, raiding the sugar barrel in the mission depository or the licorice in the medicine chest, treading carefully the black, crunchy sand walk that led to the palace, pattering down to the wharfs to see a hundred ships nodding and nudging at each other when the whalers were in port.

The Armstrong youngsters began a peanut plantation, the avails of which were to support a mission to the heathen of the South Seas. But every time a peanut got big enough to eat, they ate it. The heathen languished. A beloved cat died, and young Sam wrote its epitaph: "REQUIES-CAT IN PACE." He and his brothers thereupon lowered the American consulate flag to half mast, so that all Honolulu was asking who had died. An unbeloved cat, a tom and a prowler, he shot and buried. When it astounded him by rising and strutting away on stiff cat legs, Sam shrugged his shoulders. "I've got one of his lives, he can have the rest," he said. This was the boy who was to be better known as General Samuel Chapman Armstrong, Civil War officer and founder of Hampton Institute, the idea for which he took from his father's interest in manual labor schools.

As the children grew older, interest shifted to the wonderful moonlight rides in a straw-filled wagon drawn by the horse Boki. All the way to Punahou they went, there to serenade the fair maidens at the boarding school. Or on other moonlit nights, with the fragrant tropic breeze blowing in off the ocean, they would ride out to Waikiki and Diamond Head, fifteen or twenty couples of them cantering across the moonswept plain together.

On rainy days there was always the study, three sides of it lined with books that had grown moldy and water-stained from travels by canoe and ox cart. Sometimes the chiefs came to visit, bearing fragrant odors of *lauhala* and ginger and *maile* wreaths about their bodies. Then the best foods were prepared and the children sang for the visitors whose noble dignity even youth was conscious of. Best of all were the soirées at the palace, approached through large wooden iron-bound gates manned by two sentries who presented arms as the minister of education and his family passed through. The throne room was bright with the feather capes of the chiefs and the tall kahilis held by petty chiefs and members of the household.

Smiling, the king himself lifted little Ellen Armstrong in his arms one time and set her upon the throne. "How would you like to be a queen?" he asked. The little girl, thrilled to that ecstatic blending of solemnity and bliss known only to the young, remembered it for the rest of her life.

While the young lived their own immensely important lives, Richard toiled for the schools. In 1849 Lahainaluna Seminary finally came under his care, the mission voting to transfer it since they were short of funds for its support. In charge there was Richard's own dear friend, William Patterson Alexander. Warm and affectionate, Alexander had worked for years in beautiful but isolated Hanalei Valley on

Kauai with the help of his sweet, lovely-looking Mary Ann. Fighting
the huge cockroaches, enormous rats, mice, fleas and mosquitoes, they
had in time established an orderly household. William himself had
laid up the chimney in the cookhouse and did much of the other work
on the Yankee-looking house which still stands at the end of its long,
beautifully green lawn with the rich green sudden hills rising behind
it. Then in 1843 the Alexanders had been transferred to Lahainaluna.
And there they stayed when the seminary was formally transferred to
the charge of their friend in 1850.

The friendly relations between Armstrong and the mission brothers
had a good deal to do with the smooth management of the schools, and
with mission influence on governmental affairs. For whether they liked
it or not, the brothers were in politics. They had tried scrupulously to
avoid getting in. They had refused time and again to give political
advice to the king and the chiefs, for their whole Congregationalist-
Separatist tradition was strongly opposed to any connection between
church and state. But their very presence in the islands was a political
fact which was bound to have political effects. When they saw grasping or immoral men trying to turn events in their own favor, they
could not sit idly back, for the very religion they had come to establish was at stake.

Since the mission now had the inside track and a receptive ear in
the privy council, the Catholics inevitably felt that their schools and
scholars were being discriminated against. From time to time French
warships tried to force the government to make special arrangements
for Catholic schools. "In regard to the schools, rather than the Catholic Bishop shall have the controul [sic] of any of them (as they are
sustained entirely by government) my mind is made up," Richard wrote
his brother, "to advise that they be suspended, or the system be abolished. This will be a severe stroke upon the nation, but it will be the
less of the two evils I am confident."

In the end, after the coming of the Mormons in 1850 had introduced
a third religious group to complicate the school picture, Armstrong
recommended that schools should be combined without regard to the
religion of the pupils, doing away with any religious instruction which
would be offensive to any one of the groups. There was a good deal
of opposition, but Armstrong's idea carried.

Meanwhile he kept up his fight for the principles he believed in. "I will try to give rum, & adultery, & gambling a kick in the posteriors that they will feel," he wrote to Dr. Baldwin.

One of his kicks, however, landed in a place altogether too tender for his own safety. The king had taken to drink again, and after expostulating with him to no effect, Armstrong told the king off by way of prayer in a public service. Angry and offended, the king brought the matter to the privy council and then retired to let them talk it over. Dr. Judd said he had threatened several times to resign unless the king would stay sober. Upshot of the whole matter was that the king threatened to resign unless Armstrong was removed. Paki said he would agree to Armstrong's leaving if the king would reform; John Ii said he would not agree to it because the fault was the king's. In the end things were patched up, the king forgave his minister, and they remained friends until his death.

In addition to running his department, visiting the outer islands—sometimes for ten-week stretches—keeping an eye on the king, preaching and raising his large family, Richard Armstrong also began to buy land. On his visits about the islands he saw how former missionaries like Jonathan Green were setting a good example of careful husbandry. Hawaii needed more such Yankee farmers to raise the whole economic standard of the islands, he thought. He was for importing them, as well as encouraging missionaries to seek their own support and inducing their children to settle down instead of going off to the United States.

The matter of land purchase and tenure had become, by 1848, the most important issue in the islands.

To the descendants of the Pilgrims, who had made outright ownership of land one of their great objectives, the Hawaiian system was indefensible. Ownership of land in fee simple, thought Yankee preachers and merchants alike, was the basis of a sound economy, of habits of industry—perhaps even the key to stopping the disastrous drop in the Hawaiian population which by 1850 was to sink to little more than 80,000.

So in 1846 the government as an experiment offered lands in Makawao on Maui (Jonathan Green's area) and Manoa Valley behind Honolulu. Green undertook to explain the new plan to his people.

Since the whole idea was foreign to them, it took some explaining. Always before whenever a new order had come along, it had meant more for the chiefs, less for themselves. But in the end, with Green's urging and patient explanation, most of them took a small piece of land.

John Ii handled the land in Manoa. He got into trouble when some of what he sold was claimed by chiefs who said it was theirs. A near-scandal developed when Ii tried to recover the titles. The *News* triumphantly announced that because it had exposed the situation, the common people won out.

But this was still on a small scale. Before real progress could be made, all the lands claimed by chiefs and king would have to be redistributed. The proposal was a drastic one, and if it had not been for the groundwork laid by the missionaries in the new concepts of freedom and of democracy which they had introduced, it could not have been accomplished at all.

The great Mahele, or dividing of the lands, converted Hawaii from a feudal to an individualistic basis. Compared with the million acres of crown lands, or the million and a half in government land and an equal amount to the chiefs, the 30,000 acres which the plain people had claimed by 1855 seems like a drop in the bucket. But this was all good farming land, while much of the other was mountainous or volcanic or otherwise unadapted to small farms.

To help the work along, many mission brethren turned surveyors. During their vacations mission lads in their teens went out as chain bearers to missionary fathers, earning the money they would need when they went home to college. Emerson at Waialua urged his people to take up land, and when they got him appointed government agent, he personally surveyed eight thousand acres into homesteads.

"You have done a noble work for your people," Justice Lee wrote him.

The mission was heart and soul in this last great effort to clothe the Hawaiian people with Yankee benefits, convinced that once they owned the ground they lived on, all other benefits would ensue.

It didn't work.

No steps were taken to prevent the people from selling their land. The matter was discussed in privy council, but although the lack of experience in land ownership was recognized as a danger, the council was not willing to put a curb on outright ownership. Then, in Judd's absence during 1849–50, the floodgates were opened when aliens living in Hawaii were granted the right to hold land in fee simple.

Inevitably the big plantations operated by foreigners—Yankees mostly—began to absorb the small holdings. High prices were offered, the people were tempted. Land ownership meant little to them; it was no part of their culture. So, as Kamakau remarked, the children of Kamehameha did not get the milk, and adopted children sucked the breasts dry.

The importation of the Yankee culture had inevitably begun the destruction of the Hawaiian community. Ironically, free ownership of the land, intended to revive the dying community, had given it the death stroke.

It is dangerous to tamper with any part of a culture. Culture is a web, and to tear one part of it damages the whole. From the moment when the Hawaiians cast away their own tabu system, their culture was doomed, and many worse things could have happened to it than to have it come under the influence of a group who in all sincerity had the interest of the Hawaiians at heart. It is idle, perhaps, to wonder how the job might have been better done. Surely if the whalers and traders had been given a free hand, the result would have been disastrous.

If Dr. Judd's counsel had been followed, and foreigners prevented from buying land, perhaps the Hawaiians would in time have got on their feet. But Hawaiian culture did not demand strenuous activity and "getting ahead." It assumed that life was good for and in itself. The Hawaiians, blessed with a beautiful and bountiful land, simply could not believe that life was meant to be lived in a constant rush and fret. So they never would have "developed" their resources; they would simply have enjoyed them. And this the western world could not stand. By hook or crook, therefore, the islands were fated to be taken over.

*   *   *

The process was hastened by the discovery of gold in California. California was closer to Hawaii than to the eastern United States by a matter of months, so the impact was felt first in the islands. Early in 1848 the notices of departure, required of all residents planning to leave the islands, began appearing in *The Polynesian*. By July they filled a long, closely-printed column. Hawaiian agriculture leaped into activity as demands for sugar, butter, hams, coffee, potatoes came pouring in. Prices rose fantastically. Here, if anywhere, was the spur the Hawaiians had needed to develop their resources. Woolen blankets brought fifty to a hundred dollars apiece at the mines. On October 7 the king's own schooner, the *Kamehameha III*, sailed for California with a load of men and provisions. The stores of Honolulu had been stripped. The price of knives had jumped from 62 cents to $2.25 a dozen. Local blacksmiths were making picks by the hundred. Twenty-seven vessels were soon plying between the coast and Hawaii. Among the goldseekers was William Kanui, member of the pioneer company, who got and lost $6,000 in California. Years later he was found blind and in poverty in San Francisco. Contributions were raised to bring him home, but he arrived only in time to die, in January, 1864.

To balance the heavy exports, California sent two products which spread like wildfire throughout the islands—measles and whooping cough. The children were hit worst. To Lowell Smith, working like all the mission brothers to save the people, it seemed that most of the youngsters were being swept away. His congregation fell off from 1,500 to 100. In November alone one thousand died on the island of Oahu. Those who, tortured by a burning fever, plunged into the ocean were dead within a few hours. The land was literally decimated.

*   *   *

Through all these changes and disasters the feeling against Dr. Judd had been steadily mounting. Even his friend James Jarves had quit *The Polynesian* early in 1848. According to Wyllie the reason was that Judd had concealed from Jarves the valuable wharf rents he was enjoying, and when Jarves found it out he felt that he could no longer defend Judd in print. Moreover, claimed Wyllie, Judd had pocketed $500 which the Wilkes expedition had given him for the mission. There were, in fact, other reasons why Jarves quit—one of them being that Libby consistently refused to live with him on any but "cold, kind terms, not as a wife." He had given her a written confession of adultery with which she could have got a divorce, but they were still nominally married when James sailed for San Francisco with one of the two children on February 4, 1848. Libby nearly died to part with her son, but the family was never reunited. After negotiating a treaty of friendship, commerce, navigation and extradition which was signed at Washington on December 6, 1849, Jarves embarked on a very different career as a collector of, and writer on early Italian painting.

The charges against Judd continued to pile up. Dillon, the newly appointed French consul ("a contemptible fellow, utterly destitute of principles," according to Armstrong), wrote a long letter to Judd in which he said that Wyllie was trying to get the doctor removed from government, thus bringing an end to American influence. Get rid of Wyllie, he argued; for he is intriguing to ruin you. Dillon went on to say that he had known some of Wyllie's friends in England who were well acquainted with "his steamlike propensity to write and to talk," that his departure had been a great relief, "particularly to the Reform Club of which he had been for some years past the great bore," and that the members often wondered "what the Hawaiian people had done to merit this scourge."

I know you think France wants to stick her fork into the Sandwich Islands as a kind of plum pudding, Dillon continued. "Two thirds of the time my inclination is only to laugh at the fuss that is made about this Lilliputian kingdom." Instead of letting Wyllie oust you, he suggested, "take the department yourself two, three, six months hence. Appoint your brother in law* under secretary or law adviser, give the finance department to Mr. Paty and the customs to some respectable party whom we shall select and you need expect no trouble from me."

A strange letter for a consul to send to a minister of state!

Judd took the letter to the privy council where Wyllie saw it and naturally was furious at Dillon. But Judd and Wyllie never really trusted each other from here on.

Dillon next teamed up with Ten Eyck and General Miller to accuse Judd of trading in partnership with William Paty and of appearing in the courts as a contending party in commercial transactions. Their remonstrance to the king got this answer: Judd is already being investigated by a high commission of inquiry.

Judd had a clerk named George M. Robertson who bore a grudge

* Asher Bates, who arrived in 1848 and soon became a government attorney.

against his employer and decided to get even with him by forcing his impeachment. He brought a long list of charges against the doctor: that he usurped business belonging to other departments, treated the office help in a dictatorial manner, traded in foreign goods without a license, refused and delayed some payments and illegally paid other bills, appropriated government money to his own use, wasted government funds or failed to make a proper accounting of them, and failed to have his books audited.

These were serious charges. Paki, Kekuanaoa, Ii, Wyllie, Armstrong and C. G. Hopkins (a small, effeminate Englishman who had become editor of *The Polynesian* and was friendly with the king and chiefs) were chosen to investigate. Some of the charges were quickly thrown out as not legally impeachable offenses. On most of the others the committee found insufficient evidence. It was true, they decided, that Judd had loaned government funds without any enabling legislation, but the privy council had authorized it. He had also sold for twelve and a half cents a pound coffee which the government had received for taxes at twenty cents a pound, but this was to encourage the coffee industry. A better system of accounts should have been set up, but Judd had not defrauded the government or acted for his own gain.

"He is a faulty man, very much so, but not unprincipled," wrote Armstrong.

So for the moment Judd's head still rested on his shoulders. His enemies bided their time.

CHAPTER 24

MULTIPLYING LIKE THE JEWS IN EGYPT
1848–1850

BY 1848 THINGS WERE COMING TO A CRISIS IN THE MISSION as well as in government. No matter how spiritually minded the brethren were, they could not help being affected by the current of events—by the demand for farm products, the rise in prices, the California fever. Several of their number had long since left the mission but remained in the islands, drawing their support from the land and in some cases continuing their evangelical work. Most conspicuous among these was Jonathan Green who had made quite a thing of wheat-growing at Makawao where the land sloped upward toward the great mound of Haleakala.

"Most like 'old folks' of any I have seen, that good old stamp that one regards highly," wrote a young Yankee visitor who called on the Greens.

Across the island from Honolulu at Waialua, Peter Gulick had bought three hundred acres of land at the special price allowed to missionaries (fifty cents less per acre than the land would otherwise have sold for) in recognition of their great services to the nation. Then, for $1,000, Gulick bought one hundred head of drought-starved cattle. It was a good investment. Under his management the herd prospered.

At Ewa, below Pearl Harbor, Artemas Bishop (transferred from Kailua in 1836) had built up a spanking good herd. Levi Chamberlain thought he was altogether too forward in claiming it as his own. Yet Bishop was sending to the mission treasury as much as four or five hundred dollars a year as a result of his profits in agriculture.

Clearly the time had arrived when something definite must be decided about the brethren's relationship to the land and the herds they had developed. With the prospect before them of making more money through the management of fields and herds than they could get from the mission, the sentiment was rising for a complete break from board support.

So in 1848 they assembled in Honolulu for an old-time general meeting, bringing their wives and children. There were now 130 children in the islands, and a good many more in the United States. Some of the families had not seen each other in fifteen years. On May 26 they all went to the palace to be received by the king and queen. Asa Thurston, looking like a biblical patriarch now in his flowing beard, recalled to the king the condition of the islands twenty-eight years ago when the pioneers came, and reminded him of his duty to commit to God all the interests of his kingdom. The king was pleased with the visit, and said so. But the thing that pleased him most was "the numbers and sprightliness of the children."

It was for these children that the brethren felt the necessity of making some permanent settlement of their worldly affairs. "We multiply like the Jews in Egypt," wrote Amos Cooke to his sister. "Perhaps we are to inherit the land." These were prophetic words for a Cooke.

Armstrong never ceased to preach the mutual benefits that would result if the mission children could be induced to settle permanently in the islands. "They will form a fine moral nucleus for future time and will, it may be hoped, perpetuate the good institutions their fathers have planted," he wrote the board. And the board, echoing his confidence, wrote back to parents who were worrying about their children's future: "The great field of enterprise, now, is certainly in the part of the world where you are."

So in their deliberations the brethren tried to figure out how to meet the needs of their children without drawing upon themselves any further criticism—there had been a God's plenty already—for worldly-mindedness. Although there was a good deal of disagreement, what it came down to was this. The present system of small cash salaries ($450 to a man and wife, $500 if in Honolulu) was no longer realistic. It did not meet the rising costs of living. Missionaries could do better by raising their own flocks and crops, relying upon their congregations to help support them. It was time the Hawaiian churches took up the responsibility of supporting their pastors anyway. And as this shift from board to congregational support occurred, missionaries must be free to acquire property. Artemas Bishop proposed that members of the mission leave the service of the board one by one as they were able to get their support from their people and their land.

Through all these negotiations, the brethren were extremely sensitive to the fact that they would be criticized for land-grabbing. Some of the men feared that leaving the board would open the way to love of gain and preoccupation with getting. While the mission was hammering out a plan to meet the new conditions, the board at Boston was reaching very similar conclusions. On July 19, 1848, it recommended that a missionary taking his release from the board be given the house he lived in and a part of the land and herds of the station, if the government would confirm the land to him. This, substantially, was how the mission became a locally supported church establishment.

Artemas Bishop immediately asked to be dismissed, requesting that the herd of one hundred cattle, half of which his wife had paid for, be made over to him.

One after another the members of the mission made the shift, sending in their request for dismission and in time receiving permission from the board. To round out the program, the churches began voting to support their pastor, as Lahaina did in March, 1850, with the understanding that $1,000 would be needed. Each pastor, as Bishop had proposed, was to dissolve his connection with the board as soon as his flock could support him, but in some stations this would be impossible for years to come, unless the pastor could support himself on the land.

It was a drastic change for the mission families. In a sense they were cutting themselves off from home, since the new arrangement did not provide any funds for transporting them back to the United States. They were casting their lot in the islands, and the lives of their children too.

"We have never perhaps felt more attached to the cause in which we are laboring," they told the board in summing up their 1848 meeting, "or more closely united in the bonds of fraternal affection, and though our numbers are diminishing we are not discouraged in our work, nor are we fearing a defeat from the fewness of our number or from the hosts of the enemy, for the Lord giveth power to the faint, and to him that hath no might he encreaseth strength."

The spring of 1848 had also seen the first marriage in the islands of a mission child. Maria Whitney, having returned from America as a missionary, had met on board a young man, the Reverend John Fawcett Pogue, who took her fancy. Mother Whitney for some reason or other did not approve of the marriage. It took place, nevertheless, on May 29 during general meeting. Two days later Mercy refused to attend the mission picnic "being not yet reconciled to her daughter's marriage." Since Maria had known John Pogue for five years, and since he was an upstanding, fine-looking gentleman, it is hard to see what Mercy objected to. Perhaps it was this tension in the family that had made Maria subject to "spasms." She must have got over them, for she lived to be eighty.

As the plan for self-support went forward, the man who had done more than any other to keep the fiscal affairs of the mission in order began to weaken towards his end. Levi Chamberlain, now in his fifties, had been having trouble with his lungs for years and had taken two voyages in search of relief—one to China and one to the United States. They had done him no permanent good. Now, in the early months of 1849 he had grown so feeble that he had to stay in bed. He was not afraid of dying. His only fear was that he might live to be a burden to his family.

The blue eyes and fair hair looked faded now, the rather melancholy cast of his features made more so by the hollows beneath his high cheekbones.

On July 29 he beckoned his wife, Maria, to him, embracing her with arms grown thin and weak. Then he kissed her and said, "Farewell. Very pleasantly have we lived together for twenty-one years. Now we must separate. I commit you to the Lord." Then he kissed the children and said farewell to them—five of the seven were living at home—also bidding good-by to his friends and the doctor. He soon fell asleep without a sound, a peaceful smile on his face and not a wrinkle in his forehead.

"I never knew a better man," wrote Richard Armstrong. That simple but superlative tribute was one with which every brother in the mission could heartily agree. Conscientious to a painful degree, Levi had never demanded as much of others as he asked of himself. He had not been happy about the shift to private property, fearing that it would open the way to too much worldliness and greed.

Perhaps he was right.

* * *

While the mission was shifting its basis of support, the French consul Dillon was continuing to harass the government and its ministers. Between him and Wyllie began to rise a great pile of communications, the pages of which fairly smoked with acrimony. But when in April, 1849, he advised the king to get rid of his ministers of finance and foreign relations, the privy council decided to crack down. All questions at issue were hereafter to be referred directly to the French government, which was requested to recall Dillon. Jarves, now in the United States, was appointed a special commissioner to negotiate with the French in Paris.

When Rear Admiral Legoarant de Tromelin, commander of French naval forces in the Pacific, arrived with two ships-of-war in August, therefore, Dillon was thirsting for revenge. Together the two men presented an ultimatum on August 22. It listed a number of alleged grievances and made ten demands which were to be agreed to within three days—or else.

Since the demands included those usual with the French—low duties on liquor, separate school superintendents for Catholic schools, an official apology by government for the Lahainaluna students who had impiously dabbled their hands in holy water—they were refused.

On August 25 Tromelin sent an armed force ashore. Reaching the fort, they demanded its surrender. You have it, Governor Kekuanaoa told them. What more do you want?

Where were his soldiers?

Gone into the country, to their homes.

Their arms?

Taken with them.

Haul down your flag, they demanded.

"If you desire to have the flag down, haul it down yourself—I shall not."

The flag stayed there during the two weeks of occupation. Meanwhile the soldiers defaced the fort, spiked the ancient cannon, wrote obscenities on the walls and blackened the beach with the barrels of gunpowder they destroyed. No resistance was made, much to the amazement of the French, nor was anybody frightened. Crowds poured into the fort to see what the French would do. "Finding nothing else to fight," reported Richard Armstrong, "they went to work on the poor governor's old windows, calabashes &c. and over these they gained a most splendid victory." In addition to the fine old calabashes, furniture and other effects were smashed or stolen.

Tromelin next seized the king's yacht, the *Kamehameha III*. It was a handsome schooner, especially built in Baltimore in 1845 for sale to the king. When it beat his own schooner in a race to Lahaina, he bought it for $10,000. When Tromelin tried to sail the yacht away, however, it refused to budge. Watchers on shore had a good laugh at the French sailors who lacked the magic to sail a Yankee ship. At last the admiral sent a diver down. He found a stout line running from keel to shore.

On September 5 (1849) the squadron departed. Despite protests, the king's yacht was never returned.

Dillon also sailed away with his family, headed for France by way of San Francisco. It now appeared to the Hawaiian government that they had better send someone to France and not rely solely on Jarves, who would not have full information of the Tromelin outrage. So on September 11 Gerrit Judd departed with two young princes in tow— Lot and Alexander. The community had been drawn by the Tromelin affair into greater harmony than it had ever known before, and Judd was never more popular than when he sailed off with the young princes, now fifteen and nineteen. The king and queen, the chiefs and privy council and a vast crowd stood on the dock to see them off, and all the ships in the harbor cheered them as they glided out to sea. With Judd went secret instructions empowering him, if necessary, to negotiate the sale or transfer of the sovereignty of the islands, subject to ratification.

On his way through San Francisco Judd met Charles Eames, who had been authorized to negotiate a treaty in Hawaii. Since Judd also had negotiating powers, Eames completed the document without going on to the islands. Jarves meanwhile was negotiating another treaty at

Washington, unaware of Judd's impending arrival. In the end a new treaty embodying aspects of both was signed by Jarves at Washington December 20, 1849.

Judd was able to accomplish little or nothing in Paris, for the French government refused to alter its views on the liquor tax, the matter of Catholic schools or any other important issue.

But for Alexander, the heir apparent, the trip was a lark which also had its educative values. In France they took up fencing and French. On their return, the United States seemed dull by contrast with Europe. "This country I am much disappointed in in everything," Alexander confided to his journal. They were presented to President Fillmore, but "the old fellow's mind seemed to be on other subjects besides receiving visitors."

As they were leaving Washington, Alexander went ahead to board the train and was roughly ordered off by a conductor who apparently took him for a Negro. It was a slight he never forgot, and very possibly it retarded by more than forty years the annexation of Hawaii. No such thing had ever happened in Europe, "but in this country I must be treated like a dog, to go and come at an American's bidding," wrote Hawaii's next king.

The rest of his stay was colored by the experience. Americans, he decided, had no manners, no politeness to a stranger. Only at Dr. Judd's family home in Michigan (his people had moved west) did he find true happiness. Here the rural setting, the joyful tears of Dr. Judd's mother, the pretty girls who came to a church picnic delighted him. When the young ladies left their shawls and straw bonnets near Orchard Lake, an ox stepped up and selected a bonnet. Only the end of the ribbons stuck out to tell its fate when the party, returning, found the animal soberly ruminating the remains.

Judd and the princes reached Honolulu September 9, 1850, having been gone two days less than a year. It was England, not the United States, which had impressed them most. "In England an African can sit by Queen Victoria," Alexander remarked. He thought he knew how to interpret the lesson.

CHAPTER 25

PHYSICIAN, HEAL THYSELF
1850–1854

FROM SWEET HOME UP IN NUUANU VALLEY DR. JUDD HAD a magnificent and uninterrupted view of Honolulu and the harbor, all the way from the mission buildings to the left, past the palace and the business section and thence to Pearl Harbor and Barber's Point with the Waianae Mountains on the right. He could see, as he started downtown of a morning, that even in the year he had been away, the place had changed. Iron or picket fences were replacing the drab old adobe walls. Though swine still rooted and wallowed in the streets, and a man might even be killed by a steer breaking loose on its way to market, still Honolulu was getting to be more of a town. With its rather prim churches, its boxy mercantile houses and its shanty-like shops and offices, the place looked like a cross between a New England village and a western frontier town. The combination was natural enough, since Honolulu was half Yankee and half California. Now that California was a state—it had been admitted the very day Judd and the princes returned to Honolulu—the United States had leaped a whole continent and come months nearer to the islands.

One result, the doctor discovered, was that wages had jumped sky high. With everyone and his uncle off to the gold fields, a cook or washerwoman could now demand and get an outrageous $20 to $30 a month instead of the standard $5. To be hauled ashore from a ship in the harbor cost a dollar instead of a quarter.

Honolulu, with the whaler trade and the potato boom to bolster its confidence, was a growing community. The king had even declared it a city during the doctor's absence, designating it as his capital and giving names to twenty-nine streets.

This was well enough. But what Gerrit Judd did not like was the law permitting unnaturalized foreigners to own land in fee simple. He had fought the idea hammer and tongs, and then as soon as he was away they had passed it—and on Brother Armstrong's motion at that. It would be the ruin of Hawaii, Judd was sure.

Before going to his office in Honolulu Hale, Judd often walked down to "the beach" where along with the tall customs house and the commodious new market were a number of mercantile houses. He liked the stir and bustle of the waterfront; he had money invested there and still drew his wharf rents.

Here was Rogers, the customs guard, swearing at a man in a boat.

"What's wrong?" Judd asked.

"Why, I can't make this stupid Kanaka understand how to get that barrel of beef onto the wharf."

"Psha!" said the doctor. "Give me a rope and I will show you."

Handy in all fields, Doctor Judd made a parbuckle and hauled the barrel up onto the wharf—never knowing that it was full of rum. Rogers, bribed to overlook the fact, heaved a grateful sigh when the doctor walked away.

Enterprising Yankees, eager to avoid the high duty on liquor, often sent casks that pretended to be what they were not. One shipper sent two hundred barrels of beef from Boston. When the last cask was being landed on the wharf it fell and broke, disclosing a ten gallon keg of brandy inside. The other 199 were then opened and found to be the same.

At the waterfront Dr. Judd was likely to run into Charles Bishop, the young man who had come out with Judge Lee and who had recently replaced William Paty as collector of customs. Bishop had married the lovely Bernice Pauahi the previous June. This was Paki's accomplished daughter, a graduate of the Chiefs' School and now nineteen. Her parents had been dead set against the marriage, and so was most of Honolulu society. Mixed marriages still carried the onus of the old easygoing arrangements which had formerly characterized them. None of the chiefs came—not even Paki—and the couple did not even send round pieces of wedding cake. Only the Armstrongs were on hand from court circles. Bernice wore a simple gown of white muslin and a wreath of jasmine. The next evening they left for a trip to Kauai. On their return they moved into a small cottage but took their meals at Mrs. Ladd's—apparently cooking had not been one of the subjects taught at the Chiefs' Children's School. But after a while Bernice's parents forgave her and the young couple went to live with them in the large two-storied building on King Street where the Bank of Hawaii now stands. With its verandas running around both stories, it was one of the finest homes in the city. Paki called it Haleakala—House of the Sun.

The time would come when Honolulu society would angle for their favor, for though Bernice refused to be queen, she ultimately became heir of the Kamehameha line, acquiring vast land holdings which she placed in trust for a number of worthy charities continued to this day by the Bishop Estate.

Leaving the waterfront, then, Dr. Judd would walk to his office in Honolulu Hale, a two-storied building with the inevitable lookout on top. Passing through an arched gateway, he went up the steps and into the corner room on the lower floor which accommodated the treasury department. Wyllie, with his stacks of official papers and his never-ending correspondence, occupied the upper floor.

Shortly after his return in 1850 Judd had made up his mind that he could not get on with Wyllie any longer. The two had never been entirely compatible. Judd was a driver—a man who liked to get things done; Wyllie a negotiator and manipulator who delighted in the verbiage and complication of diplomacy. The quarrel simmered and cooked without quite coming to a boil. But it destroyed the harmony of the privy council. The two men were rather evenly matched. Judd had the advantage of Wyllie in his sound knowledge of Hawaiian. Judd was also, in Judge Lee's carefully weighed opinion, bold and cunning. "But in mind and heart, in all that is generous, liberal and manly, Wyllie is far his superior. . . . Ever since Judd came home he has been uneasy and dissatisfied. His arbitrary temper, his wounded pride, his hate of all rivals, his solicitude to promote his relatives, and his ambition to preside over the department of the Interior, all conspire to render his position grievous to himself and his friends."

Wyllie, it is clear, had more of a genius for making friends than Judd. The townspeople had grown accustomed to seeing him walk up and down to his home, Rosebank, in Nuuanu Valley—always in the same white hat and blue coat with golden crowns, his russet moustache matching a brown plush vest. "The same fussy, kind-hearted scribbling old bachelor," Lee called him. At Rosebank the chairs and tables were loaded with neat piles of letters and documents when his Tea and Twaddle Society—a group of teen-age girls he was fond of—came at his invitation to eat and play with him.

But Wyllie, a good diplomat, was not above stretching his kindness to cover both sides in a dispute. To Armstrong he could write that he had a higher regard for the Protestant missionaries and that the distinction he drew between them and the Catholics would give great offense to the latter if they knew of it. To a friend he could write, at about the same time, that though bred a Scotch Presbyterian, "from all I see around me, the Catholic Missionaries judged by the rule of Scripture, have really more of the Christian Character than the Congregationalists of the New England States, who so much abound among us." Maybe he was thinking of Judd!

While this conflict simmered, the first election of the legislature by ballot took place early in January of 1851. Before the legislature could meet, another French diplomat arrived, presenting new demands. Louis Perrin, with whom Judd had dealt in Paris, was the new consul and commissioner, and he was soon making about the same claims with which the French had bedeviled Hawaii for years. This time the king, tired of the struggle, determined to put his islands under the protection of a power strong enough to squelch the French. General Miller was sounded out on the possibility of raising the British flag over the islands if Perrin got too insistent. But the joint French-British agreement of 1843 prevented this.

On March 11, therefore, the king and John Young, as premier, signed a document which put the islands in the hands of the United States, either until the difficulties with France could be ironed out, or perpetually in case of failure to reach an agreement. The new commissioner, Luther Severance, arranged with the captain of the U.S.S. *Vandalia* then in port to defend the American flag if it was raised, even to firing on the French ship *Sérieuse* if necessary. Perrin, getting wind of what had happened, quickly agreed to a halfway settlement which satisfied neither side but at least brought an end to the squabble —and to American annexation.

*   *   *

To add to the perplexities of a harassed government, the potato boom now staggered and collapsed. By the fall of 1851 it was over. Trade with California fell off disastrously. Then came a drought, lasting nearly half a year, which put an end to agricultural prosperity for the time being. On top of this a poor whaling season threw the whole economy into a tailspin.

1852 began more hopefully with the arrival of the steamship *Constitution* which loped over to Lahaina and back, cutting down to a day or two a voyage which under sail could take weeks. (News now arrived from New York in six weeks.) Business was still dull, but there were signs of hope on the horizon. A clever Yankee mechanic named David Weston built a centrifugal machine to separate sugar from molasses, thus shortening to minutes a process which had taken weeks. Later in the year a group of business and government leaders which included Wyllie, Lee, Armstrong, Bishop, Stephen Reynolds, Lorrin Andrews and Dr. Judd formed a joint stock company to provide capital for island enterprises. Tropical crops could be produced at a profit, they felt. But co-operative effort to provide capital, management and marketing was needed. The Hawaiian plantation system had reached another step in its development.

By the middle of the year whaling was prosperous again and prices were profitably high. By November a hundred American whalers crowded the harbor, each with thirty men aboard, half of whom were generally ashore with little to do. A riot reminiscent of the old days ended in their setting fire to the town, and then helping man the fire engine to put it out. Martial law had to be proclaimed, however, and about a hundred men were locked in the fort before the fracas was broken up.

To meet the desires and tastes of the seamen, something new had been added to the Honolulu scene in the shape of public dance houses where a man could meet a girl and spin her around, in rounds or squares, to a good orchestra. Every night but Sunday, in shipping season, the houses were in full swing. The missionaries were furious.

"These dancing houses whereby they get native girls are the most perfect brothels, no doubt," Richard Armstrong complained. "But by what law can we put them down?"

The sailors spent their money freely, which was good for business. But living costs were getting too high to suit the local residents.

"You will think perhaps that I am getting rich on two thousand five hundred dollars a year," Lorrin Andrews wrote to his brother John. "So I ought to be but am not. Our expenses are considerable. Flour is now twenty dollars per barrel. Wood (fuel) from twelve to sixteen dollars per cord. We pay a hundred and fifty dollars per annum for washing and we find soap. Lumber for any kind of wood work is from 100 to 120 dollars per thousand feet. Labor among mechanics is from 3 to 5 dollars per day. . . . We have no help nor can we get any. We do our own work or it must go undone."

As for the seven children, all were well—from twenty-four-year Lorrin now a clerk on a Maui sugar plantation down to eight-year-old Mary. Lorrin senior was proud of his oldest son—"intelligent, uses both languages, English and Hawaiian, equally well, and sustains a good moral character. . . . But," father sadly added, "has no religion." Times were changing indeed!

Explaining the prevalence of foreigners in government to his brother, Lorrin continued: "The native chiefs see and understand that the present Government is the best, but they do not understand the method of its administration. . . . If the foreign officials were to withdraw from their places, the wheels of Government would not continue to run for a month; everything would be in utter confusion. The native rulers of themselves are utterly inadequate to perform the duties growing out of the offices which they hold."

There were situations, however, which even the foreign officials could not cope with.

In February of 1853 the *Charles Mallory* sailed into port with a case of smallpox aboard. It was strictly quarantined. Immediately Dr. Judd attempted, though without much success, to produce vaccine. Armstrong was ordered to get a general campaign of vaccination under way, but the result was disappointing—only two out of every two hundred were successful. Then in May the brig *Zoe* landed a chest of clothes which were sold at auction. Shortly thereafter smallpox broke out in the town and spread with frightening speed. As usual the poor Hawaiians were hardest hit.

The legislature created a health commission to which Judd, another doctor (T. C. B. Rooke) and the marshal, W. C. Parke, were appointed. Hospitals were set up where victims could be isolated. Lee, Bishop, Judd and others personally visited the afflicted to give what help they could. Yellow flags flew where the infection struck; houses were burned and dogs killed in hopes of checking the disease. It only grew worse. Those who had recovered from the disease were ordered to man the yellow carts that gathered the dead and took them to the cemetery. Bodies, said Kamakau, were stacked like cord wood while awaiting the cart, their heads and feet sticking out from the sheets that covered them.

Dr. Baldwin, appointed commissioner of public health for Maui, was determined the disease would get no foothold on his territory. To every village he sent or himself carried the message: Let no one come ashore. But as frightened people fled by canoe from pest-ridden Oahu, it became impossible to keep them out.

So the disease got in. Baldwin set up a temporary hospital outside Lahaina to which patients were carried by canoe. When the crew had delivered its unhappy cargo, they dived over the side and swam about "to wash off the disease." The doctor vaccinated furiously, went without sleep to tend his people, and when it was all over had managed to keep the death toll down to 250. On Oahu it was ten times that many according to official report, and probably much more. In October the scourge was over.

Though he did not catch the disease, the epidemic was fatal to Dr. Judd. At the height of it all a group of Judd-haters turned into an oust-Judd movement a meeting held to consider new control measures. Behind the movement stood two doctors—Lathrop and Newcomb— who had grudges against their colleague. These two men together with eleven others now played upon the fears and anxieties of the people, blaming Judd and Armstrong—quite unjustly, of course—for the epidemic. In reality it was the old hatred of mission influence "as it has tended to the enactment & enforcement of laws against intemperance, licentiousness, Sabbath desecration &c.," as Armstrong noted in his journal. "These are obnoxious to most foreign residents in Honolulu, & they wish to remove from office, all who sustain such a policy."

On July 20 another meeting authorized the "Committee of Thirteen" to draft a petition for the removal of Judd and Armstrong. While this was being circulated, another meeting was called for July 25 at Kawaiahao Church. Here respectable men like John Ii, in a gathering mostly Hawaiian, adopted counter-resolutions and circulated another petition. When the petitions reached the king, he appointed a committee of the privy council to examine them. The anti-Judd paper, the committee decided, was full of spurious Hawaiian signatures, pressing charges that were vague and unsubstantiated. So said Governor Kekuanaoa, Ii, Andrews, Prince Lot and Piikoi. Moreover, few of the haole signers were Hawaiian citizens.

A struggle now went on both within the council and within the town over Dr. Judd, and efforts were made to convince the king that if Judd were not ousted, the opposition would attempt to take over the government.

At last the king asked all four ministers—Wyllie, Armstrong, Judd and John Young—to hand in their commissions. On September 5 he reappointed all but Judd, who was replaced by Elisha Allen, until recently the American consul.

"Why Dr. Judd was dropped, I do not certainly know, not being in the councils of the chiefs for the last few days," wrote Richard Armstrong. "His general unpopularity may have helped the matter, & some private influences hostile to him, all together may have decided the case. . . . He has been for many years the butt of a fierce opposition in Honolulu; and although faulty in his manner of doing things, & often gives offence unnecessarily, yet injustice is often done him. Substantially I regard him as a good man." And Charles Bishop concurred: "Exceedingly unpopular with all parties though with all his faults a better man, and more honest than his principal accusers and enemies."

After the battle that had raged around him for years, Gerrit Judd no doubt returned with mixed feelings to his medical practice. A great load had been lifted off his shoulders, yet he had enjoyed the sense of power and importance. Getting a living from medicine for his large family would be no lark. Yet he faced it as bravely as he had faced the battles of the last ten years.

Wyllie, who may have proven the appropriateness of his name in behind-the-scenes efforts to oust Judd, wrote to Ricord soon after the event:

"It was always my view that your services were immeasurably more valuable than those of Dr. Judd, whom neither nature or education had fitted for any other office than those of petty peddling, bill discounting and the lowest kind of brokerage. As for being a statesman, he never was cut out for that.

"But with his two large estates," Wyllie continued, "one on East Maui and one on Oahu, his grazing farm on Waikiki planes [*sic*], his house and lot, which might be let for $800 a year and his famous wharf annuity of $1,000 annually, he is three times as well provided for as the late Mr. Richards, without ever having been one tithe of the service."

Well, perhaps. But Wyllie had honest reasons for disliking Judd, and he seems to have let them run away with him.

Armstrong was more than a little surprised that he had not been dropped too, though his conscience was clear. "As to my getting rich, were I called from earth today my family would be in want." The land at Haiku on Maui, given him for the work he did before becoming minister, thirty-six acres in Manoa Valley for which he had paid more than the market price, and a house worth $8,000 which the government had sold him for $5,000 were all he had got in addition to his salary. As for the house, "it was sold at a loss to the government of over $3,000; but the price I offered was all I was able or willing to give, at the time, because I thought I could do better than give any more for *such a house then.*"

"I expect little else than trouble and opposition while I remain in office," he wrote Dr. Baldwin, "and I only remain to sustain the interest for which I have and we all have so long labored—schools, morals and religion—the great things to the people, without which they must sink back to heathenism. . . . These mal-contents want to get all missionary influence, root and branch out of the government. So says Newcombe & co. Miserable! What good would they have had, but for us missionaries?"

Perhaps the ouster of Judd gave some satisfaction to David Malo, who had led the first revolt against foreigners in government. David, with his quizzical look and his broad upper lip, had finally persuaded the mission to let him minister to an independent church at Keokea in the Kula district of Maui where, as he wrote the mission at Honolulu, he was "doing his best for God." He would have been happy there except for the behavior of his third wife, Rebecca. First she took to sleeping when he wanted to pray with her and teach her. Then she took to sleeping with the wrong people. She was seen going into the church at Lahaina with a man named Manaku. They stayed there alone for two hours and afterwards David beat her with a small stick. Perhaps the stick was not big enough. Anyway, Rebecca soon left him because he tried to crack down on her fancy clothing. People were saying that she had been guilty of adultery with several others besides Manaku.

Grieving over his wife's infidelity, David nevertheless found time to set down a description of the old days which, translated into English as *Hawaiian Antiquities,* was to become the most fascinating picture of pre-missionary Hawaii. Still grieving, this good if sometimes over-passionate man died on October 21, 1853. His last request was that he be buried at the top of Mount Ball, high up behind Lahainaluna, "beyond the rising tide of foreign invasion," as he quaintly put it. The grave is there today, visited once a year by students from the same school David had attended as a grown man.

*   *   *

As early as 1849 American newspapers had begun to talk of annexing the islands and admitting them to the union as the state of Hawaii. In 1852 it was advocated for the first time in Congress as a necessary step to protect the Pacific coast and American trade routes to the Orient where Perry was now preparing to force open the empire of Japan. With Texas annexed, the Oregon question settled and New Mexico and California under the American flag, American influence was inevitably on the rise. A proposal was even forwarded to Dr. Judd from New York offering to buy the islands for $5,000,000!

Soon after California began to swarm with opportunists, rumors had begun to reach the islands of filibusters on their way to overthrow the government. In 1851 a gang of suspicious characters arrived on the *Gamecock,* rifled the mail bag during the voyage and threw many letters overboard. Preparations were made to lock them up if they became troublesome, and they soon left.

"Annexation we do not want," Richard Armstrong wrote his

brother-in-law in 1851. But by 1854 the situation had changed so that he was saying, "Our whole safety now lies in hugging close to Uncle Sam." France was threatening again, and if she went far enough, annexation would be the result. "Though it would be bad for the natives, I prefer it to French insolence, popery and brandy," said Richard.

In August, 1853, a group of prominent men including Charles Bishop and Samuel Castle (now separated from the mission) sent to the king a memorial which recommended annexation. None of the missionaries signed it. On February 6, 1854, the king signed an order instructing Wyllie to negotiate with the United States regarding annexation. Several months later the new American commissioner, David Gregg, received a commission from President Pierce which authorized him to negotiate a cession, subject to ratification.

In the meantime General Miller came charging into Armstrong's office in a perfect rage over some articles in a paper edited by Armstrong's clerk. They favored annexation. Patiently Armstrong told the old war horse that he had not even known his clerk was to edit the paper.

"He stormed & said I had gone altogether too far with this matter of annexation; that he & Mr. Perrin were not going to allow a few missionaries to annex the Islands; that I had one narrow escape & had better look out." And a good deal more, all in a passionate manner. "I managed to keep my temper," Richard noted with some satisfaction.

On August 27, 1854, Admiral Theodorus Bailey, U.S.N. sailed into Honolulu aboard the *St. Mary's* charged with "an important mission." A few days later he wrote to his brother: "I hope before I leave to be in part instrumental in adding another Star to the Constellation of the Union—but this in confidence."

One hundred years later, and more than fifty years after annexation took place, Hawaiians were still hopefully waiting for that star.

The king, meanwhile, seemed to be heartily in favor of annexation. It would relieve him of a good deal of worry and perhaps allow him to get on with his drinking (he was doing too much again) without the guilty feeling that affairs of state were embarrassed by it. Then there was Alapai, John Young's wife, to whom he had taken a fancy. He and John changed wives without the missionaries' ever getting wind of it, according to Kamakau, though Kalama continued to appear with the king on state occasions.

But the king would not do anything without the approval of his heir to the throne, young Prince Alexander Liholiho. When Alexander thought of American control, he remembered the conductor who had kicked him off a train in Washington because his skin was not white. While Commissioner Gregg waited anxiously, and many of the foreigners in Honolulu waited hopefully, the king held the question under advisement but did nothing.

There, for the moment, the matter precariously rested.

CHAPTER 26

SISTERS, COUSINS, AUNTS
1850–1854

IN THE *Honolulu Times,* AN ANTI-MISSIONARY, ANTI-government weekly which fluttered for a year and then was silent, a letter appeared in 1850 inquiring of the editor how a newcomer could hope to acquire land.

"Go to Boston and be appointed a missionary," the editor answered, "uphold the government and you will obtain land with ease."

Mercantile, non-missionary Honolulu was certain that the missionaries were inheriting the Hawaiian earth. When the privy council in August received from Wyllie and John Young a recommendation that missionaries (Protestant or Catholic) who did not already own 560 acres of land be allowed to purchase up to that amount at fifty cents an acre less than the market price, the opposition claimed that this merely proved what they had been saying all along—the way to get land was to become a missionary.

The Wyllie-Young recommendation (later approved by the privy council) limited the privilege to missionaries who had been eight years in the islands. It was based upon the belief that Hawaii would benefit from having the mission children remain as permanent residents of the islands. For the most part their parents were too poor to give them any kind of a start in life. But with land to work, they could raise cattle or cane and in time get a modest living.

No one then had any notion that the land would one day be valuable. Some missionaries bought no land at all, a few invested as much as $1,000, but most bought only a few hundred acres. Values rose at most only $2,000 to $5,000 during the life of the purchaser—hardly a way of getting rich quick. The special privileges granted missionaries had a value of about $280 to a family—hardly a princely sum. Jean Hobbs, who examined every deed and land transaction, concluded: "The popular theory that missionaries acquired land by dishonest practice is unsupported by facts." Missionaries sold their lands for nominal sums and left but small areas to their heirs.

For his labors in surveying eight thousand acres into about three hundred homesteads, John Emerson was rewarded with a gift of fifteen acres—total value $75. Now that his people had land, the next problem was how to get the products of the soil from Waialua to Honolulu. Nothing that could be called a road existed. When the government was finally persuaded to bridge the deep gulches and widen the narrow horse trail into a road, John Emerson was the only one who could do the engineering and bossing. So he became road supervisor. During his two years in office he built five bridges, grading and constructing eighteen miles of road. "The people ploughed and planted," his son recalled, "oxen were trained, carts were put on the road to transport their produce to town, and there sprang up quite a cross-country trade." Since the land was unwatered and good only for pasture, John advised his people to keep no more than eighteen head to one hundred acres. After his death the rule was disregarded, the cattle grew poor and unsalable and the people had to sell their land to get out of debt.

*   *   *

As the mission shifted from the common stock to the self-supporting system, steps were taken to convert the depository to a private business. At the general meeting in 1851 Brothers Castle and Cooke were released from the mission after agreeing to take over the goods of the depository at cost and to sell to the brethren at cost plus five (later ten) per cent. They were also to have the use of the depository and the available cash in the treasury. On June 5 the two men signed articles of partnership and the firm of Castle & Cooke was born. Sam Castle soon visited the United States to confer with the board and to establish relations for the new firm with homeside merchants.

The arrangement seems to have satisfied the partners, for the profits from the last two months of the year ran over a thousand dollars. By August, 1852, Amos Cooke noted that they had sold $7,000 worth of goods to non-missionaries at a profit of twenty-five per cent. Flour went for $24 a barrel, but to the brethren at $10. "We shall be glad to get $1,000 where some merchants get $10,000, and try to be more grateful for it than they," wrote Amos.

Brothers Hall and Dimond had also left the mission, Dimond to run a store of his own, Hall into government and then to found the firm of E. O. Hall & Son.

*　　　*　　　*

By 1852 the children who had been born of mission parents amounted to the impressive total of 283. As the offspring of parents who had always called each other "Brother" and "Sister," they had a good right to call each other "Cousin." Truly their sisters and their cousins could be reckoned up by dozens, in Gilbertian phrase—nay, even in hundreds.

Some of them were already grown men and women, returned to the islands after a mainland education, both in the single and the wedded state. Persis Thurston had returned as the wife of the Reverend Townsend Taylor who served first as seamen's chaplain at Lahaina but in 1852 had moved to Honolulu to be pastor of the Second Foreign Church. Beside Maria Whitney, two of the other girls had married ministers.

But the most romantic of the cousins was Asa Thurston who after graduating from Williams had spent two years in the gold fields of California and was now in Honolulu sporting a most "elegant mustache," high boots and a hat that bore the very breath of California. Elizabeth Jane Bishop, writing home to her brother Sereno, warned him: "Don't expect gracious advances from Asa Thurston. He probably won't call on you when you arrive . . . seeks only the company of Persis and Mr. Taylor." Jane thought him smart but shy. But the Judd girls—great beauties, as everyone agreed—were amiable to the fascinating cousin. They apparently did not find him stand-offish.

Then there was Charlie Judd who had grown up loving horses, frequently absenting himself from school when something important like a ride or a picnic came up. Seventeen now, he had been placed for a while by his father as government auditor. But "his majesty didn't choose the young duke for that post," William Goodale reported to Nevins Armstrong. So Charlie went over to Kauai with his father to auction off a batch of government-owned horses the doctor had acquired—some said at too easy a bargain.

Between the Judds and Thurstons a cloud had arisen. The two men had had an open quarrel, the upshot of which was that the Judds stopped sitting in the choir. But this did not seem to prevent the young from getting together. Besides the Judds and Thurstons, there were Henry Whitney, Orramel Gulick and Warren Chamberlain—all in their twenties.

In January, 1853, Sereno Bishop reached Honolulu with his young bride. In his metal-rimmed glasses Sereno looked earnest and scholarly as no doubt a recently ordained man should. He was in time to become principal of a revived Lahainaluna, editor of the *Friend,* map-maker, volcanologist and discoverer of "Bishop's Rings" which circled the earth when Krakatoa erupted in 1883.

Before Sereno returned to the islands, another "cousin" arrived in 1852 with his young wife, bound as a missionary to Micronesia. He was Luther Halsey Gulick, physician and ordained minister. On Sunday morning, March 28, his brother John who was studying at Punahou saw a large merchantman drop its anchor outside the harbor. No passengers—not mission people anyway—would come ashore on a Sunday, but early Monday morning John rode down to the docks. Much to his disappointment Orramel, the brother between himself and Luther, had already taken a boat and gone out to the ship. Shortly thereafter the passengers came ashore—not only Luther and his wife, but Lucy Thurston returning from her second trip to the United States, another couple, the Snows, also headed for Micronesia, and two other returning mission couples, the Parises and the C. B. Andrews. Claudius Andrews also had a bride with him— he had first come out as a single man in 1844. Moreover, he had the presence of mind to bring a spare—his wife's sister Samantha, whom he married when his first wife died in 1862. The Gulick family—six sons and one daughter—being short on women were delighted with their new sister, Louisa. They thought her cultivated but unassuming, simple and natural in her manners, "not beautiful in natural appearance but very lovely in her character." And they co-operated to introduce her to the islands.

Meanwhile, general meeting opened at Honolulu on May 8 (1852). There were now so many grown-up or teen-age cousins that they decided to have a meeting of their own. On May 22 they gathered in the old adobe schoolhouse behind Kawaiahao Church. Orramel Gulick spoke of their being cousins to each other and Asa Thurston "gave a few excellent suggestions which were quite unexpected, especially from him." He proposed that the cousins support Cousin Luther Halsey Gulick. The idea took hold, and the Hawaiian Mission Children's Society—affectionately referred to as the Cousins' Society—was formed. On July 15 the Micronesia mission sailed away on the *Caroline,* a small schooner bought for the mission by the Hawaiian congregations. The cousins, taking their responsibilities seriously, began to hem handkerchiefs, weave belts and watch-chains and raise vegetables in order to get the money they had pledged to the support of Luther.

But the meetings of the cousins were far from solemn. Because Honolulu had no street lights, they set their monthly meetings for the Saturday night nearest the full moon. Riding in from Punahou by moonlight, they would gather at one of the mission homes, some of them still too moonstruck to go beyond the porch. If they did go on in, they could take part in a discussion of some such topic as "Should Missionaries be obliged to be different from other Christians in respect of their right of holding property?" or "Is it right and expedient for missionaries and pastors of churches, at these islands, to directly advise or influence their people on political questions?" Good questions.

The society continues today as custodian of the old mission houses and of a magnificent collection of mission books and manuscripts. In 1952 it celebrated its hundredth anniversary, and it still supports missions.

The 235 living cousins mentioned in its first annual report (164 of them then in the islands, 71 on the mainland) have in the course of years grown to thousands, over sixteen hundred of whom care enough about their mission background to be life members.

* * *

While the cousins were forming their association, their fathers in general meeting were taking the final steps to cast themselves loose from the American Board. They voted to discontinue the general meeting, and in its place erected the Hawaiian Evangelical Association with power to examine and license ministers and to serve as an ecclesiastical court. After thirty-four years of missionary effort, the brethren still did not see their way to including any Hawaiian brothers. Churches were still to be supplied by vote of the clerical association, but under pastoral guidance Hawaiian *lunas* or deacons divided the big churches into smaller groups for the easier detection of delinquencies, collecting money, and holding local prayer meetings.

The American Board exerted no control whatever over the government of the Hawaiian churches, and never had. This, in view of its great outlay ($673,000 by 1849), was a remarkable evidence of faith in the men it sent out. Though board and mission had often misunderstood each other, often disagreed, and sometimes written sharply back and forth, with that irreconcilable difference of viewpoint between field and home office which goes with all large operations, yet they had jogged on together these thirty-four years, well agreed as to objectives however they might differ as to means. Now the time had come to part. By 1854, with its reconstitution as the Evangelical Association and its status as a "home mission," the Hawaiian church was essentially independent.

The same meeting which brought this about also had the painful duty of taking action on the mission's first scandal. The Reverend Samuel Dwight who had come out as a bachelor in 1848 and been assigned to the lonely station of Kaluaaha had sought relief from his loneliness in familiar relations with the girls he taught. He boarded some of them in his house, where he had been known to take them on his lap and fondle their breasts. He had caught one of these girls, Anna Mahoe, with a Hawaiian boy in her bed. For reasons unexplained Samuel Dwight thereupon hastily decided to marry her himself. Sadly the brothers read him out of the mission.

The strange thing about it is that both Hawaiians and missionaries, after thirty-four years of hearing and preaching the doctrine of Christian love, still regarded the marriage of a missionary with a Hawaiian girl as degrading to him. Charlie Judd had shown the same attitude when, with reference to Emma Rooke, granddaughter of old John Young, he wrote to Willie Armstrong: "Do you think I would marry a girl with native blood?—far from it." Yet Emma was as much haole as she was Hawaiian. Perhaps it was as well for her that Charlie felt as he did, since she became a queen by marrying Alexander shortly after he came to the throne.

Samuel Dwight spent the rest of his days in the islands, where he and Anna—who was only fifteen when he married her—raised a crop of seven children and died within a few months of each other at Honolulu. He was the only missionary to marry a Hawaiian, for which practical demonstration of the Christian doctrine that "God hath made of one blood all nations of men for to dwell on the face of the whole earth" he might better have had praise than blame. The mission children did not share Charlie Judd's prejudice, for six mission families in the second generation married Hawaiians, among them such distinguished ones as Bailey, Lyman and Wilcox. In the next generation after Charlie, the Judd family also intermarried.

Far more worrisome than Brother Dwight's preference for a Hawaiian wife was the growing strength of the Mormons in the islands. The first of their missionaries had arrived in 1850, only three years after the Mormons reached Utah. They were young, adaptable, enthusiastic, and obliged to earn their own living. By 1854 they had converted several thousand Hawaiians and begun a gathering of the saints on the little island of Lanai, where they laid out their City of Joseph, built houses, and started to raise their crops. Judge Lee reported that they were also assembling behind his house along Nuuanu stream where every Sunday they baptized by fifties and hundreds, the elect including former members of Coan's, Clark's and Lowell Smith's churches, as well as some Catholics. The brethren did not care for this additional trespass on their field, but there was not much they could do about it and in time they became accustomed to the presence of these other transplanted Yankees whose religion had been propagated by two Vermonters, Joseph Smith and Brigham Young. Mormonism became and remained one of the strongest faiths in the islands.

*   *   *

The king was suffering now from delirium tremens. He had kept a mistress openly for several years, and when she died in the smallpox epidemic he had taken heavily to drink. But late in 1854 he was resting on the other side of Oahu from Honolulu and he was not drinking. Then Queen Kalama wanted to go back to the city, the king got into a drinking bout, and when he came home insisted on sleeping outdoors. Soon he was breathing heavily.

"Wake up! Wake up!" the queen said. "You must have taken cold; let us go into the house."

Dr. Rooke was sent for and the king soon felt better. Then he took to drinking again. Nausea, convulsions, delirium followed. When the fit passed, the king knew he was dying. He asked to see his one-time counselor and friend, Dr. Judd. When Judd came, the king thanked him for all he had done.

"You are the best friend I ever had, and I ask your forgiveness for my treatment of you," he said, while the tears rolled down his cheeks. "I drank much, and I was not a good Christian; much unhappiness came after you went."

At fifteen minutes before noon on December 15 the king died. He was forty-one years old.

Those who had known him best spoke well of him. "One of the best-hearted men I ever knew," wrote Richard Armstrong in his private journal. Laura Judd said that his character, though marred by grave faults, had truly noble traits. He was a true friend, generous to a fault, tender in heart, merciful and sensitive to suffering. No drop of blood had been shed in his reign despite all the disputes that had marked it.

Orators pointed out how he had given his people schools, laws, a constitution, free title to lands. Since these were memorial addresses they did not say that while the king had given ready consent, it was the Yankee preachers who had suggested and carried out the reforms.

The historian Kamakau's tribute runs to irony. "The plover flew in peace, the rat squeaked without fear in his hole, the shark showed his teeth unmolested in the wave, there had never been such peace before," he wrote. What he meant was that under so mild a king foreigners had taken over the islands. He expressed a point of view many Hawaiians must have held. Plenty of people living in the islands today believe the missionaries robbed the Hawaiians of their land. Somehow it suits human nature to blame these good men rather than to point the finger at the lusty, devil-may-care sailors who brought disease and death, the profit-hungry merchants who brought rum backed up by guns, the opportunists like Charlton who snatched up land when the use of it was innocently offered and then held it by western laws of ownership the Hawaiians had never heard of.

"The missionaries have spoiled everything," the Spaniard Marin had said. "But without doubt, their intentions were good."

Steen Bille, a Danish naval commander who visited Hawaii in 1846 and who had no ax to grind either for or against the missionaries, wrote: "If this weak nation emerges victorious from the struggle the thanks are only due to its true allies, the North American missionaries who have settled in the islands since 1820, and to whom the nation owes thanks for all that it has so far become: a small, but free nation, with a certain degree of independence, with laws and a regular government."

Sam Armstrong, when he had grown up, gone through the Civil War and come out a general, said: "Judged by the progress of the Hawaiian people since 1820 the missionary work has been a grand success. Judged by Puritan standards of morals it has been a sad failure."

Luther Severance, American commissioner to Hawaii in the early fifties, found the missionaries about the same sort of people he knew in his home state of Maine—temperate and moral, quite as liberal as the average Yankee and more self-denying. It was their vigilance in protecting the king and keeping out rum that made them so many enemies, he said. These enemies keep repeating the same lies, and "occasionally they find a bookmaker like Herman Melville to repeat their calumnies and imbibe their prejudices."

Every grass house now had its Bible, and grace before meat was as common as it had once been in New England. A man could travel throughout the islands and into its wildest spots unarmed and without fear, which was more than could be said for California. And all this had been accomplished at less than the cost of a ship-of-war.

Said Robert Louis Stevenson: "With all their deficiency of candour, humour, and common sense, the missionaries are the best and most useful whites in the Pacific."

No wonder, in view of what they accomplished, that the old king, Kamehameha I, when asked his opinion about the haole religion, had replied:

"I should be afraid to adopt so dangerous an expedient as Christianity; for I think no Christian king can govern in the absolute manner in which I do, and yet be loved by his subjects as I am by mine: such a religion might perhaps answer very well in the course of a few generations; but what chief would sanction it in the beginning, with the risk of its subverting his own power, and involving the islands in war? I have made a fixed determination not to suffer it."

Christianity had brought an end to absolute monarchy, but it had done so in such a way that Hawaii was led into the world of nations without being submerged or destroyed. Kamehameha had been right: the spiritual revolution had led inevitably to political evolution. But the Yankee preachers who guided the movement knew that Hawaiians could not become democrats overnight. So they supported the king as symbolic father of his people, just as they themselves filled the father role in the churches.

Perhaps they held on to it too long. Rufus Anderson, secretary of the American Board, felt that the big churches under the missionaries should, about 1848 when the nation was largely converted, have been divided into smaller churches under Hawaiian pastors. The brethren, however, could not let go. They knew well enough that the most pious-appearing Hawaiians were still capable of sleeping mischievously, and they did not want to discredit the ministry with backsliders. Their paternalism carried over into plantation life where it remained even into the present century.

No one except a very prejudiced observer could deny their achievements even while regretting the blight they placed upon much that was innocently charming and beauty-loving in the Hawaiian character.

By 1850 there were twenty-two thousand church members—well over a fourth of the population. Seventeen thousand youngsters were going to school. "Civilization" had come to Hawaii.

Yet it appeared that the Hawaiians might not long be there to welcome it. Their numbers continued to drop alarmingly. (Today there are only ten thousand pure Hawaiians, though the number of part Hawaiians is rising.) Even this could not make the mission admit defeat. "If the benevolence of American Christians is destined to be disappointed in the extinction of the Hawaiian race," wrote one of the brothers, "still, they have no cause to regret their zeal and labor in behalf of a people, who have now doubtless, and are destined to have a still greater representation in the world of bliss, where, but for the introduction of the Gospel among them, none would have appeared." The Hawaiians, if they had lost their earthly paradise, had gained a better one above. So what cause had they to complain?

To Christianize Hawaii seventy-five men had been sent out, and about as many women. Many had died or gone home. Of the pioneer company only Asa Thurston still labored in the field, a strong, patient, godly man. He and Lucy, together with the Whitneys, were the only pioneer couples to end their days in Hawaii. As for Mercy Whitney, once so round-faced and young and innocent-looking, she became even beautiful as old age began to lay its hand on her. Her hair still meticulously dressed, her cap and gown always fresh and dainty, she dined frugally on baked taro and a pint of milk a day, living still in the house Sam had built in Waimea, Kauai. There, in 1872, she died.

Of the second company only Artemas Bishop still labored on. Most of the third company were still active—Dr. Judd back in his medical practice though not as a missionary, Lorrin Andrews in a judgeship, Ephraim Clark as pastor of Kawaiahao Church—though his small voice could not fill the huge building and a partition had to be put up. The later companies were still active. Titus Coan, for example, was still trying to convert both the Hawaiians and his own brethren, who never could quite believe in his wholesale conversions. The Baldwins, Alexanders, Hitchcocks, Lymans, Lyons, and all the rest were spead now throughout the islands in twenty-two mission stations.

The roster is too long to call completely. But John Emerson of Waialua on Oahu can represent them all. After all his children had grown up, Mahaulu who had also grown up in the Emerson family was talking one day to one of the sons, Oliver Pomeroy.

"There is Sam, your eldest brother," he said, bending down one finger. "He was a ranchman and raised cattle, but your father knew more about stock than Sam ever dreamed of; and there are Nat and Justin, physicians, and good ones. Nat here as president of the board of health, Justin on the Mainland, but your father was both doctor and minister and cared for the bodies as well as for the souls of his people. Then there is Joe, a surveyor for the Hawaiian government, but your father not only surveyed government lands, he sold them to the people and helped them get homesteads; and here are you, a minister and the secretary of the Hawaiian Board. Your father was our minister, preacher and spiritual leader and got close to us in our homes, teaching us how to live."

Having doubled over each of his five fingers, Mahaulu shook his fist at Oliver. "Your father combined in his one person the various vocations which you five brothers have followed," said he, "and all of you put together are not equal to the old man."

No small tribute to the country boy from Chester, New Hampshire. It was part of Hawaii's good fortune that the Yankee missionaries came mostly from the small towns and farms of New England where men still did most of their own work—knowing the ways of nature and crops and animals, raising their own food, making much of their own clothing and furniture and equipment, and also making their own amusements, educating their children in small neighborhood schools, managing their own public affairs, choosing and supporting their own pastors.

The combination of individual resourcefulness with a genius for group cohesiveness and co-operation was the mark of the Yankee in an age when cities were still the exception. That resourcefulness was an asset in the pioneer conditions the early missionaries found in the islands, and it continued to play a part as the missionaries and their sons tried to develop Hawaii economically—first of all as a means of making the people diligent, later on as a means of getting their own living.

But when they tried to re-establish the institutions they had known —church, school, government—the native culture was too strong for them. New England could not be transplanted to the islands unchanged. The result was a paternal guidance which turned into pa-

ternalism—in church government, in school organization, in constitutional monarchy.

As in the institutions, so in spirit the islands came to be a compromise between the old culture and the new. Blended with the Hawaiian aloha was the idea of Christian love and duty; with easygoing acceptance of things as they are, a drive to get things done.
The charm of the islands is in the combining of the two cultures, even
in the conflict between them. It is an imprint that will always be
there.

CHAPTER 27

DID THEY DO GOOD—OR WELL?

1854–1954

ALMOST THE FIRST THING A VISITOR TO HAWAII HEARS IS that the New England missionaries came to do good and ended by doing well. Island residents—those who know a little island history but not enough—point to the imposing downtown structures of Castle & Cooke or Alexander & Baldwin. There, they say, is tangible proof that the missionaries did very well indeed.

The fact is that in most cases the missionaries lived very simply if not abstemiously and left small estates. Sam Castle and Amos Cooke, it is true, did prosper. So did Elias Bond of Kohala on the big island. In order to keep his Hawaiian parishioners from leaving the area, he established the Kohala Sugar Plantation, went to Castle & Cooke for additional capital, and finally got the business going. For years there was no profit, but at last in 1875 a twenty-five per cent dividend was declared. Thereafter Bond's share of the profits rose to $12,000 —even to $48,000 in a year. All of this he gave away, considering himself only the steward of his Master. His large gifts to the American Board were made anonymously.

When Gerrit Judd died in 1873, he left his son Charles about two thousand acres of rural land which at that time had no great value. Sweet Home with its seven acres went to Helen, less a lot to Elizabeth. Laura also got a lot. To Albert went land and houses at the corner of Fort and Merchant streets, to Allan twenty acres in Pawaa, Waikiki. The annual wharf rent of $1,000 was still being paid by government, and the ice house property at the waterfront brought an annual $360. Investments amounting to $16,000 (including a $10,-000 life insurance policy) and a $1,000 annuity were to be administered for the benefit of the doctor's dependents.

Charles Judd became chamberlain to King Kalakaua while his brother Albert Francis became chief justice of Hawaii. The sons of Albert Francis Junior are still active in Hawaiian affairs—Henry as a minister and professor of Hawaiian, Lawrence a former governor of the territory. Dr. Judd apparently did better by his beneficiaries than most of his missionary brethren. But neither he nor any other missionary was able to leave anything like the half million acres of the non-missionary Parker ranch on Hawaii.

By 1862 three-fourths of all the real property on Oahu was under foreign control, except in the Waialua area where John Emerson's leadership in getting the Hawaiian people to take up homesteads had kept the figure down to one half. The land *was* passing into foreign hands, but not to the missionaries.

As the mission children grew up and began to make their own livings, they took the paths that were open to them—farming, merchandising, government.

Albert S. Wilcox, the son of Abner, was active in the sugar industry throughout his life, became a director of many firms, sat in the legislature and gave time and money to innumerable good causes.

Samuel M., the son of the Bethel preacher Samuel O. Damon, grew prosperous as a partner in the bank started by Charles Bishop. Representing Queen Liliuokalani at the Diamond Jubilee of Queen Victoria, he brought back a Scotch gardener who created the beautiful gardens of Moanalua known to tourists as the Damon Estate.

Lorrin A. Thurston, grandson of Asa the missionary, became eminent in Hawaii's political and cultural life as well as in industry. Developer of plantations, lawyer, newspaper publisher, minister of the interior, he represented the Hawaiian government at Washington from 1893 to 1895.

In 1865 a young man from Massachusetts broke his leg in a fall from a horse while his ship was at Honolulu. It was therefore chiefly luck which led Benjamin Franklin Dillingham to stay in Hawaii. Once settled there he married a daughter of the Reverend Lowell Smith, bought out Henry Dimond's hardware business with Alfred Castle as partner, built the Oahu Railroad, and handed on a precarious empire to his son Walter, which that young man consolidated and developed with admirable skill. Many of today's leaders similarly get their mission background from the distaff side. So Atherton Richards is descended not from William Richards but from the Cookes. Ballard Atherton, telephone executive, is also a Cooke through his grandmother Juliette Montague Cooke Atherton.

Perhaps the most distinguished of all the second generation was Sanford B. Dole, the youngster whose mother had died at his birth while she and her husband were in charge of Punahou School. To care for the baby, the mission called William and Mary Rice. Thereafter the children of the two families grew up as foster brothers and sisters. Sanford Dole, after going to the United States to attend Williams College, returned to an active life in Hawaii which culminated in his becoming president of the provisional government of 1893. With the backing of the American minister, Dole * and his friends in the Annexation Club seized the government building and read a proclamation which abrogated the monarchy. Then they sent five commissioners to Washington to negotiate annexation. But President Cleveland, after sending an investigator to the islands, was convinced that the American minister had conspired with the annexationists to overthrow the monarchy. When he tried to put Queen Liliuokalani (little Lydia of the Chiefs' Children's School) back in power, however, the provisional government refused to give up. Instead, it converted itself into a so-called republic, which carried on from 1894 until the Spanish-American War finally persuaded Congress to annex the islands in 1898.

So many mission children were involved in the government during this period that they were charged with having stolen the kingdom in order to turn it over to the United States. Two of three supreme court justices, three of four ministers of state, and two members of the Hawaiian legation at Washington were sons of missionaries. Again it was the old story: decay and incapacity had left a vacuum which these men filled because they were the most able and perhaps the most trusted.

Other mission sons made their marks in other parts of the world. General Sam Armstrong established Hampton Institute, driven by a desire to do something for the Negroes who, though liberated by

* Dole Pineapple was developed by James D. Dole, a distant relative, who came to the islands from Massachusetts in 1900.

the Civil War, could only be truly free if they were properly educated. John Thomas Gulick made important contributions to the theory of evolution. Seven other sons became ministers in the United States, and still others went as missionaries to foreign lands.

Grandsons and great grandsons continued to distinguish themselves. Hiram Bingham III is an archaeologist of note and also served as governor of Connecticut and United States Senator. Lorrin Andrews Thurston published the *Pacific Commercial Advertiser* which his son Lorrin P. Thurston now publishes. William Richards Castle was under-secretary of state in the Hoover administration. Benjamin F. Dillingham II carries on his grandfather's name and sits in the Hawaiian Senate. Luther Halsey Gulick, descendant of Peter and an authority on public administration, is city administrator of New York. The list of outstanding men in all walks of life could easily be prolonged.

In the life of the islands today—and not only their economic life —the descendants of missionaries still play a prominent part. Castles, Cookes, Alexanders and Baldwins are active in the firms bearing their names, in the various banks and businesses connected with them through interlocking directorates, and in the cultural institutions that make Honolulu an ongoing community. On Maui, Harold Rice and, on Kauai, Charles Rice are influential in business and political affairs. The Wilcox family has continued to husband the fortunes built up by Abner Wilcox's sons, Samuel Whitney and George Norton Wilcox. George, incidentally, was prime minister in 1892.

Of the seventy-five mission couples who had been sent to the field by 1854, about forty have descendants still living in the islands. Since twenty-six couples returned to the United States when their children were still young or for other reasons left no offspring in the island, this record is impressive. The children of missionaries, many of them, chose to make Hawaii their home. A much smaller group than the other haole residents of the islands, and with no particular advantages over other haoles except those they made for themselves by education or hard work, they succeeded—for a time at least—in winning a commanding position in the economic and political life of the islands. They began with little or nothing, often as surveyors, clerks, managers of other men's plantations. They worked to improve plantation methods of irrigating, cropping, milling. They acquired lands of their own, combined their resources, and sometimes prospered.

For some strange reason, the prosperity and success which would have been praised even if envied in others, was condemned in them. Children of missionaries, apparently, were expected to become missionaries themselves or at least to remain untainted by worldly possessions. Their great crime was their success. Conveniently forgetting that mission children were not missionaries, less successful haoles persisted in calling them missionaries and in trying to hold them to mission standards, as if they had no right to lives of their own. And to this day a good many people in Hawaii and elsewhere think that the missionaries grew rich and seized control of the island economy.

It was not the missionaries but their children, who were not missionaries, who reaped the benefits of being on the ground at the right time, being young and energetic, and being ready to gamble on their ability to make money in sugar. Plenty of people had lost their shirts trying to grow sugar, coffee, silk and other products. There was no guarantee that these young men would succeed. Once they had done so, of course, it looked easy. But many a prosperous plantation today began on a shoestring, hard work and faith.

Then how about the Big Five? says the island critic.

The Big Five, often mentioned by those who would like to prove that the missionaries grabbed the islands from the Hawaiians, consist of five firms (not families) only one of which was founded by missionaries. Sam Castle and Amos Cooke, after leaving the mission, began as wholesale and retail merchants (this part of their business was sold in 1898), but gradually got into the business of financing and serving the sugar plantations. The firm showed its mission origins, at least as long as the founders were alive, by applying the Golden Rule to business. Where other firms charged their clients five per cent on sales, Castle & Cooke were content with three. Where others charged one per cent a month for loans, or even more, the Castle & Cooke rate was ten per cent a year.

Castle & Cooke helped many young men get a start in sugar, among them the sons of two missionary families, Alexander and Baldwin. It was Samuel T. Alexander and Henry P. Baldwin, with assistance from Castle & Cooke, who formed the last of the Big Five firms, the only one to be founded on sugar alone.

While Dr. Baldwin was preaching and healing at Lahaina, William Alexander was teaching up on the hill behind him. Their boys, Henry and Samuel, grew up knowing the islands and the people. Starting out in a small way and risking what little they had, they joined forces and built up a successful business in sugar cane. Sam began by managing his father's little sugar plantation, while Henry Baldwin worked in the fields until he landed a job as head overseer at Waihee Plantation, Maui, where Sam had, meanwhile, become manager. In 1868, together with Wallace Alexander and a man without mission connections, they bought a plantation with the help of Castle & Cooke. From about 1870 to 1894 the affairs of Alexander & Baldwin are so interwoven with those of Castle & Cooke that it is hard to separate them. In 1893 the younger firm owed Castle & Cooke $140,000, and $300,000 elsewhere. A financial panic threatened the firm's existence, but it survived to become and remain one of the Big Five. The descendants of Sam Alexander and Henry Baldwin have carried on the firm they started and are still prominent in the life of the islands. The Baldwins are today large landholders on Maui and Lanai.

The cousins who had formed their society back in 1852 naturally felt drawn towards each other. They intermarried, joined in business ventures, and became a tightly knit social group—even a social elite. Their mission upbringing generally gave them a sense of moral obligation to the community, one form of which was the paternalistic attitude they took towards their working forces on the plantations. In a day when labor could expect little consideration, they did provide medical services, recreation and other benefits. As labor became more assertive, however, they failed to keep pace with the times, attempting to preserve their paternalistic control when it was no longer acceptable. As a result, an aggressive labor movement was able to appeal to the workers and to organize an island-wide front against the already well-organized employers. So the tight hold on the economy of the islands which was once held by the Big Five no longer exists. Now organized labor can tie up the islands, throttling them with a shipping strike or calling out all the plantation workers.

The cousins have also been replaced or refreshed to a considerable extent by new blood from the mainland. In some of the old families the original Yankee shrewdness and enterprise had run thin. Smart young men from outside have always been welcome in the island enterprises, and often they have married cousins. So the old blood lines are preserved even though some of the family names are new. Run through a list of the leading men in the Hawaiian economy, and you find that most of them—or their wives—qualify as cousins.

The majority of the stock in island enterprises is held in the islands, and a good deal of it is in the hands of cousins. Yet not one of the presidents of the Big Five is a mission descendant.

*   *   *

While the descendants of missionaries turned to business and government, what was happening to the churches?

In 1856 they had a membership of 24,000. By 1898 the number had dropped to 4,624. At Kawaiahao Church the attendance had once been so great that a demijohn of wine had to be kept beneath the communion table for replenishing the tankards. By 1903 membership in the church had dropped to 476. (It is now, 1955, over 1,000 again.) Part of the difficulty, of course, was the continuous sharp decline in the Hawaiian population. But only part. Many new faiths—Christian, Buddhist, Shinto and miscellaneous ones hardly known on the mainland—had come in. Churches under the Evangelical Association were divided along linguistic lines, so that a plantation town with Japanese, Hawaiian, Filipino and haole workers might have four churches belonging to the association, each trying to support a pastor. Statistically, the churches founded by the Yankee missionaries were on the downgrade and had been for years. While other and newer faiths were supported from the mainland, these had to rely on their own resources, or at least on what they could obtain in the islands.

Most prosperous of all is Central Union Church in Honolulu, successor of the original mission church and attended by many of the social elite who are cousins. Most of these mission descendants have a sense of civic obligation well above average, either when compared

with other haoles in the islands or with mainland communities. Yet
their influence is on the wane. They are somewhat apprehensive
about this, and about the future, for they know that the non-haole
population now far outnumbers them. They are somewhat resentful
—and rightly so—of the common belief that they stole the islands
from the Hawaiians while pretending to bring them religion. Though
some of them have gone to seed, yet on the whole they have been
the most positive and progressive force in Hawaiian life. They have
several times managed to save the islands when they appeared to be
on the verge of economic collapse. They have organized a system of
plantation management so efficient that it has so far managed (with
the help of government control of the sugar market for which they
have successfully lobbied) to keep the islands prosperous. They have
pioneered in agricultural research through the Hawaiian Sugar Planters' Association, developed new products to employ the rising population, increased plantation efficiency to meet rising wage scales.

It is hard to imagine what Hawaii would have been without them
—without the cohesiveness they felt as cousins, which brought them
together and made co-operation possible when non-co-operation
would have brought disaster. They are often accused of being monop-
olists, yet the pecular nature of the island economy—its isolation
from the mainland, its necessary concentration on a few crops, its
dependence on shipping, the need of absolute efficiency in order to
operate at a profit—seems to make a degree of monopoly essential.

*   *   *

Whatever you may think of them, the missionaries came with a
noble vision of the dignity of man and the love and righteousness of
God. They *knew* that their faith was the only true one, and they
panted to save the heathen by teaching them the one faith which led
to everlasting salvation. Yet they were not content to establish a
theology only. Their faith had moral consequences and material results. They believed that man was apt to transgress and that he must
build his life so as to minimize the danger of going astray. They tried
to teach, not only a belief in God, but a code of conduct. They themselves tried to follow, even to the common stock system, the way
of life they believed the first Christians to have practiced. For it was

their faith that if God's way were truly followed, men would surely live in unity and blessedness everywhere on earth. This ideal of a beloved community they tried their best to raise up on sound foundations in one of the loveliest spots on earth.

It was a vision so different from anything the Hawaiians knew that they never did understand it fully. But they knew the missionaries were good men, having their welfare at heart. If only they had also known how to enjoy life—to lie in the sun or glide shoreward on a skimming surf board, to deck the body with flowers or exercise it in the innocent delights of love!

Might there have been a middle way? Might the easygoing, generous, nature-loving island character have been saved while all the dark things—infanticide and sacrificial murders, feudal oppression and food tabus and superstition—were removed?

When the missionaries arrived in 1820, the Hawaiians had already been in contact with haoles long enough to see what the contact was bringing them. It was bringing drunkenness, shameless cheating, and venereal disease horrible beyond words.

For a drastic situation a drastic remedy was needed. By good luck, or by the will of Providence, the Yankee mission arrived at the critical moment. It arrived with a plan which it believed to have universal validity and which, with its clearly spelled out rules, offered salvation to a dying race. The brethren suffered from the limitations of their age. They could not distinguish between what was eternal in the Christian message and what was nineteenth century New England. So they felt that Hawaiians must take the Christian message as they taught it, with no allowances for cultural differences.

But now in our time the Hawaiian way of life with its accent on ease and relaxation has again become respectable. The missionaries thought it immoral; we yearn for it as an end in itself. In the islands it is expressed in the word *aloha*—which means not only love, but a warm-hearted regard for all men, a willingness to accept differences without discrimination, to match the natural beauty of the islands with responsive good humor and good will. The word is used to explain the friendliness between men of the many different races that have peopled the islands. It has become a social ideal—a word around which the people of the islands can rally as the symbol of their unity. It is almost a magic word, for friction when it appears can frequently be smoothed by an appeal to remember and practice the spirit of aloha.

So in these beautiful islands of the Pacific a Yankee version of the faith of Jesus, a Jew, as fortified by Greek philosophy and reformulated by the Swiss Calvin, has blended with the indigenous Hawaiian aloha to bring harmony to a community made up of men from Japan, China, the Philippines, Europe and America. It is not a perfect community, since it is human, but it is a remarkably harmonious one. For this it has to thank its Yankee background as well as its Hawaiian.

"God hath made of one blood all nations of men, to dwell on the face of the earth in unity and blessedness." So William Richards, missionary from the little Massachusetts hill town of Plainfield, had written in Hawaii's first constitution. It was a noble hope. It was also the statement of a faith well designed to be the guide of a young nation.

A hundred years ago the missionaries who had gone into government came to the conclusion that Hawaii would prosper best under the American flag, in which it was assumed that the islands would be represented by a star. Over fifty years ago the hope sprang again when Hawaii was admitted as a territory, with the understanding that statehood would not be far away. The islands still wait for this consummation, because some United States senators do not believe that God has indeed made all men of one blood, and because they believe that skin color rather than education and cultural influences determine such matters as loyalty and ability.

Honolulu is as American as San Francisco, Des Moines or Boston. The islands, despite their tropic charm, have a Yankee quality still. After a hundred years the mark of the mission is still there— not in congregations of five thousand, to be sure, but in the laws, the institutions, the descendants, the enterprise and energy, the tone of the whole.

In the heart of Honolulu, surrounded by a coral wall, the old mission houses still stand—the old white clapboard house where Bingham lived, the little coral print shop, the thick-walled coral house

Levi Chamberlain built. Past them streams the modern traffic of a busy city. But they are still there in the heart of it all. And so are Bingham and Richards, and Judd and Armstrong, and all the rest—forevermore.

APPENDICES

SOME IMPORTANT HAWAIIANS, 1820-1854

(For Missionaries, see p. 339)

Boki. Governor of Oahu, 1819–1829. Brother of Prime Minister Kalanimoku

Haalilio. Cousin and ambassador of Liholiho

Hoapili. Governor of Maui, 1836–40. Husband to Keopuolani. Father to Liliha

Honolii, John. Mission assistant, with first company

Hopu, Thomas. Assistant to first mission group

Ii, John. Counselor to Liholiho. Faithful Christian

Jackson, Susan. Wife of Stephen Reynolds

Kaahumanu. A widow of Kamehameha I. Virtual head of government, 1820–32

Kaikioewa. Governor of Kauai, 1824–40. Nephew of Kalanimoku

Kalakua. A widow of Kamehameha I. A wife of Hoapili

Kalama. Wife of Kauikeaouli

Kalanimoku (Billy Pitt). Prime Minister

Kamamalu. A wife and half sister of Liholiho

Kamakau. Historian

Kamehameha I. Uniter of the islands. Died 1819

Kamehameha II. See Liholiho

Kamehameha III. See Kauikeaouli

Kamehameha, Lot. Son of Kinau and Kekuanaoa. Later Kamehameha V

Kanui, William. Mission assistant, with first company

Kapiolani. Defier of Pele. Wife of Naihe

Kapule. A wife of Kaumualii, king of Kauai

Kauikeaouli. Kamehameha III

Kaumualii. King of Kauai

Kealiiahonui. Son of Kaumualii, king of Kauai. A husband to Kaahumanu

Keeaumoku (Cox). Governor of Maui. Brother of Kaahumanu

Kekauluohi. A wife of Liholiho, then of Kanaina. Premier, 1839–45

Kekauonohi. A wife of Liholiho

Kekuanaoa. Governor of Oahu, 1836–47

Keopuolani. A wife of Kamehameha I. Mother of Liholiho and Kauikeaouli. Later a wife of Hoapili

Kinau. Daughter of Kamehameha I. A wife of Liholiho and later of Kekuanaoa. Premier, 1832–39

Kuakini (John Adams). Governor of Hawaii, 1820–45

Liholiho. Kamehameha II. Son of Kamehameha I and Keopuolani

Liholiho, Alexander. Kamehameha IV. Son of Kinau and Kekuanaoa

Liliha. Wife of Boki. Governor of Oahu, 1829. Daughter of Hoapili

Likelike. A wife of Kalanimoku

Lunalilo, William. Son of Kekauluohi and Kanaina. King after Kamehameha V

Malo, David. Preacher and official

Nahienaena, Princess. Sister of Liholiho and Kauikeaouli

Naihe. A leading chief on Hawaii. Husband of Kapiolani

Namahana. A wife of Kamehameha I

Paki. Captain of the Honolulu fort

Pauahi. A wife of Liholiho, then of Kekuanaoa

Pauahi, Bernice. Daughter of Konia and Paki. Married Charles Bishop

MEMBERS OF THE SANDWICH ISLANDS MISSION, 1819–1854

Based upon the Missionary Album published by the Hawaiian Mission Children's Society, Honolulu, 1937

COM-PANY*	NAME	BORN	DIED	IN THE ISLANDS	PRINCIPAL STATIONS
5	Alexander, William Patterson	1805	1884	1832–1882	Waioli, Wailuku
5	——, Mary Ann McKinney	1810	1888	1832–1888	same
11	Andrews, Claudius Buchanan	1818	1877	1844–1876	Kaluaaha, Makawao
11	——, Anna Seward Gilson	1823	1862	1852–1862	Makawao
11	——, Samantha Gilson	1828	1904	1852–1878	Makawao
3	Andrews, Lorrin	1795	1868	1828–1868	Lahainaluna
3	——, Mary Ann Wilson	1804	1879	1828–1879	same
8	Andrews, Seth Lathrop, M.D.	1809	1893	1837–1848	Kailua
8	——, Parnelly Pierce	1807	1846	1837–1846	same
5	Armstrong, Richard	1805	1860	1832–1860	Wailuku, Honolulu
5	——, Clarissa Chapman	1805	1891	1832–1880	same
8	Bailey, Edward	1814	1903	1837–1888?	Wailuku
8	——, Caroline Hubbard	1814	1894	1837–1888?	same

* 12 companies were sent out. Those for whom no number is given arrived individually. Marriages contracted after a member left the mission are not included.

COM-PANY	NAME	BORN	DIED	IN THE ISLANDS	PRINCIPAL STATIONS
4	Baldwin, Dwight, M.D.	1798	1886	1831–1886	Lahaina
4	——, Charlotte Fowler	1805	1873	1831–1873	*same*
1	Bingham, Hiram	1789	1869	1820–1840	Honolulu
1	——, Sybil Moseley	1792	1848	1820–1840	*same*
2	Bishop, Artemas	1795	1872	1823–1872	Kailua, Ewa, Honolulu
2	——, Elizabeth Edwards	1796	1828	1823–1828	Kailua
3	——, Delia Stone	1800	1875	1828–1875	Kailua, Ewa, Honolulu
	Bishop, Sereno Edwards	1827	1909	1827–1909	Lahaina, Honolulu
	——, Cornelia A. Sessions	1826	1920	1853–1920	*same*
2	Blatchely, Abraham, M.D.	1787	1860	1823–1826	Kailua
2	——, Jemima Marvin	1791	1856	1823–1826	*same*
8	Bliss, Isaac	1804	1851	1837–1841	Kohala
8	——, Emily Curtis	1811	1866	1837–1841	*same*
9	Bond, Elias	1813	1896	1841–1896	Kohala
9	——, Ellen Mariner Howell	1817	1881	1841–1881	*same*
7	Brown, Lydia	1780	1865	1835–1865	Wailuku, Lahaina
8	Castle, Samuel Northrup	1808	1894	1837–1894	Honolulu
8	——, Angeline Lorraine Tenney	1810	1841	1837–1841	*same*
	——, Mary Tenney	1819	1907	1843–1907	*same*
1	Chamberlain, Daniel	1782	1860	1820–1823	Honolulu
1	——, Jerusha Burnap	1786?	1879	1820–1823	*same*
2	Chamberlain, Levi	1792	1849	1823–1849	*same*
3	——, Maria Patton	1803	1880	1828–1880	*same*
5	Chapin, Alonzo, M.D.	1805	1876	1832–1835	Lahaina
5	——, Mary Ann Tenney	1804	1885	1832–1835	*same*

COM-PANY	NAME	BORN	DIED	IN THE ISLANDS	PRINCIPAL STATIONS
3	Clark, Ephraim Weston	1799	1878	1828–1864	Lahainaluna, Honolulu
3	——, Mary Kittredge	1803	1857	1828–1857	*same*
	——, Sarah Helen Richards	1812	1887	1859–1864	Honolulu
7	Coan, Titus	1801	1882	1835–1882	Hilo
7	——, Fidelia Church	1810	1872	1835–1872	*same*
	——, Lydia Bingham	1834	1915	1834–1915	Hilo, Honolulu
8	Conde, Daniel Toll	1807	1897	1837–1856	Hana
8	——, Andelucia Lee	1810	1855	1837–1855	*same*
8	Cooke, Amos Starr	1810	1871	1837–1871	Honolulu
8	——, Juliette Montague	1812	1896	1837–1896	*same*
	Damon, Samuel Chenery	1815	1885	1842–1885	Honolulu
	——, Julia Sherman Mills	1817	1890	1842–1890	*same*
4	Dibble, Sheldon	1809	1845	1831–1845	Lahainaluna
4	——, Maria M. Tomlinson	1808	1837	1831–1837	*same*
	——, Antoinette Tomlinson	1809	1897	1840–1849	*same*
6	Diell, John	1808	1841	1833–1840	Honolulu
6	——, Caroline Platt	1807	1901	1833–1840	*same*
7	Dimond, Henry	1808	1895	1835–1895	Honolulu
7	——, Anne Maria Anner	1808	1893	1835–1893	*same*
9	Dole, Daniel	1808	1878	1841–1878	Honolulu, Koloa
9	——, Emily Hoyt Ballard	1808	1844	1841–1844	Honolulu
8	——, Charlotte Close Knapp	1813	1874	1837–1874	Honolulu, Koloa
12	Dwight, Samuel Gelston	1815	1880	1848–1880	Kaluaaha
	——, Anna Mahoe	1839	1879	1839–1879	*same*
	Ellis, William	1794	1872	1822–1824	Honolulu
	——, Mary Mercy Moor	1793	1835	1823–1824	*same*

COM-PANY	NAME	BORN	DIED	IN THE ISLANDS	PRINCIPAL STATIONS
2	Ely, James	1798	1890	1823–1828	Honolulu
2	——, Louisa Everest	1792	1848	1823–1828	*same*
5	Emerson, John S.	1800	1867	1832–1867	Waialua
5	——, Ursula Sophia Newell	1806	1888	1832–1888	*same*
5	Forbes, Cochran	1805	1880	1832–1847	Kaawaloa, Lahaina
5	——, Rebecca Duncan Smith	1805	1878	1832–1847	*same*
6	Fuller, Lemuel	1810	?	1833 only	Honolulu
2	Goodrich, Joseph	1794	1852	1823–1836	Hilo
2	——, Martha Barnes	1801	1840	1823–1836	*same*
3	Green, Jonathan Smith	1796	1878	1828–1878	Makawao, Wailuku
3	——, Theodosia Arnold	1792	1859	1828–1859	*same*
	Gulick, Luther Halsey, M.D.	1828	1891	1828–1870	Honolulu
	——, Louisa Lewis	1830	1894	1852–1870	*same*
3	Gulick, Peter Johnson	1796	1877	1828-1874	Waimea (Hawaii), Waialua
3	——, Fanny Hinckley Thomas	1798	1883	1828–1874	*same*
7	Hall, Edwin Oscar	1810	1883	1835–1883	Honolulu
7	——, Sarah Lyons Williams	1812	1876	1835–1876	*same*
5	Hitchcock, Harvey Rexford	1800	1855	1832–1855	Kaluaaha
5	——, Rebecca Howard	1808	1890	1832–1890	*same*
1	Holman, Thomas, M.D.	1793	1826	1820–1821	Kailua
1	——, Lucia Ruggles	1793	1886	1820–1821	Kailua
1	Honolii, John		1838		
1	Hopu, Thomas				
11	Hunt, Timothy Dwight	1821	1895	1844–1848	Lahainaluna
11	——, Mary Halsted Hedges	1821	1861	1844–1848	*same*

COM-PANY	NAME	BORN	DIED	IN THE ISLANDS	PRINCIPAL STATIONS
8	Ives, Mark	1809	1885	1837–1850	Kaawaloa
8	——, Mary Ann Brainerd	1810	1882	1837–1853	*same*
8	Johnson, Edward	1813	1867	1837–1867	Waioli
8	——, Lois S. Hoyt	1809	1891	1837–1891	*same*
4	Johnstone, Andrew	1794	1859	1831–1859	Honolulu
4	——, Rebecca Worth	1792	1879	1831–1879	*same*
3	Judd, Gerrit Parmele	1803	1873	1828–1873	Honolulu
3	——, Laura Fish	1804	1872	1828–1872	*same*
2	Kalaioulu, Richard		1835		
2	Kamooula, William				
1	Kanui, William		1864		
12	Kinney, Henry	1816	1854	1848–1854	Waiohinu
12	——, Maria Louisa Walsworth	1822	1858	1848–1858	*same*
8	Knapp, Horton Owen	1813	1845	1837–1845	Honolulu
8	——, Charlotte Close	1813	1874	1837–1874	Honolulu, Koloa
2	Kupelii				
8	Lafon, Thomas, M.D.	1801	1876	1837–1842	Koloa
8	——, Sophia Louisa Parker	1812	1844	1837–1842	*same*
8	Locke, Edwin	1813	1843	1837–1843	Waialua
8	——, Martha Laurens Rowell	1812	1842	1837–1842	*same*
1	Loomis, Elisha	1799	1836	1820–1827	Honolulu
1	——, Maria Theresa Sartwell	1796	1862	1820–1827	*same*
5	Lyman, David Belden	1803	1884	1832–1884	Hilo
5	——, Sarah Joiner	1805	1885	1832–1885	*same*
5	Lyons, Lorenzo	1807	1886	1832–1886	Waimea, Hawaii
5	——, Betsey Curtis	1813	1837	1832–1837	*same*
8	——, Lucia Garratt Smith	1808	1892	1837–1892	*same*
8	McDonald, Charles	1812	1839	1837–1839	Lahaina
8	——, Harriet T. Halstead	1810	1901	1837–*c.*1843	*same*

COM-PANY	NAME	BORN	DIED	IN THE ISLANDS	PRINCIPAL STATIONS
3	Mills, Samuel J. (Paloo)				
8	Munn, Bethuel	1803	1849	1837–1841	Kaluaaha
8	——, Louisa Clark	1810	1841	1837–1841	*same*
3	Ogden, Maria	1792	1874	1828–1874	Wailuku, Honolulu
9	Paris, John Davis	1809	1892	1841–1892	Kona
9	——, Mary Grant	1807	1847	1841–1847	Kau
	——, Mary Carpenter	1815	1896	1852–1896	Kona
6	Parker, Benjamin Wyman	1803	1877	1833–1877	Kaneohe, Lahaina
6	——, Mary Elizabeth Barker	1805	1907	1833–1907	*same*
3	Phelps, John E. (Kalaaauluna)				
11	Pogue, John Fawcett	1814	1877	1844–1877	Lahainaluna, Honolulu
	——, Maria Kapule Whitney	1820	1900	1820–1881	*same*
2	Popohe, Stephen				
9	Rice, William Harrison	1813	1862	1841–1862	Punahou
9	——, Mary Sophia Hyde	1816	1911	1841–1911	*same*
2	Richards, William	1793	1847	1823–1847	Lahaina
2	——, Clarissa Lyman	1795	1861	1823–1849	*same*
5	Rogers, Edmund Horton	1806	1853	1832–1853	Honolulu
3	——, Mary Ward	1799	1834	1828–1834	*same*
7	——, Elizabeth Hitchcock	1802	1857	1835–1857	*same*
10	Rowell, George Berkeley	1815	1884	1842–1884	Waimea (Kauai)
10	——, Malvina Jerusha Chapin	1816	1901	1842–1884	*same*
1	Ruggles, Samuel	1795	1871	1820–1834	*same*
1	——, Nancy Wells	1791	1873	1820–1834	*same*
3	Shepard, Stephen	1800	1834	1828–1834	Honolulu

COM-PANY	NAME	BORN	DIED	IN THE ISLANDS	PRINCIPAL STATIONS
3	——, Margaret Caroline Slow	1801	?	1828–1835	*same*
	Shipman, William Cornelius	1824	1861	1854–1861	Waiohinu
	——, Jane Stobie	1827	1904	1854–1904	*same*
	Smith, Asa Bowen	1809	1886	1842–1846	Waialua
	——, Sarah Gilbert White	1813	1855	1842–1846	*same*
10	Smith, James William, M.D.	1810	1887	1842–1887	Koloa
10	——, Melicent Knapp	1816	1891	1842–1891	*same*
6	Smith, Lowell	1802	1891	1833–1891	Honolulu
6	——, Abigail Willis Tenney	1809	1885	1833–1885	*same*
8	Smith, Marcia Maria	1806	1896	1837–1853	Punahou
5	Spaulding, Ephraim	1802	1840	1832–1836	Lahaina
5	——, Julia Brooks	1810	1898	1832–1836	*same*
2	Stewart, Charles Samuel	1795	1870	1823–1825	Lahaina
2	——, Harriet Bradford Tiffany	1798	1830	1823–1825	*same*
2	Stockton, Betsey *c.* 1798		1865	1823–1825	*same*
3	Tahiti, Henry				
	Taylor, Townsend Elijah	1818	1883	1848–1854	Lahaina
	——, Persis Goodale Thurston	1821	1906	1821–1906	*same*
1	Thurston, Asa	1787	1868	1820–1868	Kailua
1	——, Lucy Goodale	1795	1876	1820–1876	*same*
4	Tinker, Reuben	1799	1854	1831–1840	Honolulu
4	——, Mary Throop Wood	1809	1895	1831–1840	*same*
3	Tyler, George (Kieuaa)				
8	Van Duzee, William Sanford	1811	1883	1837–1839	Kaawaloa

COM-PANY	NAME	BORN	DIED	IN THE ISLANDS	PRINCIPAL STATIONS
8	——, Oral Hobart	1814	1891	1837–1839	*same*
	Wetmore, Charles Hinckley, M.D.	1820	1898	1849–1898	Hilo
	——, Lucy Shelden Taylor	1819	1883	1849–1883	*same*
1	Whitney, Samuel	1793	1845	1820–1845	Waimea, Kauai
1	——, Mercy Partridge	1795	1872	1820–1872	*same*
11	Whittlesey, Eliphalet	1816	1889	1844–1854	Hana
11	——, Elizabeth Keane Baldwin	1821	1876	1844–1854	*same*
8	Wilcox, Abner	1808	1869	1837–1869	Waioli
8	——, Lucy Eliza Hart	1814	1869	1837–1869	*same*

SOURCES

In writing this book my aim has been to find first-hand evidence for every adjective, attitude, movement and quoted word, but without losing the story, the drama which is as authentically a part of history as the "facts."

Since the method involves constant reference to hundreds of sources, it is manifestly impossible to provide a note to every source without doubling the length of the book. As an example, the description of the mission house on page 74 was drawn together from the Loomis and Chamberlain journals, Lucy Thurston's *Life and Times,* the *Missionary Herald,* and a typescript compilation in the Hawaiian Mission Children's Society library titled, "Mission Houses Honolulu."

As a compromise between documenting every adjective and supplying no information as to sources, the following material has been provided for those who are curious. Those who are content with the story itself may ignore all that follows.

In addition to those mentioned further on, I am indebted to the following residents of Hawaii for special courtesies: Riley Allen, Miss Janet Bell, Miss Ethel Damon, Mrs. Kathleen Dickenson Mellen, Mrs. Mary Pukui, Mrs. Violet A. Silverman, Mr. and Mrs. Gregg Sinclair, Miss Mabel Wilcox. Other friends too numerous to name made our stay forever memorable.

Much of the research and all of the index are the work of my wife, Marion Collins Smith.

The staffs of the Albany State Library and Williams College Library were invariably helpful.

The principal collections are identified by the following abbreviations:

ABC   American Board of Commissioners for Foreign Missions, in Houghton Library of Harvard University

AH   Archives of Hawaii, Honolulu

Bp   Bishop Museum, Honolulu

HHS   Hawaiian Historical Society. Its library is housed together with that of

HMCS   Hawaiian Mission Children's Society, behind the old mission houses in Honolulu

LC   Library of Congress

UH   University of Hawaii

SELECT BIBLIOGRAPHY

1. BOOKS AND PAMPHLETS

1. Alexander, Arthur C. *Koloa Plantation*. Honolulu, 1937
2. Alexander, James M. *Mission Life in Hawaii*. Oakland, 1888
3. Alexander, Mary Charlotte. *Dr. Baldwin of Lahaina*. Berkeley, 1953
4. ——. "Lahaina Missionary Premises" (n.p., n.d.)
5. ——, and Charlotte Peabody Dodge. *Punahou 1841–1941*. Berkeley, 1941
6. ——. *William Patterson Alexander*. Honolulu, 1934
7. Alexander, W. D. *A Brief History of the Hawaiian People*. New York, 1899
8. *Ancient Hawaiian Civilization*. Honolulu, 1933
9. Anderson, Rufus. *The Hawaiian Islands*. Boston, 1864
10. ——. *History of the Sandwich Islands Mission*. Boston, 1870
11. Armstrong, C. C. "Reminiscences of a Missionary Chair." San Francisco, 1886
12. [Armstrong.] *Richard Armstrong, America—Hawaii*. Hampton, Va., 1887
12a. Arnold, S. G. "The Call of Dr. Judd." [A poem] Mount Pleasant, D.C., 1886
12b. Ashdown, Inez. "The Story of Lahaina." n.p., 1947

13. Baker, Ray Jerome. *Honolulu in 1853*. Honolulu, 1950
14. Ball, John. *Autobiography*. Glendale, Cal., 1925
15. [Bates, George Washington.] *Sandwich Island Notes*. New York, 1854
16. Bille, Steen. *Report on the Corvette Galathea's Circumnavigation*. (Published 1851 in Danish; English translation in typescript, HMCS.)
17. Bingham, Hiram. *Bartimeus of the Sandwich Islands*. New York [1865]
18. ——. *A Residence of Twenty-one Years in the Sandwich Islands*. Hartford and New York, 1847
19. Bingham, Hiram II. "Address at Kawaiahao Church." Honolulu, 1903
20. Bishop, Sereno Edwards. *Reminiscences of Old Hawaii*. Honolulu, 1916

21. Blackman, William Fremont. *The Making of Hawaii*. New York, 1906
22. Bradley, Harold Whitman. *The American Frontier in Hawaii*. Stanford, 1942
23. Brewer, Charles. *Reminiscences*. Jamaica Plain, 1884
24. Castle, Samuel N. *An Account of the Visit of the French Frigate L'Artémise*. Honolulu, 1839. (This is a booklet of 63 pp. There is also a sheet with the same title written by officers of the U. S. East India squadron which defends the missionaries.)
25. *The Centennial Book, 1820–1920*. Honolulu, 1920
26. *Charlton Land Claims*. [Six pamphlets] Honolulu, 1844–47
27. Cheever, Henry T. *Life in the Sandwich Islands*. New York, 1851
28. Coan, Titus. *Life in Hawaii*. New York, 1882
29. Coan, Mrs. Titus [Lydia Bingham]. *A Brief Sketch of . . . Mrs. Sybil Moseley Bingham*. n.p., n.d. [1895]
30. Cook, James, and James King. *A Voyage to the Pacific Ocean*. London, 1785
31. Cook, John. *Reminiscences*. Honolulu, 1927
32. Cooke, Amos Starr, and Juliette Montague. *The Chiefs' Children's School*. Honolulu, 1937. Ed. Mary Atherton Richards

33. Damon, Ethel M. *Father Bond of Kohala*. Honolulu, 1927
34. ——. *Koamalu*. Honolulu, 1931
35. ——. *The Stone Church at Kawaiahao*. Honolulu, 1945
36. Damon, Samuel C. "A Jubilee Sermon." Honolulu, 1883
37. Dibble, Sheldon. *History of the Sandwich Islands*. Lahainaluna, 1843
38. Doyle, Emma Lyons, ed. *Makua Laiana. The Story of Lorenzo Lyons*. Honolulu, 1945
39. Duhaut-Cilly, A. *Voyage autour du monde*. Paris, 1834
40. Dwight, E. W. *Memoir of Obookiah*. New York, n.d.

41. Ellis, William. *Journal of a Tour around Hawaii*. Boston, 1825
42. Elwes, Robert. *A Sketcher's Tour round the World*. London, 1854
43. Emerson, Nathaniel B. *Unwritten Literature of Hawaii*. Washington, 1909
44. Emerson, Oliver Pomeroy. *Pioneer Days in Hawaii*. Garden City, 1928

45. Frear, Mary Dillingham. *Lowell and Abigail*. New Haven, 1934
46. Frear, Walter F. *Anti-Missionary Criticism*. Honolulu, 1935

47. Gelett, Charles Wetherby. *A Life on the Ocean*. Honolulu, 1917
48. Golovnin, V. *Puteshestvie Vokrug Sveta*. St. Petersburg, 1822. (Hawaiian portion of this Russian voyage translated and in typescript, HMCS.)

49. [Graham, Mrs. Maria.] *Voyage of H. M. S. Blonde to the Sandwich Islands.* London, 1826

49a. Green, J. S. *Notices . . . of the late Bartimeus L. Puaaiki.* Lahaina-luna, 1844

50. Gulick, Reverend and Mrs. Orramel Hinckley. *The Pilgrims of Hawaii.* New York, 1918

50a. Halford, Francis John. *9 Doctors & God.* Honolulu, 1954

51. Hewitt, John H. *Williams College and Foreign Missions.* Boston, 1914

52. Hobbs, Jean. *Hawaii: A Pageant of the Soil.* Stanford, 1935

53. Hohman, Elmo Paul. *The American Whaleman.* New York, 1928

54. Holman, Lucia Ruggles. *Journal.* Honolulu, 1931 (Bishop Museum Special Publication 17)

55. Hopkins, Manley. *Hawaii: the Past, Present, and Future of Its Island-Kingdom.* London, 1862

56. Hunnewell, James. *Journal of the Voyage of the "Missionary Packet," Boston to Honolulu.* Cambridge, 1880

57. Jarves, James Jackson. *History of the Hawaiian or Sandwich Islands.* Boston, 1843

58. ——. *Scenes and Scenery in the Sandwich Islands.* Boston, 1844

59. Judd. *Fragments.* [A series of six small volumes of excerpts from various Judd journals and letters] Honolulu, 1903, 1911, etc.

60. Judd, Laura Fish. *Honolulu: Sketches of Life . . . in the Hawaiian Islands.* New York, 1880

61. Koskinen, Aarne A. *Missionary Influence as a Political Factor in the Pacific Islands.* Helsinki, 1953

62. Kuykendall, Ralph S. *The Hawaiian Kingdom.* Honolulu, 1938

63. Ledyard, John. *A Journal of Capt. Cook's Last Voyage. . . .* Hartford, 1783

64. Loomis, Elisha. *Journal.* Honolulu, 1937 [mimeographed]

65. Loomis, Albertine. *Grapes of Canaan.* New York, 1951

66. Ludlow, Helen W. "Clarissa Chapman Armstrong." n.p., n.d.

67. Lyman, Henry M. *Hawaiian Yesterdays.* Chicago, 1906

68. Lyman, Nettie Hammond. *History of Haili Church.* n.p., 1942 [mimeographed]

MISSION PUBLICATIONS:

69. "Constitution of the Original Hawaiian Church" [3 printed pages]

70. "The Duty of the Present Generation to Evangelize the World." Honolulu, 1836 [The famous "Circular" sent with Richards to the United States]

71. *General Letters to the Sandwich Islands Mission* [From the American Board; printed from time to time; 2 bound volumes in HMCS covering 1831–60]

72. Hawaiian Evangelical Association. *Annual Reports.* 1854–

73. Hawaiian Mission Children's Society. *Annual Reports.* 1852–

74. ——. *Jubilee Celebration.* Honolulu, 1887

74a. *Hawaiian Mission Children's Society, 1852–1952.* Honolulu, 1952

75. "Instructions of the Prudential Committee of the American Board of Commissioners for Foreign Missions to the Sandwich Islands Mission." Lahainaluna, 1838 [Collects instructions sent with each company]

76. Maternal Association. "Names of Members and Children." 1854

77. *Minutes of General Meetings of the Sandwich Islands Mission* [In HMCS these are bound together: Vol. I, 1830–37; Vol. II, 1838–53]

78. "Refutation of the Charges . . . against the American Missionaries. . . ." 1843

79. "The Three Old Mission Houses." [4 page sheet] 1951

80. Macrae, James. *With Lord Byron at the Sandwich Islands in 1825.* Honolulu, 1922

81. Malo, David. *Hawaiian Antiquities.* Honolulu, 1903

82. Martin, John. *An Account of the Natives of the Tonga Islands. . . .* London, 1818

83. Mathison, Gilbert Farquhar. *Narrative of a Visit to . . . the Sandwich Islands.* London, 1825

84. Maurer, Oscar E. "Three Early Christian Leaders of Hawaii." Honolulu, 1945

85. Mellen, Kathleen Dickenson. *The Magnificent Matriarch.* New York, 1952 [The life of Kaahumanu]

86. *Missionary Album.* [Invaluable reference, listing all the missionaries with brief biographies and portraits] Honolulu, 1937

87. Morgan, Theodore. *Hawaii: A Century of Economic Change 1778–1876.* Cambridge, Mass., 1948

88. Morison, Samuel Eliot. *The Maritime History of Massachusetts 1783–1860.* Boston, 1921

89. *A Narrative of Five Youth from the Sandwich Islands.* New York, 1816

90. Nellist, George F. *Men of Hawaii.* Honolulu, 1935

91. ——. *The Story of Hawaii and its Builders.* Honolulu, 1925

92. Oliver, James. *Wreck of the Glide.* New York & London, 1848

93. Parke, W. C. *Personal Reminiscences.* [For the sailor riot of 1852] Cambridge, Mass., 1891

94. Parker, Mrs. E. M. Wills. *The Sandwich Islands as they are.* . . . San Francisco, 1852
95. Pratt, High Chiefess. *Keoua.* Honolulu, 1920 [Chiefs' genealogies]
96. *Report of the Proceedings and Evidences of Messrs. Ladd & Co.* . . . Honolulu, 1847
97. Reynolds, J. N. *Voyage of the U. S. Frigate Potomac 1831–34.* New York, 1835
98. Richards, Mary Atherton. *Amos Starr Cooke and Juliette Montague Cooke.* Honolulu, 1941
99. [Richards, William.] *Memoir of Keopuolani.* Boston, 1925
100. Ruschenberger, W. S. *Narrative of a Voyage Round the World.* . . . Philadelphia, 1838

101. Simpson, Alexander. *The Sandwich Islands, Progress of Events since their Discovery.* London, 1851
102. Simpson, Sir George. *An Overland Journey Round the World.* London, 1847
103. Skogman, C. *Fregatten Eugenies Resa . . . 1851–1853* [Translation of Hawaiian portion by Meiric Dutton, Honolulu, 1954]
104. Smith, Emma L. *Journal Book 1850–1851.* Honolulu, 1923
105. Smith, Jared. *The Big Five.* Honolulu, 1942
106. Starr, Edward C. *A History of Cornwall, Connecticut.* New Haven, 1926
107. Steegmuller, Francis. *The Two Lives of James Jackson Jarves.* New Haven, 1951
108. Stevens, Sylvester. *American Expansion in Hawaii 1842–1898.* Harrisburg, 1946
109. Stewart, C. S. *Private Journal of . . . a Residence in the Sandwich Islands.* Boston, 1839
110. ——. *A Visit to the South Seas.* . . . New York, 1831
111. Strong, William E. *The Story of the American Board.* Boston, 1910
112. Sullivan, Josephine (ed. K. C. Leebrick). *A History of C. Brewer & Company Ltd.* Boston, 1926
113. *Suspension of Anthony Ten Eyck, Esq.* Honolulu, 1848

114. Thurston, Lucy G. *Life and Times.* Ann Arbor, 1882, and Honolulu, 1934
115. Tinker, Reuben. *Sermons.* New York, 1856 [Includes biographical sketch]
116 Tyerman, Daniel, and George Bennet. *Journal of Voyages & Travels . . . in the South Sea Islands.* Boston, 1832

117. Vancouver, George. *A Voyage of Discovery to the North Pacific Ocean.* . . . London, 1798

118. von Holt, Ida Elizabeth Knudsen. *Stories of Long Ago.* Honolulu, 1953

119. Westervelt, W. D. *Legends of Maui—a Demigod of Polynesia.* Honolulu, 1910

120. Wheeler, Daniel. *Extracts from the Letters and Journals.* Philadelphia, 1840

121. Wight, Elizabeth Leslie. *The Memoirs of Elizabeth Kinau Wilder.* Honolulu, 1909

122. Wilcox, Abner and Lucy. *Letters from the Life of Abner and Lucy Wilcox* (ed. Ethel M. Damon). Honolulu, 1950

123. Wilkes, Charles. *Narrative of the U. S. Exploring Expedition during the Years 1838–1842.* [Five volumes and atlas] Philadelphia, 1845

124. Williston, Samuel. *William Richards.* Cambridge, Mass., 1938

125. Withington, Antoinette. *The Golden Cloak.* Honolulu, 1953

126. Wright, Louis B., and Mary Isabel Fry. *Puritans in the South Seas.* New York, 1936

127. Wyllie, R. C. "Answers to Questions Proposed by His Excellency, R. C. Wyllie . . . to all the Missionaries in the Hawaiian Islands, May, 1846." Honolulu [1848]

2. Periodicals

The files of the following periodicals have been particularly valuable. Specific reference to some of the articles occurring in them will be found in the Notes which follow. It is impossible to acknowledge specific indebtedness in every instance.

128. *The Friend.* Originally *The Friend of Temperance and Seamen.* Published continuously in Honolulu since 1843, its files are full of valuable material on Hawaiian life and history.

129. *Hawaiiana.* Nine volumes of miscellaneous periodical items bound together under this title in HMCS.

130. *Hawaiian Almanac & Annual* (Thrum's Annual). Currently continued under the title *All About Hawaii.*

131. Hawaiian Historical Society. Valuable *Annual Reports* and *Papers,* beginning 1892.

132. *Hawaiian Spectator.* 1838 and 1839 only

133. *Honolulu Advertiser* (and predecessor, *Pacific Commercial Advertiser*) and

134. *Honolulu Star-Bulletin*
     Leading Hawaiian newspapers, which frequently print material about Hawaiian history.

135. *Honolulu Times.* Weekly newspaper, 1849–50

136. *The Missionary Herald.* Published in Boston since 1805. Full of valuable material about the Hawaiian mission, especially during the early years. Dates are sometimes confused because of the months (sometimes more than a year) letters took to travel home.
137. *Paradise of the Pacific.* Honolulu, 1888–
138. *The Polynesian.* Weekly newspaper beginning 1840 and continuing (with lapse 1842–43) throughout the period covered in this book.
139. *Sandwich Island [sic] Gazette.* Weekly, 1836–39
140. *Sandwich Island Mirror.* Monthly, 1839–40. Especially the *Suppliment [sic]* of 15 January 1840.
141. *Sandwich Islands News.* Weekly, 1846–48 with hiatus

Of the many scattered articles consulted, the following were most useful:

Coan, Titus. "The Natives of Hawaii," *Annals* of the American Academy of Political and Social Science, XVIII (July, 1901), 9-17
Dunstan, J. Leslie. "The Churches in Hawaii," *Social Process in Hawaii,* XVI (1952), 34-39
Manby, Thomas. "Journal," *Honolulu Mercury,* 29 August 1949
Ruggles, Samuel and Nancy. "From a Missionary Journal," *Atlantic Monthly,* CXXXIV (November, 1924), 648-57
Société de Propagation de Foi. *Annales,* Lyons, 1840

3. UNPUBLISHED MATERIAL

For fresh insights into this period of Hawaiian history it is essential to examine the magnificent manuscript collections of the Mission Historical Library (combining the resources of the Hawaiian Historical Society and the Hawaiian Mission Children's Society), the Archives of Hawaii, and the files of the American Board of Commissioners for Foreign Missions now on deposit in the Houghton Library of Harvard University. I am deeply indebted to Miss Bernice Judd, Librarian of the HMCS, to Mrs. Willowdean Handy, Librarian of the HHS, and to Miss Carolyn E. Jakeman of the Houghton Library for guiding me through their collections, and to Miss Mary Walker, Librarian of the American Board, for arranging special privileges in connection with the board's rich collection.

To list the hundreds of manuscript items in these and other collections would be impossible. Instead, a general description of the material in each collection will be followed by specific references in the Notes to quoted sources.

HAWAIIAN MISSION CHILDREN'S SOCIETY LIBRARY

Letters, diaries, journals and accounts of all the missionaries are preserved here in manuscript. Some materials have also been typed. Some valuable non-missionary journals are also found here.

Among the many journals and letters consulted, those by the following were especially helpful: Mr. and Mrs. Lorrin Andrews, Mr. and Mrs. Richard Armstrong, Dr. Dwight Baldwin (including a large file of letters to him from many of the brethren), Mr. and Mrs. Hiram Bingham, Artemas Bishop, Mr. and Mrs. Levi Chamberlain, the charming childhood journals of Mary and Nathan Chamberlain, Daniel Chamberlain, Ephraim Clark, letters to and from the Cookes, Titus Coan, John Colcord, Louisa Everest Ely, Cochran Forbes, Mr. and Mrs. Jonathan Green, Peter J. Gulick, Lucia Ruggles Holman, Mary Ann Brainerd Ives, Kamakau, Mr. and Mrs. Elisha Loomis, David B. Lyman, Chester Smith Lyman, Stephen Reynolds, William Richards, Mr. and Mrs. Samuel Ruggles, Charles S. Stewart, Mr. and Mrs. Asa Thurston, Reuben Tinker, Joel Turrill Correspondence (letters of C. R. Bishop and William L. Lee), Mr. and Mrs. Samuel Whitney.

HMCS also has a valuable collection of church records, including among many others those of Hilo, Lahaina and Oahu which provided information regarding church discipline, government, and membership.

Also a number of folders containing little essays or *Kumumanao* (Fundamental Thoughts) by Hawaiians including Lahainaluna students, some of which are accompanied by manuscript translations by the Reverend Henry P. Judd.

Three typescript books supplied information on the Hilo Boarding School: Mildred Osmundson Gordon: *A History of the Hilo Boarding School* (Unpublished M.A. thesis, University of Hawaii, 1936); Nettie Hammond Lyman: *Notes on the Hilo Boarding School* (1935), and *Letters of David Lyman* to Dibble and Anderson regarding the Hilo School.

Manuscript books containing the General Meeting Minutes, the Minutes of the Prudential Meetings of the Mission Family, the Journal of the Sandwich Islands Mission, "Answers by the Sandwich Islands Missionaries to the Questions in the Circular of 1833," and Records of the Maternal Association of the Sandwich Islands Mission were also usefully consulted.

AMERICAN BOARD OF COMMISSIONERS FILES IN THE HOUGHTON LIBRARY

Especially valuable are the lengthy letters, reports and journals sent from Hawaii to the board; letters of candidates for missionary posts, memoranda of talks with returned missionaries. In the early years much of the material sent back was by Hiram Bingham, but there are also many other letters of value, especially those from islands other than Oahu. Also the Minutes of the Prudential Meetings of the Mission, General Meeting records and the journal of Edwin Locke.

The Houghton Library also has the Hunnewell Papers, and letters of John C. Jones in the Josiah Marshall Papers.

Citations from the ABC papers in the Notes carry the numerical designation by which they are located in the collection, for example: ABC 19.1 v. 1.

ARCHIVES OF HAWAII

A large collection of papers and letters designated FO & Ex (Foreign Office & Executive) was examined, especially those relating to Judd, the Charlton claims, annexation, mission lands, Wyllie, and Dillon's strange attempt to intrigue with Judd against Wyllie.

Other documents examined include the Journals of William Richards, Henry Sheldon's "Reminiscences of Honolulu 35 Years Ago" (a typescript collecting eighty-four articles from the *Saturday Press*), the extant portion of Don Francisco de Paula Marin's Journal translated by Wyllie, and a collection of documents dealing with the impeachment charges against Dr. Judd. Photostat copies of the Armstrong Papers in the Library of Congress were also examined here.

The will of Dr. Judd was examined at the Supreme Court.

HAWAIIAN HISTORICAL SOCIETY

The typescript of an unpublished life of Admiral Theodorus Bailey by Francis R. Stoddard provided information on the annexation scheme of 1854.

Several manuscripts gave graphic pictures of life in Hawaii: Estrella Mott's description of Honolulu in 1848; several journals and letters by Gorham D. Gilman, a young Yankee trader; reminiscences of Honolulu by Emma Theodora Paty Yates; the interesting, though anonymous, "1848 Honolulu as it is Notes for Amplification."

Alexander Liholiho's private journal of his European tour is kept here.

BISHOP MUSEUM

First in importance is S. M. Kamakau's "History of Hawaii" which the museum plans to publish. John Ii's "An Expression of Affection for Ka-imi-haku (Lover of Chiefs)," translated by Mary Pukui, is also useful. The collection of Hawaiian Ethnological Notes provided some miscellaneous information. A letter of Luther Severance to Hannibal Hamlin, 31 January 1852, contains a good estimate of the missionaries.

OTHER SOURCES

Several unpublished theses were read at the University of Hawaii, including George Theodore Becker's "Lahainaluna 1831-77" (1938).

Mrs. Frederick Edgecomb generously permitted the examination of letters written by Hiram and Sybil Bingham and a journal of Sybil's.

Mrs. Gordon Smith kindly supplied letters written by the Artemas Bishop family.

Professor Ralph Kuykendall opened up his extensive collection of Hawaiiana to supply the court-martial records covering the Percival affair, letters of Ladd & Co. to Brinsmade during his European trip, copies of letters in the Bancroft Library at the University of California relating to Hawaiian commerce, and extracts from Finch's cruise in the *Vincennes,* taken from Navy Department files.

In the Wailuku Library, Maui, are two typescripts, "The Hana Mission Station" and "The Wailuku Mission Station," by E. E. Pleasant.

NOTES

For each chapter references are given to works that were generally useful, followed by specific citations for quoted material. To conserve space, each printed work and periodical has been numbered in the bibliography and is identified by that number below. For example, *123:* 18, 342 means that on page 123 of this book the quoted material is from Bingham's *Residence* (number 18), page 342.

Chapter 1 (p. 9)

For Hawaiian antiquities 7, 8, 30, 81. I must mention by name Ralph Kuykendall's indispensable *The Hawaiian Kingdom* (62) which I have used as a standard reference throughout. The landfall and surrounding incidents: 18, 75, 114, 136; the Mission Journal (ABC & HMCS), Loomis and Bingham Journals (HMCS), Ruggles Journal (see periodical listings), Hunnewell letters (Houghton).

9: Samuel & Nancy Ruggles, "From a Missionary Journal," *Atlantic Monthly,* vol. 134 (Nov. 1924), pp. 648-57. *10:* 114, 24; 75. *16:* 43; 114, 26 & 30.

Chapter 2 (p. 20)

10, 18, 22, 27, 29, 40, 44, 48, 52, 54, 62, 65, 69, 88, 89, 126, 136. Journals of Maria Loomis, Daniel Chamberlain; Bingham letters to Ruggles (HMCS). Mission Journal (ABC). Minutes of Prudential Committee, ABC 19.3 v. 2. Harwood Diaries, Bennington Museum in Vermont (for Bingham's early years).

22: 40, 26. *24:* 89, 20. *25:* 89, 37; ABC 6 v. 2. *27:* 29; ABC 6 v. 2, 3 Oct. 1819. *28:* 114, 6. *29:* ABC 6 v. 2, 16 Sep. 1819. *30:* ABC 6 v. 2, 17 Aug. 1819; 23 Aug. 1819; 4 Sep. 1819. *32:* ms. Journal (HMCS). *33:* 48.

Chapter 3 (p. 34)

18, 37, 54, 57, 109, 114, 136. Journals of Maria Loomis, Artemas Bishop and Daniel Chamberlain (HMCS). Mission Journal (ABC). Kamakau (Bp.).

37: 136 (1821), 117; 114, 36. *38:* ABC 19.1 v. 1, 39. *39:* Kamakau (Bp.). *42:* ABC 19.1 v. 1; 114, 42. *44:* 114, 42. *45:* 114, 50.

Chapter 4 (p. 47)

18, 27 (the Hoapili story), 29 (Sybil's chair), 37, 58, 65, 109, 136. Journals of Sybil Bingham, Daniel Chamberlain, the Loomises (HMCS), and of Marin (AH), Ruggles (op. cit.) and Mission (ABC). Kamakau (Bp.), Hawaiian Ethnological Notes (typed, Bp.) on superstitions regarding missionaries; N. B. Emerson, "The Honolulu Fort," HHS 8th Annual Report; Bruce Cartwright, "Honolulu in 1809–1810," *Paradise of the Pacific*, vol. 38 (Dec. 1925), p. 59 on Oliver Holmes. Minutes of the Prudential Committee on the Kanui case (ABC). "History of the Defection of Dr. Holman," ABC 19.1 v. 1.

49: 18, 93. *50:* Journal 22 Apr. 1820 (HMCS). *51:* 18, 106. *52:* ABC 19.1 v. 1, 6 June 1820; Loomis Journal, 8 July 1820 (HMCS). *53:* Sybil Bingham Journal, 24 June 1820 (HMCS). *54:* 29. *56:* 136 (1821) 169 et seq.; Ruggles Journal (op. cit.). *57:* ABC 19.1 v. 1, 76 and Ruggles Journal. *60:* 50a, 56; Elisha & Maria Loomis Journals, 2 Sep. 1820 (HMCS). *61:* ABC 19.1 v. 1, 100. *62:* 27, 77. *64:* ABC 19.1 v. 1, 142.

Chapter 5 (p. 66)

18, 50a, 114, 136. Journals of Mission (ABC & HMCS), Loomis, Whitney (HMCS), Ruggles (op. cit.), Marin (AH), Holman (Bp.). Kamakau (Bp.). "Mission Houses Honolulu" (HMCA, typed volume). Josiah Marshall letters (Houghton). "History of the Defection . . ." (ABC, op. cit.). John M. Lydgate, "Ka-umu-alii, the Last King of Kauai," HHS 24th Annual Report. Ethel Damon, "George Prince Kaumualii," HHS 55th Annual Report. End of tabu: 37, 57, 18, 22, Kumumanao (HMCS)and W. D. Alexander, "Overthrow of the Ancient Tabu System," HHS 25th Annual Report.

69: ABC 19.1 v. 1, 177; 18, 129. *70:* ABC 19.1 v. 1, 117 and 191. *71:* 136. *72:* 114, 57; Mission Journal 18 Mar. 1821 (HMCS); *76:* do., 22 May 1821. *77:* Alexander, HHS 25th Report, op. cit.; Kumumanao (HMCS); 18, 135. *78:* Marshall letters (Houghton), J. C. Jones to Marshall, 6 July, 5 Oct. & 23 Dec. 1821. *79:* 18, 146. *81:* Jones to Marshall, 23 Dec. 1821; ABC 19.1 v. 1, 16 Nov. 1821.

Chapter 6 (p. 83)

18, 57, 83, 114, 116, 126, 136. "Mission Houses Honolulu" (op. cit.), Marin, Mission, and Loomis Journals and Marshall letters cited above, Sybil Bingham's Journal (owned by Mrs. Frederick Edgecomb), E. S. Handy, "Cultural Revolution in Hawaii," *The Friend*, Oct. 1931, pp. 227 et seq.

84: 18, 157. *86:* Maria Loomis Journal 5 Mar. 1822 (HMCS). *87:* 116, 66. *89:* 114, 66; Sybil Bingham Journal 1821–1823 (Edgecomb).

90: Sybil Bingham to Wm. Beals 29 [Aug.] 1822 (HMCS); 18, 172; ABC 19.1 v. 1, 335. *91:* Jones to Marshall, 16 Nov. 1822 & 9 Mar. 1823 (Houghton); 114, 67. *92:* 114, 69.

Chapter 7 (p. 94)

18, 41, 57, 99, 109, 114, 124, 136. Mission Journal (ABC), ABC 6 v. 4 for new arrivals, Kamakau (Bp.), Luisa Ely Journal (HMCS), Sybil Bingham Journal (Edgecomb), Marin Journal (AH). Bishop to Chamberlain 2 July 1823 (HMCS).

94: 29; 18, 175. *95:* 18, 176-8; Journal 12 Feb. 1823 (Edgecomb). *98:* ABC 19.1 v. 1, 394. *99:* ABC 6 v. 4. *100:* 99; 136 (1825), 40; 18, 194. *101:* 136 (1825), 69; 99; 41, 77. *103:* 41, 44 et seq. *104:* ABC 19.1 v. 1, 434 (3 Oct. 1823). *105:* 18, 200. *107:* ABC 19.1 v. 1, Bingham to Evarts, 21 Nov. 1823; 18, 203; Kamakau (Bp.).

Chapter 8 (p. 108)

18, 20, 44, 49, 64, 109, 136. Journals: Chamberlain, Whitney (HMCS). Kamakau.

108: Hunnewell Papers 5 June 1824 & 29 Aug. 1823 (Houghton). *109:* 18, 207-8. *111:* 21, 65; 18, 214. *112:* 18, 224. *114:* 109, 246; 18, 234. *116:* 64, 28 June 1824. *118:* ABC 19.1 v. 2, 26 Mar. 1825 & 18, 255.

Chapter 9 (p. 120)

17, 18, 49, 64, 80, 109, 136. Chamberlain Journal (HMCS); Minutes of Prudential Meetings (HMCS); ABC 19.3 v. 2 (Records of General Meetings); Navy Department Office of Judge Advocate General Court Martial Records, vol. 23, 1830, nos. 523 to 531: Proceedings of a Court of Inquiry etc. in the case of Lieut. Jno. Percival (hereafter Percival Inquiry).

120: 18, 204. *121:* 18, 259. *122:* 18, 262. *124:* 18, 265. *125:* 136 (1827), 204. *126:* 49, 168. *127:* 136 (1826), 169. *128:* 64, 48. *129:* 18, 282; Percival Inquiry, 211 et seq.

Chapter 10 (p. 130)

18, 41, 65. Percival Inquiry; Reynolds Journal; Chamberlain Journal (HMCS). ABC 19.1 v. 2, Bingham's account of the *Dolphin* riot, 11 Feb. 1830; Richards' account, 19.1 v. 3, 6 Dec. 1827.

130: 18, 284. *131:* 18, 286 et seq. *132:* ABC 19.1 v. 2, 11 Feb. 1830; 18, 287. *133:* Percival Inquiry. *134:* Jones to Marshall 5 May 1826 (Houghton). *135:* ABC 8.5, conversation with Ellis, 26 April 1825. *136:* Chamberlain Journal, 13 Nov. 1826 (HMCS). *137:* 65, 297; 18, 303. *138:* ABC 19.1 v. 3, 250 et seq. *139:* 65, 300. *140:* 65, 302-3; 18, 303.

Chapter 11 (p. 141)

18, 29, 62, 136. Reynolds Journal. ABC 19.1 v. 3, 6 Dec. 1827
(Richards' 26 page account of the Lahaina outrage). Chamberlain to
Whitney-Ruggles, 17 Dec. 1827 (HMCS).
142: ABC 19.1 v. 2 (Whitney's Kauai Journal), 2 Apr. 1826; 118, 73.
143: Bishop to Chamberlain, 17 July 1824 and 27 Oct. 1825 (HMCS).
145: Reynolds Journal, 8 Feb. 1827; do., 19 June 1827. *146:* Sybil Bingham to Nancy Ruggles, n. d. (HMCS); 18, 310; Marshall Papers, 20
July 1827 (Houghton). *147:* Chamberlain Journal, 20 July 1827
(HMCS). *148-9:* ABC 19.1 v. 2, Chamberlain to Board, 1 Nov. 1827;
ibid., v. 3, Richards to Board, 6 Dec. 1827. *150:* Bishop to Chamberlain,
30 Oct. 1827 (HMCS). *151:* Chamberlain to Whitney-Ruggles, 17 Dec.
1827 (HMCS); ABC 19.1 v. 2, 15 Dec. 1827. *152:* ibid.

Chapter 12 (p. 153)

18, 50a, 60, 68, 110, 114. ABC 19.1 v. 2 (numerous letters relating
to this period); Chamberlain and Mary Andrews Journals (HMCS);
Reynolds Journal; FO & Ex Letter Book, 1825–1834 (AH); Navy Department Extracts from Captain William B. Finch's Cruise in the U. S. S.
Vincennes.
153: Reynolds Journal, 30 Mar. 1828. *154:* 60, 6 and 11. *155:* ABC
19.1 v. 2 (Bingham), 12 June 1828; Theodosia Green's Journal, 1827–
28 (HMCS); 114, 93. *157:* ABC 19.1 v. 2, 15 Oct. 1828; Sybil to Sophia,
23 Oct. 1828 (Edgecomb). *158:* 18, 345. *159:* 18, 352; FO & Ex Letter
Book, 1825–34, 25 Nov. 1829 (AH). *160:* 18, 352. *161:* Navy Dept.
Finch Extracts (op. cit.). *162:* Chamberlain Journal, 9 June 1829; John
Ii, "An Expression of Affection for Ka-imi-haku" (Bp.).

Chapter 13 (p. 163)

18, 44, 50a, 59 vol. 2, 68, 109, 118. Lyman & Gulick Journals
(HMCS); ms. letters of Bishop (Mrs. Gordon Smith); "Mission Houses
Honolulu" (HMCS); George Theodore Becker, "Lahainaluna 1831–1877"
(UH); Société pour la Propagation de la Foi, *Annals,* Lyons, 1840.
164: Clark Journal (HMCS). *165:* ABC 19.1 v. 5, Jonathan Green to
David Green, 17 July 1830. *167:* 18, 375; Bingham to Chamberlain,
13 July 1830 (HMCS); ABC 19.1 v. 5 (Goodrich), 5 Mar. 1831. *168:*
Bishop to Chamberlain, 9 Dec. 1828 (HMCS). *169:* 112. *170:* D. B.
Lyman Journal, 12 July 1846 (HMCS); ABC 19.1 v. 1, 192 (24 Mar.
1821). *171:* "The Association" Records, 1830 (HMCS). *172:* Bingham
to Chamberlain 14 Sep. 1830 (HMCS). *173:* 112 quoting Pierce to
Hunnewell, 8 Mar. 1831; 59, v. 3, 1 Apr. 1831; 18, 413. *174:* 136
(1832), 115. *175:* Andrews to Chamberlain, 2 Jan. 1833 (HMCS); 59,
v. 2, 1 Oct. 1838.

Chapter 14 (p. 177)

6, 38, 44, 57, 66, 92, 97, 115. W. D. Alexander, "The Oahu Charity School," HHS 16th Annual Report; *Sailor's Magazine,* 1834 (HMCS); Becker's "Lahainaluna," op. cit. ABC 19.1 v. 4, Hilo General Letter 14 Oct. 1833; ibid., v. 6, Spaulding, 23 Oct. 1832.

178: 18, 432; ABC 19.1 v. 5, Bingham to Anderson, 22 May 1833; 18, 433. *180:* 57, 300; 18, 448; 57, 301. *182:* 59, v. 2, 23 Oct. 1833. *183:* Reynolds Journal, 10 Jan. 1833. *186:* Sybil to Lucy, 4 May 1834 (Edgecomb). *187:* Andrews to Chamberlain, 2 Nov. 1834 and ff. (HMCS). *188:* ibid., 9 Jan. 1835. *189:* Tinker Diary, 16 Feb. 1834 (HMCS); Bishop to Ruggles, 8 Nov. 1834 (HMCS).

Chapter 15 (p. 190)

18, 33, 38, 60, 74, 122, 130, 136. Lahaina Church Records (HMCS); Records of the Maternal Association (HMCS); manuscripts relating to General Meeting of 1836 (HMCS); Chamberlain Journal (HMCS); Edwin Locke Journal, ABC 19.3 v. 3; Société pour la Propagation de la Foi, *Annals* (op. cit.); Sanford B. Dole, "The General Meeting," HHS 27th Annual Report.

191: ABC 19.1 v. 4, Andrews, 16 Nov. 1835; Green quoting Dibble, 16 Nov. 1836 (HMCS). *194:* Records of the Maternal Assn., 21 May 1840 (HMCS). *196:* Mss. relating to 1836 General Meeting (HMCS); Richards, 1 Aug. 1837 (HMCS). *197:* 60, 60; 50a, 162. *198:* 38, 3; Ruggles, 22 Nov. 1836 (HMCS). *199:* Andrews, 11 Dec. 1835 (HMCS); Cooke to Ruggles, 11 Aug. 1837 (HMCS). *200:* ABC 19.1 v. 9, 13 Dec. 1837; 18, 506. *201:* Bingham to Judd, 13 July 1837 (HMCS); ABC 19.3 v. 3, Locke Journal.

Chapter 16 (p. 202)

10, 20, 22, 28, 38, 57, 58, 67, 68, 122, 123, 136. Coan letters, Lyman Journal and letters, Hilo Church Records, Revised Minutes of Delegate Meeting of the Sandwich Islands Mission, all HMCS. ABC 19.1 v. 8, general letters from mission. Reynolds Journal.

202: 122, 88-9. *204:* Coan to Chamberlain 1 Nov. 1841 (HMCS). *205:* 28, 50 and 46 passim. *206:* 122, 164; 28, 56. *207:* 122, 90. *209:* 38, 128; 12, 22. *212:* 139, 15 July 1837.

Chapter 17 (p. 213)

About the Judds: 121 & M. A. Chamberlain, "Memories of the Past and Present" (HMCS typescript). Kinau's death: 58. Kekauluohi: 123. Church government: Anderson to Mission, 10 June 1840 and Minutes of General Meetings (HMCS). Salaries: ABC 19.1 v. 8, 8 June 1839; 75 (mission letter of 3 Dec. 1836). *Artemise* affair: 3, 24, 107, 139, Chamberlain (HMCS) and Reynolds Journals. For information on Liliha,

Kinau and Kekauluohi: the Kamakau manuscript (Bp.). Baldwin Correspondence (HMCS) for various events.

213: 121, 7-8. *216:* Minutes of General Meetings, 1839 (HMCS); Anderson to Mission, 10 June 1840 (HMCS). *217:* ABC 19.1 v. 6, 8 June 1839; 75, 114. *218:* Reynolds Journal, 25 June 1839. *219:* 18, 535; 3, 98. *220:* Reynolds Journal, 11-12 July 1839; 18, 545; 139, 13 July 1839; 18, 547. *221:* 19 July 1839 (Bernice Judd Notes, HMCS); Baldwin Correspondence, 18 Aug. 1839 (HMCS).

Chapter 18 (p. 224)

18, 32, 95, 98, 121. Ellen Armstrong Weaver, "Memories of the Old Palace," *Friend* (1920), 105-6. John Ii, "An Expression of Affection" (Bp.). C. S. Lyman Journal, 11 April 1847 (HMCS). ABC 19.1 v. 4, July 1834, pp. 16-17 (ages and identity of children).

224: 32, 1 June 1839. *225-6:* 130 (1907), 175. *226:* 98, 3 Jan. 1840. *228:* 32, 60; 32, 15 July 1841. *229:* 32, 107. *231:* 121.

Chapter 19 (p. 232)

On the eruption: 28, 136 (1841), 285. First twenty years: 136 (1842), 100; 10; 28. Hoapili's death: 27, 50. 58. Schools: 62, 136 (1841), Becker's "Lahainaluna" (op. cit.). Bingham departure: 29, 66, 114, Reynolds Journal. Armstrong: An important collection of his letters is found in the Library of Congress. Wilkes visit: 50a; 123; 136 (1841), 360. The Constitution: 62, 123, Kamakau (Bp).

235: Baldwin Correspondence, 10 Sep. 1842 (HMCS) and 29 Jan. 1840. *236:* ibid., 15 Aug. 1840. *237:* ABC 19.1 v. 8, 1 June 1840; Reynolds Journal, 3 [5?] Aug. 1840; Armstrong Papers, 18 July 1844 and 5 Mar. 1842 (LC). *238:* 114, 148; Thurston to Hall, 16 Aug. 1841 (HMCS); Thurston to Chamberlain, 11 Sep. 1840 (HMCS). *239:* 138, 20 Dec. 1840. *242:* 60, 102.

Chapter 20 (p. 243)

50a, 58, 60, 67, 71, 77, 122, 136. Chamberlain and Reynolds Journals, Becker's "Lahainaluna", Kamakau.

243: FO & Ex, 16 Jan. 1841 (AH). *244:* Nancy Ruggles to Ebenezer Brown, 3 June 1833 (HMCS). *245:* Kamakau. *246:* 122, 38; 136 (1842), 241. *247:* Reynolds Journal, 18 June 1841; Richards to Wilkes, 15 Mar. 1841 (AH). *249:* 77. *250:* Andrews letters, 1842 and 25 Feb. 1842 (HMCS). *252:* 44, 132; 58, 33. *253:* Andrews to Chamberlain, 19 Feb. 1843 (HMCS). *254:* 29; Bingham to Mission, 26 Feb. 1842 (HMCS).

Chapter 21 (p. 255)

37; 59, vol. 3; 60. Gorham Gilman Journal (HHS). For Ricord's western trek, Bradford Smith, *A Dangerous Freedom,* 119.

255: 3, 97. *256:* 71, 28 Oct. 1842; ABC 19.1 v. 11, 20 Mar. 1843. *257:* Richards Journal, 26 Dec. 1842 (AH); *Messages and Papers of the Presidents* (ed. James D. Richardson), iv, 212. *258:* Reynolds Journal, 14 Feb. 1843; 62, 215. *259:* 121, 63. *260:* 28, 107. *262:* Gorham Gilman Journal (HHS). *263:* 71, 14 Mar. 1843; ABC 19.1 v. 9, 28 Apr. 1843; Smith to Baldwin, 23 Oct. 1843. *264:* 59, vol. 3, 10 Nov. 1831.

Chapter 22 (p. 267)

6, 16, 60, 84, 96, 107, 113. Chamberlain and C. S. Lyman Journals (HMCS); Kamakau (Bp); *Dictionary of American Biography* (for Judge Lee); Sheldon's "Reminiscenses" (AH); "1848 Honolulu as it is Notes for Amplification" (HHS, Anonymous).

269: 103 (no pagination); Armstrong Papers, [?] Nov. 1843 (LC). *270:* FO & Ex, Judd to Pearce, 1 Jan. 1845 (AH); Baldwin Correspondence, 23 June 1845 (HMCS). *271:* ibid., 21 July and 9 June 1845. *273:* 3 May 1846 (HMCS); Kamakau, ch. 25 (Bp); 14 Sep. 1845 (HMCS). *274:* 138, 21 Feb. 1846. *275:* 141, 9 June 1847. *276:* Armstrong Journal (HMCS); 113, 5. *278:* 141, 12 May 1847; 60, 170. *279:* 98, 20 Sep. 1848; Mercy Whitney to her children, 23 Feb. 1846 (HMCS); 6, 260. *280:* Journal, 11 Apr. 1847 (HMCS); ABC 19.1 v. 14 (Armstrong), 10 Oct. 1847; 71, 10 Apr. 1846.

Chapter 23 (p. 281)

12, 44, 50, 52, 60, 87. Clarissa Armstrong Journal, Peter Gulick Autobiography (HMCS); papers relating to Judd impeachment (AH); Ethnological Notes and Kamakau (Bp); Sheldon "Reminiscences" (AH); Gorham Gilman "Notes of a Tour on Oahu 1848" (HHS); Armstrong Papers (LC).

281: ABC 19.1 v. 13, Armstrong to Board, May 1848; Armstrong to Lyman, 25 Feb. 1848. *282:* ABC 19.1 v. 16, Lowell Smith, 14 June 1848; Ellen Armstrong Weaver, "Reminiscences of Stone House," *Southern Workman,* Oct. 1904, 544-9. *283:* Ellen Armstrong Weaver, "Memories of the Old Palace," *Friend,* 1920, 105-6. *284:* 22 Aug. 1849 (LC). *285:* Baldwin Correspondence, 12 Jan. 1852 (HMCS). *286:* 44, 146. *289:* FO & Ex, Dillon to Judd, 11 Aug. 1848 (AH). *290:* Armstrong to Lyman, 10 Apr. 1849 (HMCS).

Chapter 24 (p. 291)

33, 71, 77. Chamberlain Journal (HMCS); Alexander Liholiho's Journal and Gorham Gilman's Journal of a trip to Maui (1843) (HHS).

291: Gilman, Trip to Maui (HHS). *292:* ABC 19.1 v. 13, 26 May 1848; 98, 14 Mar. 1849; ABC 19.1 v. 14, 21 Dec. 1848; 71, 24 Oct. 1849. *293:* ABC 19.1 v. 13, 2 June 1848. *294:* Chamberlain Journal, 31 May 1848 (HMCS); Maria Chamberlain letter, 16 Aug. 1849 (HMCS);

Armstrong Journal, 29 July 1849 (HMCS). *295:* Sheldon "Reminiscences" (AH). *296:* Armstrong to Lyman, 3 Sep. 1849 (HMCS). *297:* Alexander Liholiho Journal (HHS).

Chapter 25 (p. 298)

3, 50a, 59 vol. 2, 84. Armstrong Journal (HMCS) and Papers (LC); Baldwin Correspondence and Turrill Correspondence (HMCS).

299: Sheldon's "Reminiscences" (AH). *300:* Lee to Turrill, 11 Oct. 1851 (HMCS). *301:* ibid., 15 Jan. 1853; FO & Ex, 11 Nov. 1851 (AH). *302:* Armstrong to Baldwin, 28 Oct. 1852 (HMCS). *303:* Lorrin to John Andrews, 30 Oct. 1852 (HMCS). *304:* Armstrong Journal, 20 July 1853 (HMCS). *305:* ibid., 5 Sep. 1853; Bishop to Turrill, 7 Oct. 1853 (HMCS); FO & Ex, Wyllie to Ricord, 12 Oct. 1853 (AH). *306:* Armstrong Journal, 5 Sep. 1853 (HMCS); Armstrong to Baldwin, 13 Sep. 1853 (HMCS); Malo, 16 Apr. 1853 (HMCS). *307:* Armstrong to Chapman, 8 Oct. 1851 (LC). *308:* ibid., 24 Apr. 1854; Armstrong Journal, 11 Mar. 1854 (HMCS); Manuscript life of Adm. Theodorus Bailey by Francis R. Stoddard (HHS).

Chapter 26 (p. 310)

On mission lands: 15, 38, 44, 52, 126, 128 (vol. 51, no. 5). On Castle & Cooke: 77. 98. Children's Society: 50, 59, 67, 73, 74a; M. A. Chamberlain, "Memories of the Past" (HMCS); Armstrong Papers (LC); Bishop letters owned by Mrs. Gordon Smith. On church organization: Minutes of the Meeting of the Hawaiian Evangelical Association, 1854 (HMCS); ABC 19.1 v. 15, E. W. Clark on ecclesiastical organization at the Sandwich Islands. Dwight affair: ABC 19.1 v. 13. King's death: 60, 121; Armstrong Journal (HMCS); Kamakau (Bp); Emma Paty Yates, "Reminiscences of Honolulu" (HHS), Sheldon "Reminiscences" (AH).

310: 135, 2 Jan. 1850. *311:* 52, 101; 44, 144. *312:* 98, 11 Nov. 1852. *312:* Elizabeth to Sereno Bishop, 31 Mar. 1852 (Mrs. Gordon Smith). *313:* Armstrong Papers, 16 Oct. 1851 (LC). *314:* 74a, 2 and 5; 73, 1854 report. *316:* Armstrong Papers, 13 Feb. 1853 (LC). *317:* Kamakau (Bp); 121, 107; Armstrong Journal, 24 Dec. 1854 (HMCS). *318:* 128, 1 May 1850; 16, 53 (typescript); Severance to Hamlin, 31 Jan. 1852 (Bp); 87, 95. *319:* 82, xlvii. *320:* 127. *321:* 44, 169.

Chapter 27 (p. 323)

21, 33, 34, 50, 90, 91, 106. 128, vol. 51 no. 5 p. 34 and vol. 52 no. 1 p. 2. J. Leslie Dunstan, "The Churches in Hawaii," *Social Process in Hawaii,* XVI (1952), 34-9. Hiram Bingham II, Address at Kawaiahao (HMCS). 134, 4 Feb. 1928 and 22 Jan. 1955. Dr. Judd's Will (dated 18 Dec. 1872) Supreme Court 497.

INDEX

INDEX

Adams, Alexander, 156
Adams, Governor. *See* Kuakini
Adams, John Quincy, 160
Alexander, Mary Ann McKinney, 188, 284
Alexander, Samuel T., 327-28
Alexander, Wallace, 328
Alexander, William Patterson, 188, 279, 283-84
Alexander & Baldwin, 323, 326, 328
Alexander Liholiho. *See* Kamehameha IV
Allen, Anthony, 53
Allen, Elisha, 305
Allen, Capt. Joseph, 61, 70
American Bible Society, 24, 38, 57
American Board of Commissioners for Foreign Missions (A.B.C.F.M.), 10, 23, 24, 195, 199, 203, 211, 216-17, 249, 256, 270, 293, 315, 319, 323
American Seamen's Friend Society, 184
Amherst College, 266
Anderson, Rufus, 22, 216, 256, 319
Andover Theological Seminary, 23, 26, 105, 164, 202, 276
Andrews, Anna Gilson, 313
Andrews, Claudius B., 313
Andrews, Lorrin, 165, 174-75, 184-85, 187-88, 190-92, 199, 249-51, 253, 273, 302, 303, 305, 320
Andrews, Lorrin, Jr., 303
Andrews, Mary, 154, 303
Andrews, Samantha Gilson, 313
Andrews, Sarah, 250
Annexation, 307-09, 325
Annexation Club, 325
Armstrong, Clarissa Chapman, 188, 193, 209, 230, 237-38, 269
Armstrong, Ellen, 283
Armstrong, Mary Jane, 282
Armstrong, Nevins, 313
Armstrong, Richard, 188, 193, 209, 230, 237-38, 253, 271, 276, 280-85, 289-90, 292, 296, 299, 302-08, 317
Armstrong, Samuel Chapman, 283-84, 318, 325
Armstrong, Willie, 316
Artemise, 219, 222, 226
Atherton, Ballard, 325
Atherton, Juliette Montague Cooke, 325
Auna, 86-87, 89

Bachelot, Father Alexis, 175-76, 200-01
Bailey, Adm. Theodorus, 308
Baldwin, Charlotte Fowler, 186
Baldwin, Dwight, 177, 186, 217, 248, 255, 271-72, 304, 328
Baldwin, Henry P., 327-28
Bartimeus, 127, 252
Bates, Asher, 289
Beals, William, 51-52, 62, 89, 90, 112
Becket, 78
Belgian Company of Colonization, 274
Bennet, George, 86, 89
Bennington, Vermont, 18, 25, 164
Bethel Church, 184, 265, 275-76, 324
Big Five, 169, 327-29
Bille, Commander Steen, 318
Bingham, Elizabeth, 167
Bingham, Hiram, 18, 25-26, 31-32, 35-38, 41, 47-51, 53-55, 58-60, 63-64, 66-72, 75-77, 81-82, 85-86, 91, 96, 109, 113-14, 122, 128, 132-33, 135, 137, 139, 146, 151, 157, 167, 172, 178, 187, 200-01, 215, 218-19, 236-39, 250, 253-54
Bingham, Hiram II, 186
Bingham, Hiram III, 326
Bingham, Jeremiah, 113, 126
Bingham, Lucy, 146, 167, 186
Bingham, Sophia, 90, 113, 146, 157
Bingham, Sybil Moseley, 27, 32, 39, 52, 52, 54-55, 58, 61, 63, 82, 89,

94-95, 113, 117, 126, 146, 156-57, 167, 186, 236-38, 253-54

Bishop, Artemas, 103-05, 126-27, 143, 150, 168, 219, 249, 271, 291, 293, 320

Bishop, Bernice Pauahi, 225, 227, 229-30, 299-300

Bishop, Charles, 230, 277, 299, 302, 304-05, 308, 324

Bishop, Delia Stone, 168

Bishop, Elizabeth Edwards, 96, 104, 155

Bishop, Elizabeth Jane, 312

Bishop, Sereno, 312-13

Bishop Estate, 300

Blanchard, Captain, 10, 35, 40, 47, 73

Blatchely, Abraham, 101, 105, 134, 135, 141

Bliss, Emily Curtis, 198

Bliss, Isaac, 198

Blonde, 121-25

Boki, 48-51, 54, 58, 61, 67-69, 79, 106-07, 121-22, 123, 133, 135-36, 144, 151, 155, 162, 250

Bond, Elias, 323

Brewer, C., & Co., 169, 244, 270

Brinsmade, Peter, 200, 219, 221, 239, 244, 248, 255, 264, 274-76, 278

Brintnal, Capt. Caleb, 21

British claims in Hawaii, 140, 200-01, 243, 248, 255-60, 264, 301

Brown, George, 263, 270-72, 276

Brown, Lydia, 193

Buchanan, James, 276

Buckle, Capt. William, 127-28, 147-50

Burnham, Charles, 184-85

Butler, Mr. (Lahaina), 45, 83, 99, 136

Byng, Hon. Frederick, 120

Byron, George Anson, Lord, 121, 123-26

Canning, George, 120

Carysfort, 257, 261

Castle, Alfred, 324

Castle, Angeline Tenney, 246

Castle, Mary Tenney, 246

Castle, Samuel, 246, 308, 311, 323, 327

Castle, William Richards, 326

Castle & Cooke, 246, 311-12, 323, 326-28

Catholicism, 147, 172, 174-75, 199-

201, 212, 218-21, 234, 236, 284, 295, 297, 301

Central Union Church, 329

Chamberlain, Daniel, 28, 32, 53, 59, 63-64, 73-75, 80, 89, 93, 96

Chamberlain, Daniel, Jr., 32, 35

Chamberlain, Dexter, 32, 59-60

Chamberlain, Jerusha, 28, 29

Chamberlain, Levi, 105, 110, 117, 122, 145, 150, 153, 156, 169, 172, 181, 211, 217, 250, 253, 269, 291, 294-95

Chamberlain, Maria Patton, 156, 269, 294

Chamberlain, Mary, 32

Chamberlain, Nancy, 32

Chamberlain, Nathan, 32, 59

Chamberlain, Warren, 313

Chapin, Alonzo, 177

Charlton, Richard, 121, 123, 134-35, 138-40, 144, 147-51, 158-60, 182, 200-01, 243-44, 256, 260, 263-64, 269, 271, 273-74

Chiefs' Children's School, 224-31, 260, 299-300, 325

Clark (Clarke), Capt. Elisha, 147-48

Clark, Ephraim, 164-66, 172, 185, 209, 320

Cleopatra's Barge, 64, 66, 79-80, 99

Cleveland, Grover, 325

Coan, Fidelia Church, 203, 207

Coan, Titus, 202-07, 212, 232, 235, 260, 320

Columbia, 20

"Committee of Thirteen," 304-05

Congregationalism, 31, 128, 171, 216-18, 233-34, 253, 284, 301, 315, 319-20

Constellation, 260, 262

Constitution, 302

Cook, Capt. James, 11, 20

Cooke, Amos, 199, 221, 224-31, 271, 292, 311-12, 323, 325, 327

Cooke, Joseph, 226

Cooke, Juliette Montague, 193, 224-31, 246, 279

Cornwall, Conn., 24-26, 212

Cox. *See* Keeaumoku

Damon, Samuel C., 265-66, 324

Damon, Samuel M., 324

Daniel, 127-28, 150

Davis, Betty, 78

Davis, Isaac, 78

Davis, Capt. William Heath, 21, 52, 80, 91
Dibble, Sheldon, 185, 191
Diell, John, 184, 265, 276
Dillingham, Benjamin Franklin, 324
Dillingham, Benjamin F. II, 326
Dillingham, Walter, 324
Dillon, Guillaume Patrice, 289, 295-96
Dimond, Henry, 312, 324
Dole, Daniel, 250-51
Dole, Emily, 250-51
Dole, James D., 325
Dole, Sanford B., 251, 325
Dolphin, 130-34
Dominis, John, 138
Dublin, 261
Dudoit, Jules, 200-01, 219, 222, 270
Duty of the Present Generation to Evangelize the World, The, 195-96
Dwight, Anna Mahoe, 315-16
Dwight, Edwin W., 22, 24
Dwight, Samuel, 315-16
Dwight, Timothy, 22

Eames, Charles, 296
Ebbets, Capt. John, 138
Ellis, William, 86-89, 95, 96, 101, 103-04, 106-07, 109, 117
Ely, James, 104, 110, 136, 143, 157
Ely, Louisa Everest, 110
Emerson, John S., 186, 251-52, 271, 286, 311, 320, 324
Emerson, Oliver Pomeroy, 320-21
Emerson, Samuel, 321
Emerson, Ursula Newell, 186, 251-52
Ewa, Oahu, 291

Fillmore, Millard, 297
Finch, Capt. William Bolton, 160-61
Forbes, Cochran, 271
French, Capt. William, 161, 183
French claims in Hawaii, 147, 200-01, 219-21, 248, 264, 274, 284, 295-97, 301, 308
Friend of Temperance and Seamen, The, 265, 313

General Meeting, 155, 172, 174, 186, 193-95, 198, 211, 215, 249, 271, 282, 292, 315
George IV of England, 121
Gilman, Gorham, 262
Goodale, William, 313

Goodrich, Chauncey, 30
Goodrich, Joseph, 103-04, 110, 118, 143, 167-68, 178, 203
Gray, Capt. Robert, 20
Green, Ashbel, 99
Green, Jonathan, 165, 168, 189, 193, 285-86, 291
Green, Theodosia, 155
Gregg, David, 308-09
Grimes, Capt. Eliab, 138
Guizot, François Pierre Guillaume, 264
Gulick, Fanny, 154
Gulick, John, 313
Gulick, John Thomas, 326
Gulick, Louisa, 313
Gulick, Luther Halsey (1828–1891), 313-14
Gulick, Luther Halsey (1892–   ), 326
Gulick, Orramel, 313-14
Gulick, Peter, 168, 271, 291

Haalilio, 145, 200, 255-58, 264, 271, 274
Haiku, Maui, 188, 306
Hall, E. O., & Son, 312
Hall, Edwin O., 262, 312
Hancock, John, 20
Hawaiian Antiquities, 307
Hawaiian Bible, 157, 168, 177, 211, 215
Hawaiian Clerical Association, 96
Hawaiian Evangelical Association, 315, 329
Hawaiian games, 14-15
Hawaiian gods, 64, 69, 118-19, 232
Hawaiian language, 76, 83-84, 187, 208, 215
Hawaiian laws, 128-30, 150-51, 173, 192, 217-18, 235-36, 242, 272, 278
Hawaiian Mission Children's Society, 314, 328-29
Hawaiian population, 195, 285, 319-20, 329
Hawaiian Spectator, The, 222
Hawaiian Sugar Planters' Association, 330
Haystack Monument, 23, 98
Hellespont, 193
Hilo, Hawaii, 104, 109-10, 118, 143, 167-68, 203-06
"History of the Defection of Dr. Thomas Holman," 75

Hoapili, 62, 100, 102, 115, 122, 147-49, 173-74, 190, 235
Hobbs, Jean, 310
Holman, Lucia, 18, 29, 33-34, 39-40, 42-44, 59-60, 63
Holman, Thomas, 29, 42-44, 59-60, 63, 75-76, 80
Holmes, Charlotte, 53, 81
Holmes, Hannah, 52, 62, 91, 134-35, 145, 155, 201, 212, 246
Holmes, Jennie, 53
Holmes, Mary, 53
Holmes, Oliver, 50, 51-52, 62, 127
Holmes, Polly, 52, 214
Honolii, John, 12, 17, 24, 110, 212
Honolulu
    description of, 91, 163, 233, 239-41, 265-66, 267, 298
    mission station, 40, 42, 54, 61, 126, 157-58, 160-61, 164, 169-70, 172-74, 199, 233-34, 252-53
Honolulu Times, 310
Honuaula, Maui, 252
Hooper, William, 218, 275, 278
Hopkins, C. G., 290
Hopu, Delia, 92
Hopu, Thomas, 9, 12, 17, 21-26, 31, 35, 37, 42, 43, 45, 59, 60, 85, 92, 105, 111, 172, 212
Hula, 16, 64-65
Hulumanu ("Bird Feathers"), 179, 181
Hunnewell, James, 12, 16, 52, 70, 83, 108, 137, 150, 169, 173
Hunnewell, Joseph, 108
Hunnewell, Susan, 12, 108, 137, 169

Ii, John, 44, 77, 132-33, 162, 181, 227-29, 235, 256, 262, 268, 285-86, 290, 305
Ii, Sarai, 227-29, 268

Jackson, Sally, 61
Jackson, Susan, 156, 163-64, 184
Jarves, Elizabeth Russell Swain, 221-22, 238, 244, 265, 288-89
Jarves, James Jackson, 221-22, 238, 243-44, 252, 265, 275-76, 288-89, 295-97
John Palmer, 147-48
Johnstone, Andrew, 182
Jones, John C., 76, 78, 80-81, 91, 108, 117, 134-35, 137, 145, 146, 155, 159, 161, 183, 201, 212

Jones Thomas ap Catesby, 136-40
Judd, Albert Francis, 323-24
Judd, Albert Francis, Jr., 324
Judd, Allan, 323
Judd, Charles, 312-13, 315-16, 323-24
Judd, Elizabeth Kinau, 213-14, 229, 268, 323
Judd, Gerrit, 153, 156, 167, 177-78, 213-14, 225, 231, 236, 241-42, 245, 247, 255-56, 259-60, 263-66, 269-71, 273-78, 285, 287-90, 296-300, 302-07, 313, 317, 320, 323
Judd, Gerrit, Jr., 167
Judd, Helen (Nelly), 229, 323
Judd, Henry, 324
Judd, Laura Fish, 153-54, 156, 197, 213-14, 259-60, 262, 267-69, 272, 278, 317, 323
Judd, Lawrence, 324

Kaahumanu, Elizabeta,, 76-77, 80-86, 89-90, 94, 107, 109, 111-13, 120, 122, 123, 125-26, 128-29, 131, 135, 139-40, 144-45, 147-49, 151, 154, 164-67, 173, 175, 177-79, 200
Kaawaloa, Hawaii, 110, 143
Kahaalaia, 67, 114, 179
Kaikioewa, 115, 174, 225
Kailua, Hawaii, 34-44, 59-60, 64, 75, 92, 103-05, 135, 143, 168, 199, 238, 291
Kalaikoa, 190
Kalakaua, David, King, 229, 324
Kalakua, 34-35, 77-78, 102
Kalama, 179, 197, 210, 235, 266-68, 309, 317
Kalanimoku (Billy Pitt), 17-18, 35-36, 40, 64, 67-69, 77, 84, 97, 100, 101, 107, 111-15, 122, 124-25, 128-29, 133, 134, 137, 140, 144
Kaluaaha, Molokai, 315
Kamakaeha, Lydia. *See* Queen Liliu-okalani
Kamakau, S. M., 70, 106-07, 112, 222, 273, 287, 304, 309, 317
Kamamalu, Queen, 37, 43, 66, 88-89, 96-97, 106-07, 120-21, 124
Kamamalu, Victoria, 229, 267, 272
Kamehameha I, 13, 16, 17, 21, 36, 47, 48, 56, 125, 210, 319
Kamehameha II (Liholiho), 16, 37-44, 57, 59, 60, 66-67, 69-73, 76-80, 86-89, 94-95, 101-02, 106-07, 120-22, 124

Kamehameha III (Kauikeaouli), 44-45, 97, 116, 122, 124, 158, 162, 165-67, 173, 179-81, 191, 192, 197, 200-01, 210, 214, 220-21, 235, 242, 243, 248-49, 258, 261-63, 267, 272-73, 285, 305, 308-09, 317

Kamehameha IV (Alexander Liholiho), 225-26, 229-31, 296-97, 309, 316

Kamehameha V (Lot Kamehameha), 225-26, 228-31, 296-97, 305

Kamehameha III (yacht), 288, 296

Kamooula, William, 98

Kanaina, 225

Kanui, William, 24, 42, 51, 58, 252, 288

Kaomi, 145, 179-80

Kapiolani, 79, 105, 110, 118-19, 125, 128, 167, 244-46

Kapule, 56-57, 85, 114, 128

Kauikeaouli. *See* Kamehameha III

Kaumakapili, Oahu, 119, 221, 241

Kaumualii, King of Maui, 56-57, 63, 76-80, 84-85, 111-13

Kaumualii, Prince George (Tamoree), 12, 24-26, 31, 33, 38, 50, 56-57, 58, 78, 113-15, 134

Kawaiahao Church, 227, 237-39, 252-53, 272, 281, 305, 314, 320, 329

Kawaihae, Hawaii, 17, 67, 166

Kealiiahonui, 78, 125, 128, 171

Kearney, Lawrence, 260-61

Keeaumoku (Cox), 83-85, 89, 112

Keikenui, 280

Kekaaniau, Elizabeth, 229

Kekaaniau, James, 229

Kekauluohi (Auhea), 214-16, 220, 222, 225, 235, 262, 268, 272

Kekauonohi, 97, 136

Kekuaiwa, Moses, 225-26, 228-30

Kekuanaoa, 121, 145, 157, 179, 200, 218-20, 222, 225-26, 230, 235, 240-41, 243, 256, 261, 267, 278, 290, 295, 305

Kelii, 225

Keokea, Maui, 306

Keopuolani, 69, 85, 99-101

Kilauea Crater, 118-19, 232, 241-42

Kinau, 97, 145, 175, 179-80, 192, 201, 212-14, 225, 272

Kinau, John, 229

Kohala, Hawaii, 187, 198, 323

Kohala Sugar Plantation, 323

Konia, 225

Kuakini (Governor Adams), 36, 83-85, 88, 103, 105, 110-12, 151, 156-57, 167-68, 173-74, 199, 235, 272

Kumu Hawaii (Hawaiian Teacher), 189

Laanui, 186

Ladd & Co., 247, 255, 259, 264, 274-76, 278

Lahaina, Maui, 45, 59-60, 98-100, 102, 111, 122, 127-28, 136, 144, 147-48, 152, 157, 165, 174, 185, 190, 210, 235-36, 248, 249, 251, 255, 267, 272-73, 280, 293, 304, 312, 328

Lahainaluna Maui, 174-75, 184-85, 207, 210, 234, 249-52, 283-84, 295, 307, 313

Lahilahi, 145, 155, 201, 212

Lama Hawaii (Hawaiian Luminary), 185

Lanai (island), 165, 316, 328

Laplace, Capt. C. P. T., 219-21, 234, 264, 274,

Lathrop, Dr. George A., 304

Ledyard, John, 20

Lee, William Little, 277, 286, 299, 300, 302, 304, 316

Leleihoku, 197

Leoiki, 127, 147-50

Leopold I of Belgium, 264

Lewis, Isaac, 81

Liholiho. *See* Kamehameha II

Likelike, 67-68

Liliha, 58, 67, 79, 106, 121-22, 123, 165, 172-74, 180, 222

Liliuokalani, Queen (Lydia Kamakaeha), 229, 324, 325

Loeau, Jane, 227, 229-30

London Missionary Society, 86

Loomis, Elisha, 29, 49, 59, 60, 63-64, 67-68, 73-74, 83-84, 96, 116, 117, 142

Loomis, Levi, 59

Loomis, Maria Sartwell, 29, 32, 50, 52, 59, 68, 70, 81, 86, 104

Lot. *See* Kamehameha V

Lunalilo, William, (later king Lunalilo) 225, 228-29

Lyman, Chester, 280

Lyman, David, 202-04, 208, 271

Lyman, Sarah Joiner, 202, 207-08

Lyons, Betsy Curtis, 198

Lyons, Lorenzo, 198, 208-09
Lyons, Lucia Smith, 208

Mackintosh, Stephen, 212
Maheha, Abigail, 227, 229-30
Mahele, Great (Land division), 285-87
Maigret, Louis D., 201
Makawao, Maui, 285, 291
Malo, Bathesda, 236
Malo, David, 190, 233, 235-36, 252, 268, 272-73, 306-07
Malo, Rebecca, 307
Manuia, 133, 154
Marin, Don Francisco de Paula, 48, 51, 71, 77, 88, 154, 318
Marin, Mary, 62, 71
Marquesas Islands, 188
Marshall, James F. B., 244, 259-60, 264-65, 275
Marshall, Josiah, 80
Mary Frazier, 197
Maternal Association, 194-95
Meek, Capt. John, 138
Melville, Herman, 188, 318
Micronesia, 313-14
Middlebury College, 22, 26, 254
Miller, Gen. William, 263-64, 268, 270-73, 289, 301, 308
Mills, Samuel J., 22-24, 159
Missionary Packet, 137, 146, 155, 169
Molokai (island), 165
Monroe Doctrine, 258
Mormons, 284, 316
Morse, Samuel F. B., 25, 26

Nahienaena, Princess, 97, 100, 116, 122, 124, 144, 161-62, 172, 179, 181, 185, 189-91, 197
Naihe, 40, 79, 97, 105, 110, 173-74, 244
Naihekukui, 179
Namahana, Lydia, 122, 132-33, 135-36
Newcomb, Dr. Wesley, 304, 306
Nukuhiva, Marquesas, 188

Oahu Charity School, 182-83, 270
Ogden, Maria, 165
Opukahaia (Obookiah), 21-26

Pacific Commercial Advertiser, 326
Paki, 173, 225, 268, 285, 290, 299-300
Paris, John Davis, 313

Parke, W. C., 304
Parthian, 153
Paty, William, 270, 289, 299
Pauahi, 97-98, 102, 134, 145
Paulet, George, 257-62
Peacock, 136, 139, 239
Percival, Lt. John, 130-33
Perrin, Louis, 301, 308
Pierce, Franklin, 308
Pierce, Henry A., 169, 173
Pigot, Capt. William J., 49, 51, 52
Piikoi, 305
Pitt, Billy. See Kalanimoku
Pogue, John Fawcett, 294
Polynesian, The, 233, 238, 240, 243-44, 265, 270, 272, 274, 288, 290
Presbyterianism, 216, 233, 253
Princeton, 98
Printing, 83-84, 106, 126, 142, 160, 166, 177, 185, 187-88, 215, 234
Pulunu, 51
Punahou School, 250-52, 283, 325

Quakers (Friends), 61, 70

Reynolds, Stephen, 129, 138-39, 143-45, 150, 155, 163-64, 183-84, 212, 214, 218, 220, 222, 229, 233, 237, 244, 246-48, 256, 258, 269, 274, 302
Rice, Charles, 326
Rice, Harold, 326
Rice, Mary, 251, 325
Rice, William, 251, 325
Richards, Atherton, 325
Richards, Clarissa Lyman, 98, 128
Richards, James, 23
Richards, William, 23, 98, 102, 122, 128, 136-39, 142-43, 147-50 165, 172, 181, 188, 191, 193, 196-97, 210-11, 217-19, 222, 230, 235-36, 247, 255-58, 264, 271, 274, 279, 281, 325, 332
Ricord, John, 264-65, 267-68, 270, 273, 275, 277-78, 305
Rives, Jean, 41, 107, 120, 147
Robertson, George M., 289-90
Rogers, Edmund Horton, 187
Rooke, Dr. C. B., 304, 317
Rooke, Emma (Queen Emma), 229, 316
Royal School, 230
Ruggles, Nancy Wells, 9, 29, 32, 34, 39, 63, 146, 186, 244-45

Ruggles, Samuel, 9, 17, 25, 29, 32, 49-50, 55-57, 59, 60, 63, 78, 110, 118, 125, 143, 167-68, 186, 198
Russians in Hawaii, 33, 47, 56

Sandalwood trade, 21, 69, 108, 139, 169-70
Sandwich, George, 76
Sandwich Island Gazette, 211-12, 220
Sandwich Islands News, 275-78, 286
Scheffer, George, 56
Severance, Luther, 301, 318
Shepard, Stephen, 153
Short, Patrick 175-76, 200
Simpson, Alexander, 256, 258-60
Simpson, Sir George, 255-56
Smith, Lowell, 199, 221, 223, 235, 241, 263, 270-71, 273, 288, 324
Smith, Marcia, 250-51
Society Islands, 76
Society of Inquiry on the Subject of Missions, 23
Southard, Samuel, 160
Stevenson, Robert Louis, 318-19
Stewart, Charles, 98-99, 102, 116, 160-61
Stewart, Harriet Bradford Tiffany, 99, 125-26
Stockton, Betsy, 98-99, 102, 126
Sumner, Capt. Charles, 197

Tabu, 13-14, 16, 77, 87-88, 130, 287
Tahiti, 76-77, 78, 86, 89
Tamoree, Prince George. *See* Kaumualii, George
Taylor, Townsend, 312
Ten Eyck, Anthony, 276, 289
Thaddeus, 9, 16-19, 27, 31-35, 38, 42, 43, 47, 55, 58, 72
Thames, 96, 99
Thomas, Admiral Richard, 257, 261-63
Thouars, Capt. A. du Petit, 200-01
Thurston, Asa, 18, 27-28, 31-32, 35-38, 42-45, 59, 60, 64, 66-67, 72-74, 91, 96, 103-05, 110, 150, 238, 292, 313, 320
Thurston, Asa, Jr., 312-14
Thurston, Lorrin Andrews, 324, 326
Thurston, Lorrin P., 326
Thurston, Lucy, 105, 194, 238
Thurston, Lucy Goodale, 10, 16-17, 27-28, 42-45, 60, 71-72, 74, 89, 92, 116, 155, 168, 238, 313, 320

Thurston, Persis, 105, 146, 194, 238, 312
Tinker, Reuben, 183, 188-89, 211
Tromelin, Rear Admiral Legoarant de, 295-96
Tyerman, Daniel, 86, 89
Tyler, John, 257-58

Union College, 22
United States, relations with Hawaii, 20-21, 136-37, 139-40, 160-61, 239, 248, 255-58, 263, 264, 289, 296-97, 301, 307-09, 332

Van Buren, Martin, 197, 212
Vancouver, George, 42
Vincennes, 160, 239
Virginia, 274

Waiakea, Hawaii. *See* Hilo
Waialua, Oahu, 186, 251-52, 286, 291, 311, 320, 324
Wailuku, Maui, 185, 189, 193, 209, 238, 252
Waimea, Hawaii, 167, 177, 208
Waimea, Kauai, 55-57, 63, 78-80, 113, 320
Waioli, Kauai, 188
Waldo & Benson, 280
Walsh, Robert A., 212, 220-21
Ward, Mary, 165
Waterwitch, 108, 110
Webster, Daniel, 257, 263
Weston, David, 302
Whaling, 91, 302
Whitney, Emily, 186
Whitney, Henry, 113, 142, 313
Whitney, Maria, 63, 113, 141, 279, 294, 312
Whitney, Mercy Partridge, 30, 32-33, 52, 63, 113, 141-42, 168, 294, 320
Whitney, Samuel, 30, 32-33, 49-50, 55-57, 59, 63, 96, 114, 141-42, 168, 279, 320
Whitney, Samuel, Jr., 113, 142
Wilcox, Abner, 202-03, 207, 324, 326
Wilcox, Albert S., 324
Wilcox, George Norton, 326
Wilcox, Samuel Whitney, 326
Wildes, Capt. Dixey, 111-12, 138
Wilkes, Lt. Com. Charles, 239-42, 288
Williams College, 22, 98, 199, 202, 221, 312, 325

Winship, Jonathan, 21
Winship, Nathan, 21, 48-49
Wood, Robert W., 245
Wyllie, Robert Chrichton, 268, 271, 273-75, 288-90, 295, 300-02, 305-06, 308, 310

Yale College, 22, 23, 24, 28, 30
Young, Alapai, 308-09
Young, James, 106, 121
Young, John, 36, 40-42, 137, 268, 316
Young John (Keoni Ana), 268, 272, 301, 305, 308-09, 310

Date Due

U.S.S. MIDWAY
CVA-41